Criminal Procedure and the Supreme Court

Criminal Procedure and the Supreme Court

A Guide to the Major Decisions on Search and Seizure, Privacy, and Individual Rights

Edited by
ROLANDO V. DEL CARMEN
AND CRAIG HEMMENS

Contributing Authors:
VALERIE BELL
DAVID BRODY
SUE CARTER COLLINS
CLAIRE NOLASCO
JEFFERY T. WALKER
MARVIN ZALMAN

ROWMAN & LITTLEFIELD PUBLISHERS, INC.
Lanham • Boulder • New York • Toronto • Plymouth, UK

Published by Rowman & Littlefield Publishers, Inc.
A wholly owned subsidiary of The Rowman & Littlefield Publishing Group, Inc.
4501 Forbes Boulevard, Suite 200, Lanham, Maryland 20706
http://www.rowmanlittlefield.com

Estover Road, Plymouth PL6 7PY, United Kingdom

British Library Cataloguing in Publication Information Available

Library of Congress Cataloging-in-Publication Data

Criminal procedure and the Supreme Court : a guide to the major decisions on search and seizure, privacy, and individual rights / edited by Craig Hemmens and Rolando V. del Carmen ; contributing authors, David Brody . . . [et al.].
    p. cm.
  ISBN 978-1-4422-0156-9 (cloth : alk. paper) — ISBN 978-1-4422-0158-3 (electronic : alk. paper)
  1. Searches and seizures—United States—Cases. 2. Civil rights—United States-—Cases.
  3. Privacy, Right of—United States—Cases. 4. Criminal procedure—United States—Cases.
  5. Criminal investigation—United States—Cases. 6. United States. Supreme Court. [1. Judges—United States—Biography.] I. Hemmens, Craig. II. Del Carmen, Rolando V. III. Brody, David C.
  KF9630.C75 2010
  345.73'05—dc22   2010005880

Printed in the United States of America

Contents

Acknowledgments

Rolando V. del Carmen thanks Craig Hemmens, coeditor and chapter author, for all the work he did for this book. Without Craig, the book would never have materialized. He contacted authors and coordinated and detailed the work for the book. Thanks also go to Rolando's wife, Josie, and his daughter, Jocelyn, both of whom have given him their utmost encouragement and support throughout his years of teaching.

Craig Hemmens thanks his coeditor, Rolando V. del Carmen, and all of the contributing authors. Without them, this book would not have been written. Rolando had the idea for the book, and he encouraged Craig to recruit folks to participate. All of the contributing authors have been a pleasure to work with—happily accepting their chapter assignments, doing quality work, and submitting their chapters ahead of schedule! It doesn't get any better than that for an editor. Craig also acknowledges Mary, Emily, Amber, and Max. As much as he loves the law, he loves you more.

Rolando and Craig also thank Suzanne Staszak-Silva and all of the fine folks at Rowman & Littlefield. Suzanne saw the value in this book and has been supportive from the outset. Lastly, we thank all of our students—without you we would not have the opportunity to get paid to study, teach, and write about these important and interesting cases that have dotted the American jurisprudential landscape over the years.

Introduction

THE PURPOSE OF THIS STUDY

As any faculty and student know, criminal-procedure books in criminal justice abound with cases and topics relevant to how suspects and defendants are processed en route to punishment. In these tomes numerous cases are cited and their holdings summarized, but few are discussed in great depth. By contrast, criminal-procedure books used in law schools feature full-length cases but are woefully short on case discussion or updates. Students are left to themselves to ascertain the significance of each case and where it stands in importance in the hierarchy of all cases on a topic. This book seeks to combine both approaches, choosing the most significant cases in criminal procedure, ranking them, discussing the decision in totality (including dissenting and concurring opinions), and updating and then placing them in perspective. It features a vertical rather than a horizontal approach to learning criminal procedure. The result is fewer cases under review but greater author guidance and in-depth coverage of leading decisions. This approach to learning is different but effective and fills a need.

Ranking cases is a novel approach to studying United States Supreme Court decisions. There is no compelling justification for it except that it arouses curiosity and can lead to further reflection and inquiry. There is, however, a mundane excuse for the use of rankings even in the halls of academe: The reality is that we live in a world of lists. Newspapers, magazines, and even academic journals are often replete with rankings of the Top However Many Somethings of whatever category is under discussion. Colleges and universities are assigned status based on perceived prestige, as are undergraduate and graduate programs among the various disciplines. Academic priorities in educational institutions are ranked, as are academic journals. Sports teams are rated each week, just as professional firms and practitioners are on a yearly basis. Lists and rankings are ubiquitous in a media-driven society and invite attention in an age of information overload. The upside of lists is that they fill a need to quickly assess the importance of something based on somebody else's perception or study; the downside is that they are usually judgmental and can be misleading, if not downright flawed. Properly used, however, rankings constitute a starting point for inquiry but should not be considered the final word. They can be useful tools for discussion and debate but should not be proxies for personal informed choices.

This book features a list and discussion of the top twenty cases in criminal procedure. These cases are placed in context, analyzed, and updated. Criminal procedure is governed by United States Supreme Court decisions and is "nationalized," meaning that the core of criminal-procedure rules is similar from one state or jurisdiction to another. The United States Supreme Court has decided hundreds of cases on criminal procedure since the Court's creation in Article Three of the United States Constitution. These cases differ in importance and impact regarding how defendants are processed and eventually punished. Twenty cases, ranked in importance, is an acceptable beginning and challenges the reader to better understand the way the police and courts deal with suspects and defendants. This selection of cases is, however, merely the tip of the iceberg, so to speak, in a sea of cases in American criminal procedure. There are a lot more to be studied and analyzed, as would be true in any area of law.

HOW THE CASES WERE CHOSEN

Subjectivity is inevitable in any nonquantified list. The list in this book is subjective and based mainly on our teaching backgrounds and collective experience—we each hold a number of law degrees and have years of teaching experience on the graduate and undergraduate levels. We chose each case based on its perceived impact on police work and daily police interaction with the public. For example, *Miranda v. Arizona* is considered case number one because it impacts policing in a meaningful way every day as no other case does. Law-enforcement officers are all familiar with Miranda warnings, of necessity, as is most of the public. In fact, every case in this list of twenty is (or should be) familiar to police officers and the public in principle, though the specifics may not be well understood. For example, *Carroll v. United States* (case number seven) defines the limits of motor-vehicle searches, a daily occurrence in the United States. Although neither the police nor the public may be aware of the specifics of this case, *Carroll's* prescribed principles for motor-vehicle searches have been in use since 1925, when the case came before the Court. And while the editors' specific case rankings may differ among scholars and law-enforcement personnel, there should be little doubt that every case in this list has had a significant effect on policing and court procedure and thus deserves to be studied closely.

Any such list inevitably omits cases that may be more significant in the judgment of others. The choices in this book are explained by three considerations: (1) our subjective, perhaps flawed, judgment has led us to omit or include a case, (2) an omitted important case may recently have been overruled and is no longer the authority after having been the leading case for a long time, or (3) the decision may be recent, and its impact on policing has yet to be determined and hence is unsuitable for extended discussion. Exemplars for the latter two considerations are the cases *New York v. Belton* and *Arizona v. Gant*. The first case, *Belton*, decided in 1981, held that the "police may search the passenger compartment of a vehicle and any containers therein as a contemporaneous incident of a recent occupant's lawful arrest." That case had an immediate massive impact on police-public contact because it greatly expanded the power of the police to search motor vehicles. *Belton* remained authoritative for twenty-eight years before being either repealed (according to the dissent) or at least narrowed (according to the majority) by *Gant*, which was decided on April 21, 2009. Because this more recent case covers police searches of motor vehicles, *Gant* will likely influence police behavior in the immediate future, but how extensively and for how long remains to be seen (the case was decided on a four-to-one-to-four vote in the Supreme Court). Thus *Belton* and *Gant* are not included among the top twenty.

The terrorist attacks in New York City, Washington, D.C., and Pennsylvania on September 11, 2001, and subsequent global events placed national security in the forefront of domestic concerns. Hence national security has more recently merited inclusion as a topic in criminal-procedure books. No case on that topic, however, is included in this book for two reasons: (1) thus far most United States Supreme Court decisions on national security have addressed the issue of court jurisdiction (where suspects are to be tried and by what court), a peripheral concern in policing cases, and (2) the domestic "war on terror," although doubtless crucial, is primarily the responsibility of the national government and not of state or local police. In some cases, national-security agents and the police do interact and collaborate, but that is still the exception rather than the rule. This area of law, however, may increase in importance if federal-state collaboration increases in the effort to stamp out domestic terrorism.

BOOK ORGANIZATION

As the table of contents shows, the twenty cases are divided sequentially into eight parts, as follows:

Part I: Reasonable Expectation of Privacy and Probable Cause

Part II: The Exclusionary Rule

Part III: Stop and Frisk

Part IV: Arrest

Part V: Searches of Places and Things

Part VI: Motor Vehicles

Part VII: Interrogation and Lineups

Part VIII: Police Liability

This grouping mirrors the usual table of contents in textbooks on criminal procedure. It starts with the cases on reasonable expectation of privacy and probable cause because these legal concepts pervade criminal procedure. Reasonable expectation of privacy has assumed greater importance in an age of electronics and ever-changing technological advances. *Probable cause* is arguably the most important term in policing and must be thoroughly understood by law-enforcement officials in order for them to perform their job properly; similarly, it must be understood by the public, who seek to protect their rights and civil liberties when in contact with the police. The exclusionary rule is basic in policing and applies when a case comes to court. The rule was extended to state criminal proceedings in *Mapp v. Ohio* (1961), which is, arguably, the second-most important case in criminal procedure after *Miranda v. Arizona*. The eight parts close with a case addressing police liability, a topic of relatively recent origin but of constant concern to police officers and departments. Taken together, the twenty cases discussed and their eight categorizations constitute the core of legal issues in policing.

CHAPTER ORGANIZATION

To achieve a degree of uniformity in chapter format, the writers in this book organize their chapters, whenever feasible, as follows:

Case Introduction
   The Facts
   The Issue before the Court
   The Court's Holding
   The Majority Opinion
   The Dissenting Opinion
   Case Significance

Further Analysis

Update Cases

The Current Scope of Police or Court Authority on the Topic

Other Considerations

The Future

Conclusions

Nonetheless, variation in chapter organization exists but has been minimized to every extent possible. Each chapter also includes suggested titles for further reading, and a brief biography of the writer of the majority opinion is included in the appendix. Although judicial decision making is often a complex process and results from professional interaction, it is hard to deny that a justice's ideological and personal background sometimes influences the outcome of cases despite protestations to the contrary. Reading a brief biography of the majority-opinion writer humanizes the decision and puts a face on an otherwise abstracted and impersonal process.

We hope that focusing on these top twenty cases helps readers understand these decisions and how they have shaped and refined important aspects of criminal procedure. This case-centered approach is unique among current criminal-justice books. Our aim is to enhance each reader's appreciation of the role of the Supreme Court in law enforcement and the importance of case law in expanding the scope of or setting limits on law enforcement in the American system of criminal justice.

Rolando V. del Carmen
Craig Hemmens

REASONABLE EXPECTATION OF PRIVACY AND PROBABLE CAUSE

Katz v. United States

SUE CARTER COLLINS

INTRODUCTION

In the twenty-first century, technology reigns supreme. The advent of computers, cellular telephones, and Internet technology has made the ability to engage in electronic communications commonplace. With just a few keystrokes on a computer it is possible to be in instant contact with someone on the other side of the world. Through the use of Internet service providers like Yahoo! one can send instant messages and use voice over Internet protocol (VoIP) to bypass the traditional telephone system and communicate electronically with others. Although the U.S. Postal Service still delivers some pieces of mail, the use of electronic-mail (e-mail) communications is rapidly replacing it. Not only can a person send and receive e-mail instantly, for both the environmentally conscious and the criminal element there is the added benefit of being able to avoid a paper trail by storing information in cyberspace.

Although these technological advances bring with them great freedoms, they have been accompanied by significant governmental erosion of individual rights. For instance, have you ever wondered if the "private" conversations that you have on your cell phone are constitutionally protected? Have you considered whether there is a constitutional right to privacy in your e-mail communications or instant messages? If you are the subject of a criminal investigation, can law-enforcement agencies access electronically stored messages that have been password protected?

This chapter explores the realm of electronic surveillance. It begins with an analysis of *Katz v. United States*, 389 U.S. 347 (1967), the premier Supreme Court decision on electronic surveillance. It next provides a basic overview of federal legislation and case law in this area. The chapter concludes with a discussion of the future of electronic surveillance and its impact on individual rights in the post–9/11 era.

THE CASE OF *KATZ V. UNITED STATES* (1967): ELECTRONIC SURVEILLANCE

The Facts

Charles Katz was convicted on a federal indictment that charged him with transmitting betting information by telephone across state lines. At his trial, the government presented evidence of Katz's end of the conversation, which FBI agents overheard when they attached an electronic listening and recording device to the outside of the public phone booth where Katz made the calls. The telephone booth was constructed partially of glass so that Katz was as visible after entering the booth as he would have been if he had remained outside.

Katz appealed his conviction, arguing that the recordings were unlawfully obtained in violation of the Fourth Amendment. The appellate court rejected this contention because the FBI had not physically entered the phone booth where Katz placed the calls. The court based its ruling on two cases: *Olmstead v. United States*, 277 U.S. 438 (1928), which held that conversations were not subject to Fourth Amendment protection; and *Goldman v. United States*, 316 U.S. 129 (1942), which held that electronic surveillance that did not involve physical penetration into a protected area was not a constitutional violation. The Supreme Court granted certiorari to consider the question presented.

The Issue before the Court

Is a public telephone booth a constitutionally protected place such that evidence obtained by attaching an electronic listening and recording device to the outside of the booth is a violation of the user's right to privacy?

The Majority Opinion

Katz was argued before the Court on October 17, 1967, and decided on December 18 of the same year. Justice Stewart wrote the majority opinion, expressing the views of seven members of the Court. Katz contended that the government violated his Fourth Amendment right to privacy by attaching a

protected area is necessary before a search and seizure can be said to be violative of the Fourth Amendment of the Unites States Constitution."

In what was probably a surprise to both Katz and the government, Justice Stewart rejected this formulation of the issues, stating that the parties had attached too much significance to the characterization of the phone booth from which Katz placed his calls. Katz had argued that the phone booth was a constitutionally protected area; the government had argued that it was not. Stewart dismissed both contentions, stating that when viewed in the abstract the focus on whether an area is constitutionally protected deflects attention from the real problem, which is whether an individual has exhibited a subjective expectation of privacy that society considers reasonable. Declaring that "the Fourth Amendment protects people not places," Stewart held that "what a person knowingly exposes to the public, even in his own home or office, is not a subject of Fourth Amendment protection. . . . But what he seeks to preserve as private, even in an area accessible to the public, may be constitutionally protected."

In further reliance on *Olmstead*, the government argued that the activities of its agents should not be subject to Fourth Amendment requirements because the wiretap did not physically penetrate the telephone booth from which Katz placed his call. After noting that the government's reliance on the trespass doctrine was misplaced, Stewart overruled *Olmstead* and *Goldman* and stated, "We have since departed from the narrow view on which that rested. Indeed, we have expressly held that the Fourth Amendment governs not only the seizure of tangible items but extends as well to the recording of oral statements, overheard without any 'technical trespass under . . . local property law'" (*Silverman v. United States*, 365 U.S. 505 [1961]). Regarding the search in *Katz*, Stewart held that "the government's activities in electronically listening to and recording [Katz's] words violated the privacy upon which he justifiably relied while using the telephone booth and thus constituted a 'search and seizure' within the meaning of the Fourth Amendment. The fact that the electronic device employed to achieve that end did not happen to penetrate the wall of the booth can have no constitutional significance."

Stewart also rejected the government's argument that the actions of its agents should be retroactively validated because they exercised restraint and did no more than they could have done under a properly issued warrant. Noting that the restraint imposed was by the agents themselves and not by a judicial officer, Stewart reiterated that "the [Fourth] Amendment requires adherence to judicial processes . . . and searches conducted outside the judicial process, without prior approval by judge or magistrate, are per se unreasonable under the Fourth Amendment—subject only to a few specifically established and well-delineated exceptions."

Justice Harlan concurred with Stewart's assessment that "the Fourth Amendment protects people, not places," and stated that the relevant inquiry is "just what protection does it afford?" Articulating the standard that is still used today, Harlan said, "The rule that has emerged from prior decisions is that there is a twofold requirement: first . . . a person [must] have exhibited an actual (subjective) expectation of privacy, and second . . . the expectation [must] be one that society is prepared to recognize as 'reasonable.'" In *Katz*

> the critical fact . . . is that "one who occupies [a telephone booth], shuts the door behind him, and pays the toll that permits him to place a call is surely entitled to assume" that his conversation is not being intercepted. . . . The point is not that the booth is "accessible to the public" at other times . . . but that it is a temporarily private place whose momentary occupants' expectations for freedom from intrusion are recognized as reasonable.

Justice Black disagreed completely with the majority opinion and stated he would not have overruled *Olmstead*. He took the position consistent with the plain meaning of the Fourth Amendment's language and the intent of the Constitution's framers, that the Fourth Amendment simply does not apply to eavesdropping. Stating that the particularity requirement makes it clear that the amendment applies only to tangible things, Black observed that "a conversation overheard by eavesdropping, whether by plain snooping or by wiretapping, is not tangible and, under the normally accepted meaning of the words, can neither be searched nor seized." Further, Black noted, the language of the amendment refers "to something already in existence so that it can be described. Yet the Court's interpretation would have the amendment apply to overhearing future conversations, which by their very nature are nonexistent until they take place." Black continued, "How can one 'describe' a future conversation? And, if one cannot, how can a magistrate issue a warrant to eavesdrop on one in the future?" Stating that he see could "no way in which the words of the Fourth Amendment [could] be construed to apply to eavesdropping," Black refused to "distort the words of the amendment in order to 'keep the Constitution up to date' or 'to bring it into harmony with the times.'" In his opinion, "the Fourth Amendment protects privacy only to the extent that it prohibits unreasonable searches of 'persons, houses, papers, and effects.'"

Case Significance

In *Katz* the Court articulated a new standard governing the use of electronic surveillance that is still used today. Stating that the Constitution protects people, not places, the Court concluded that the legal premises on which the "trespass doctrine" was based had been so eroded that the standard could no longer be controlling. The Court expressly overturned *Olmstead* and *Goldman*, which together held that electronic surveillance that did not involve physical penetration into a protected area was not a violation of the Fourth Amendment. The net effect of the Court's decision in *Katz* is that individuals who exhibit an objectively reasonable expectation of privacy enjoy broad Fourth Amendment protection of their activities and conversations that is "portable" in nature and accompanies them wherever they go.[1] Indicative of this, the Court stated that "no less than an individual in a business office, in a friend's apartment, or in a taxicab, a person in a telephone booth may rely upon the protection of the Fourth Amendment."

THE BROADENING SCOPE OF POLICE AUTHORITY TO CONDUCT ELECTRONIC SURVEILLANCE: HOW FAR CAN THEY GO?

Electronic surveillance is regulated by the United States Constitution, federal laws, and state statutes. Since September 11, 2001, when America was traumatized by domestic terrorist attacks, Congress has granted law-enforcement agencies greater power and authority to intercept communications using electronic devices. Subsequent to the rule of law announced in *Katz*, Congress implemented a complex statutory scheme consisting of Title III of the Omnibus Crime Control and Safe Streets Act of 1968 (Title III), the Electronic Communications and Privacy Act of 1986 (ECPA), and the Communications Assistance for Law Enforcement Act of 1994 (CALEA). Additionally, as a direct response to the events of September 11, Congress passed the USA Patriot Act, which amends Title III and expands the government's authority to conduct electronic surveillance in cases involving suspected domestic and foreign terrorists. It is axiomatic that when the government's power to regulate the people is expanded, the rights of individuals are restricted. This section provides a brief overview of the federal legislation that authorizes electronic surveillance and its impact on individual rights.

Title III of the Omnibus Crime Control and Safe Streets Act of 1968

Title III of the Omnibus Crime Control and Safe Streets Act of 1968 is the primary legislation governing wiretaps and electronic surveillance. The purpose of the statute is to allow authorized surveillance while simultaneously maintaining an individual's privacy. Title III regulates all "nonconsensual" electronic surveillance (when none of the parties have consented to the interception) except "national security" eavesdropping. The statute specifies that law-enforcement officers may not tap or intercept wire communications, or use electronic devices to intercept private conversations, unless there is a court order authorizing the wiretap or consent has been given by one of the parties to the conversation. Where police act pursuant to a court order a state statute must exist that authorizes issuance of the order. If such legislation does not exist a judge cannot validly authorize a wiretap or any form of electronic surveillance. Where the police electronically record a conversation pursuant to consent given by a participating party the consent is not valid if state law prohibits it. A police officer who willfully conducts electronic surveillance or uses or discloses information in violation of Title III is subject to federal criminal prosecution including imprisonment and a fine. Title III also has its own exclusionary rule. Evidence obtained in violation of the statute is not admissible in any state or federal prosecution. Although states may further restrict police authority to conduct electronic surveillance they may not increase it in violation of Title III.

The Electronic Communications and Privacy Act of 1986 (ECPA)

Congress passed the Electronic Communications and Privacy Act (ECPA) in 1986. This statute amends Title III. The purpose of the ECPA is to safeguard electronic communications from government intrusion and prohibit Internet and electronic service providers from accessing the content of these communications without the consent of the Internet user or the electronic service customer who originated the conversation. The statute covers new forms of communications such as in-transit and stored e-mails, voice mails, computing services, and wireless telephones. The ECPA also establishes rules that protect an individual's "privacy relative to the use of cell phones, radio paging, customer records, and satellite communications"; "amends the law of nonconsensual interception of wire communications . . . and oral communications by a concealed microphone or electronic device"; specifies the procedures that law-enforcement officers must follow to obtain authorization to use pen registers and trap-and-trace devices;[2] and, "prescribes the procedures that law enforcement officers must follow to obtain stored communications . . . such as telephone toll records and unlisted telephone subscriber information."[3] The ECPA also expanded the power of law enforcement agencies to conduct electronic surveillance under specified circumstances.

The Communications Assistance for Law Enforcement Act of 1994 (CALEA)

In 1994 Congress passed the Communications Assistance for Law Enforcement Act (CALEA) to keep pace with advancements in technology. The act supplements and amends Title III and the ECPA relative to the government's ability to conduct electronic surveillance using pen registers, trap-and-trace devices, and content interceptions. The act's purpose is "to make clear a telecommunications carrier's duty to cooperate in the interception of communications for law enforcement purposes" while (1) safeguarding law-enforcement agencies' ability to carry out authorized intercepts, (2) protecting individual privacy in the face of increasingly powerful technology, and (3) protecting the development of new communications services and technologies.

Enacted amid growing concern about cellular telephone communications, CALEA mandates that the cell-phone industry design systems that comply with the act's requirements and make it easier for the FBI to monitor calls. The Federal Communications Commission (FCC) was tasked with determining the specific standards applicable to electronic monitoring. Pursuant to FCC rules, with the aid of telecommunications carriers law-enforcement agencies may

- track the general location of a cell-phone user by identifying which cellular antennas the phone used to transmit the beginning and ending of the call,
- identify all participants on a conference call and continue to monitor their conversations even after the target of the investigation is no longer on the phone, and
- determine if cell-phone users are using telephone features such as call forwarding and call waiting.[4]

In sum, CALEA attempts to protect individual rights while simultaneously granting law-enforcement agencies significant authority to monitor and access electronic communications.

The USA Patriot Act

Perhaps the most sweeping expansion of police authority to conduct electronic surveillance is found in the USA Patriot Act. Congress passed the Patriot

Act in an atmosphere of fear after terrorists attacked America on September 11, 2001. The purpose of the act is to address communications issues within and between government agencies regarding information sharing on counterterrorism measures and intelligence and to increase the investigative powers of certain agencies. Since its enactment, the Patriot Act has had a significant impact on surveillance and privacy laws. While an exhaustive review of this complex statute is beyond the scope of this chapter, following are brief summaries of key provisions regulating electronic surveillance.

Section 201 of the act grants "authority to intercept oral, wire, or electronic communications relating to terrorism." Federal agents are allowed to bypass the normal probable-cause requirement when obtaining a search warrant to seize communications thought to be related to terrorism or intelligence investigations. If a person is suspected of a terroristic crime, suspicion alone is sufficient to obtain a wiretap for the person's communications. The government also may wiretap the communication devices of American citizens suspected of terrorism.

Section 202 of the act permits the government to obtain warrants for computer-based offenses related to domestic terrorism. Such warrants are not limited to intelligence investigations and may extend to criminal investigations.

Section 203 of the act provides that disclosure of intercepted communications related to "foreign intelligence or counterintelligence" may be made to "any federal law-enforcement, intelligence, protective, immigration, national-defense, or national-security official" for use in the performance of official duties.

Section 204 of the act revised Title III and the Stored Communications Act. Stored up voice-mail communications may be accessed by the government with a search warrant rather than the more rigorous wiretap order. Voice mails also are governed by section 209, which allows courts to issue nationwide search warrants; however, voice recordings on an answering-machine tape are beyond the reach of the statute.

Section 206 of the act expands the government's power to obtain roving wiretaps. Although roving wiretaps have been used in criminal cases since 1986, unlike statutory requirements in prior years, section 206 does not compel law-enforcement officers to identify the actual target.

Section 216 extends the power of law-enforcement agencies to set up pen registers and trap-and-trace devices, and the installation of devices used to document computer routing, addressing, and signaling information. Although a court order is required to install such devices, the statute permitting monitoring only requires a government attorney to certify that the information to be acquired is pertinent to an ongoing criminal investigation; the act does not require a showing of probable cause or oversight by a judge.

Section 217 allows government agents to intercept the communications of a "computer trespasser" as long as the owner or operator of a "protected computer" agrees to the interception. A protected computer is any computer that is used for "interstate or foreign commerce or communication." This section allows surveillance of the intruder's communications without judicial oversight.

Section 220 of the act allows courts to issue search warrants that have nationwide application. This section increases the range of surveillance orders and makes it difficult for those served with the warrant to object to legal or procedural defects.

In summary, the current federal statutory scheme accords law-enforcement agencies sweeping authority to conduct electronic surveillance. Title III, the ECPA, and CALEA regulate the electronic tracking, monitoring, and interception of wire and oral communications. The USA Patriot Act governs information sharing among select agencies and electronic surveillance involving domestic and foreign terrorism. Proponents claim that these statutes are necessary to fight the war on crime and combat terrorism; however, opponents see them as major intrusions on individual rights. Although each statute contains provisions that purport to protect individual privacy rights, in general when resolving Fourth Amendment claims involving electronic surveillance, lower courts typically rule in favor of the government, finding no constitutional violations as long as there is a valid warrant.

SEARCH-WARRANT REQUIREMENTS

The criteria used to determine when a surveillance warrant is issued and whether such warrants are valid were first announced by the Supreme Court in *Berger v. New York*, 388 U.S. 41 (1967). There the Court struck down a New York statute authorizing the use of electronic surveillance by law-enforcement officers. Holding that the Fourth and Fourteenth Amendments are violated by legislation that provides a "blanket grant of permission to eavesdrop . . . without adequate judicial supervision or protective procedures," the Court set forth guidelines for obtaining a valid warrant. *Berger* was decided several months before *Katz* and one year prior to Congress's enacting Title III. Its provisions are legislatively incorporated into the statute.

In order to obtain a valid warrant authorizing any form of electronic surveillance law-enforcement officers must comply with Title III requirements. Only federal district and appellate court judges and their state counterparts may issue surveillance orders. Except when an emergency exists that threatens the national security, an electronic surveillance warrant may not be issued without a properly authorized application. The application must be made in writing and under oath. It also must include the identity of the officer making the application and the individual authorizing it, as well as a "full and complete statement" of the circumstances constituting probable cause. Specific requirements that officers must meet when seeking a warrant include

1. identifying the crime that was committed,
2. providing a particular description of the facilities or place where the interception is to be made or used,
3. specifying the type of communication sought to be intercepted,
4. identifying the person, if known, who is committing the offense and whose conversation is to be intercepted, and
5. stating "whether other investigative methods have been tried or failed or why they reasonably appear to be unlikely to succeed if tried or to be too dangerous."

At the time the warrant is issued the court order must specify that the interception will be executed "as soon as practicable [and] conducted in such a way as to *minimize the interception of communications not otherwise subject to interception.*" The order also "must terminate upon attainment of the authorized objective, or . . . in thirty days," but may be extended upon a renewed showing of probable cause. Once the order is obtained, officers may lawfully enter the premises to install the listening device and eavesdrop on conversations; no additional search warrant is required.

SIGNIFICANT CASES INVOLVING ELECTRONIC SURVEILLANCE
The law on electronic surveillance is still evolving; however, existing case law seems to divide itself rather neatly into two categories: (1) cases in which the Court has held that a search warrant was not required to monitor a beeper or tracking device, and (2) cases in which the Court has held that a search warrant is needed prior to installing a surveillance device or capturing electronic communications. This section reviews significant cases in these areas.

No Search Warrant Required

The Supreme Court has long held that law-enforcement officers, while investigating crimes, may utilize common technology such as flashlights or binoculars to enhance their senses without violating the Fourth Amendment (*United States v. Knotts*, 460 U.S. 276 [1983]). Pen registers and trap-and-trace devices are included in this category because they do not violate a person's reasonable expectation of privacy since they only capture telephone numbers not conversations.[5]

Pen Registers

In *Smith v. Maryland*, 442 U.S. 735 (1979), the police suspected that Smith had committed a robbery and made a warrantless request to the phone company, which installed a pen register to record numbers dialed from Smith's phone. Smith was tried, convicted, and sentenced to prison based on the phone-call log and other evidence obtained by the police. The Supreme Court accepted review of the case to consider the "restrictions imposed by the Fourth Amendment on the use of pen registers." Finding that no Fourth Amendment violation had occurred, the Court held that no warrant was needed since the "petitioner in all probability entertained no actual expectation of privacy in the phone numbers he dialed. . . . Even if he did, his expectation was not 'legitimate,'" since he had to convey the number dialed to the phone company in order to complete the call. The Court concluded that "a person has no reasonable expectation of privacy in information he voluntarily turns over to third parties."

Beepers and Electronic Tracking Devices

As is true with pen registers, generally courts have held that the warrantless use of beepers and tracking devices does not violate the Fourth Amendment. Indicative of this, in *United States v. Knotts*, 460 U.S. 276 (1983), officers obtained consent from a chemical company to install a beeper in a container of chloroform prior to its purchase by Armstrong. The officers visually surveilled and monitored the signal to determine the location of the container as it was carried in an automobile to a cabin in a rural area. Based on this information officers obtained and executed a search warrant for the cabin where they discovered an illicit drug lab. Knotts, the owner of the cabin, was convicted of conspiracy to manufacture controlled substances. The Court rejected his appeal, holding that the use of the beeper was not a search; rather, "visual surveillance from public places along [the] route or adjoining Knotts's premises would have sufficed to reveal all of these facts. . . . Nothing in the Fourth Amendment prohibited the police from augmenting [their] sensory faculties . . . with such enhancement as science and technology afforded them."

The *Knotts* decision struck a blow in favor of law enforcement and against individual rights. It left two questions unanswered:

> (1) whether installation of a beeper in a container of chemicals with the consent of the original owner constitutes a search or seizure within the meaning of the Fourth Amendment when the container is delivered to a buyer having no knowledge of the presence of the beeper, and (2) whether monitoring of a beeper falls within the ambit of the Fourth Amendment when it reveals information that could not have been ascertained through visual surveillance.

The Court addressed these questions one year later in *United States v. Karo*, 468 U.S. 705 (1984). Answering the first question in the negative, the Court held that the mere transfer of a can containing an unmonitored beeper "infringed no privacy interest" and therefore was not a search since "it conveyed no information at all." The Court answered the second question in the affirmative holding that just as it would be an unreasonable search to surreptitiously enter the premises to ascertain if the container was there,

> for purposes of the Fourth Amendment, the result is the same where, without a warrant, the government surreptitiously employs an electronic device to obtain information that it could not have obtained by observation from outside the cartilage of the house. The beeper tells the agent that a particular article is actually located at a particular time in the private residence and is in the possession of the person or persons whose residence is being surveilled. Even if visual surveillance has revealed that the article to which the beeper is attached has entered the house, the later monitoring not only verifies the officers' observations but also establishes that the article remains in the premises.

The net effect of the holdings in *Knotts* and *Karo* is that the police may place a beeper in a container and track its whereabouts as long as it remains in a public area. Once the beeper enters a protected area the police must obtain a warrant in order to continue to track its presence and location. Unlike the decision in *Knotts*, the Court in *Karo* drew the line at the doorway of the residence in favor of individual rights.

Search Warrant Required

Consistent with the decision in *Karo,* in 2001 the Supreme Court held that without a warrant the government may not surreptitiously use an electronic device to obtain information that it could not have gathered by observation from outside the cartilage of the house. The Court's decision in *Kyllo v. United States,* 533 U.S. 27 (2001), heralded another major win for individual rights.

Thermal-Imaging Device

In *Kyllo v. United States* federal agents suspected the defendant of growing marijuana in his home. Knowing that indoor growing operations require the use of high-intensity heat lamps, agents used a thermal imager to scan the house without first obtaining a warrant. The scan only took a few minutes and was conducted by an agent who parked across the street from the house. The scan showed that the roof over the garage and the side of Kyllo's house was substantially warmer than the rest of his residence and the adjoining homes of his neighbors. Armed with information obtained from informants, utility bills, and thermal imaging, the agents obtained a search warrant for Kyllo's home, which resulted in the discovery of an indoor growing operation containing more than one hundred plants. Kyllo was indicted and convicted. On appeal, the lower courts ruled against him finding that use of the thermal imager did not violate the Fourth Amendment since no reasonable expectation of privacy existed in the hotspots on the roof and the exterior wall of the house.

The Supreme Court granted certiorari to consider "whether the use of a thermal-imaging device aimed at a private home from a public street to detect relative amounts of heat within the home constitutes a 'search' within the meaning of the Fourth Amendment." Noting that the interior of a person's home has long been accorded a reasonable expectation of privacy, the Court stated that "to withdraw protection of this minimum expectation would be to permit police technology to erode the privacy guaranteed by the Fourth Amendment." In a ruling that favored individual rights the Court held that "where, as here, the government uses a device that is not in general public use, to explore details of the home that would previously have been unknowable without physical intrusion, the surveillance is a 'search' and is presumptively unreasonable without a warrant."

THE FUTURE OF ELECTRONIC SURVEILLANCE IN THE POST–9/11 ERA

In the post–9/11 era it is anticipated that many issues related to electronic surveillance will involve some aspect of cell-phone usage, computer usage, e-mail, and video or cyber technology. These issues, which are slowly making their way through the judicial system, have not been addressed by the Supreme Court; therefore they lack final resolution. For example, although most cell-phone users view their conversations as "private" matters between the caller and the recipient, in general lower courts have refused to find that the parties enjoy a reasonable expectation of privacy under the Fourth Amendment. Similarly, while it has become commonplace to communicate by e-mail, participate in social networks, and conduct research, business, and other activities using Internet services, persons engaging in these activities should be aware that little or no Fourth Amendment protection may apply to their activities. Indicative of this, in *United States v. Forrester*, 512 F.3d 500 (9th Cir. 2008), the Ninth Circuit Court of Appeals ruled that the IP addresses and the e-mails to and from addresses are analogous to the addresses on a letter in the mail, and therefore individuals have no right of privacy in this information. Knowledge of this type will allow police agencies to ascertain valuable information about individuals ranging from their beliefs and values to the types of books read and whether they're involved in criminal activities. The content of the e-mail itself enjoys limited protection depending upon how long it is stored and whether storage takes place on an Internet provider's network such as Yahoo! or is downloaded to the owner's laptop computer; however, even the content of e-mails may be accessed pursuant to a valid warrant.[6]

Some courts have held that, unlike e-mail communications, the senders and receivers of instant messages have a reasonable expectation of privacy in them (*United States v. Maxwell*, 45 M.J. 406 [C.A.A.F. 1996]). The rationale supporting this ruling is that, like telephone conversations, once a message is sent it is lost forever. On the other hand, courts have refused to recognize a reasonable expectation of privacy in university computers or networks, city networks without password protection, online bulletin boards, and chat rooms.[7] This means that individuals who use these devices do so at their own risk.

Concerns about crime and terrorism have increased the use of video surveillance in public places. For example, many cities now use video cameras to deter crime and apprehend traffic violators. It is generally believed that such surveillance does not involve a Fourth Amendment violation since there is no privacy interest in what is exposed to the public. Additionally, it has been suggested that application of the plain-view doctrine to video surveillance may be limited in three ways: "(1) the police cannot use cameras posted in public places to monitor places where there is an expectation of privacy, (2) police cannot use zoom lenses to magnify individuals or their belongings to a degree that is invasive, and

(3) police cannot use cameras on such a broad scale as to conduct mass searches without suspicion."[8] While these limitations appear to be reasonable in that they permit achievement of law enforcement's objectives while simultaneously protecting individual rights, it remains to be seen whether the Supreme Court ultimately will rule in this manner.

CONCLUSIONS

Katz signaled a significant break with the past by repudiating the trespass doctrine and holding that the Fourth Amendment protects people not places. By recognizing the existence of a constitutional right of privacy the Court ruled in favor of individual rights; however, the ruling in *Katz* was not the end of the story. Since 1968, Congress has enacted significant legislation broadening law-enforcement agencies' authority to conduct electronic surveillance of criminal suspects and ordinary citizens who *may* be involved in domestic or foreign terrorism. The breadth of the power relegated to law-enforcement agencies by these statutes, especially Title III and the USA Patriot Act, is more encompassing than society has ever experienced. In light of this, citizens must remain vigilant to prevent police abuses; however, such vigilance is nearly impossible, since court orders are issued in private and electronic surveillance is conducted in secret shrouded by the authority of the courts and the government.

FURTHER READING

Jeremy Brown, "Pan, Tilt, Zoom: Regulating the Use of Video Surveillance of Public Places," *Berkeley Technical Law Journal* 23 (2008): 755–82.

Deborah Buckner, "Internet Search and Seizure in *United States v. Forrester*: New Problems in the New Age of Pen Registers," *BYU Journal of Public Law* 22 (2008): 499–517.

Rolando V. del Carmen, *Criminal Procedure: Law and Practice*, seventh ed. (Belmont, Calif.: Thomson-Wadsworth, 2007).

Archal Oza, "Amend the ECPA: Fourth Amendment Protection Erodes as E-mail Gets Dusty," *Boston University Law Review* 88 (2008): 1043–73.

Illinois v. Gates

DAVID BRODY

INTRODUCTION

The use of confidential informants and anonymous tips by police has been a controversial practice for many years. Because many informants are themselves criminals, it is understandable that information they provide is treated cautiously. On the other hand, as they may well be on the forefront of an illegal enterprise and therefore have firsthand knowledge of inside information regarding a past, ongoing, or future crime, the tips provided by informants may be the key to arrests and convictions of dangerous criminals.

While obtaining information from confidential sources is an accepted aspect of police work, the manner in which the leads are used is a source of great controversy. One such discussion regards how courts should weigh information provided by informants in determining whether or not probable cause exists for the issuance of a search or arrest warrant. In 1983, in the case of *Illinois v. Gates* (462 U.S. 213 [1983]), the Supreme Court ruled that information from confidential informants can form the basis for probable cause if under a totality of the circumstances presented to a judge or magistrate there is a substantial basis for believing the informant's information and believing there is probable cause that a crime occurred or that evidence of criminal activity will be found at a certain place.

Use of Informants' Tips Prior to *Gates*

Before examining the standard established by the Court for using information from anonymous informants in determinations of probable cause in

Illinois v. Gates, it is important to consider the evolution of the law pertaining to search-warrant requirements. The starting point for this analysis is the 1933 case of *Nathanson v. United States* (290 U.S. 41 [1933]). In *Nathanson*, in a search-warrant application, the only underlying basis for probable cause provided by a customs officer was his sworn statement "that he had cause to suspect and did believe that" contraband was at a certain location. In invalidating the search warrant, the Supreme Court held that a search warrant may not be issued "upon mere affirmance of suspicion or belief without disclosure of supporting facts or circumstances." The Court went on to hold that "under the Fourth Amendment an officer may not properly issue a warrant to search a private dwelling unless he can find probable cause therefore from facts or circumstances presented to him under oath or affirmation. Mere affirmance of belief or suspicion is not enough."

In *Draper v. United States* (358 U.S. 307 [1959]) the Supreme Court ruled that hearsay could be used to establish probable cause. The *Draper* Court held that a tip from a previously reliable informant, describing a suspect in great detail and predicting that the suspect would be in possession of narcotics at a specific time and place, furnished probable cause for Draper's warrantless arrest. The Court based its decision on the fact that since the police had confirmed the informant's detailed description of Draper, they could reasonably deduce that he also was carrying the drugs. As such, the Court held that an informant's tip can establish probable cause if it is substantially corroborated by police.

One year after deciding *Draper*, the Court held that a tip from an informant could furnish probable cause for issuance of a search warrant in *Jones v. United States* (362 U.S. 257 [1960]). *Jones* significantly expanded *Draper* by holding that a tip, standing alone, could be sufficient to establish probable cause, with or without independent police corroboration. The Court held that an informant's tip could serve as a basis for a warrant only "so long as a substantial basis for crediting the hearsay is presented." In *Jones*, the Court emphasized that the informant's leads were based on personal knowledge and that he had previously given the police accurate information. That being said, the Court did not elaborate on how lower courts should determine the sufficiency and veracity of information obtained from an informant in a warrant application.

Several years later the Court departed from the vagueness of the substantial-basis standard and adopted a more rigid, formalistic standard. In *Aguilar v. Texas* (378 U.S. 108 [1964]), the Supreme Court reaffirmed the rule that a warrant may be issued on the basis of hearsay. The Court explicitly held, however, that a warrant application must contain specific facts upon which the informant had concluded that criminal activity had occurred. To consider whether this information amounted to a substantial basis to accept the informant's tip in making a probable-cause determination, the Court established a two-pronged test: The two prongs to be considered, which must be established in an affidavit provided as part of a warrant application, involve the informant's (1) basis of knowledge and (2) veracity or reliability.

To satisfy the "basis of knowledge" prong, a search- or arrest-warrant affidavit must present a neutral judge or magistrate with a statement about how the informant obtained his knowledge. This frequently involves a consideration of whether it was by personal observation or in some other dependable manner and not through mere rumor.

The "veracity prong" requires the police to provide the judge or magistrate with facts that would establish the informant's credibility or the reliability of his information. The primary way of satisfying the veracity prong is by showing that the informant had previously provided the police with accurate information. In *Aguilar*, a search warrant was issued based on a police officer's statement that he had "received reliable information from a credible person and do believe that [narcotics] are being kept at the above-described premises for the purpose of sale and use." As there was no indication that the informant had personal knowledge about the situation described, nor was there a basis for establishing the informant's credibility, the Court held that the affidavit failed to provide sufficient information to establish probable cause.

In *Spinelli v. United States* (393 U.S. 410 [1969]), the Court not only reaffirmed the two-prong test established in *Aguilar* but also provided clarification on its application. In addressing the basis-of-knowledge prong, the Court held that the affidavit filed in support of the search-warrant request should state the underlying circumstances on which the informant based his conclusion that criminal activity was afoot. Importantly, the Court held that in the absence of a statement detailing how the information was obtained, the basis-of-knowledge prong may be satisfied if the information contained in the tip describes the criminal activity in sufficient detail that indicates it is based on actual knowledge rather than rumor or guesswork.

As for the veracity prong, lack of information regarding the basis for finding the informant reliable could be overcome by independent police corroboration of some of the details contained in the tip. By corroborating some statements provided by the informant, the Court held that other information provided can be seen as more trustworthy.

When viewed together, the standards that were derived in *Aguilar* and *Spinelli* are known as the *Aguilar-Spinelli* test. This test established a bright-line rule for courts to follow. While it decreased uncertainty regarding what a search-warrant application needed to establish probable cause when making use of information from a confidential informant, the rigid manner in which courts applied it caused significant levels of frustration. By requiring that both the basis-of-knowledge and veracity prongs be proven independently, courts found that many warrants could not be issued despite overwhelming evidence for one of the prongs but inadequate information to satisfy the other. This frustration led the Supreme Court to establish an alternative test for determining when information provided by an informant can establish probable cause.

THE CASE OF *ILLINOIS V. GATES* (1983)

The Facts

According to *Illinois v. Gates* (462 U.S. 213 [1983]), on May 3, 1978, the Bloomingdale Police Department received an anonymous handwritten letter, which read as follows:

> This letter is to inform you that you have a couple in your town who strictly make their living on selling drugs. They are Sue and Lance Gates, they live on Greenway, off Bloomingdale Rd. in the condominiums. Most of their buys are done in Florida. Sue his wife drives their car to Florida, where she leaves it to be loaded up with drugs, then Lance flys down and drives it back. Sue flys back after she drops the car off in Florida. May 3 she is driving down there again and Lance will be flying down in a few days to drive it back. At the time Lance drives the car back he has the trunk loaded with over $100,000.00 in drugs. Presently they have over $100,000.00 worth of drugs in their basement.

The Bloomingdale Police Department decided to pursue the tip. Investigation by the police uncovered that a Lance Gates lived at the stated address in Bloomingdale; that "L. Gates" had made an airline reservation to fly to West Palm Beach, Florida, on May 5; that Gates flew to Florida on the scheduled flight; that Susan Gates was staying at a hotel in Florida at this time; and that Susan and Lance Gates left the hotel the next morning driving their own car heading northbound.

Bloomingdale Police Department Detective Mader signed an affidavit stating the foregoing facts and submitted it to a judge with a copy of the anonymous letter. The judge issued a search warrant for the Gateses' residence and for their automobile. At 5:15 A.M. on March 7, Lance Gates and his wife returned to their home in Bloomingdale, driving the car in which they had left West Palm Beach some twenty-two hours earlier. The Bloomingdale police were waiting for them. Armed with the warrant the police searched the trunk of the Mercury, where they uncovered approximately 350 pounds of marijuana, and the house, where they discovered marijuana, weapons, and other contraband. The Gateses were placed under arrest.

Prior to trial, the Illinois Circuit Court ordered that the evidence seized from the Gateses' house and car be suppressed, on the grounds that the affidavit submitted to the circuit judge failed to support the necessary determination of probable cause. The court based this decision on the fact that there was insufficient information contained in the affidavit to establish the veracity of the writer of the anonymous letter. Additionally, there was no indication of the basis for the letter writer's knowledge of the Gateses' activities. The court found that the corroboration of innocent details was not sufficient to meet the standards established under the *Aguilar-Spinelli* test. The Illinois Appellate Court and the Illinois Supreme Court affirmed the decision.

The Issue before the Court

Must a warrant based on information from a confidential informant satisfy both prongs of the *Aguilar-Spinelli* test to be considered constitutional?

The Court's Holding

No. If after considering the totality of the circumstances surrounding a warrant application there is a substantial basis for finding the existence of probable cause, the two prongs of the *Aguilar-Spinelli* test need not be satisfied.

The Majority Opinion

Justice William Rehnquist wrote the majority opinion in which five other justices joined. The underlying premise of the majority opinion was that probable cause is a "practical, nontechnical conception" and "a fluid concept—turning on the assessment of probabilities in particular factual contexts—not readily, or even usefully, reduced to a neat set of legal rules." The *Aguilar-Spinelli* test was contrary to this conception of probable cause. The rigid application of the two-pronged approach seriously impeded the ability of law enforcement to make use of anonymous tips because rarely can the reliability of an informant be known or documented.

Justice Rehnquist acknowledged the importance of considering an informant's basis of knowledge and veracity but stated that the Illinois Supreme Court, as well as other courts, had applied too rigid and technical an analysis in making probable cause determinations. As a consequence, the Court held that it was abandoning the use of the *Aguilar-Spinelli* test for determining whether an informant's tip established probable cause. Rather, courts should go beyond the rigid requirements of the two-pronged test and consider the "totality of circumstances" in making probable-cause determinations.

Under the "totality-of-circumstances test" an informant's basis of knowledge and veracity are still important in determining probable cause. However, they are not independent requirements; rather, they are "closely intertwined issues" that aid a judge in evaluating the overall reliability of an informant's tip. Instead of assessing an informant's basis of knowledge and creditability in isolation, a judge or magistrate should look at all the circumstances set forth in the affidavit and make a practical, common-sense decision as to whether there is probable cause.

After setting out the totality-of-circumstances test, the Court applied it to the facts of the case before them and reversed the Illinois Supreme Court. The Court found that by themselves the facts gathered through the independent police investigation at least suggested that the Gateses were involved in drug trafficking. Furthermore, Justice Rehnquist wrote that in considering the reliability of the informant the magistrate could have relied "on the anonymous letter, which had been corroborated in major part." This corroboration reduced the chances that the informant provided untruthful information. Finally, Justice Rehnquist reasoned, "the anonymous letter contained a range of details relating not just to easily obtained facts and conditions existing at the time of the tip but to future actions of third parties ordinarily not easily predicted." The Court concluded that where an informant had access to this kind of precise information "it was not unlikely that he also had access to reliable information of the Gateses' alleged illegal activities." Therefore, the Court held that "the judge issuing the warrant had a 'substantial basis for . . . conclud[ing]' that probable cause to search the Gateses' home and car existed."

The Concurring Opinion

Justice Byron White concurred with the Court's judgment but wrote a separate concurring opinion. He believed that it was not necessary to abandon the two-pronged test. He argued that the warrant was appropriately issued under the *Aguilar-Spinelli* framework. Justice White found that the investigation conducted in *Gates* demonstrated that the informant's tip was trustworthy and would satisfy the *Aguilar-Spinelli* test. This was due primarily to the fact that with police corroboration of the predications contained in the tip a magistrate could reasonably infer that the informant obtained the information in a reliable way.

Justice White also voiced concern that the majority opinion did not provide a standard by which a magistrate could make a probable-cause decision. In his opinion, any standard used to assess the reliability of an informant's tip in the issuance of a warrant should "expressly require, as a prerequisite to issuance of a warrant, some showing of facts from which an inference may be drawn that the informant is credible and that his information was obtained in a reliable way." Believing the Court had failed to do this, while agreeing in the judgment, Justice White was not willing to abandon the *Aguilar-Spinelli* test and accept the totality-of-circumstances standard.

The Dissenting Opinions

Justice William Brennan wrote a dissenting opinion, which was joined by Justice Marshall. In his dissent Justice Brennan argued that the Court acted hastily in abandoning the *Aguilar-Spinelli* framework. He stated that there was no indication that the two-pronged test was not working, but rather it preserved the role of the magistrate in considering warrant applications. The two-pronged test required that police provide a neutral magistrate with specific information that could be independently analyzed under a workable standard. By replacing such a standard with a totality-of-circumstances approach, the Court removes the necessary guidance under which magistrates and judges can make probable-cause determinations.

Justice Brennan concluded his dissent with harsh words for what he perceived to be the real basis for the majority opinion.

> The Court's complete failure to provide any persuasive reason for rejecting *Aguilar* and *Spinelli* doubtlessly reflects impatience with what it perceives to be "overly technical" rules governing searches and seizures under the Fourth Amendment.

Words such as "practical," "nontechnical," and "commonsense," as used in the Court's opinion, are but code words for an overly permissive attitude towards police practices in derogation of the rights secured by the Fourth Amendment. Everyone shares the Court's concern over the horrors of drug trafficking, but under our Constitution only measures consistent with the Fourth Amendment may be employed by government to cure this evil.

Justice Stevens also wrote a dissenting opinion. His dissent focused on the significance of an inaccuracy in the anonymous letter. He believed that the inaccuracy was significant because it cast doubt on the informant's belief that there was contraband in the Gateses' home, it made the Gateses' conduct seem less unusual, and it raised doubt about the reasonableness of relying on the letter as a basis for issuing a search warrant.

Further Analysis

The majority opinion in *Gates* is to some extent self-contradictory. While the Court held that it was abandoning the *Aguilar-Spinelli* test, it based the totality-of-circumstances test largely on the criteria contained in the two-pronged test it abandoned. Although the Court acknowledged that an informant's basis of knowledge and veracity were critical to the probable-cause analysis, it did not approve of the manner in which the criteria were being evaluated by lower courts. By adopting the totality-of-circumstances test, the Court left it up to individual courts to establish what would constitute a substantial basis for finding probable cause based on an anonymous informant's tip.

As stated by the dissenting opinion of Justice Brennan, the overarching shortcoming of *Gates* is that it did not "provide any meaningful guidelines to magistrates in their probable-cause determinations." Rather than abandoning the *Aguilar-Spinelli* test, the Court could have used *Gates* as an opportunity to voice its disapproval of overly technical and rigid application of the test. In so doing, it could have maintained the structure upon which magistrates could base their probable cause decision.

Under the *Aguilar-Spinelli* test, law-enforcement personnel had to meet clear standards to obtain a warrant based on an anonymous tip. As relying on informants can be fraught with peril, requiring an explicit basis for examining and accepting the validity of an anonymous tip served the purpose of shielding individuals from unwarranted intrusions on their privacy and liberty. By removing the requirement for evidence of both an informant's basis of knowledge and veracity, the Court significantly altered the balance between law enforcement and individual interests at issue.

Case Significance

Illinois v. Gates is an important case in the development of Fourth Amendment law. In abandoning the requirements of the *Aguilar-Spinelli* test it signaled to lower courts and the law-enforcement community that in balancing the needs of law enforcement with the privacy interests of citizens, the Court was making a dramatic shift toward the former. By viewing Fourth Amendment protections and standards as technicalities and courts that applied them as being unduly rigid, the Court gave a green light to more aggressive use of confidential informants and other tactics in the growing war on drugs. Moreover, it largely insulates a magistrate's probable-cause determination from appellate review in all but cases involving the most bare-boned, conclusory warrant applications.

The significance of the *Gates* test was evidenced in the 1990 case *Alabama v. White* (496 U.S. 325 [1990]). In *White* the Supreme Court applied the totality-of-circumstances test to investigatory stops based on reasonable suspicion. Specifically, the Court held that in considering whether an anonymous tip, coupled with police follow-up investigation, provides reasonable suspicion to justify a warrantless investigatory stop, courts should consider the totality of circumstances present at the time of the stop.

AFTERMATH OF *GATES*

Although *Gates* watered down the information necessary to establish probable cause based on information from an anonymous tip, lower courts must ensure that warrant applications include more than the conclusory statements of law-enforcement officers. Justice Rehnquist did state that sufficient information must be presented to the magistrate to allow that official to determine probable cause; the official's action cannot be a mere ratification of the bare conclusions of others. In order to ensure that such an abdication of the magistrate's duty does not occur, courts must continue to conscientiously review the sufficiency of affidavits on which warrants are issued. Once warrant applications meet a minimal threshold, however, they are likely to pass muster when subjected to the totality-of-circumstances standard.

While the lower federal courts readily adopted the totality-of-circumstances standard, the reaction of state courts was somewhat mixed. A significant majority of state supreme courts have adopted the totality-of-circumstances test as laid out in *Gates*. That being said, nearly a dozen states have chosen not to adopt the totality-of-circumstances test but instead require information akin to what was required under the *Aguilar-Spinelli* test. Nine state supreme courts have interpreted their state constitutions to have stricter requirements for the finding of probable cause than what is required under the United States Constitution. Three other states have enacted statutes that require that the components of the two-pronged test be established before a warrant can be issued based on an informant's tip.

Regardless of which standard is used by a court in determining whether an anonymous tip establishes probable cause, there are several factors frequently considered by magistrates and appellate court judges.

1. *Presence of self-verifying detail.* The inclusion of incriminating facts of such specificity that it can be reasonably inferred that the informant obtained the information in a reliable way. Spinelli held that this could be an indirect manner of establishing the basis of knowledge. It is still useful under the totality-of-circumstances test.
2. *Admission by informant against penal interest.* A tip given by an informant that implicates him or her in a crime is more reliable since it is unlikely a person would make a statement to police incriminating oneself unless it was true regarding a third party.
3. *Corroboration of details contained in tip.* The more details are corroborated, as in *Gates*, the more likely it is to be found reliable.
4. *Past performance of informant.* Past instances where an informant has proven to be reliable will buttress his or her credibility for other warrant affidavits.
5. *Informant's motive to be truthful.* A person who has a motive to be honest is more likely to be seen as credible. Typically, this involves information obtained as part of an immunity deal or a plea bargain, under which all benefits to the informant are withdrawn if he or she provides false information.
6. *Staleness of information.* Information that is based on personal observations or other sources should be contemporaneous to the warrant application. Information from the past is likely to be considered stale and of limited value.

CONCLUSIONS

In considering whether or not probable cause is present to justify the issuance of a warrant courts strive to balance competing Fourth Amendment interests. Since the adoption of the *Aguilar-Spinelli* two-pronged test for considering warrant applications based on hearsay information, courts had been frustrated by the test's rigidity. In response to this frustration in *Illinois v. Gates* the Supreme Court adopted the totality-of-circumstances test on the grounds that it equitably balanced competing Fourth Amendment interests. Whether or not *Gates* achieves this balance is debatable. It does enhance the ability of police to make use of confidential informants. It also provides courts with increased flexibility and discretion in considering warrant applications. At the same time, it removes usable standards for police and courts to base the issuance of warrants and leaves the door open for the increased use of confidential informants without adequate checks on veracity and reliability. How one considers and balances these factors is up to individual preferences.

FURTHER READING

Jodi Levine Avergun, "The Impact of *Illinois v. Gates*: The States Consider the Totality of the Circumstances Test," *Brooklyn Law Review* 52 (1987): 1127–69.

Joseph D. Grano, "Probable Cause and Common Sense: A Reply to the Critics of *Illinois v. Gates*," *University of Michigan Journal of Law and Legal Reform* 17 (1984): 465–521.

Max Minzner, "Putting Probability Back into Probable Cause," *Texas Law Review* 87 (2009): 913–78.

Charles E. Moylan Jr., "*Illinois v. Gates*: What It Did and What It Did Not Do," *Criminal Law Bulletin* 20 (1984): 93–118.

II

THE EXCLUSIONARY RULE

Mapp v. Ohio

Sue Carter Collins

INTRODUCTION

The adoption and application of the exclusionary rule has generated significant controversy stemming primarily from the fact that its use prevents consideration of evidence indicative of a defendant's guilt. In the long-ago spoken works of then Judge, later Justice, Cardozo, under the exclusionary rule the "criminal is to go free because the constable has blundered" (*People v. Defore*, 242 N. Y. 13, 21 [1926]). Prior to 1961 when the Court decided *Mapp v. Ohio*, 367 U.S. 643 (1961), the exclusionary rule applied only to agents of the federal government. The states were free to decide for themselves what criminal procedures would be applied in state trial courts. The enactment of different federal and state rules led to flagrant abuses of individual rights caused by unlawful police searches and seizures. The Court's landmark decision in *Mapp v. Ohio* closed the last remaining door that allowed illegally seized evidence to be used in state court. Detractors of the exclusionary rule have vociferously criticized its use. Although the Court has recognized several exceptions, the exclusionary rule continues to be a significant factor impacting police operations and procedures today.

The chapter begins with a comprehensive analysis of the *Mapp* decision. Following is a discussion of the exclusionary rule's purpose and scope, as well as an examination of its exceptions. The chapter concludes with the prediction that, despite opponent's claims that the rule is ineffective, in all likelihood it is here to stay.

THE CASE OF *MAPP V. OHIO* (1961): THE EXCLUSIONARY RULE

The Facts

According to *Mapp v. Ohio* (367 U.S. 643 [1961]), Dolly Mapp and her daughter were at home on May 23, 1957, when three Cleveland police officers knocked on the door and demanded entry. The Mapps lived on the top floor of a two-story boarding house. The officers believed that a person who was wanted for questioning in connection with a recent bombing was hiding out in the house and that a large amount of paraphernalia pertinent to the bombing was present. After telephoning her attorney, Mapp refused to let the officers in without a search warrant. On failing to gain entry, the officers set up surveillance on the house and waited three hours until they were joined by four additional officers.

With reinforcements present, the officers again demanded entry. By this time Mapp's attorney had arrived but was denied access to his client. When Mapp did not open the door immediately in response to the officers' command, they used force to gain entry. On sighting the officers in the hallway, Mapp demanded to see a search warrant. When one officer held up a piece of paper that he claimed was a warrant, Mapp snatched the paper and hid it in her bosom. Thereafter, a struggle ensued during which the officers recovered the paper and handcuffed Mapp for being "'belligerent' in resisting their official rescue of the 'warrant' from her person." Mapp was then taken by force to her bedroom where the officers searched several items including a dresser, chest of drawers, closet, and suitcases. On finding nothing illegal in the bedroom, the officers searched the remainder of the second-floor residence before making their way down to the basement where they discovered a trunk containing obscene materials.

Mapp was tried and convicted of possessing obscene literature. At the trial, the prosecutor failed to produce a search warrant or to explain its absence. The Ohio Court of Appeals affirmed Mapp's conviction. Citing *Wolf v. Colorado*, 338 U.S. 25 (1949), for the proposition "that in a prosecution in a state court for a state crime the Fourteenth Amendment does not forbid the admission of evidence obtained by unreasonable search and seizure," the state argued that even if the evidence was unlawfully seized the prosecution was not prevented from using it at trial. Although the Ohio Supreme Court opined that a "'reasonable argument' could be made that the conviction should be reversed because of the offensive methods used by the police to obtain the evidence," the court ruled otherwise because "the evidence had not been taken 'from the defendant's person by the use of brutal or offensive physical force.'"

The Issue before the Court

Is evidence obtained in violation of the Fourth Amendment protection against unreasonable searches and seizures admissible against the accused in a state criminal prosecution?

The Majority Opinion

Mapp was argued March 29, 1961, and decided on June 19, 1961. Justice Clark wrote the majority opinion expressing the views of five members of the Court. In a landmark decision that overruled *Wolf v. Colorado*, the Court held that "all evidence obtained by searches and seizures in violation of the Constitution is, by that same authority, inadmissible in a state court" (*Mapp v. Ohio*, 367 U.S. 643 [1961]).

Clark based the decision on both principled and pragmatic considerations. He began the analysis by revisiting the Court's decision in *Boyd v. United States*, 116 U.S. 616 (1886). He noted that in *Boyd* the Court held that the doctrines of the Fourth and Fifth Amendments "apply to all invasions on the part of the government and its employees of the sanctity of a man's home and privacies of life. It is not the breaking of his doors and the rummaging of his drawers that constitutes the essence of the offence but the invasion of his indefeasible right of personal security, personal liberty, and private property." Declaring that these constitutional protections are to be liberally construed, Clark observed that it is the duty of the Court to protect against encroachments. He also noted that to this end, in *Weeks v. United States*, 232 U.S. 383 (1914), the Court held for the first time that evidence seized by the government in violation of the Constitution is barred from use in a federal prosecution. The *Weeks* Court reasoned that the use of such evidence involves a "denial of the constitutional rights of the accused." Related to this, Clark noted that since the Court announced the exclusionary rule there have been conflicting opinions regarding whether the rule is derived from the Constitution or merely a rule of evidence. In an attempt to set the record straight he stated, "the plain and unequivocal language of *Weeks*—and its later paraphrase in *Wolf*—to the effect that the *Weeks* rule is of constitutional origin, remains entirely undisturbed."

The Dissenting Opinion

Justice Harlan authored the dissenting opinion, with concurrences from Justice Frankfurter and Justice Whittaker. Harlan began the dissent with a strong declaration against the actions of his judicial brethren. Stating that *Mapp* provided no basis for reexamining *Wolf*, Harlan argued that "in overruling the *Wolf* case the Court . . . has forgotten the sense of judicial restraint which . . . [is to be considered when] deciding whether a past decision of this Court should be overruled." Further, Harlan disagreed with the majority's identification of the controlling issue. He stated that *Mapp* had presented the Court with two questions of constitutional dimension—whether illegally seized evidence was constitutionally admissible in state court, an issue that would require reexamination of the holding in *Wolf*, or whether the Ohio statute that made mere knowing possession or control of obscene material a crime was an unconstitutional violation of free thought and expression as guaranteed by the Fourteenth Amendment.

Noting that the first question was raised by the appellant in the court below but only as a subordinate point, Harlan argued that the proper issue before the Court was the constitutionality of the Ohio statute. It was this issue that was decided by the lower court, set forth in Mapp's jurisdictional statement, and briefed and argued before the Supreme Court. Thus Harlan opined, "I think it fair to say that five members of this Court have "simply 'reached out' to overrule" *Wolf*. As further support for his argument Harlan noted that as recently as 1949 three members of the *Mapp* majority had "expressly subscribed" to the *Wolf* doctrine.

Further Analysis

The decisions in *Weeks* and *Wolf* set the stage for the Court's review of *Mapp*. Prior to 1961, the law was unmistakable that evidence illegally seized by federal agents could not be used in federal court. Although the holding in *Weeks* clearly prohibited federal agents from using in court evidence they had illegally seized, it did not address whether evidence illegally seized by state officials could be used in federal cases. Thus, the *Weeks* decision gave rise to the "silver-platter doctrine," which permitted state officials, often at the behest of federal officials, to violate search-and-seizure procedures and turn over illegally seized evidence to federal prosecutors for use in federal court (*Bryars v. United States*, 273 U.S. 28 [1927]).

A second issue not addressed by the *Weeks* Court was whether the Fourth Amendment protection against illegal searches and seizures is incorporated in the Fourteenth Amendment Equal Protection Clause and thereby applicable to both the state and federal governments. The Court answered this question thirty-five years later when it granted certiorari in *Wolf v. Colorado*, 338 U.S.

25 (1949). The specific issue in *Wolf* was whether "a conviction by a state court for a state offense den[ies] the 'due process of law' required by the Fourteenth Amendment, solely because evidence that was admitted at the trial was obtained under circumstances which would have rendered it inadmissible in a prosecution for violation of a federal law." Although the *Wolf* Court recognized that "the security of one's privacy against arbitrary intrusion by the police—which is at the core of the Fourth Amendment—is basic to a free society . . . [and] therefore implicit in 'the concept of ordered liberty' and as such enforceable against the states through the Due-Process Clause," it nevertheless decided that "the *Weeks* exclusionary rule would not be imposed upon the states as an 'essential ingredient' of that right." In other words, the Court in *Wolf* affirmed the rule of law in *Weeks* but held that "the Fourteenth Amendment does not forbid the admission of evidence obtained by an unreasonable search and seizure" in a prosecution in a state court for a state crime. The Court grounded its decision on the facts of the case and evidence that numerous jurisdictions had considered the *Weeks* rule and rejected it. Also significant to the Court's decision in *Wolf* was the fact that these jurisdictions had developed other ways to protect the right to privacy including "the remedies of private action and such protection as the internal discipline of the police, under the eyes of an alert public opinion."

The Supreme Court accepted review of *Mapp* to reassess the validity of *Wolf*'s holding. After examining the facts on which *Wolf* was based the Court found that they were no longer relevant. Writing for the majority, Justice Clark pointed out that although prior to *Wolf* (1949) almost two-thirds of the states opposed the exclusionary rule, since that time more than half of them had by "legislative or judicial decision wholly or partly adopted or adhered to the *Weeks* rule."

Regarding the second reason given by the *Wolf* Court for failing to apply the exclusionary rule to the states (i.e., that other means of protecting the right to privacy are available), Clark noted that California was one of many states that had since adopted the exclusionary rule because "other remedies have completely failed to secure constitutional compliance with the constitutional provisions." Similar failures had occurred in other states. Clark also observed that the "silver-platter doctrine" had been repudiated by the Court one year earlier in *Elkins v. United States*, 364 U.S. 206 (1960). In that case the Court found that "the controlling principles" governing search and seizure "seemed clear" until *Wolf* announced that "the Due Process Clause . . . does not itself require state courts to adopt the exclusionary rule." Accordingly, Clark opined that *Mapp* provided an appropriate opportunity to reexamine the Court's decision in *Wolf*.

In announcing the Court's holding, Clark stated,

[We] are led by [our analysis] to close the only courtroom door remaining open to evidence secured by official lawlessness in flagrant abuse of that basic right [to privacy] reserved to all persons as a specific guarantee against the very same unlawful conduct. We hold that all evidence obtained by searches and seizures in violation of the Constitution is, by the same authority, inadmissible in a state court.

The effect of this ruling is to apply the exclusionary rule to the states with the same force as it is applied to the federal government. To rule otherwise, Clark contended, "would be to grant the right but in reality to withhold its privilege and enjoyment." Further, Clark said, the Court's decision that

the exclusionary rule is an essential part of both the Fourth and Fourteenth Amendments is not only the logical dictate of prior cases, but it also makes very good sense. . . . Presently a [federal] prosecutor may make no use of evidence illegally seized, but a state's attorney across the street may, although he is supposedly operating under the same enforceable prohibitions of the same amendment. Thus, the state, by admitting evidence unlawfully seized, serves to encourage disobedience to the federal Constitution which it is bound to uphold.

For his final point Clark addressed the matter of judicial integrity. Noting there are those who argue that the exclusionary rule allows "the criminal . . . to go free" (*People v. Defore*, 242 N.Y. 13, 21 [1926]), Clark responded that while this will undoubtedly occur in some cases, "nothing can destroy a government more quickly than its failure to observe its own laws, or worse its disregard of the charter of its own existence." Besides, both the FBI and the federal courts have operated under the *Weeks* exclusionary rule for more than half a century, yet there has been no suggestion that either has been rendered ineffective. To allow the states a shortcut to conviction makes "the entire system of constitutional restraints on which the liberties of the people rest" null and void. Therefore Clark concluded, "Our decision, founded on reason and truth, gives to the individual no more than that which the Constitution guarantees him, to the police officer no less than that to which honest law enforcement is entitled, and, to the courts, that judicial integrity so necessary in the true administration of justice."

Speaking on behalf of the dissenting justices, Harlan took issue with the majority opinion on multiple fronts. In addition to suggesting that review was improvidently granted, Harlan contended that the majority's argument for extending the exclusionary rule to the states rested on faulty ground. Specifically undercutting the majority's argument that "'the factual grounds upon which *Wolf* was based' have since changed, in that more states now follow the *Weeks* exclusionary rule than did so at the time *Wolf* was decided," was a recent survey which found that "at present one-half of the states still adhere to the common-law nonexclusionary rule, and one, Maryland, retains the rule as to felonies." This aside, Harlan asserted that the real concern "is not with the desirability of that rule but . . . whether the states are free to follow it or not" as they may choose. The fact that there are different views among the states simply emphasizes that this is a debatable issue. Accordingly, Harlan concluded that far from supporting the majority's holding, the facts on which the majority rely points away from the need to "replac[e] voluntary state action with federal compulsion."

Harlan also took issue with the majority's argument that imposing the exclusionary rule on the states makes "very good sense." He contended that the Court had overstepped its authority by attempting to achieve "procedural symmetry" for the sake of "administrative convenience" between state and federal courts. Noting that the Fourteenth Amendment does not authorize the Court "to mould state remedies . . . to suit its own notions of how things should be done," Harlan asserted that states are sovereign entities and each is authorized to determine the specific procedures to be used in trial court.

Harlan rejected as inapposite the majority's analogy that "the overruling of *Wolf* is supported by established doctrine that the admission in evidence of an involuntary confession renders a state conviction Constitutionally invalid." Although he acknowledged that a statement obtained from an accused who is illegally detained is "as much as unlawfully seized evidence, illegally obtained," he countered with the fact that "this Court has consistently refused to reverse state convictions resting on the use of such statements."[1]

On a final note, Harlan pointed out that the majority opinion "is in fact an opinion only for the *judgment* overruling *Wolf* and not for the basic rationale by which four members of the Court have reached that result." Specifically, although Justice Black concurred with the result, he did not adopt the majority opinion that the exclusionary rule derives from the Constitution itself; rather, he joined the opinion only on the assumption that the "end result can be achieved by bringing the Fifth Amendment to the aid of the Fourth." In light of this, Harlan responded, "whatever the validity of the 'Fourth-Fifth Amendment' correlation which the *Boyd* case . . . found . . . we have only very recently again reiterated the long-established doctrine of this Court that the Fifth Amendment privilege against self-incrimination is not applicable to the states."

Case Significance

Before *Mapp*, it was left up to each state to decide whether to preclude the use in court of evidence unlawfully obtained by state police. *Mapp* definitively established that the provisions of the Fourth Amendment were made applicable to the states by virtue of the Fourteenth Amendment to the United States Constitution. After *Mapp*, it was clear that the *Weeks* exclusionary rule, which previously applied only to federal officers, also prohibited state officers from using illegally seized evidence in state courts. *Mapp* is one of a select few criminal cases that has revolutionized the way law-enforcement officers and prosecutors conduct business on a daily basis. As one legal scholar notes, it "is perhaps the second-most important law-enforcement case ever decided by the Court (the first was *Miranda v. Arizona*)."[2]

THREE PURPOSES OF THE EXCLUSIONARY RULE

The primary purpose of the exclusionary rule is to deter police misconduct by removing incentives for officers to violate constitutional guarantees (*Elkins v. United States*, 364 U.S. 206 [1960]). The rule also serves two additional purposes: first, "it enable[es] the judiciary to avoid the taint of partnership in official lawlessness," and, second, it "assur[es] the people—all potential victims of unlawful government conduct—that the government would not profit from its lawless behavior, thus minimizing the risk of seriously undermining popular trust in government" (*United States v. Calandra*, 414 U.S. 338 [1974]). Therefore, the net effect of the exclusionary rule is to preserve the people's privacy rights while simultaneously ensuring that the judicial process will remain unsullied.

THE CURRENT SCOPE OF THE EXCLUSIONARY RULE

Although *Mapp* involved a residential search, the exclusionary rule has been applied in a multitude of contexts—from searches and seizures of "persons" to searches and seizures of "houses, papers, and effects," including motor vehicles and containers—to prevent the use in state and federal court of evidence illegally obtained in violation of the Fourth Amendment. Illegally obtained evidence may include contraband, fruits of the crime (criminal proceeds), tools and instruments used to commit crimes, "mere evidence" (items that are not inherently criminal in nature but that connect a person to a crime such as clothes, shoes, or hats), and unlawfully obtained confessions. The exclusionary rule applies to both primary and derivative evidence. Primary evidence, such as the obscene literature seized in *Mapp*, is evidence obtained as a direct result of an illegal act by police; derivative evidence is obtained indirectly as a result of the primary unlawful act.

The Court first announced the "fruit of the poisonous tree" doctrine, which requires courts to suppress unlawfully obtained derivative evidence, in 1920 in *Silverthorne Lumber Co. v. United States*, 251 U.S. 385 (1920). This doctrine is based on the proposition that the government should not be permitted to benefit from information or evidence derived from unlawfully obtained evidence because the original bad act taints the subsequent evidence or information. In other words, if the tree is bad, the fruit that it produces also is bad; however, the Court will not prevent the government from prosecuting a defendant using evidence obtained through lawful means from an independent source.

Although the "fruit of the poisonous tree" doctrine originated in *Silverthorne Lumber Co.*, it is perhaps best known for its association with *Wong Sun v. United States*, 371 U.S. 471 (1963). *Wong Sun* involved a federal narcotics investigation that resulted in the unlawful arrest of Hom Way. Based on information obtained during the investigation the agents also arrested Toy, Yee, and Wong Sun. The defendants were each arraigned and released on recognizance. Several days later they were interrogated at the station and asked to sign written statements. Although Toy and Wong Sun refused to sign, Wong Sun admitted that the statement attributed to him was accurate. In a jury trial, Wong Sun and Toy were found guilty of transportation and concealment of heroin. The evidence against them consisted of Toy's statements made at the time of his arrest, some heroin found on Yee, and Toy's and Wong Sun's pre-trial statements. The primary issue in the case was the admissibility of evidence obtained by federal agents against Toy, Yee, and Wong Sun pursuant to an unlawful arrest. The Court held that the exclusionary rule bars the admission of any physical evidence that is unlawfully obtained as well as any derivative evidence regardless of the source. Applying the "fruit of the poisonous tree" doctrine, the Court concluded that the statements made by Toy and the heroin taken from Yee were inadmissible in court; however, the statement made by Wong Sun was properly admitted. Even though Wong Sun's arrest was unlawful because the agents lacked probable cause, his unsigned statement "was not the fruit of that arrest." Rather, the fact that he was released and returned voluntarily to make the statement was sufficient to dissipate the taint.

STANDING

In numerous cases subsequent to *Mapp* courts have affirmed that the exclusionary rule applies to any "fruits" of a constitutional violation including tangible, physical evidence that is seized in an illegal search, confessions or admissions made by suspects pursuant to an unlawful arrest or detention, and items seen or words overheard during the commission of an unlawful act. Nevertheless, not every accused is entitled to the exclusionary rule's protection. Rather, persons who allege a violation of their Fourth Amendment rights must first prove they have standing to challenge admissibility of the evidence against them.

Standing is a legal concept used to determine if a person has a privacy interest in the area searched or the evidence seized. The general rule is that a person may challenge the admissibility of evidence only if he or she has a reasonable expectation of privacy in these items (*Katz v. United States*, 389 U.S. 347 [1967]). For example, in *Minnesota v. Carter*, 525 U.S. 83 (1998), the Court held that the defendants' reasonable expectation of privacy was not violated when a police officer peered through a gap in closed blinds at an apartment window because the defendants were there for a "business purpose—to package drugs." A different outcome was reached in *United States v. Pollard*, 215 F. 3d 643 (6th Cir. 2000), where the defendant had been friends with the apartment lessee for several years, sometimes spent the night there, left clothes there, and occasionally ate there.

EXCEPTIONS TO THE EXCLUSIONARY RULE

Despite the continued viability of the exclusionary rule, the Supreme Court has identified several exceptions. In addition to the "purged taint" exception articulated in *Wong Sun*, the Court also has recognized "independent source," "inevitable discovery," and "good faith" exceptions. This section discusses these exceptions.

Purged-Taint Exception

Under the purged-taint exception unlawfully obtained evidence is still admissible if a defendant dissipates the taint through an intervening voluntary act of free will. For example, in *Wong Sun v. United States*, 371 U.S. 471 (1963), the Court held that the defendant's statement was not the fruit of his unlawful arrest because, subsequent to arraignment and while released on his own recognizance, Wong Sun voluntarily met with police and made the statement. In *Brown v. Illinois*, 422 U.S. 590 (1975), the Court identified three factors that reviewing courts should consider when determining if the taint of an unlawful act has been sufficiently attenuated: (1) how much time has elapsed between the initial illegality and obtaining the evidence, (2) the presence or absence of any intervening circumstances, and (3) the purpose and flagrancy of the police misconduct. Since *Brown*, courts have applied these criteria when determining whether to admit physical evidence, confessions, and the testimony of witnesses whose identity was discovered through unlawful means.

Independent-Source Exception

The independent-source exception provides that even if the police engage in illegal activity, the evidence is still admissible in court if it is lawfully obtained from an independent source. The Court laid the groundwork for the creation of this exception in *Silverthorne Lumber Co. v. United States*, 251 U.S. 385 (1920), when it held "that the exclusionary rule applies not only to the illegally obtained evidence itself, but also to other incriminating evidence derived from the primary evidence. . . . If knowledge of [such facts] is gained from an independent source, they may be proved like any others."

The rationale underlying the independent-source exception is that although the government should not be allowed to profit from police misconduct, it should not be penalized by being put in a worse position than it would have been in had the misconduct not occurred. Similarly, neither should the defendant be put in a better position than he would have been in had the police misconduct not occurred. For example, in *United States v. Crews*, 445 U.S. 463 (1980), a woman who was robbed gave police a description of her assailant. A man meeting the suspect's description was arrested for truancy and photographed while in custody but was never charged with that offense. On being shown the photograph, the victim identified Crews as her assailant. Crews was then indicted and tried for armed robbery. During the trial, the victim made an in-court identification of Crews as her assailant. Crews moved to suppress the identification arguing that his body was a form of evidence that was only available to the state because of the illegal arrest for truancy. Although the lower court suppressed the in-court identification, the Supreme Court reversed, holding

> that the victim's in-court identification of the defendant was not suppressible as having been derived from the defendant's illegal arrest, since . . . the victim's identity had been known by the police prior to the arrest, and the victim's capacity to identify the defendant as the perpetrator of the crime for which he stood trial had

not been biased by the unlawful police conduct, which had taken place after the victim had developed the capacity to make such identification.

In other words, the in-court identification was admissible because it was obtained from an independent source.

Inevitable-Discovery Exception

The inevitable-discovery exception allows courts to admit illegally obtained evidence if the government can prove that the evidence inevitably *would have been* discovered through lawful means even though police misconduct occurred. The premier case exemplifying this doctrine is *Nix v. Williams*, 467 U.S. 431 (1984). Williams was arrested in Davenport, Iowa, for murdering a ten-year-old girl in Des Moines. Some of the missing child's clothing and other items of evidence were found at a rest stop between the two cities. The police initiated a large-scale search in the surrounding area. Meanwhile, Williams surrendered to police in Davenport and, after being arraigned, was returned to Des Moines.

Prior to beginning the trip the transporting officers assured Williams's attorney that he would not be questioned; however, once the trip began an officer initiated conversation with Williams, saying that if the body wasn't found before the snowstorm came they might never find it. "And since we will be going right past the area . . . I feel that we could stop and locate the body, that the parents of this little girl should be entitled to a Christian burial for the little girl who was snatched away from them on Christmas [Eve] and murdered." Williams subsequently led the officers to the child's body. When police called off the search, a team of volunteers was two and a half miles from the location where the body was found.

Williams was tried twice and convicted twice for first-degree murder. He appealed the first conviction on the ground that evidence used against him was the "fruit" of his statements, which were elicited by the officers. A divided Supreme Court agreed, holding that Williams's statements had been obtained in violation of the right to counsel (*Brewer v. Williams*, 430 U.S. 387 [1977]).

At the second trial the prosecution did not seek to use Williams's statements as evidence or introduce the fact that he had directed police to the body. Instead, the state offered forensic evidence of the body's condition and argued that if the search had not been suspended the body "would have been discovered 'within a short time.'" Williams appealed his second conviction to the Supreme Court, which affirmed the lower court's decision. Announcing an "inevitable discovery" exception to the exclusionary rule, the Court stated, "it is clear that the search parties were approaching the actual location of the body, and we are satisfied . . . that . . . the body inevitably would have been found." The inevitable-discovery exception typically applies to situations where the police are already engaged in a course of lawful conduct designed to obtain the evidence. It does not apply to speculative conduct where the court is asked to assume that the evidence eventually *could* have been found.

The Good-Faith Exception

The Supreme Court first announced the good-faith exception in *United States v. Leon*, 468 U.S. 897 (1984). The issue in *Leon* was whether "evidence obtained by officers acting in reasonable reliance on a search warrant issued by a detached and neutral magistrate but ultimately found to be unsupported by probable cause" should be admissible in the prosecution's case in chief. Refusing to suppress the evidence, the Court held that suppression would not serve the remedial purposes of the exclusionary rule, which is "to deter police misconduct rather than punish the errors of judges and magistrates." The Court found no evidence that application of the rule would have a "significant deterrent effect on the issuing judge or magistrate." Stating that it is the magistrate's responsibility to determine whether a warrant application establishes probable cause, the Court noted that "in the ordinary case, an officer cannot be expected to question the magistrate's probable-cause determination or his judgment that the form of the warrant is technically sufficient. 'Once the warrant issues, there is literally nothing more the policeman can do in seeking to comply with the law.'"

Elaborating further on its holding, the Court stated that the good-faith exception is not intended to be applied indiscriminately; rather, "the officer's reliance on the magistrate's probable-cause determination and on the technical sufficiency of the warrant he issues must be objectively reasonable." The Court noted that in the following circumstances the good-faith exception will not apply and suppression remains the appropriate remedy:

1. the magistrate issuing the warrant is deliberately misled by information in the affidavit that the officer knew or should have known was false,
2. the magistrate wholly abandons his judicial role,
3. the warrant affidavit is so lacking in probable cause that an objective belief in its existence is unreasonable, and
4. the warrant fails to specify the place to be searched or the things to be seized.

Since the good-faith exception was first announced, the Court has applied the rule and refused to suppress evidence in several different circumstances. For instance, on the same day that the Court decided *Leon*, it also decided *Massachusetts v. Sheppard*, 468 U.S. 981 (1984). Both cases involved the issuance of a warrant by a neutral and detached magistrate. The difference between the cases was that *Leon* involved the use of a questionable informant while *Sheppard* involved the use of an improper warrant form. In each case a magistrate determined that probable cause existed and issued what the officers believed were valid warrants. The Court also has applied the good-faith exception in cases where the error was committed by a court employee (*Arizona v. Evans*, 514 U.S. 1 [1995]), the police reasonably believed that the person giving them consent to enter a residence had authority to do so (*Illinois v. Rodriguez*, 497 U.S. 117 [1990]), and the state statute on which the officer relied to gain warrantless entry to a wrecking yard was later declared unconstitutional (*Illinois v. Krull*, 480 U.S. 340 [1987]). The Court's rationale for refusing to exclude the evidence in these cases was twofold: first, the officers did everything they could to comply with the law, and, second, the mistake or error was not made by a member of law enforcement.

In its most recent decision addressing the good-faith exception the Court seems to have backed away from holding that for the good-faith exception to apply the individual making the mistake must not be affiliated with law enforcement. In *Herring v. United States*, 129 S. Ct. 695 (2009), the defendant went to the police station to retrieve property from his impounded car. As he was leaving he was arrested a short distance from the station based on a warrant that, it was subsequently learned, should have been removed from the sheriff's database five months earlier. Although Herring protested the validity of the warrant, a search incident to arrest revealed a weapon and controlled substances. Herring sought to suppress the evidence, but the trial court refused stating that the police had acted on a good-faith belief that the warrant was still outstanding. Because "the conduct in question [was] a negligent failure to act" that was "attenuated from the arrest," the Supreme Court held that the benefit of suppressing the evidence "would be marginal or nonexistent" at best.

WHEN THE EXCLUSIONARY RULE WILL NOT APPLY
A defendant may challenge the admissibility of evidence at numerous points during the criminal process, from the pretrial motion to suppress to the appeal of his conviction on the basis of erroneously admitted evidence, and even after conviction in a habeas-corpus proceeding.[3] There are, however, some proceed-

ings in which the Court has held that the exclusionary rule will not apply. For example, the exclusionary rule does not apply to probation-revocation hearings (*Pennsylvania Board of Probation and Parole v. Scott*, 524 U.S. 357 [1998]), civil trials (*United States v. Janis*, 428 U.S. 433 [1976]),[4] or deportation hearings (*Immigration and Naturalization Service v. Lopez-Mendoza*, 468 U.S. 1032 [1984]). The rule also is inapplicable in cases where the evidence is illegally seized by private citizens and turned over to the police (*Burdeau v. McDowell*, 256 U.S. 465 [1921]), the search violates an agency rule but not the Constitution (*South Dakota v. Neville*, 459 U.S. 553 [1983]), grand-jury proceedings in which questions relate to illegally seized evidence (*United States v. Calandra*, 414 U.S. 338 [1974]), and cases where police violate the knock-and-announce rule (*Hudson v. Michigan*, 547 U.S. 586 [2006]).[5] The Court's rationale for refusing to apply the exclusionary rule in such cases is that to do so would impose significant social costs on society by detracting from the truth-finding process. Additionally, application of the rule under these circumstances would not further its primary purpose, which is to deter police misconduct.

WHAT DOES THE FUTURE HOLD FOR THE EXCLUSIONARY RULE?

Throughout its history the exclusionary rule has been the subject of great controversy. For as many arguments as there are in favor of applying the rule, there are an equal number of arguments against it. For instance, proponents argue that the exclusionary rule is effective in securing the privacy rights of individuals, preventing police misconduct, promoting police professionalism, and enhancing the integrity of the justice system. They acknowledge that it results in the release of a small number of guilty persons but counter that it prevents government agents from profiting from wrongdoing. On the other hand, opponents argue that the exclusionary rule bars the use of evidence that is directly probative of an individual's guilt resulting in the criminal's going free because of the officer's unlawful act. This levies a significant cost that society should not be made to pay for an individual officer's actions. Additionally, as Chief Justice Warren Burger noted, "there are large areas of police activity which do not result in criminal prosecution—hence the rule has virtually no applicability and no effect in such situations" (*Bivens v. Six Unknown Named Agents of Federal Bureau of Narcotics*, 403 U.S. 388 [1971]). On a final note, opponents contend that the rule is not constitutionally derived, nor is there any evidence of its effectiveness. Rather, the exclusionary rule is a uniquely American creation that is not found in other nations.

Despite the apparent philosophical resistance to the exclusionary rule, and the encroachments resulting from the exceptions, there is no evidence that the Court will overrule it. What is more likely is that, where circumstances warrant, the Court will continue to implement narrowly crafted exceptions on a case-by-case basis. Consistent with this prediction, one should not expect that there will be revolutionary changes in the law. Rather, given the diverse array of exceptions that currently exist, the Court, in all likelihood, will strive to work within the narrow confines of the rule's existing framework.

CONCLUSIONS

The exclusionary rule is a judicially created rule designed to protect an individual's Fourth Amendment privacy interests against unreasonable searches and seizures. The primary purpose of the rule is to deter police misconduct. Initially the rule applied only to federal agents; however, in 1961, in *Mapp v. Ohio*, the Court extended the rule to prohibit the use in state court of evidence unlawfully seized by state agents. When applied, the exclusionary rule prohibits the admission of both primary and derivative evidence that is obtained as a result of police misconduct. Since its inception, there has been significant debate about whether the exclusionary rule should be abolished or continue to exist. Despite critics' claims that the rule is ineffective, there is no indication that the Court will overrule it. Rather, in recent years the Court has adopted a series of exceptions (i.e., purged taint, inevitable discovery, independent source, and good faith) that address law-enforcement concerns while simultaneously remaining true to the rule's deterrent purpose.

FURTHER READING

Rolando V. del Carmen, *Criminal Procedure Law and Practice*, seventh ed. (Belmont, Calif.: Thomson Higher Learning, 2007).

Rolando V. del Carmen and Jeffery T. Walker, *Briefs of Leading Cases in Law Enforcement*, seventh ed. (Newark: Anderson Publishing, 2008).

Kenneth J. Melilli, "What Nearly a Quarter Century of Experience Has Taught Us about *Leon* and 'Good Faith,'" *Utah Law Review* 2 (2008): 519–62.

Cliff Roberson, *Constitutional Law and Criminal Justice* (Boca Raton, Fla.: CRC Press, 2009).

III

STOP AND FRISK

Terry v. Ohio

ROLANDO V. DEL CARMEN

INTRODUCTION

"Stop and frisk" is a long-established practice in policing. It happens when an officer stops a person in a public place or an automobile, asks questions about his or her identity and activities, and then frisks the person for weapons if the officer fears for his or her safety. Although now considered routine, there was a time when its constitutionality was assumed rather than based on Court approval. Some states, by law, authorize officers to stop and frisk; other states and some federal courts have upheld the practice in judicial decisions even in the absence of statutory or agency authorization. Whether authorized by state law or validated through judicial decisions, however, stop and frisk has long been deemed an essential and necessary part of policing.

While the term *stop and frisk* may denote a continuous act because the phrase is almost always used together, the reality is that they are two completely separate acts and are best understood if considered and analyzed separately. They are similar in that a stop and a frisk must be based on reasonable suspicion and conducted with a warrant. They are different, however, in purpose and justification. A stop is valid only if an officer has reasonable suspicion that a suspect has committed a crime or is about to commit a crime. For example, if a suspect is stopped because he or she fits a criminal profile, the stop is invalid. In contrast, a frisk has only one purpose: officer protection. A frisk for any other purpose is invalid even if evidence of a crime is later discovered. Such evidence must be excluded during trial because of the exclusionary rule, which holds that evidence illegally obtained cannot be used during trial to prove the guilt of the accused. For example, assume that a frisk is conducted by an officer for the purpose of finding evidence of drug possession or use. That frisk is invalid and the incriminating evidence obtained is not admissible at trial because the purpose of the frisk was not officer protection.

Since the two acts are separate, a valid stop does not automatically lead to a valid frisk. Thus, if after questioning by the officer there is no reason to believe that the person is involved in or about to commit a crime, the suspect must be released. However, if in the process of questioning the officer reasonably believes that the person is armed and dangerous, the suspect may be frisked even if there is no reason to believe the suspect is involved in a crime.

Stop and frisk is an effective and efficient tool in policing because it constitutes a screening and monitoring procedure for past or potential offenders. Although not as benign as an officer merely asking questions of a suspect, it is not as highly intrusive as an arrest. Given its intermediate status, questions arise whether it comes under the full protection of the Fourth Amendment. If ensconced fully within the Fourth Amendment, then it amounts to an arrest and would need probable cause to be valid. If it falls under the Fourth Amendment, but is considered less than an arrest, then to what extent is it protected against unreasonable searches and seizures? Those questions were answered by the Court in *Terry v. Ohio* (392 U.S. 1 [1968]). *Terry* was decided in favor of the police and considered one of the most significant cases in law enforcement because it governs a sensitive area in police patrols. It is used daily in policing and considered an effective tool in crime prevention and officer protection. Without it, police efforts aimed at proactive policing are severely curtailed.

THE CASE OF *TERRY V. OHIO* (1968)

The Facts

According to *Terry v. Ohio* (92 U.S. 1 [1968]), Martin McFadden was a Cleveland police detective who had been with the department for thirty-nine years and a detective for thirty-five of those years. On October 31, 1963, he was assigned as a plainclothes officer to patrol downtown Cleveland. At about 2:30 that afternoon, he saw two men (John Terry and Richard Chilton) standing on the corner of Huron Road and Euclid Avenue. He did not know them but later testified that he "had developed routine habits of observation over the years and that he would 'stand and watch people or walk and watch people at many intervals of the day.'" The detailed facts in this case are important because the Court based its decision on the reasonableness of the police-citizens regarding the circumstances of the case. According to the majority opinion, this was what happened that afternoon:

He (McFadden) saw one of the men leave the other one and walk southwest on Huron Road, past some stores. The man paused for a moment and looked in a store window, then walked on a short distance, turned around, and walked back toward the corner, pausing once again to look into the same store window. He rejoined his companion at the corner, and the two conferred briefly. Then the second man went through the same series of motions, strolling down Huron Road, looking in the same window, walking on a short distance, turning back, peering in the store window again, and returning to confer with the first man at the corner. The two men repeated this ritual alternately between five and six times apiece—in all—roughly a dozen trips. At one point, while the two were standing together on the corner, a third man approached and engaged them briefly in conversation. This man then left the two others and walked west on Euclid Avenue. Chilton and Terry resumed their measured pacing, peering, and conferring. After this had gone for ten to twelve minutes, the two men walked off together, heading west on Euclid Avenue, following the path taken earlier by the third man.

By this time Officer McFadden, based on his extensive police experience, believed that something bad was about to happen. He suspected that the two men were casing a job and a possible a stick-up and considered it his duty as a police officer to investigate further. He also testified that he had fears that the men may have a gun. Deciding to take action, Officer McFadden followed Chilton and Terry and saw them stop to talk to the same person who had earlier conferred with them in the street corner. McFadden approached the three men, whom he did not know. After identifying himself as a police officer, he asked for their names. The men "mumbled something," whereupon McFadden grabbed Terry, spun him around, and patted the outside of his clothing. In the left breast of Terry's overcoat, Officer McFadden felt a pistol. He seized the weapon and ordered the three men to "face the wall with their hands raised." He patted down the clothing of the other two men and found a weapon in Chilton's overcoat, which was also seized. He then arrested all three men, placed them in a police wagon, and took them to the police station.

Chilton and Terry were formally charged with carrying concealed weapons and subsequently convicted. During trial, both men argued that the guns seized from them should not have been admitted as evidence, saying that the seizure without probable cause was unconstitutional. Both waived jury trial and were adjudged guilty. The Supreme Court of Ohio dismissed their appeal on the ground that it did not involve any "substantial constitutional question." The Court granted certiorari to determine whether the admission of the revolvers in evidence during trial violated defendants' constitutional rights under the Fourth Amendment. Although defendants Terry and Clinton were tried and convicted together, Clinton died after the writ of certiorari was granted. Terry's conviction was the only case left for the Court to review.

The Issue before the Court

Is the police practice of stopping and frisking suspects without probable cause constitutional?

The Court's Holding

Stop and frisk without probable cause is constitutional. The police have the authority to stop a person for questioning even without probable cause to believe that the person has committed a crime. This investigatory stop is not an arrest and is permissible if prompted by observation of unusual conduct that leads to a reasonable suspicion that criminal activity has taken place or is about to take place. After the stop, the suspect may be frisked if the officer reasonably believes that he or she is in danger.

The Majority Opinion

Chief Justice Earl Warren delivered the opinion of the Court on an eight-to-one vote. First, he noted that the case "presents serious questions concerning the role of the Fourth Amendment in the confrontation on the street between the citizen and the policeman investigating suspicions circumstances." He added, "We would be less than candid if we did not acknowledge that this question thrusts to the fore difficult and troublesome issues regarding a sensitive area of police activity—issues which have never before been squarely presented to this Court." In a case decided a year earlier, the Court had held that "the Fourth Amendment protects people, not places" (*Katz v. United States*, 389 U.S. 347 [1967]). The basic issues, Chief Justice Warren said, were whether a stop was equivalent to an arrest and whether frisk constituted a search under the Fourth Amendment. If they did, then Officer McFadden's actions were unconstitutional because he lacked probable cause. If the search was illegal, the evidence seized should have been excluded during trial because of the exclusionary rule.

On the constitutionality of the stop, Chief Justice Warren said that crime prevention and detection is of general government interest, adding that "it is this interest which underlies the recognition that a police officer may in appropriate circumstances and in an appropriate manner approach a person for purposes of investigating possibly criminal behavior even though there is no probable cause to make an arrest." He maintained that it was "this legitimate investigative function Officer McFadden was discharging when he decided to approach [the] petitioner and his companions." Reviewing the circumstances that led to the stop, the chief justice then concluded that "it would have been poor police work indeed for an officer of thirty years' experience in the detection of thievery from stores in this same neighborhood to have failed to investigate this behavior further."

The constitutionality of the frisk, which the chief justice averred, was the "crux of the case"; he asked whether there was justification for McFadden's invasion of Terry's personal security by searching him for weapons. Concluding that what Officer McFadden did was reasonable, Chief Justice Warren said:

> Certainly it would be unreasonable to require that police officers take unnecessary risks in the performance of their duties. American criminals have a long tradition of armed violence, and every year in this country many law-enforcement officers are killed in the line of duty, and thousands more are wounded. Virtually all of these deaths and a substantial portion of the injuries are inflicted with guns and knives.

More importantly, he set this criterion for a reasonable frisk: "When an officer is justified in believing that the individual whose suspicious behavior he is investigating at close range is armed and presently dangerous to the officer or to others, it would appear to be clearly unreasonable to deny the officer the power to take necessary measure to determine whether the person is in fact carrying a weapon and to neutralize the threat of physical harm." At the end of the majority opinion and by way of summary, Chief Justice Warren wrote:

> We . . . hold today that where a police officer observes unusual conduct which leads him reasonably to conclude in light of his experience that criminal activity may be afoot and that the persons with whom he is dealing may be armed and presently dangerous, where in the course of investigating this behavior he identifies himself

as a policeman and makes reasonable inquiries, and here nothing in the initial
stages of the encounter serves to dispel his reasonable fear for his own or others'
safety, he is entitled for the protection of himself and others in the area to conduct
a carefully limited search of the outer clothing of such persons in an attempt to
discover weapons which might be used to assault him. Such a search is a reasonable
search under the Fourth Amendment, and any weapons seized may properly be
introduced in evidence against the person from whom they were taken.

Seldom is a Court decision on a law-enforcement procedural issue clearer and
more prescriptive than the above. As a consequence, subsequent cases seldom
challenged the purpose of a stop or the reason for a frisk. *Terry* was unequivocal
about the reasons for those acts and when and how they should take place. There
was not much room left for questions or misunderstanding.

The Dissenting Opinion

The sole dissenter in *Terry* was Justice William Douglas, one of the most notable
liberal justices to have ever graced the Court. He sided with Terry, saying that he
agreed with the majority that Terry was seized and searched under the Fourth
Amendment. Justice Douglas insisted on the presence of probable cause before
any such seizure or searches could be conducted. Rejecting the lower standard of
reasonable suspicion used by the majority, he said, "The term *probable cause* rings
a bell of certainty that is not sounded by phrases such as *reasonable suspicion.* The
infringement on personal liberty of any 'seizure' of a person can only be 'reasonable' under the Fourth Amendment if we require the police to possess 'probable
cause' before they seize him." He closed by saying, "There have been powerful
hydraulic pressures throughout our history that bear heavily on the Court to
water down constitutional guarantees and give the police the upper hand. That
hydraulic pressure has probably never been greater than it is today." To Justice
Douglas, there was no justification for using a lesser standard than probable cause,
adding that the majority decision gave the police more power than that wielded by
a magistrate. In essence, while judges cannot issue warrants based on reasonable
suspicion, police officers under *Terry* had the power to search and seize a person
on less than probable cause. He found this unacceptable.

Case Significance

Terry v. Ohio is important for three reasons. First, it authorized arrests and
frisks without a warrant or probable cause as a constitutional practice, thus

greatly enhancing the power and authority of law-enforcement officers in police-citizen encounters and made police patrols a more potent means of policing. As noted above, stops and frisks derive authorization from laws, court cases, or agency policies. Prior to *Terry*, stops and frisks had never been challenged under the Fourth Amendment prohibition against unreasonable searches and seizures. That challenge came in *Terry*, and the police won.

Second, the Court acknowledged that not all police-citizen encounters constitute a seizure. There are innocent and innocuous contacts between the public and the police that fall outside the confines of the Fourth Amendment and are therefore constitutionally unprotected. Third, the Court noted that there exists a midway standard for certainty between mere suspicion (a standard that justifies initiating an investigation) and probable cause (a standard that justifies an arrest). That intermediate standard is "reasonable suspicion." It has been added to the legal repertoire of the Court and has been used since then in other Fourth Amendment cases where probable cause is not needed or where mere suspicion does not suffice.

Justice Harlan correctly predicted in his concurring opinion that "what is said by this Court today will serve as initial guidelines for law-enforcement authorities and courts throughout the land as this important new field of law develops." That "new field of law" has indeed been further developed by the Court in other Fourth Amendment cases over the years since *Terry* was decided in 1968. "Reasonable suspicion" has become a familiar and convenient refrain in policing.

It is generally recognized that policing is difficult and challenging, particularly in democratic societies where government officers are pledged to respect individual rights and uphold the rule of law. Violations of constitutional rights can lead to lawsuits against police officers and their agencies. Imagine how much more challenging policing would be if probable cause and a warrant were required in stop-and-frisk cases.

Noted authors Wayne R. LaFave, Jerold H. Israel, and Nancy J. King assert that the *Terry* case makes three main contributions to a better understanding of the Fourth Amendment.[1]

1. "The Court's conclusion that restraining a person on the street is a 'seizure' and an exploration of the outer surfaces of his clothing is a 'search' without regard to the labels which police or others choose to put on those activities." Thus, in stop-and-frisk cases substance trumps labels.

2. The "Court's further development of its recently adopted balancing test as a means for judging the constitutionality of unique practices." The authors note that in a case decided the year before *Terry*, the Court used a balancing test to resolve an issue involving housing inspections without probable cause (*Camara v. Municipal Court*, 387 U.S. 523 [1967]). The Court in the *Camara* case held that warrants for housing inspections could be issued without probable cause "if appropriate legislative or administrative standards for area or periodic inspections" are met. The same lower standard was used for stop-and-frisk cases, thus enhancing the power of the police.

3. The Court's statement that the exclusionary rule "is powerless to deter invasions of constitutionally guaranteed rights where the police either have no interest in prosecuting or are willing to forgo successful prosecution in the interest of serving other goals." This was the Court's response to the claim by *Terry* that giving the police power to stop and frisk would encourage the police to use these encounters to harass minority groups. This statement reflects the Court's pragmatic and realistic approach to the debate on the effectiveness of the exclusionary rule as a tool to deter police misconduct.

In sum, in addition to authorizing stops and frisks as legitimate tools in law enforcement, the *Terry* case also reaffirmed a doctrine (the balancing test) used in prior cases as a workable measure by which to judge the constitutionality of nontraditional intrusions into a suspect's right to privacy or under the Fourth Amendment prohibition against unreasonable searches and seizures.

Further Analysis

In its decision, the majority stated that it faced a legal issue of first impression for the Court. The Court's analysis acknowledged the need to draw a distinction between a "stop" and an "arrest," and a "frisk" and a "search." It noted this difference as crucial to the decision: a stop and a frisk amounted to mere "minor inconvenience and petty indignity" when compared to an arrest. On the other hand, the Court acknowledged the need to "strictly circumscribe" the authority of the police. Clearly, the Court saw need for balance in resolving issues of police-citizen encounters. The whole scenario was characterized in the majority opinion as follows:

Street encounters between citizens and police officers are incredibly rich in diversity. They range from wholly friendly exchanges of pleasantries or mutual[ly] useful information to hostile confrontations of armed men involving arrests or injuries, or loss of life. . . . Encounters are initiated by the police for a wide variety of purposes, some of which are wholly unrelated to a desire to prosecute for crime. Doubtless some police "field interrogation" conduct violates the Fourth Amendment. But a term refusal by this Court to condone such activity does not necessarily render it responsive to the exclusionary rule.

After defining the nature of police-citizen confrontation in an investigative situation, the Court then addressed the core of the case. The main issue to be resolved was: Is it always unreasonable for a policeman to seize a person and subject him or her to a limited search for weapons unless there is probable cause for an arrest?

Taking a careful look at the facts, the Court concluded that the stop of Terry was a form of a seizure and the frisk a form of a search under the Fourth Amendment. The Court said that it could not be blind to a law-enforcement officer's need to protect him- or herself and other prospective victims of violence in situations where they did not have probable cause to make an arrest. In view of the government's interest in crime investigation, the Court held that "there was justification for McFadden's invasion of Terry's personal security by searching him for weapons in the course of that investigation." The Court then set the rule for officer conduct in these encounters, saying, "when an officer is justified in believing that the individual whose suspicious behavior he is investigating at close range is armed and presently dangerous to the officer or to others, it would appear to be clearly unreasonable to deny the officer the power to take necessary measures to determine whether the person is in fact carrying a weapon and to neutralize the threat of physical harm."

Court decisions are sometimes burdened with vagueness and imprecision. That cannot be said of the Court's decision in *Terry*. The last paragraph of the majority opinion, as quoted above, set unambiguous guidelines for what should be done in stop-and-frisk cases.

First Stage: The Stop

These are the requirements for a valid stop:

1. *Circumstances.* The police officer must observe unusual conduct that leads him or her reasonably to conclude, in the light of his or her experience, that criminal activity is about to take place or has taken place.
2. *What the police can do.* The officer must identify himself or herself and make reasonable inquiries.

The above rules, in effect, laid out the sequence of the stop as follows: observe, approach, and identify, then ask questions.

Second Stage: The Frisk

If after the stop and in the course of the investigation the officer is reasonably concerned about safety, then he or she may do the following:

1. Conduct a pat-down search of the person's outer clothing, and/or
2. Confiscate anything that feels like a weapon. Anything that does not feel like a weapon cannot be confiscated.

An arrest follows if an illegal weapon is recovered from the suspect.

Seldom has a Court decision on police matters been so clear, descriptive, and prescriptive. In no uncertain terms, the Court told the police when to conduct stops and frisks and how to do it.

THE MEANING OF *REASONABLE SUSPICION*

Reasonable suspicion is the minimum degree of certainty required in stop-and-frisk cases. The majority opinion in *Terry* did not memorialize this legal phrase but instead used other terms such as *reasonable cause to believe* and *reasonably prudent man*. In his dissent, Justice Douglas used the term *reasonable suspicion* but did not define it. What, then, is the meaning of *reasonable suspicion*? Surprisingly, it has not been authoritatively defined by the Court.

In one case, however, the Court said that "reasonable suspicion is a less-demanding standard than probable cause not only in the sense that reasonable suspicion can be established with information that is different in quantity or contest from that required to establish probable cause, but also in the sense that reasonable suspicion can arise from information that is less reliable than that required to show probable cause" (*Alabama v. White*, 496 U.S. 325 [1990]). Despite this lower standard, reasonable suspicion must be grounded on specific, objective facts and logical conclusions based on the officer's experience. It cannot be based on mere hunch (which has 0 percent certainty) or suspicion (which may have 10 percent certainty). Reasonable suspicion is wedged between suspicion and probable cause in the hierarchy of certainty needed for the police to be able to act legally. On a scale of one to ten, suspicion would likely be a one or two, reasonable suspicion a three or four, and probable cause a four or five. Whatever the numerical equivalent, it is clear that reasonable suspicion is a less-demanding standard of certainty than probable cause. As is true with other legal terms, however, reasonable suspicion (as is probable cause) is ultimately subjective. What may be reasonable suspicion to one officer, judge, or appellate court may not be so to another. Thus, it may be a distinction without much of a difference.

LEGAL ISSUES RELATED TO *TERRY V. OHIO*

Since *Terry v. Ohio*, the Court has decided other issues related to stops and frisks. Among the more important issues are the following.

When Is a Person Considered Seized under the Fourth Amendment?

In *Terry*, the Court considered the suspects to have been seized under the Fourth Amendment and said they were therefore entitled to constitutional protection. A broader question is raised: when is a person considered seized under the Fourth Amendment? The Court provided guidance when it said that "Only when the officer, by means of physical force or show of authority, has in some way restrained the liberty of a citizen may we conclude that a seizure has occurred."

In a case decided twelve years later, the Court further clarified when a seizure occurs when it said, "We conclude that a person has been 'seized' within the meaning of the Fourth Amendment only if, in view of all of the circumstances surrounding the incident, a reasonable person would have believed that he was not free to leave" (*United States v. Mendenhall*, 446 U.S. 544 [1980]). The Court gave examples of when the person might be considered seized, even though he or she did not attempt to leave or was not free to leave. These include "the threatening presence of several officers, the display of a weapon by an officer, some physical touching of the person of the citizen, or the use of language or tone of voice indicating that compliance with the officer's request might be compelled."

In the absence of such evidence, "other inoffensive contact between a member of the public and the police cannot, as a matter of law, amount to a seizure of that person." In sum, seizure occurs if a reasonable person based on a totality of the circumstances would not have felt free to leave. What constitutes a seizure is determined, ultimately, on a case-by-case basis. Who decides what a "reasonable person" is under this standard? The answer: the trier of fact in a particular case, meaning the jury or judge that hears the case. This can be a subjective standard that may vary from one judge or jury to another.

What Encounters Are Not Considered a Seizure?

There are encounters the Court does not consider a seizure and therefore are not protected by the Fourth Amendment. Such encounters include the following:

- The police asking questions of individuals on the street to gather general information. These are nonintrusive situations that do not cause discomfort or inconvenience to the general public and are deemed a part of an individual's civic duty.
- The police asking questions of witnesses to a crime. This is considered general on-the-scene questioning where the police do not as yet have a suspect or are not yet focused on any person being questioned.
- The police asking a driver to get out of a car after being stopped (*Pennsylvania v. Mimms*, 434 U.S. 106 [1977]).
- The police boarding a bus and asking questions that a person is free to refuse to answer (*Florida v. Bostick*, 501 U.S. 429 [1991]).
- The police riding alongside a person to see where he is going (*Michigan v. Chesternut*, 486 U.S. 657 [1988]).

In each of these cases, the encounters with the police are minimally invasive and therefore did not come under the Fourth Amendment. The Court considers police-public contacts as situations where a person could have walked away from the police or would otherwise feel free to leave.

What Is the Duration of a Stop in Order for It to Be Valid?

Subsequent cases have raised the issue of the allowable length of a stop in stop-and-frisk cases. There is no definite time limit for the length of an investigatory stop; instead specific circumstances should be taken into account (*United States v. Sharpe*, 470 U.S. 675 [1985]). A general rule is that an investigatory stop must not last any longer than necessary under the circumstances to achieve its purpose. In sum, the standard is reasonableness. In *Sharpe*, the Court found it reasonable for the police to detain a truck driver for twenty minutes. The driver was suspected of carrying marijuana in a truck camper. The length of the stop was caused in part by the driver attempting to evade the stop, causing the two officers pursuing him to be separated. The officer who performed the stop had to wait fifteen minutes for his more-experienced partner to arrive before making the search. The Court held the search valid, saying that to determine whether a detention is reasonable in length, the court must look at the purpose to be served by the stop and the time reasonably needed to carry it out.

In another case, however, the Court held that a ninety-minute detention of an air traveler's luggage was deemed excessive (*United States v. Place*, 462 U.S. 696 [1983]). In that case, the suspect's luggage was detained long enough to enable a trained dog to sniff for marijuana. The Court concluded that the initial seizure was unjustified under *Terry v. Ohio* but added that the ninety-minute delay exceeded the permissible limits of an investigative stop. It stressed that "although we decline to adopt any outside time limitation for a permissible *Terry* stop, we have never approved a seizure of the person for the prolonged ninety-minute period involved here and cannot do so on the facts presented by this case."

It is difficult, if not futile, to state exactly how much time suffices for a valid stop, since circumstances vary so considerably. What we do know is that the Court uses the test of reasonableness, meaning whether the stop is longer than necessary under the circumstances to achieve its purpose. This is determined on a case-by-case basis.

What Is the Extent of a Frisk in Order for It to Be Valid?

As noted earlier, *Terry v. Ohio* is both a stop and a frisk case. These are in sequence but are totally separate acts. In *Terry*, the Court said that where the officer has reasonable suspicion to conclude that in light of his experience "the person with whom he is dealing may be armed and presently dangerous" and "where nothing in the initial stages of the encounter serves to dispel his reasonable fear for his own or others' safety, he is entitled for the protection of himself and others in the area to conduct a carefully limited search of the outer clothing of such persons in an attempt to discover weapons which might be used to assault him." A frisk that goes beyond that allowed in *Terry* is invalid.

The standard set by the Court for a frisk is clear; nonetheless, it underwent refinement in *Minnesota v. Dickerson*, 508 U.S. 366 (1993). In *Dickerson*, the Court held that a frisk that went beyond that prescribed in *Terry* was not valid. In that case, the suspect was asked to stop and submitted to a pat-down search. The search revealed no weapons, but the officer found a small lump in Dickerson's pocket. On the witness stand, the officer admitted that at first he did not know what it was, so he "squeezed, slid, and otherwise manipulated" the pocket contents. Only after doing that did he know it was crack cocaine. Dickerson was charged and convicted. He appealed his conviction, saying that the seizure of the contraband was invalid. The Court agreed, saying that the officer went beyond the bounds of a *Terry* frisk when he "squeezed, slid, and manipulated" the pocket contents to determine what it was. Only after that did he realize it was crack cocaine. The Court said the officer went beyond a mere pat-down of the outer clothing of the suspect to determine if the suspect has a weapon which may endanger the officer.

Anything that does not feel like a weapon during a frisk cannot be confiscated. In short, a frisk cannot be used as a "fishing expedition" to obtain evidence that might be used against the suspect. It has one purpose and one purpose only: officer protection. If used for anything else, the frisk is invalid and anything seized during the frisk cannot be used as evidence during trial.[2]

Are Stops Based on Racial Profile Valid?

Racial profiling has generated intense controversy between minority groups and law-enforcement agencies. It occurs when a government law-enforcement officer stops a person on the basis of a set of identifiers, one of which is race or ethnicity. The process is known in some places as stopping a person for DWB (driving while black) or DWH (driving while Hispanic). The Court has not directly addressed this issue, certainly not in *Terry*. But it is safe to say that stopping a motorist based on race alone is unconstitutional because it is unfair, unwarranted, and discriminatory. The more difficult question, however, is whether race can be taken as one factor in the "totality of circumstances" when determining reasonable suspicion for purposes of a stop. Again, the issue has not been resolved by the Court, but lower court decisions differ. Some lower courts say it is valid, other courts consider the practice unconstitutional. Until resolved by the United States Supreme Court, differences in lower-court decisions will persist. Racial profiling is banned by state law or police-agency policy in many states. It is also banned in federal law enforcement, except for identifying possible terrorism suspects and other threats to national security.

THE CURRENT SCOPE OF POLICE AUTHORITY TO STOP AND FRISK, BASED ON DECIDED CASES

Over the years, the Court has decided important cases on the power of the police to conduct stop and frisk. In chronological order, they follow.

A stop and frisk may be based on information provided by another individual: In *Adams v. Williams* (407 U.S. 143 [1972]), an officer was approached by an informant while patrolling a high-crime area. The informant, who had provided the officer with reliable information in the past, told the officer that Adams, who was in a nearby car, had narcotics and was carrying a gun in his waistband. The officer went to the car, tapped on the window, and asked Adams to open the door. Instead, when Adams rolled down the window, the officer reached inside the car and removed the revolver. A search incident to the arrest yielded more weapons and some heroin. During trial, Adams sought to exclude the evidence seized, saying there was no reasonable ground for a stop and frisk because the officer did not have any personal information about Adams's having a gun. On appeal, the Court upheld the conviction, saying that reasonable grounds for a stop and frisk do not rest solely on an officer's personal observations. Information obtained from a reliable informant may also constitute reasonable suspicion.

A suspect who is stopped cannot be forced by the police to answer questions: A stop is usually followed by a series of questions from the officer. The Court has ruled that suspects cannot be forced to answer but that the refusal may provide the officer sufficient justification to frisk because it may fail to dispel suspicions of danger to the officer (*Florida v. Royer*, 460 U.S. 491 [1983]). The refusal may also help establish probable cause to arrest, provided other circumstances are present.

For example, a suspect refuses to answer questions, is nervous, appears to be hiding something, and smells of alcohol. Taken together, these circumstances may provide probable cause for arrest.

Reasonable suspicion based on a wanted poster is sufficient for a valid stop: In *United States v. Hensley*, 469 U.S. 221 (1985), the defendant was wanted for questioning about an armed robbery in St. Bernard, Ohio. The police issued a wanted flyer to other police departments in the area. Knowing of the flyer, officers in nearby Covington, Kentucky, stopped the car the defendant, Hensley, was driving. A search revealed firearms in the car. Hensley was arrested, charged, and convicted. He appealed his conviction, saying the evidence should have been suppressed because the stop was illegal since there was no probable cause. The Court disagreed, saying that the police had reasonable suspicion (based on the wanted flyer) that the individual in the car committed a felony. The evidence was admissible during trial.

There is no specified time limit for the length of an investigatory stop; instead, specific circumstances should be taken into account: In *United States v. Sharpe*, 470 U.S. 675 (1985), agents of the U.S. Drug Enforcement Administration (DEA) detained Sharpe while they conducted a limited investigation of and were chasing another car which was also suspected of criminal activity. Sharp was arrested approximately forty minutes after his car was stopped. The Court said that the detention was reasonable in view of the circumstances. The Court added that there is no rigid time limit for the length of an investigatory stop. Instead, the following should be taken into account: (1) the purpose of the stop, (2) the reasonableness of the time used for the investigation that the officers wanted to conduct, and (3) the reasonableness of the means of investigation used by the officers. Although not all delays are considered valid, the delay in this case was considered reasonable because of the circumstances.

An anonymous tip that a person is carrying a gun is not, without more information, sufficient to justify a stop and frisk: In *Florida v. J. L.,* 529 U.S. 266 (1999), police responded to an anonymous tip that a young black male was standing at a certain bus stop wearing a plaid shirt and carrying a gun. Officers saw a person matching that description standing at the bus stop with two other persons. They frisked him and found a pistol. The police also frisked the other persons, but found nothing. Other than the anonymous tip, the officers had no reason to suspect any of the three people of illegal conduct. Arrested, tried, and convicted, J. L. appealed his conviction, saying that the frisk based on an anonymous tip alone was invalid. The Court agreed, saying that the anonymous tip by itself, without anything else, did not amount to reasonable suspicion.

A suspect's presence in a high-crime area, combined with unprovoked flight upon observing police officers, constitutes sufficient grounds for officers to investigate further: In *Illinois v. Wardlow,* 528 U.S. 119 (2000), narcotics officers in Chicago went to an area known for heavy narcotics trafficking. An officer noticed Wardlow standing next to a building, holding an opaque bag. Wardlow saw the officers and immediately fled. The officers followed him. When Wardlow stopped, the officers patted him down, based on the officer's experience that weapons were common in that area of narcotics trafficking. A handgun was found, and Wardlow was arrested. He appealed his conviction, claiming that his actions (fleeing a high-crime area upon seeing police officers) did not create a reasonable suspicion that justified a stop and frisk. The Court upheld his conviction, saying that Wardlow's presence in a high-crime area, together with his unprovoked flight upon seeing the police officers, gave them sufficient grounds to stop him to determine if criminal activity was afoot. The Court stressed, however, that the determination of reasonable suspicion must be based on commonsense judgment and inferences of human behavior.

During a stop, an officer may require a suspect to provide his or her name; the suspect may be arrested for refusing to comply with the request: In *Hiibel v. Sixth*

Judicial District Court of Nevada, 542 U.S. 177 (2004), an officer in Nevada re-ceived a telephone call from a person who reported that he saw a man assault a woman "in a red and silver GMC truck on Grass Valley Road." The officers went to the scene and found a truck matching that description. The officers saw a man standing by the truck and a woman sitting inside. One of the officers approached the man and explained that they were investigating a reported assault. The man appeared to be drunk. When asked if he had any identification, the man refused to provide it. The suspect was arrested pursuant to a Nevada law that allows officers to detain a person suspected of committing a crime to ascertain his or her identity. Tried and convicted, the defendant, Hiibel, appealed, saying that his arrest was unconstitutional. The Court disagreed, holding that requiring a suspect to disclose his or her identity does not violate the Fourth Amendment prohibition against unreasonable searches and seizures or the Fifth Amendment prohibition against self-incrimination.

CONCLUSIONS

Stops and frisks are tactics used by law-enforcement agencies to prevent crime, apprehend offenders, and protect officers. Its use is frequent, routine, and perva-sive. It is efficient and effective, but it can also be abused. For example, the New York Police Department reportedly stopped and frisked 531,000 people in 2008. Of that number, 31,665 resulted in arrests and 34,081 led to the issuance of sum-mons.[3] In 2009, a lawsuit was filed by the American Civil Liberties Union to stop the practice, alleging massive violations of individual rights.[4] Lawsuits seeking total discontinuance of stops and frisks will likely fail, although agency practices that tolerate flagrant abuses might be curtailed or stopped by the courts.

Although often taken as one continuous act, stops and frisks are two separate acts and have different purposes. The purpose of a stop is to determine if a crime has been committed, is being committed, or is about to be committed; the pur-pose of a frisk is completely different—it is officer protection. In *Terry v. Ohio*, the Court held that stop and frisk is valid without a warrant and in the absence of probable cause as long as reasonable suspicion is present. This means that stops and frisks come under Fourth Amendment protection but are justified by a dif-ferent level of certainty because they are not as intrusive or invasive as arrest.

Terry v. Ohio is one of the most important cases ever decided in favor of law enforcement. Had the Court decided differently, the search-and-seizure authority of law-enforcement officers would have been clipped and law en-forcement made more difficult and dangerous. There are current allegations that stops and frisks are abused by the police in certain departments and used as instruments of harassment. That may be true in some places and, where true, would invite judicial oversight. It is hard to imagine a situation, however, when either stops or frisks would be prohibited completely or authorized only based on a warrant and probable cause. That would diminish the power of the police to a degree that might endanger them or compromise public safety. Despite susceptibility to abuse, stops and frisks have long been important tools in policing that most of the public accepts as promoting community safety. Whether current stop-and-frisk practices need further scrutiny and refinement by the courts is hard to tell. For now, however, *Terry v. Ohio* has worked well and served a society that constantly seeks an acceptable balance between public security and individual rights.

FURTHER READING

Fred E. Imbau, "Stop and Frisk: The Power and Obligation of the Police," *Journal of Criminal Law and Criminology* 89 (1999): 1445–1522.

Jerome H. Skolnick, "*Terry* and Community Policing," *St. John's Law Review* (Summer 1998), http://findarticles.com/p/articles/miqa3735/is199807/?tag=content;coll.

"Stop and Frisk Law: A Guide to Doctrines, Tests, and Special Circumstances," www.apsu.edu/oconnort/3000/3000/ect03.htm.

George C. Thomas III, "*Terry v. Ohio* in the Trenches: A Glimpse at How Courts Apply 'Reasonable Suspicion,'" *St. John's Law Review* (Summer 1998), http://findarticles.com/p/articles/miqa3735/is199807/?tag=content;coll.

5

Minnesota v. Dickerson

ROLANDO V. DEL CARMEN*

INTRODUCTION

Minnesota v. Dickerson (508 U.S. 366 [1993]) is the leading case on the limits of a frisk by police officers. It has its origin in the case of *Terry v. Ohio* (392 U.S. 1 [1968]), the first stop-and-frisk case decided by the Court twenty-five years earlier. In *Terry*, the Court held that the police have the authority to detain a person briefly for questioning even without probable cause to believe that the person has committed a crime. This investigatory stop does not constitute an arrest and is constitutional if supported by: (1) police observation of unusual conduct leading to a reasonable suspicion that criminal activity may have taken place or is about to take place, and (2) the officer being able to point to specific and articulable facts that would justify his or her reasonable suspicion. After a valid stop, the officer may frisk the suspect if the officer reasonably suspects personal danger or danger to other persons. The last paragraph of the majority opinion in *Terry v. Ohio* summarizes the rules prescribed by the Court in that case for stop and frisk and sets the foundation for *Minnesota v. Dickerson*. Said the Court,

> We . . . hold today that where a police officer observes unusual conduct which leads him reasonably to conclude in light of his experience that criminal activity may be afoot and that the person with whom he is dealing may be armed and presently dangerous, where in the course of investigating this behavior he identifies himself

---

*Parts of the discussion in this whole chapter are taken, with modification, from Rolando V. del Carmen, *Criminal Procedure: Law and Practice*, eighth ed. (Wadsworth: Cengage Learning, 2010), 124–46.

as a policeman and makes reasonable inquiries, and where nothing in the initial stages of the encounter serves to dispel his reasonable fear for his own or others' safety, he is entitled for the protection of himself and others in the area to conduct a carefully limited search of the outer clothing of such persons in an attempt to discover weapons which might be used to assault him. Such a search is a reasonable search within the Fourth Amendment, and any weapons seized may properly be introduced in evidence against the person from whom they are taken.

The above excerpt sets unambiguous guidelines for two separate acts by the police: the stop and the frisk. While the decision declared that a frisk based on reasonable suspicion (less than probable cause) is constitutional, it did not define the precise limits of a frisk. *Terry*, however, provided clear guidelines for what the police should do.

For the stop, the police are to follow this sequence:

1. Observe the suspect,
2. Approach and identify, and
3. Ask questions of the suspect.

For the frisk (which should take place only if the answers do not dispel the officer's concern for safety), the following procedure is to be followed:

1. Conduct a pat-down of the suspect's outer clothing,
2. If a weapon is felt, confiscate it, and arrest the suspect (optional), and
3. Conduct a fully-body search after the arrest (optional).

In *Terry*, the Court made it clear that although the term *stop and frisk* may imply that the two acts always go together, they are actually two separate acts, each with its own legal requirements for validity. Thus, a valid stop does not automatically mean that a valid frisk can be conducted. An invalid stop, however, leads to an invalid frisk, but a valid stop in itself does not automatically lead to a valid frisk. To be valid, both must be based on "reasonable suspicion," a lower degree of certainty than "probable cause."

A frisk is a mere pat-down for a weapon; anything beyond that is invalid. Moreover, a frisk must be limited initially to a pat-down of a person's clothing. Only an object that feels like a weapon may properly be seized. The object may turn out not to be a weapon, but if it feels like one, the frisk is justified. Conversely, if the object does not feel like a weapon, it cannot be seized. For example, assume that after a valid stop based on reasonable suspicion an officer has a reasonable fear that the suspect may be armed. She then frisks the suspect and in the process feels something soft that cannot possibly be considered a weapon. The officer cannot seize that object, and, if seized, the object is not admissible as evidence in court even if it turns out to be drugs or other illegal items.

While *Terry v. Ohio* made clear when and what an officer could do after a stop, doubts persisted as to the outer limits of a frisk. *Minnesota v. Dickerson* addressed this issue and further clarified what officers can and cannot do during a frisk, thus bringing further clarity and giving more substance to *Terry v. Ohio*.

THE CASE OF *MINNESOTA V. DICKERSON* (1993): A SEQUEL TO *TERRY V. OHIO* (1968)

The Facts

According to *Minnesota v. Dickerson* (508 U.S. 366 [1993]), on the evening of November 9, 1989, two police officers in Minneapolis, Minnesota, were on patrol in a marked police car. They saw Dickerson leaving a twelve-unit apartment building where the officers had previously responded to complaints of drug sales and had executed several search warrants on its premises. The building was considered to be a "notorious crack house." Upon seeing the squad car and making eye contact with one of the officers, Dickerson abruptly turned around and walked in the opposite direction. The police officer saw Dickerson turn and enter an alley on the other side of the apartment building. Based on Dickerson's suspicious actions and the building being known for crack-cocaine traffic, the officers stopped him so they could investigate further.

The officers followed Dickerson into the alley and ordered him to stop and submit to a pat-down search. The search did not yield any weapon, but one of the officers felt a "small lump" in Dickerson's nylon jacket. During trial, the officer testified as follows: "As I pat-searched the front of his body, I felt a lump, a small lump, in the front pocket. I examined it with my fingers, and it slid, and it felt to be a lump of crack cocaine in a cellophane." Based on this, the officer "reached into respondent's pocket and retrieved a small plastic bag containing one-fifth of one gram of crack cocaine." Dickerson was arrested and charged with possession of a controlled substance.

He repeatedly sought to exclude the evidence seized, maintaining that his Fourth Amendment right against unreasonable search and seizure was violated by the illegal search. His motion to suppress was denied by the trial court, but on appeal the Minnesota Court of Appeals reversed and excluded the evidence, saying that although the stop by the officers was valid, the officers "had overstepped the bounds allowed by *Terry* in seizing the cocaine." The Minnesota Supreme Court affirmed the decision of the Minnesota Court of Appeals. The exclusion of the evidence seized was appealed by the government to the United States Supreme Court. The Court granted certiorari, saying it wanted "to resolve a conflict among the state and federal courts over whether contraband detected through the sense of touch during a pat-down search may be admitted into evidence."

The Issue before the Court

Two related issues faced the Court: (1) Is contraband detected through the sense of touch during a pat-down search admissible as evidence during trial, and (2) was the seizure by the officer of the small plastic bag containing one-fifth of one gram of crack cocaine in this case constitutional? On the first issue, the Court said yes, but on the second issue the Court said no.

The Court's Holding

Contraband detected through the sense of touch during a pat-down search is admissible as evidence during trial. But a frisk that goes beyond that allowed under *Terry v. Ohio* is invalid. In this case, the frisk was invalid because instead of a mere pat-down search for weapon allowed under *Terry*, the officer "squeezed, slid, and otherwise manipulated the packet's content" before knowing it was crack cocaine. What the officer did exceeded the bounds of a frisk set in *Terry v. Ohio*.

The Majority Opinion

The opinion was divided into four parts. Justice Byron White wrote the opinion for a unanimous Court for parts I and II, but there were concurring opinions and a dissent for parts III and IV. Justice Scalia filed a concurring opinion; Chief Justice Rehnquist joined the Court's opinion for parts I and II but filed an opinion with which Justice Blackmun and Justice Thomas joined, concurring to portions and dissenting to others in parts III and IV. Part I of Justice White's majority opinion reviewed the facts and history of the case. In part II, Justice White reviewed *Terry v. Ohio* and its implications for *Dickerson*.

In section A of part II, Justice White reiterated that stops and frisks, although forms of search and seizure, are exceptions to the probable-cause and warrant requirements. He restated what the Court said for a valid frisk in *Terry*: "When an officer is justified in believing that the individual whose suspicious behavior he is investigating at close range is armed and presently dangerous to the officer or to others," the officer may conduct a pat-down search "to determine whether the person is in fact carrying a weapon." The tone for Justice White's opinion was set by his statement, early in the opinion, that "if the protective search goes beyond what is necessary to determine if the subject is armed, it is no longer valid under *Terry* and its fruits will be suppressed." It was clear, categorical, and prescriptive.

In section B of part II, Justice White addressed the issue as to whether evidence detected through the sense of touch during a pat-down search is admissible at trial. The *plain-view doctrine*, he concluded, was applicable to this case. He defined that doctrine as follows: "If police are lawfully in a position from which they view an object, if its incriminating character is immediately apparent, and if the officers have a legal right of access to the object, they may seize it without a warrant. The same rule applies to cases in which an officer discovers contraband through the sense of touch during an otherwise lawful search." He reasoned that "if a police officer lawfully pats down a suspect's outer clothing and feels an object whose contour or mass makes its identity immediately apparent, there has been no invasion of the suspect's privacy beyond that already authorized by the officer's search for weapons; if the object is contraband, the warrantless seizure would be justified by the same practical consideration that inhere in the plain-view context."

After reviewing basic constitutional rules in part II, Justice White then applied these principles to the facts in the *Dickerson* case. Having earlier concluded that evidence obtained through the sense of touch is governed by the same principle as that of plain view, he then focused on whether the frisk itself was constitutional, saying, "thus the dispositive question before this Court is whether the officer who conducted the search was acting within the lawful bounds marked by *Terry* at the time he gained probable cause to believe that the lump in respondent's jacket was contraband." Justice White agreed with the findings of the Minnesota Supreme Court, which found after a close examination of the record that the officer's own testimony "belies any notion that he 'immediately'" recognized the lump as crack cocaine. Instead, the Minnesota Supreme Court concluded, the officer determined that the lump was contraband only after "'squeezing, sliding, and otherwise manipulating the contents of the defendant's pocket'—a pocket which the officer already knew contained no weapon." This was the crucial part of the Court's finding. Based on this finding of fact, Justice White concluded that "it is clear that the court was correct in holding that the police officer in this case overstepped the bounds of the 'strictly circumscribed' search for weapons allowed under *Terry*." He pronounced the frisk invalid and held that the crack cocaine seized by the police officer was not admissible at Dickerson's trial.

The Concurring Opinions

Justice Scalia wrote a concurring opinion expressing doubt whether the frisk that resulted in the seizure of the crack cocaine complied with the standard set in *Terry*. He declared that there was "no clear support" in American jurisprudence or at common law for physically searching the suspect as the officer did. Although he did not favor the "mode of analysis" in *Terry v. Ohio*, he admitted he could not say its results were wrong. Besides, he said that the constitutionality of the frisk in the present case "was neither challenged nor argued." Thus he agreed with the majority's conclusion that the search was lawful.

Chief Justice Rehnquist wrote an opinion, concurring in part and dissenting in part, with which Justice Blackman and Justice Thomas concurred. The chief justice agreed with parts I and II of the majority opinion (thus the unanimous decision as to these parts) but said he would have vacated the judgment of the Supreme Court of Minnesota and remanded the case to that court for further proceedings. He agreed with the majority that "the dispositive question before the Court is whether the officer who conducted the search was acting within the lawful bounds marked by *Terry v. Ohio*." But he believed that the finding of facts by the Minnesota Supreme Court was "imprecise and not directed expressly to the question of the officer's probable cause to believe that the lump was contraband." Because he lacked confidence in the analysis used by the Supreme Court of Minnesota (which, he said, differed significantly from that adopted by the United States Supreme Court), he would have preferred to vacate its judgment and remand the case for further proceedings in light of the Court's opinion.

Case Significance

Although decided more than two decades later, *Minnesota v. Dickerson* was the first follow-up case of significance to *Terry v. Ohio* on non-motor-vehicle frisks. In *Terry*, the Court held that the police may stop and frisk a suspect without warrant or probable cause if they have reasonable suspicion that the person has just committed or is about to commit a crime.[1] *Dickerson* focuses on the "frisk" part of stop and frisk and set further boundaries for a frisk. In *Terry*, the Court held that a frisk has one purpose and one purpose only: officer protection. Moreover, the officer can merely pat-down the suspect for a weapon, nothing beyond that. In *Dickerson*, the Court held that the officer's action went beyond that allowed in *Terry*, saying that he did not merely conduct a pat-down but instead "squeezed, slid, and otherwise manipulated the pocket's content." During the initial pat-down, the officer felt a "small lump" in the suspect's pocket but admitted it was not a weapon. He knew it was crack cocaine only after he "squeezed, slid, and manipulated" it. Clearly the officer went beyond the limits of a pat-down frisk. Probable cause was likely established after he squeezed, slid, and manipulated, but not before that. The legality of his actions during and before that was limited strictly by what is allowable for a frisk as set in *Terry*.

Dickerson is significant because it sets further boundaries on what an officer can do in the course of a frisk and under what circumstances. Stops and frisks are conducted by law-enforcement officers on a daily basis. It is an important preventive and protective aspect of police patrol and one of the routine practices in any law-enforcement agency. Defining its proper limits is important as a guide in police work to prevent arbitrariness and abuse. Absent clear and well-set boundaries, the frisk of a person can easily turn into a "fishing expedition" for evidence by the police. Its potential for abuse is huge and can be pervasive, thus the need for controls. The Court in *Dickerson* sent this message: frisks are for a limited purpose. Anything beyond police protection is prohibited.

Further Analysis

What if the cop testified differently? Central to the Court's decision in *Dickerson* was the testimony of the police officer during trial. On the witness stand, the officer admitted he knew that the object he felt inside the suspect's jacket was not a dangerous weapon. This admission ruled out officer protection as the justification for the continued search. He then proceeded to "squeeze, slide, and manipulate" the object so that he could determine whether or not it was contraband, which indeed it was. What he did amounted to a fishing expedition and went outside the purpose of a frisk as set in *Terry*. Thus the Court excluded the evidence at trial.

The Court's decision might have admitted the evidence, however, had the officer testified differently. He could have said that when he felt the lump he knew it was not a weapon but that he had probable cause to believe right then—from his experience as a police officer and the place where the encounter took place— that the lump was cocaine. Had the officer said this, the evidence would likely have been admissible based on probable cause. Under these circumstances, the seizure could have been considered valid, not under stop and frisk but based on probable cause. A frisk can turn in an instant into a valid search if, in the course of the frisk, the officer develops probable cause to believe that the object felt is contraband. In these instances, however, the seizable nature of the object must be "immediately apparent" to the officer for the seizure to be valid. The Court in *Dickerson* said,

> Although the officer was lawfully in a position to feel the lump in respondent's pocket, because *Terry* entitled him to place his hands upon respondent's jacket, the court below determined that the incriminating character of the object was not immediately apparent to him. Rather, the officer determined that the item was contraband only after conducting a further search, one not authorized by *Terry* or by any other exception to the warrant requirement.

If the officer had been honestly convinced and then testified that he had believed that what he felt in Dickerson's jacket, although he knew it was not a weapon, was in fact contraband, then the result could have been different. Probable cause would likely have been an issue during trial, but it is ultimately a subjective concept in that what may constitute probable cause to one judge or appellate court may not be probable cause to another. Given the officer's extensive experience and the surrounding circumstances in this case, he could have been deemed highly credible. There is a temptation, given what may be at stake in drug cases, for officers in frisk cases to take this perjurious route to legitimize what otherwise was an exploratory search. It then becomes an issue of police integrity and a question of fact to be determined by a judge or appellate court. Although this alternative is susceptible to misuse, nothing prevents an officer from testifying in good faith during trial that what he or she felt during the pat-down search, given the totality of circumstances, was contraband and therefore occasioned probable cause. Whether this in fact establishes probable cause is ultimately a judgment to be made by the trier of fact.

THE PLAIN-FEEL DOCTRINE
Aside from further defining the limits of a frisk, *Minnesota v. Dickerson* is also significant in that for the first time the Court officially recognized the *plain-feel doctrine* (also known as *plain touch*) in law enforcement. The plain-feel doctrine holds that probable cause can be established through the use of the sense of touch

rather than through the sense of sight. American courts have long recognized the more established doctrine of plain view. This doctrine holds that items in plain sight are subject to seizure by officers without warrant or probable cause as long as other requirements are present. *Dickerson* officially recognized plain feel as a variant of the plain-view doctrine, thus giving a name and judicial recognition to a doctrine that had long been accepted in lower courts as one of the ways by which probable cause can be established. In the context of *Dickerson*, the plain-feel doctrine states that "if the officer, while staying within the narrow limits of a frisk for weapons, feels what he has probable cause to believe is a weapon, contraband, or evidence, the officer may expand the search or seize the object."[2]

OTHER CASES ON THE LIMITS OF A FRISK

Other than a case decided by the Court in 2009 (which involved the frisk of a passenger of a motor vehicle and which is discussed below), there have not been many significant cases over the years since *Dickerson* addressing issues related to frisks. It was simply assumed that frisks based on reasonable suspicion are automatically valid. This may have much to do with the clarity of the Court's decision in *Terry*, which mandated that frisks must have one single purpose only—officer protection—and that the frisk is limited to a mere pat-down for a weapon. These guidelines are unambiguous and convenient for departments to include in their official policy. They are easy for officers to follow, although in some cases (as in the blurring of lines between probable cause for contraband and the admission of no danger to the officer) the guidelines may be susceptible to being blurred.

The one major case on the limits of a frisk was in fact decided by the Court on the same day as *Terry v. Ohio*. In that case, *Sibron v. New York* (392 U.S. 41 [1968]), the Court held the search of a suspected narcotics dealer to be "unreasonable" because it was not based on a concern for officer safety. In *Sibron*, the police followed the suspect for several hours and observed him talking with several narcotics addicts. Officer Martinez then stopped and questioned him. The officer told the suspect, "You know what I am after," whereupon the suspect reached into his pocket. Simultaneously, the officer "thrust his hands into Sibron's pocket" and seized several heroin envelopes.

During the trial for drug trafficking, Sibron sought to exclude the heroin, saying it was the product of an unconstitutional search. Sibron was subsequently convicted and appealed. The Court held the seizure invalid saying that Sibron's conversation with drug addicts in itself did not constitute probable cause that could justify a warrantless search. Moreoever, Officer Martinez could not justify the seizure as resulting from a valid frisk because he admitted he had no reason to suspect Sibron of concealing any weapon. Said the Court,

> The police officer is not entitled to seize and search every person whom he sees on the street or of whom he makes inquiries. Before he places a hand on the person of a citizen in search of anything, he must have constitutionally adequate, reasonable grounds for doing so. In the case of self-protective search for weapons, he must be able to point to particular facts from which he reasonably inferred that the individual was armed and dangerous.

What, then, does *Dickerson* add to what we learned from *Sibron* twenty-five years earlier? Simply this: *Sibron* informed officers when a legal frisk can take place (when an officer has reasonable suspicion about his or her safety), whereas *Dickerson* reaffirms that the frisk is limited to a pat-down for weapons and cannot go beyond that. *Sibron* identifies the *purpose* of a frisk, whereas *Dickerson* further sets the *limits* of a frisk. Taken together, these two cases provide officers definitive frisk guidelines. It is hard to be more specific and detailed than what the Court laid out in these cases; they do not leave much room for misinterpretation by police officers.

FRISKS INVOLVING MOTOR VEHICLES: *ARIZONA V. JOHNSON* (2009)

For a long time, no case of importance was decided by the Court on the limits of a frisk involving automobiles since *Dickerson* was decided in 1993. In January 2009, however, the Court decided *Arizona v. Johnson*, No. 07-1122 (2009), an important case involving motor vehicles. In *Johnson*, the Court ruled that a police officer may frisk a passenger of a motor vehicle if the officer has reasonable suspicion that the passenger may be armed and dangerous even in the absence of reasonable suspicion that the suspect has just committed a crime or is about to commit a crime. In *Johnson*, a car in which Johnson was riding in the back seat was pulled over by an antigang police patrol. Johnson was questioned, and the police learned that he came from "a place [the officer] knew was home to a Crips gang." They also learned that he had served time in state prison for burglary. Johnson was asked to get out of the car for further questioning. Seeing that Johnson wore a blue bandana and had a scanner in his pocket, the officer "patted him down for officer safety." The pat-down yielded a pistol and a small bag of marijuana, which the officer seized. Convicted at trial for weapons and drug possessions, Johnson later appealed to the Court saying that the seizure was illegal. The issue on appeal was narrow but significant:

Can an officer, who stops a vehicle for a minor traffic violation, frisk a passenger who he has reason to suspect could be armed and dangerous in the absence of reasonable suspicion that a crime was committed or being committed?

In a unanimous decision, penned by Justice Ginsburg, the Court held the seizure valid. The Court stated that pat-down searches are valid if the police "harbor reasonable suspicion that a person subjected to the frisk is armed and therefore dangerous to the safety of the police and public" *even if the police have no reason to believe that the person had committed, was committing, or was about to commit an offense.*

The decision was unanimous although the vehicular stop was merely for a minor traffic violation (a license-place check revealed that the vehicle registration had been suspended for an insurance-related violation) and no serious offense was involved. Given the reason for the stop, there were no reasonable grounds to believe that anybody in the vehicle had committed or was committing a criminal offense—the usual justification for stopping a motor vehicle prior to a frisk or search. The Court added that traffic stops are "especially fraught with danger to police officers," who can minimize danger to themselves by exercising "unquestioned command of the situation."

The Court then cited three previously decided cases to support its decision. The first (*Pennsylvania v. Mimms*, 434 U.S. 106 [1977]) holds that "once a motor vehicle has been lawfully detained for traffic violations, the police officer may order the driver to get out of the vehicle without violating the Fourth Amendment." The second (*Maryland v. Wilson*, 519 U.S. 408 [1997]) extends the *Mimms* ruling to passengers as well as drivers based on "the same weighty interest in officer safety." The third and more recent case (*Brendlin v. California*, 551 U.S. 249 [2007]) holds that a passenger, like the driver, is also seized from the moment the police orders the driver and the car to stop on the side of the road. The Court defended the rule saying that "the additional intrusion on the passenger is minimal" and that a passenger's motivation to use violence during a stop to prevent apprehension is just as great as that of the driver. More to the issue, however, is a fourth case (*Knowles v. Iowa*, 525 U.S. 113 [1998]), where the Court, in a dictum ("a statement, remark, or observation"), stated that officers who conduct a routine traffic stop may "perform a pat-down of a driver and any passengers upon reasonable suspicion that they may be armed and dangerous."

In sum, police officers have the same authority to stop and frisk motor-vehicle drivers and passengers as they have in non-motor-vehicle cases because the danger to the officer in motor-vehicle cases is just as great, if not greater. This is allowed even if the police have no reasonable suspicion that the person frisked committed a crime or is about to commit a crime. This decision further un-couples a stop from a frisk and reifies the principle that stops and frisks, although related, are two separate acts. In *Johnson*, the stop requirement (that a person has committed or is about to commit a crime) is not applied to a frisk (which has one purpose: officer protection and the safety of others). The Court holds that a frisk stands on its own without being burdened by the requirement for a valid stop. Thus, in *Johnson*, the two related acts have moved further apart.

In the case of motor-vehicle (as distinguished from non-motor-vehicle) frisks there is an intervening act after the vehicle is stopped and before the frisk. This is the order by the officer for the driver or passenger to get out of the car so that the passenger can be frisked. The Court held this in *Mimms* to be allowable because the degree of the intrusion involved in the order to "get out of the car" is mini-mal. Thus the intervening act of asking the driver to get out of the car constitutes no legal barrier to stops and frisks involving motor vehicles.

CONCLUSIONS

Dickerson sets two important principles in policing: (1) Contraband detected through the sense of touch during the pat-down search is admissible as evidence during trial, and (2) a frisk that goes beyond a mere pat-down for weapons is invalid. These two guidelines are well recognized in courts and embedded in police manuals. Plain feel as a way of establishing probable cause had long been recognized in lower court cases, but its formal recognition by the United States Supreme Court did not happen until *Dickerson*. American jurisprudence has long held that probable cause is established through the use of the five senses. These are sight (seeing a robbery taking place), hearing (hearing a gunshot from a suspect), smell (a police dog smelling marijuana), taste (an officer tasting something alcoholic), and touch. *Dickerson* makes clear that the sense of touch (plain feel) also establishes probable cause, although not in this case because the officer went beyond the limits of a frisk.

Further setting the limits of a frisk is the more significant principle in *Dick-erson*. The setting of a clear limit serves two important functions in policing: First, it gives police officers and departments clear guidance about the extent of a frisk, which is that nothing beyond a mere pat-down for a weapon is valid.

Second, and more importantly, it protects the public from fishing expeditions by the police during a frisk. The rule is clear: anything that does not feel like a weapon cannot be seized in a frisk. This prevents explorations for evidence by the police. Admittedly, there are ways by which this limitation might be bended or breached, but it is legal only if the officer is honestly convinced that probable cause exists or is illegal if the officer perjures his or her testimony in an effort to secure a conviction.

What of the future? The lack of critical scholarly articles or practitioner outcries for further refinement denotes that *Minnesota v. Dickerson* hardly needs further clarification. This is even more the case after the recent Court decision in *Arizona v. Johnson* (2009), which expands police power. It can be left alone by the Court for decades to come and still serve the police and the public well. In *Dickerson*, the Court balanced the need to prevent law breaking against the need to protect individual rights in a way acceptable to proponents of both. This is no minor accomplishment by a Court in a democratic society where finding a proper balance between government power and individual civil liberties is often elusive—a goal constantly sought but hardly ever attained.

FURTHER READING

Louis DiPietro, "The 'Plain Feel' Doctrine: Frisking Suspects," *The FBI Law Enforcement Bulletin* (February 1994).

David A. Harris, "Driving while Black and All Other Traffic Offenses," *Journal of Criminal Law and Criminology* (Winter 1997): 544–605.

D. Kalk, "Stop-and-Frisk Limitations Exist," *The Law Enforcement Magazine* 21, no. 12 (December 1997): 44–45.

Susanne M. MacIntosh, "Fourth Amendment: The Plain Touch Exception to the Warrant Requirement," *Journal of Criminal Law and Criminology* (Winter–Spring 1994): 743–75.

Robert T. Thetford, "Plain Feel, A Second Week: When Is It Used and What Should Officers Know Before Using This Technique?" www.icje.org/id64_m.htm.

IV

ARREST

6

Chimel v. California

C L A I R E N O L A S C O

INTRODUCTION

Prior to the case of *Chimel*, there were no clear guidelines as to the scope and extent of a permissible search incident to a lawful arrest. Although prior case law allowed for this type of search as a valid exception to the warrant requirement of the Fourth Amendment, the Supreme Court vacillated on the justifications for the search, the objects that could be seized, and the exact boundaries of the area that could be searched.

Chimel is significant in three aspects: first, it laid down the twin justifications of a search incident to a lawful arrest—namely, officer safety and preservation of evidence; second, it defined a proper search as one that is "contemporaneous" and not "remote in time and place from the arrest"; and, third, the area that could be searched must be "within his immediate control" or the immediate vicinity where he "might reach to grab" or "gain possession" of any weapon or evidence that can be used against him. The more limited phrase "immediate control" restricted the contemporaneous-area search that could be conducted by police officers and overruled prior decisions that all areas within "the arrestee's control" could be searched as an incident to arrest.

THE CASE OF *CHIMEL V. CALIFORNIA* (1969)

The Facts

According to *Chimel v. California* (395 U.S. 752 [1969]), police officers arrived at the house of Chimel to execute an arrest warrant against him for burglary of a coin shop. The officers identified themselves to Chimel's wife, who allowed them to enter the house and wait for his arrival from work. When Chimel arrived, the officers placed him under arrest and requested permission to "look around." Although Chimel refused, the officers informed him that the search could be conducted "on the basis of a lawful arrest." The officers searched the entire three-bedroom house, including the attic, the garage, and a small workshop. They conducted an extensive search of the master bedroom and sewing room, asking Chimel's wife to open drawers and physically handle the contents so that they could view the objects more thoroughly for evidence of the burglary. The officers seized various items admitted in evidence against Chimel and used for his conviction. He appealed, claiming that the evidence was unconstitutionally seized. Both the California Court of Appeals and the California Supreme Court affirmed his conviction, claiming that although the arrest warrant was invalid because the supporting affidavit set out conclusions rather than facts, the officers obtained the warrant in good faith and had probable cause to arrest Chimel. They also affirmed the legality of the search as incident to a lawful arrest. The United States Supreme Court granted certiorari.

The Issue before the Court

Was the warrantless search of Chimel's entire house constitutionally justified as a search incident to his arrest?

The Court's Holding

Voting seven to two, the Court held that the search of Chimel's house violated the Fourth and Fourteenth Amendments. The Court ruled that searches "incident to arrest" are limited to the area within the immediate control of the person arrested, where he or she may obtain a weapon to use against police officers or where he or she can conceal or destroy evidence. While police could reasonably search and seize evidence on or around the arrestee's person, they were prohibited from searching the entire three-bedroom house without a search warrant.

The Majority Opinion

Justice Stewart wrote the majority opinion for the Supreme Court. He initially reviewed the Court's case law allowing searches incident to a lawful arrest as an exception to the warrant requirement of the Fourth Amendment. He pointed out that the first time the Supreme Court considered the possibility of a search of the person lawfully arrested was a dictum in the case of *Weeks v. United States,*

232 U.S. 383 (1914). The Supreme Court opined that the case of *Weeks v. United States* did not involve an "assertion of the right on the part of the government, always recognized under English and American law, to search the person of the accused when legally arrested to discover and seize the fruits and evidences of the crime." The Supreme Court subsequently considered the scope of the area that can be searched incident to an arrest in the case of *Carroll v. United States*, 267 U.S. 132 (1925), stating that a person lawfully arrested for an offense can be searched for "whatever is found upon his person or in his control which it is unlawful for him to have and which may be used to prove the offense." The area that may be searched incident to an arrest and the objects that may be seized were further defined in *Agnello v. United States*, 269 U.S. 20 (1925), where the Supreme Court held that police officers who make a lawful arrest can contemporaneously search the person arrested and the place where the arrest is made to discover "things connected with the crime as its fruits or as the means by which it was committed" as well as "weapons or other things" that may be used to "escape from custody."

Decisions on the constitutionality of searches incident to arrest vacillated in terms of the scope of the area that may be searched. In *Marron v. United States*, 275 U.S. 192 (1927), the Supreme Court upheld the legality of a search of a closet not listed in the search warrant for a warehouse where liquor and certain articles were manufactured. The officers in this case arrested the person in charge and inspected the closet where they found and seized an incriminating ledger. The Court said that since the agents made a lawful arrest, they could "contemporaneously" search without warrant "all parts of the premises used for the unlawful purpose" in order "to find and seize things used to carry on the criminal enterprise."

In *Go Bart Importing Co. v. United States*, 282 U.S. 344 (1931), police officers searched the office of persons whom they had arrested, seizing items inside a desk, a safe, and other parts of the office. The Supreme Court declared the warrantless search and seizure unconstitutional since no crime was committed in the officers' presence and since the officers "had an abundance of information and time to swear out a valid warrant."

The Supreme Court similarly upheld the search of a four-room apartment in *Harris v. United States*, 331 U.S. 145 (1947) where police officers searched a desk and seized an envelope containing forged government documents. Subsequently, it declared unconstitutional the search of a distillery contemporaneous to the arrest of one of the coconspirators, claiming that the officers had "more than enough time" before the raid to obtain a search warrant.

In *United States v. Rabinowitz*, 339 U.S. 56 (1950), the Supreme Court upheld the constitutionality of a warrantless search by police officers of the entire one-room business office of the arrestee. At the time of arrest, the police officers searched the office, desk, safe, and file cabinets of the arrestee, seizing 573 forged stamps that were used as evidence at the arrestee's trial. The Court stated that a warrantless search incident to a lawful arrest may generally "extend to the area that is considered to be in the possession or under the control of the person arrested."

The Court noted that previous cases, including *United States v. Rabinowitz*, were "hardly founded on an unimpeachable line of authority" and proceeded to explain the permissible extent of a search incident to a lawful arrest. They clarified that when an arrest is made, the arresting officer can search the person arrested to "remove any weapons that the latter might seek to use in order to resist arrest or affect his escape." In addition, the arresting officer may "search for and seize any evidence on the arrestee's person in order to prevent its concealment or destruction." The area that may be searched must be within the arrestee's "immediate control" or "the area from within which he might gain possession of a weapon or destructible evidence." The Court further clarified that a search incident to an arrest must be contemporaneous and not "remote in time and place from the arrest."

Justice Harlan concurred in the opinion of the Court, adding that as a result of *Mapp v. Ohio*, 367 U.S. 643 (1961), "every change in Fourth Amendment law must now be obeyed by state officials facing widely different problems of local law enforcement."

The Dissenting Opinion

Justice White, with whom Justice Black joined, dissented from the majority opinion, arguing that the warrantless search of the three-bedroom house of Chimel contemporaneous with his arrest should be upheld as constitutional for the following reasons: first, there was probable cause for both the search and the arrest; second, exigent circumstances existed concerning possible removal or destruction of evidence; and third, there was satisfactory opportunity to dispute the issue of probable cause in a subsequent hearing. Unlike the majority, the dissent did not seek to clarify what constituted areas "within the control of the arrestee" that can be searched incident to a lawful arrest.

Justice White argued that the Court has "always held" that a warrantless search is reasonable when there is probable cause to search and it is "impracticable for one reason or another to get a search warrant." He stated that in this case, it was "unreasonable to require police to leave the scene of an arrest in order to obtain a search warrant" when they already had "probable cause to search" and there was "clear danger" that evidence may have been concealed or destroyed before they returned with a warrant.

He stated that the analysis should focus on two issues: first, the validity of Chimel's arrest without a valid warrant, which the majority assumed; and, second, the constitutionality of the warrantless search incident to his arrest. On the first issue, he pointed to a line of decisions and laws that allowed law-enforcement officers, such as the United States marshal, the Federal Bureau of Investigation, the Secret Service, and the narcotics law-enforcement agency, to make warrantless arrests even where there was time to obtain them as long as they had "reasonable grounds to believe that the person arrested has committed or is committing a felony." On the second issue, he opined that the "fact of arrest" creates an "exigent circumstance" justifying a warrantless search since the police "lawfully gained entry" to Chimel's house and "delaying the search to secure a warrant would have involved the risk of not recovering the fruits of the crime." He then points out that the arrestee can always challenge the constitutionality of a warrantless search incident to an arrest in a subsequent adversary proceeding.

Case Significance

Prior to *Chimel*, case law yielded varying results on the permissible scope of a search incident to a lawful arrest. Although there was a consensus that the officer could search the person of the arrestee, there was no definite ruling on the extent of the area search that may be conducted contemporaneously with the arrest. In *Carroll v. United States*, 267 U.S. 132 (1925), the Supreme Court allowed an area search for objects on the arrestee's person or in his control "which it is unlawful for him to have and which may be used to prove the offense." The Court further expanded the allowable area search in *Agnello v. United States*, 269 U.S. 20 (1925), stating that the arresting officer may search "the place where the arrest is made" to find and seize evidence "connected with the crime as its fruits or as the means by which it was committed" and also for "weapons and other things" that could be used by the arrestee to escape. The Court, however, varied in its interpretation of the extent of the area that could be searched, upholding area searches of a four-bedroom apartment in *Harris v. United States*, 331 U.S. 145 (1947), a one-room business office in *United States v. Rabinowitz*, 339 U.S. 56 (1950), and a liquor saloon in *Marron v. United States*, 275 U.S. 192 (1927).

The Court, in contrast, declared unlawful area searches of an office in *Go Bart Importing Co. v. United States*, 282 U.S. 344 (1931), and a distillery in *Trupiano v. United States*, 334 U.S. 699 (1948).

In *Chimel*, the Court for the first time clarified the justification for, and scope of, the area that may be searched incident to a lawful arrest. The Court held that two justifications existed for this type of warrantless search: namely, officer safety and preservation of evidence. The Court also overruled prior cases that upheld searches incident to arrest of any area "in the control" of the person arrested, limiting the allowable scope of such search to the arrestee's person as well as the areas "within his immediate control." It interpreted the area "within his immediate control" as the immediate vicinity where the suspect "might reach to grab" or "gain possession" of any weapon or evidence that can be used against him. The Court further noted that there was no justification for "routinely searching any room other than that in which an arrest occurs" or for searching through "all the desk drawers or other closed or concealed areas in that room itself." In addition, the Court established the temporal scope of the search, citing *Preston v. United States*, 376 U.S. 364 (1964), where a contemporaneous search was allowed as long as the search was "not remote in time or place from the arrest."

Further Analysis

In *Chimel*, the Court sought to create a clear standard by which to determine the lawfulness of searches incident to an arrest. It established a limited search-incident-to-arrest exception to the warrant requirement of the Fourth Amendment, taking into consideration its rationale and historical origins. They quoted with approval Justice Frankfurter's dissent in *Rabinowitz* (339 U.S. 56 [1950]) that the Fourth Amendment's prohibition against unreasonable searches and seizures must be read in "light of the history that gave rise to the words—a history of abuses so deeply felt by the Colonies as to be one of the potent causes of the Revolution." The Court emphasized that the warrant requirement is not a "mere formality" and that "absent some grave emergency" police officers must apply for a warrant before a neutral magistrate. The Fourth Amendment provides for a warrant requirement not to "shield criminals nor to make the home a safe haven for illegal activities" but to enable "an objective mind" to weigh the need to invade an individual's privacy to enforce the law.

The government in *Chimel* argued that it was "reasonable" to search a person's house when the suspect is arrested in it. The Court believed that this argument proposes a subjective view regarding the acceptability of certain actions of law enforcement and was not based on considerations underlying the Fourth Amendment. According to the Court, the test of reasonableness of a search-incident exception must be based on the "reason underlying and expressed by the Fourth Amendment: the history and experience which it embodies and the safeguards afforded by it against the evils to which it was a response." Thus, although the reasonableness of a search depends on "the facts and circumstances—the total atmosphere of the case, those facts and circumstances must be viewed in the light of established Fourth Amendment principles." Otherwise, a subjective test of reasonableness would result in Fourth Amendment protection approaching an "evaporation point."

SIGNIFICANT CASES SINCE *CHIMEL*

The Court clearly sought to limit the search-incident-to-arrest exception in *Chimel*. Subsequent decisions, however, continued to define and expand the parameters of what police officers could search as an incident to a lawful arrest.

Rulings That Affirm *Chimel* (Chronologically)

Full-body search of the arrestee is lawful: Regardless of the nature of the offense for which the arrestee was placed under lawful custody, the police officer has the right to fully and thoroughly search the person of the arrestee (*United States v. Robinson*, 414 U.S. 218 [1973]). This absolute authority to conduct a body search exists even if the offense for which the arrestee was held in custody does not require any supporting evidence and even if the police officer does not believe that the arrestee is armed and dangerous. The Court stated that every arrested offender poses a potential threat to an arresting officer. The officer must be allowed to conduct full-body searches of the arrestee to complete the arrest and ensure officer safety. The Court further stated that the officer's decision as to how and where to search the person of the arrestee is a "quick ad hoc judgment" that the Fourth Amendment "does not require to be broken down in each instance into an analysis of each step in the search." This discretion "does not depend on what a court may later decide was the probability that in a particular arrest situation" weapons or evidence would be found on the arrestee's person.

Several hours' delay in the search of arrestee's clothing after his arrest is valid: A delay of several hours in the search of the arrestee's clothing is valid if the "normal processes incident to arrest and custody had not been completed" and the "delay in seizing the clothing was not unreasonable" (*United States v. Edwards*, 415 U.S. 800 [1974]). In *Edwards*, the arrestee was booked and held in custody

late in the evening. The officers did not immediately search the arrestee's clothing until the next day, approximately ten hours after the arrest, when they were
able to purchase substitute clothing for him. They then searched the clothing
that the arrestee had turned over to them. The Court held that once an accused
has been "lawfully arrested" and placed in custody, his personal effects seized
at the "place of detention" may lawfully be searched and seized without a warrant despite a reasonable delay. The police officers have authority to search the
arrestee's personal effects (i.e., his clothing) even after the lapse of a substantial
time between his arrest and the seizure of property for use as evidence.

A body search prior to arrest can be a valid search incident to arrest: A body
search of a suspect prior to his arrest is valid as long as police officers had probable cause to arrest him and in fact "formally arrested" him immediately after the
search (*Rawlings v. Kentucky*, 448 U.S. 98 [1980]). In *Rawlings*, police officers executed a search warrant for a house occupied by Rawlings and his friends. When
the officers instructed one of Rawlings's friends to empty her purse, the officers
discovered a huge amount of illegal drugs. Rawlings "immediately claimed
ownership of the controlled substances." Police then conducted a body search
of Rawlings. The Court ruled that "once he admitted ownership of the drugs"
found in his friend's purse, the police officers had probable cause to arrest him.
Since the officers immediately arrested Rawlings, the search that occurred prior
to the arrest was still a valid search incident to an arrest.

An area search prior to arrest is not a valid search incident to arrest: A warrantless search of a bag that an individual throws onto the hood of his car is not a
valid search incident to arrest even if police officers immediately arrest him after
discovering drug paraphernalia inside (*Smith v. Ohio*, 494 U.S. 541 [1990]). In
Smith, an individual was carrying a bag when he exited a private residence. When
police officers tried to stop him, he threw the bag onto the hood of his car. The
officers opened the bag, found drug paraphernalia, and placed him immediately
under arrest. The state supreme court admitted the drug paraphernalia as evidence to convict him, stating that the search was valid as incidental to a lawful
arrest. The Supreme Court, however, ruled that the area search of the bag could
not be justified as a search incident to a lawful arrest.

Rulings That Modify *Chimel* (Chronologically)

*Search of passenger compartments incident to the arrest of a recent occupant of
the vehicle is valid:* When an officer lawfully arrests a recent occupant of a vehicle,
he can search the entire passenger compartment incident to that arrest (*Thorn-*

ton v. United States, 541 U.S. 615 [2004]). An individual can be considered a "recent occupant" of the vehicle regardless of whether the officer first makes contact while the individual is inside or outside the vehicle. The Court conceded that "an arrestee's status as a recent occupant may turn on his temporal or spatial relationship to the car at the time of arrest and search."

Vehicle search is not valid where the arrestee has been secured and cannot access its interior and when evidence of the offense of arrest cannot possibly be found in the vehicle: Police officers cannot validly search a vehicle incident to an arrest of a "recent occupant" when the arrestee has already been "handcuffed and secured in separate patrol cars" and "cannot access the interior of the vehicle" (*Arizona v. Gant*, 129 S. Ct. 1710 [2009]). A valid area search is limited to the area from which the arrestee "might gain possession of a weapon or destructible evidence." The Court also stated that "circumstances unique to the automobile context justify a search incident to arrest when it is reasonable to believe that evidence of the offense of arrest might be found in the vehicle." Police officers cannot validly search the car in the case of *Gant* since they could not "reasonably have believed that evidence of the offense for which the individual was arrested (i.e., driving with a suspended license) might have been found in the car."

Cases since *Chimel* follow the Court's delineation of the scope of searchable area incident to arrest. Subsequent cases have also affirmed the lawfulness of these types of searches to ensure officer safety and preserve evidence. The Court, however, has provided a more relaxed standard for the timing of the search, allowing a lapse of time before or after the arrest as long as it is justified under the circumstances. The Court also clarified the types of offenses that cannot lead to valid incidental searches, namely traffic citations where any further search would not yield corroborating evidence for the offense of arrest. In cases after *Chimel*, the Court introduced the concept of "recent occupant" of a vehicle and allowed incidental searches of a vehicle where there was urgent need to preserve evidence.

Maryland v. Buie (1990): Searching "Areas Incident to a Lawful Arrest" Compared with "Protective Sweeps"

A lawful arrest of a suspect allows police officers to conduct an incidental search and a protective sweep, where the circumstances require it. The Court has defined a protective sweep as a "quick and limited search" of the premises, incident to an arrest and usually conducted to ensure officer safety. It is "narrowly confined to a cursory visual inspection of those places in which a [dangerous] person might be hiding" (*Maryland v. Buie*, 494 U.S. 325 [1990]). Important distinctions arise between searches incident to a lawful arrest and protective sweeps. The Court in *Buie* clearly defined the rationale for both types of searches, the areas that may be searched, and the manner of search.

In *Buie*, two armed men, one of them wearing a red running suit, robbed a pizza parlor. That same day, police officers obtained arrest warrants for respondent Jerome Edward Buie and his suspected accomplice and placed Buie's house under police surveillance. Two days later, six officers proceeded to Buie's house to execute the arrest warrant. Once inside, several officers searched the first and second floors. One of them announced that he would "freeze" the basement so that no one could come up and surprise them. The officer twice shouted into the basement, ordering anyone down there to come out. Eventually, Buie emerged from the basement and was arrested, searched, and handcuffed. Another police officer entered the basement "in case there was someone else" down there and found a red running suit similar to the one used in the robbery.

The trial court denied Buie's motion to suppress the running suit as evidence and convicted Buie for robbery with a deadly weapon and using a handgun in the commission of a felony. The Court of Special Appeals of Maryland affirmed the trial court's denial of the suppression motion. The court stated that police officer "did not go into the basement to search for evidence but to look for the suspected accomplice or anyone else who might pose a threat to the officers on the scene." The Court of Appeals of Maryland reversed the judgment, holding that the running suit was inadmissible because the officer who conducted the "protective sweep of the basement" did not have probable cause to believe that a "serious and demonstrable potentiality for danger exists."

The majority opinion applied the *Terry v. Ohio* (392 U.S. 1 [1968]) balancing test by weighing the burden on Buie's Fourth Amendment interests of the search of his basement against the immediate interests of the police in protecting themselves from the danger posed by hidden weapons as well as dangerous persons who could "unexpectedly launch an attack."

The Court distinguished the nature of possible searches incident to an arrest and set two distinct standards. First, with respect to spaces immediately adjoining the place of arrest, police officers, "as an incident to the arrest," could "look in closets and other spaces . . . from which an attack could be immediately launched." Such warrantless search of immediately adjoining spaces could be conducted "as a precautionary matter and without probable cause or reasonable suspicion." Thus, police officers could conduct routine full-blown searches of such adjoining spaces in order to ensure their safety.

For areas that extend beyond the places "immediately adjoining" the place of arrest, police officers must establish "articulable facts which taken together with the rational inferences from those facts" would lead a "reasonably prudent officer" to believe that the adjoining areas are likely to harbor an individual "posing a danger to those on the arrest scene." The Court emphasized that such a "protective sweep, aimed at protecting the arresting officers, if justified by the circumstances, is nevertheless not a full search of the premises but may extend only to a cursory inspection of those spaces where a person may be found." This cursory inspection cannot last longer than necessary "to dispel the reasonable suspicion of danger" or "to complete and depart from the premises."

The Court further distinguished its ruling in *Chimel v. California* (395 U.S. 752 [1969]), which held that a warrantless search of a house incident to an in-home arrest could not extend beyond the arrestee's "person" and areas "within his immediate control." First, *Chimel* involved a "full-blown, top-to-bottom search of an entire house for evidence of the crime for which the arrest was made." *Buie*, in contrast, involved a "more limited intrusion contemplated by a protective sweep." Second, the justification for the search incident to arrest in *Chimel* was the threat "posed by the arrestee" while the justification in *Buie* was "the safety threat posed by the house, or more properly by unseen third parties in the house."

CONCLUSIONS

The Court in the *Chimel* case tried to limit the search-incident-to-arrest exception based on the history and reasons underlying the Fourth Amendment. Prior to the approval of the Fourth Amendment, law enforcement frequently conducted warrantless searches and searches authorized under general warrants and writs of assistance. They had broad discretion to conduct investigative searches without judicial oversight. The Fourth Amendment aims to protect citizens against arbitrary and unlimited government searches.

Chimel emphasized that the Fourth Amendment requires police officers to apply for a warrant before a neutral magistrate prior to conducting a search. This requirement is not a mere "formality" that courts could overlook and exceptions should be granted only "in some grave emergency." Exceptions such as the search incident to arrest should thus be clearly defined and limited. The scope of the search must be "strictly tied to and justified by the circumstances which rendered its initiation possible." The Court did not allow a broader exception because the "exigencies of arrest" do not justify it.

The Court provided a clear guideline for searches conducted by law enforcement incident to arrest. Cases decided after *Chimel* used two justifications for this type of search: officer safety and preservation of evidence. By limiting the extent of searchable area to those within the arrestee's "immediate control," law enforcement is prohibited from conducting arbitrary and unlimited searches. The Court in *Maryland* clarified the scope and extent of protective sweeps, by allowing police officers to search areas not immediately adjoining the place of arrest only when they have reason to believe that these areas are likely to harbor a dangerous third person. Only a cursory and limited inspection, however, may be conducted in protective sweeps unlike searches incident to lawful arrests, which may be full-blown and thorough.

The guidelines established by *Chimel* enable law enforcement to determine the extent of the search that they may validly conduct without violating the mandates of the Fourth Amendment. By limiting these types of searches, they are prohibited from conducting arbitrary searches and exercising broad discretion. *Chimel* provides logic to the search-incident-to-arrest exception, establishing a clear framework that organizes and supplants prior case law on the matter.

FURTHER READING

Henry J. Abraham, *Justices and Presidents: A Political History of Appointments to the Supreme Court*, third ed. (New York: Oxford University Press, 1992).

Helaine M. Barnett, Janice Goldman, and Jeffrey B. Morris, "A Lawyer's Lawyer, a Judge's Judge: Potter Stewart and the Fourth Amendment," *University of Cincinnati Law Review* 51 (1982): 509–91.

Helaine M. Barnett and Kenneth Levine, "Mr. Justice Potter Stewart," *New York University Law Review* 40 (1965): 526–82.

Daniel M. Berman, "Mr. Justice Stewart: A Preliminary Appraisal," *University of Cincinnati Law Review* 28 (1959): 401–55.

Rolando V. del Carmen, *Criminal Procedure: Law and Practice* (Belmont, Calif.: Wadsworth/ Cengage Learning, 2010).

K. Deters, "The 'Evaporation Point': *State v. Sykes* and the Erosion of the Fourth Amendment through the Search Incident to Arrest Exception," *Iowa Law Review* 92 (2007): 1901–27.

S. Fox, "Protective Sweep Incident to a Lawful Arrest: An Analysis of Its Validity under the Federal and New York State Constitutions," *Touro Law Review* 8 (1992): 761–95.

John P. Frank, "Frank Murphy," in *The Justices of the United States Supreme Court: Their Lives and Major Opinions*, ed. Leon Friedman and Fred L. Israel (New York: Chelsea House Publishers, 1997).

Kermit L. Hall, ed., *The Oxford Companion to the Supreme Court of the United States* (New York: Oxford University Press, 1992).

R. Moran, "Motorists Are People Too: Recalculating the Vehicular Search Incident to Arrest Exception by Prohibiting Searches Incident to Arrests for Nonevidentiary Offenses," *Criminal Law Bulletin* 44 (2008): 3–20.

J. Samaha, *Criminal Procedure* (Belmont, Calif.: Thomson Wadsworth, 2008).

J. Scheb and J. Scheb II, *Criminal Law and Procedure* (Belmont, Calif.: Thomson Wadsworth, 2008).

J. Tomkovicz, "Divining and Designing the Future of the Search Incident to Arrest Doctrine: Avoiding Instability, Irrationality, and Infidelity," *University of Illinois Law Review* (2007): 1417–76.

A. Trupp, "*Maryland v. Buie*: Extending the Protective Search Warrant Exception into the Home," *Journal of Contemporary Law* 17 (1991): 193–210.

Tinsley E. Yarbrough, "Justice Potter Stewart: Decisional Patterns in Search of Doctrinal Moorings," in *The Burger Court: Political and Judicial Profiles*, eds. Charles M. Lamb and Stephen C. Halpern (Urbana: University of Illinois Press, 1991), 375–406.

7

United States v. Robinson

CLAIRE NOLASCO

INTRODUCTION

In *Chimel v. California*, 395 U.S. 752 (1969), the Supreme Court laid down the twin justifications for a search incident to a lawful arrest: namely, officer safety and preservation of evidence. While conceding the authority of law enforcement to conduct a body search of the person arrested, the Court limited the permissible area that can be searched by law-enforcement officers to the area within the arrestee's "immediate control" or the vicinity where the arrestee can reach for or grab weapons or evidence connected with the offense for which the person was arrested.

The *Chimel* case raised further issues that went unresolved until the landmark case of *Robinson* was decided. These issues were (1) whether law enforcement had to perceive or subjectively fear that the arrestee was concealing weapons or evidence within the searchable areas and (2) whether a search incident to a lawful arrest was constitutional only where the offense of arrest might possibly yield further evidence in these areas. *Robinson* is significant in two aspects: first, it granted law enforcement the absolute right to conduct searches incident to a custodial arrest based on probable cause; and, second, it established such right regardless of (1) whether the offense of arrest could yield further evidence within the searchable areas and (2) the subjective fears or perceptions of law enforcement that weapons or evidence were in fact concealed in these areas.

THE CASE OF *UNITED STATES V. ROBINSON* (1973)

The Facts

According to *United States v. Robinson* (414 U.S. 218 [1973]), on April 19, 1968, a police officer stopped a vehicle driven by Robinson for a "routine spot check." After examining Robinson's driver's permit and vehicle registration card, the officer allowed Robinson to proceed. Since the documents contained some discrepancies, the officer checked police records and discovered that Robinson's permit had been revoked. Four days later, the same police officer saw Robinson driving the same vehicle and placed him under arrest for "operating after revocation and obtaining a permit by misrepresentation," an offense under state law.

In accordance with police procedures, he began to search Robinson. The officer felt a package on Robinson's left pocket, pulled it out, and opened it. The cigarette package contained fourteen gelatin capsules of heroin. The evidence was admitted in Robinson's trial in the United States District Court for the District of Columbia where he was convicted of possession and facilitation of concealment of heroin. The court of appeals reversed, holding that the heroin was obtained in violation of the Fourth Amendment of the United States Constitution. The United States Supreme Court granted certiorari.

The Issue before the Court

Was the search valid even if the police officer did not subjectively perceive that the arrestee was concealing weapons or evidence on his person and regardless of whether the offense of arrest does not require further evidence of the crime?

The Court's Holding

Voting six to three, the Court held that both the search of the arrestee's person and the seizure of evidence was valid under the Fourth Amendment. The Court held that, "while thorough," the search was not conducted in an "extreme or patently abusive" manner and that "it is the fact of custodial arrest which gives rise to the authority to search." Thus, it did not matter in this case that the police officer did not "indicate any subjective fear of the respondent or that he did not himself suspect that the respondent was armed."

The Majority Opinion

Justice Rehnquist wrote the majority opinion for the Court. Based on prior Court decisions, he stated that a lawful arrest carries with it two incidental rights: the right to search the person of the arrestee and the right to search the area within the immediate control of the arrestee. Although the first incidental right has been "settled from its first enunciation," the Court has varied in its interpretation of the extent of the area that may be searched. Justice Rehnquist then proceeded to discuss case law, granting law-enforcement officers the unqualified right to search the person of the arrestee incident to a lawful arrest for either "weapons" that may be used to endanger the officer's safety or evidence that the arrestee may conceal or destroy (*Chimel v. California*, 395 U.S. 752 [1969]; *Adams v. Williams*, 407 U.S. 143 [1972]).

The court of appeals applied the restrictions of *Terry v. Ohio*, 392 U.S. 1 [1968]) to this case, holding that a police officer cannot fully search the person of the arrestee but must instead conduct "a limited frisk of the outer clothing and remove such weapons" that the officer may "reasonably believe and ascertain that the suspect has in his possession." The court of appeals reasoned that since the arrestee was held for the offense of "driving with a revoked license," there would be no further evidence of such crime that can be discovered through searching the arrestee. Any further search could only be justified by the need to discover weapons to ensure "officer safety."

The Supreme Court stated that the principles of *Terry* (involving a limited protective frisk for weapons) should not be applied to a search incident to an arrest for probable cause. According to the Court, there is a "distinction in purpose, character, and extent between a search incident to an arrest and a limited search for weapons." A search incident to a probable-cause arrest implies a full-blown search for weapons, while a protective frisk for weapons without probable cause must "be strictly circumscribed by the exigencies which justify its initiation." The protective frisk implies "something less than a full search" and must thus be limited in scope so as to merely allow the police officer to discover weapons that endanger his safety. The Court further stated that the "absence of probable fruits or further evidence" of the particular offense for which the probable-cause arrest was made does not justify a reduction of a search based on probable cause to the limited protective frisk described in *Terry*.

The court of appeals also relied on *Peters v. New York* (392 U.S. 40 [1968]), in which the Court ruled that the search of the arrestee's person was valid because it did not involve an "unrestrained and thorough-going examination of Peters and his personal effects." The court of appeals interpreted this as a limitation on the right to search the person of the arrestee. The Court rejected this interpretation, stating that the arresting officer has a "traditional and unqualified authority" to search the "arrestee's person."

The Court clarified that previous statements on the "unqualified authority to search incident to a lawful arrest are dicta [the part of a judicial opinion which is merely a judge's editorializing and does not directly address the specifics of the case at bar; extraneous material which is merely informative or explanatory]." Hence, the Court is not "foreclosed by principles of stare decisis [legal principle that prior decisions must be followed; when a point has been settled by prior court decision, it forms a precedent which is not afterwards to be departed from]" from framing a new rule regarding the nature of the right to search incident to a probable-cause arrest. The Court, citing Cardozo's decision in *People v. Chiagles* (237 N.Y. 193 [1923]), distinguished between a lawful and unlawful search incident to an arrest. Search of a person is "unlawful" when the "purpose of the search is to discover grounds as yet unknown for arrest or accusation." Search of the person becomes lawful "when grounds for arrest and accusation have been discovered and the law is in the act of subjecting the body of the accused to its physical dominion."

The Court refused to distinguish among custodial arrests for various offenses, such as driving with revoked licenses and other crimes. Noting that all custodial arrests, regardless of offense type, expose the officer to the same danger and contact with the arrestee, the Court stated that "all custodial arrests" must be treated "alike" for purposes of "search justification."

The court of appeals further held that each case must be examined to determine whether the justifications for search incident to an arrest existed. The Court rejected this, holding that a "case-by-case adjudication" is unnecessary and instead opted for a bright-line rule that granted law enforcement the absolute right to search the arrestee after a full custodial arrest. The Court said that the "police officer's determination" as to the circumstances of the search is a "quick ad hoc judgment which the Fourth Amendment does not require to be broken down in each instance into an analysis of each step in the search." This search authority does not depend on a court's subsequent determination of the probability that weapons or evidence would be found on the arrestee's person.

The Court concluded that a "custodial arrest of a suspect based on probable cause is a reasonable intrusion under the Fourth Amendment; that intrusion being lawful, a search incident to arrest" does not require additional justification. The "fact of lawful arrest" establishes the "authority to search," and a full-body search of the arrestee is not only an "exception to the warrant requirement of the Fourth Amendment" but also a "reasonable search under that amendment."

The Dissenting Opinion

Justice Marshall, with whom Justices Douglas and Brennan joined, dissented from the majority opinion, opining that the search in this case was unconstitutional. He objected to the majority's grant of absolute authority to search incident to a lawful arrest. Instead, he argued that under prior decisions of the Court on Fourth Amendment issues there is "no formula for the determination of reasonableness" and that "each case is to be decided on its own facts and circumstances." He also disagreed that the "quick ad hoc judgment of a police officer" should not be subject to review or control by the judiciary. According to him, the Fourth Amendment requires that law-enforcement practices be subjected to the "more detached, neutral scrutiny of a judge who must evaluate the reasonableness of a particular search or seizure in light of particular circumstances." He emphasized that because the search-incident-to-arrest doctrine is an exception to the warrant requirement, it does not "preclude further inquiry into the reasonableness of the search."

He then cited existing state and federal court decisions holding that, without special circumstances, an officer cannot conduct a full search of a person incident to a lawful arrest for "violation of a motor-vehicle registration" or other "routine traffic violations." In the case of traffic arrests, the officer must "have reasonable grounds to believe that a search was necessary for his own safety or to prevent an escape." He also proposed that the Court adopt a case-by-case adjudication to "determine whether a full arrest" was made for "purely legitimate reasons" or only as a "pretext for searching the arrestee."

He proposed that the right to a search incident to traffic arrests be limited to the protective frisk for weapons established in *Terry*. He argued that *Chimel* provides for two justifications for searches incident to an arrest: officer safety and preservation of evidence. Since any further search in traffic arrests would not yield evidence of traffic violations, the only justification would be to remove weapons that the arrestee might use to harm the officer. Any search must thus be confined in scope to an "intrusion reasonably designed to discover guns, knives, clubs, or other hidden instruments" that can be used by the arrestee. A search for weapons is justified only when the officer has "cause to believe" that he or she is dealing with a dangerous individual. In this case, the officer "had no reason to believe" and did not in fact believe that the cigarette package taken from Robinson contained a weapon; hence, the search was invalid.

Case Significance

Prior to *Robinson*, it was unclear whether a police officer could conduct a body search incident to an arrest for an offense where any further search would yield no evidence. Another unresolved issue was whether the search incident to arrest was justified only if the officer subjectively perceived that the arrestee actually carried weapons or was concealing evidence.

These issues were settled in *Robinson* where the Court held that a body search incident to any custodial arrest is valid even if (1) the arrest is for an offense that would not have any supporting evidence and (2) the officer has no reason to believe that the arrestee is dangerous or concealing evidence. The Court held that the fact of arrest creates the police officer's right to search the arrestee's person. The rule means that police could conduct a search upon arrest for any kind of offense, including minor offenses such as traffic violations. Under *Robinson*, the officer also does not need to justify any incidental search by showing that he or she subjectively perceived or feared that the arrestee was actually concealing weapons or evidence.

The Court established, however, the necessity of a custodial arrest prior to the exercise of the absolute right to search. The Court emphasized that it is the "proximity, stress, and uncertainty" arising from the arrest situation and not "the grounds for arrest" that justify the warrantless incidental search. Law-enforcement officers are precluded from conducting searches incident to nonarrest situations, such as after issuing traffic citations. The exposure-to-danger rationale of searches incident to arrest arises due to the officer's prolonged contact and exposure to the suspect after a full custodial arrest. Thus, any situation that does not lead to a custodial arrest does not involve the same danger.

Further Analysis

The Court in *Robinson* held that a body search may be conducted after any custodial arrest regardless of the perceived threat faced by a police officer or the possibility of discovering fruits or further evidence of the particular crime for which the arrest is made. Police officers are granted an unqualified right to search after making a custodial arrest, regardless of the nature of the offense for which the arrest was made. The Court's ruling in *Robinson* justifies searches incident to arrests even for minor offenses, such as misdemeanor and petty offenses. According to the Court, there is no basis to distinguish the search authority based on the underlying offense for which the suspect is arrested. The Court believed that it is not valid to assume that persons arrested for minor offenses such as driving with revoked licenses are "less likely to possess dangerous weapons than those arrested for other crimes." The Court stated that any custodial arrest exposes the officer to the same danger in contrast to a nonarrest stop-and-frisk situation of *Terry* where there is "relatively fleeting contact" between suspect and officer.

The police officer's right to search only arises after he makes a custodial arrest by placing a person under his or her custody. When an officer does not make a custodial arrest but merely issues a citation for speeding, there is no incidental right to search because the twin justifications of officer safety and preservation of evidence do not arise (*Knowles v. Iowa*, 525 U.S. 113 [1998]). Also, the timing of the incidental search is irrelevant as long as the arrest occurs immediately after the search. Police officers can conduct an incidental body search of the suspect prior to his or her arrest as long as they had probable cause for the arrest and in fact "formally arrested" him or her immediately after the search (*Rawlings v. Kentucky*, 448 U.S. 98 [1980]).

SIGNIFICANT CASES SINCE *ROBINSON* (CHRONOLOGICALLY)

Subsequent cases have further defined the nature and scope of searches incident to a custodial arrest. The most significant rulings are outlined in the following.

Arrest for failure to carry and produce a driver's license while driving provides basis for a valid incidental search: A full search of the defendant's person after his lawful custodial arrest for failure to possess and produce a valid vehicle-operator's license did not violate the Fourth and Fourteenth Amendments (*Gustafson v. Florida*, 414 U.S. 260 [1973]). It was immaterial that (1) there were no police-department policies that required "taking the defendant into custody or conducting the full-scale body search," (2) there were "no mandatory minimum sanctions for the offense of driving without having possession of a license," (3) the officer "did not indicate any subjective fear of the defendant" or "suspect that he was armed" or (4) the search could yield further evidence of the offense of driving without having possession of a license.

An officer cannot conduct a vehicle search incident to the issuance of a traffic citation: A warrantless search incident to arrest can only be conducted if the person searched has been taken into lawful custody. When an officer does not make a custodial arrest but merely issues a citation for speeding, "the concern for officer safety is not present to the same extent, and the concern for destruction or loss of evidence is not present at all" (*Knowles v. Iowa*, 525 U.S. 113 [1998]). The Court stated that the twin rationales provided in *Chimel*, officer safety and preservation of evidence, did not apply to mere stops and traffic citations. The Court reasoned that threat to officers is insufficient since a person receiving the citation is less likely to be hostile than one who is arrested and the citation incident is a brief encounter compared to arrest situations. Also, the "need to discover and preserve evidence" does not exist in a traffic stop, because once a person is stopped for speeding and issued a citation, "all evidence necessary to prosecute that offense had been obtained."

Arrest based on probable cause but prohibited by state law provides sufficient basis for an incidental search: Police did not violate the Fourth Amendment when they made an arrest based on probable cause but prohibited by state law or when they performed a search incident to the arrest (*Virginia v. Moore*, 128 S. Ct. 1598 [2008]). In this case, Moore was stopped by police officers who suspected he was driving with a suspended license. After confirming that his license was suspended, they arrested him for the misdemeanor even though under Virginia law they should have only issued him a summons. A search subsequent to arrest revealed evidence of crack cocaine, which resulted in Moore's conviction by the trial court. The state supreme court reversed, holding that the search violated the Fourth Amendment because the arresting officers should have issued a citation under state law and the Fourth Amendment does not permit search incident to citation.

The Court held that "when an officer has probable cause to believe a person committed even a minor crime, the arrest is constitutionally reasonable." The Court cautioned against changing the rules when a state chooses to protect privacy interests beyond the requirements imposed by the Fourth Amendment. The Court ruled that "an arrest based on probable cause serves interests that justify seizure." Arrest ensures that a suspect "appears to answer charges and does not continue a crime." It also "safeguards evidence" and allows police officers to "conduct an in-custody investigation." A state's "more restrictive search-and-seizure policy" does not render "less-restrictive ones unreasonable" or "unconstitutional." The Court conceded that states are "free to require their officers to engage in nuanced determination of the need for arrest as a matter of their own law." The Fourth Amendment, however, should reflect "administrable bright-line rules." The Court believed that "incorporating state-arrest rules into the Constitution would make Fourth Amendment protections as complex as the underlying state law and variable from place to place and time to time."

The Court stated that officers "may perform searches incident to constitutionally permissible arrests in order to ensure their safety and safeguard evidence." Although officers who merely issue citations are not exposed to the same danger faced by those who make custodial arrests and thus do not have authority to search, the officers in this case already arrested Moore and therefore faced the risks that provide "adequate basis for treating all custodial arrests alike for purposes of search justification."

Cases decided after *Robinson* affirm the legality of searches incident to lawful custodial arrests and clarify the timing of the search relative to the arrest. The legality of searches incident to the issuance of traffic violations was further addressed in subsequent cases, including the case of *Knowles v. Iowa*.

Knowles v. Iowa: The Court Prohibits Searches Incident to Traffic Citations

Knowles was stopped in Newton, Iowa, for driving eighteen miles above the twenty-five-miles-per-hour speed limit. The police officer issued a citation, although under Iowa law he had the option to arrest him. After conducting a full search of the car, the officer found a bag of marijuana and a "pot pipe" that was used as evidence in Knowles's conviction under state law for dealing with controlled substances.

Under Iowa law at that time, peace officers "having cause to believe that a person has violated any traffic or motor vehicle–equipment law" had the option of either arresting the suspect or issuing a citation in lieu of arrest. The law also provides that the issuance of a citation in lieu of an arrest "does not affect the officer's authority to conduct an otherwise lawful search." The Iowa Supreme Court interpreted this provision as giving authority to officers to conduct a full-blown search of an automobile and driver in cases where police officers opt to issue a citation. The Iowa Supreme Court upheld the constitutionality of the search. The United States Supreme Court granted certiorari and reversed the decision of the Iowa Supreme Court.

The issue in this case was whether the search authorized under state law violates the Fourth Amendment. The Court held that a full custodial arrest is required before officers can conduct any incidental search. The search incident to arrest is justified by two historical rationales, officer safety and preservation of evidence. These rationales for the search-incident-to-arrest exception do not exist when officers issue traffic citations. First, the threat to officer safety from issuing a traffic citation is not present in the same manner as when the officer makes a custodial arrest of a suspect. A custodial arrest involves "danger to an officer" because of "the extended exposure which follows the taking of a suspect into custody and transporting him to the police station." The danger to the officer arises from the "fact of the arrest and its attendant proximity, stress, and uncertainty and not from the grounds for arrest." A routine traffic stop, on the other hand, is a relatively brief encounter and "is more analogous to a so-called 'Terry stop' . . . than to a formal arrest." The Court conceded that officer safety may also be a concern in a routine traffic stop. However, the particular circumstances of traffic stops may justify only the "minimal additional intrusion of ordering a driver and passengers out of the car" but does not "by itself" justify a full-blown search.

Second, the need to discover and preserve evidence does not exist when police officers issue traffic citations. When a police officer stops a vehicle and issues a traffic citation, "all the evidence necessary to prosecute that offense had been obtained." Any additional search would not yield "further evidence of excessive speed" or the traffic violation that gave rise to the citation.

CONCLUSIONS

The *Robinson* case clarified certain issues left unresolved in *Chimel*, specifically (1) whether law enforcement had to perceive or subjectively fear that the arrestee was concealing weapons or evidence within the searchable areas and (2) whether a search incident to a lawful arrest was constitutional only where the offense of arrest might possibly yield further evidence in these areas. In *Robinson*, the Court granted law enforcement the absolute right to conduct searches incident to a custodial arrest based on probable cause regardless of the underlying offense. The fact of arrest created the absolute right to search.

Subsequent decisions clarified the custodial-arrest requirement necessary for a valid incidental search. *Knowles v. Iowa* further prohibited searches incidental to the issuance of traffic citations since the twin justifications for a search (officer safety and preservation of evidence) did not exist. *Virginia v. Moore* allowed a police officer to make an arrest for traffic violations although prohibited by state law and to conduct a search incident to the arrest. The fact of arrest and not "the ground for arrest" justifies any subsequent search due to the "proximity, stress, and uncertainty" of the situation.

One consequence of the *Robinson* rule and subsequent decisions is that law-enforcement officers may decide to make arrests even for relatively minor offenses such as traffic violations and petty misdemeanor offenses. Even though only a minor infraction is involved, the officer might resort to the drastic option of arresting the suspect in order to justify the search. The situation in *Virginia v. Moore*, for example, required that police officers only issue a summons to the suspect instead of placing him under arrest. The Court's ruling in that case grants wide discretion to police officers when conducting arrests, even though they may be contrary to state law.

FURTHER READING

Henry J. Abraham, *Justices and Presidents: A Political History of Appointments to the Supreme Court*, third ed. (New York: Oxford University Press, 1992).

Clare Cushman, ed., *The Supreme Court Justices: Illustrated Biographies, 1789–1995*, second ed., Supreme Court Historical Society (Washington, D.C.: Congressional Quarterly Books, 1995).

Rolando V. del Carmen, *Criminal Procedure: Law and Practice* (Belmont, Calif.: Wadsworth/ Cengage Learning, 2010).

K. Deters, "The 'Evaporation Point': *State v. Sykes* and the Erosion of the Fourth Amendment through the Search Incident to Arrest Exception," *Iowa Law Review* 92 (2007): 1901–27.

D. Dripps, "The Fourth Amendment and the Fallacy of Composition: Determinacy versus Legitimacy in a Regime of Bright-Line Rules," *Mississippi Law Journal* 74 (2004): 341–423.

John P. Frank, Leon Friedman, and Fred L. Israel, eds., *The Justices of the United States Supreme Court, 1789–1969: Their Lives and Major Opinions* (New York: Chelsea House Publishers, 1969).

Kermit L. Hall, ed., *The Oxford Companion to the Supreme Court of the United States* (New York: Oxford University Press, 1992).

David L. Hudson, *The Rehnquist Court: Understanding Its Impact and Legacy* (New York: Raeger Publishers, 2006).

W. Logan, "An Exception Swallows a Rule: Police Authority to Search Incident to Arrest," *Yale Law and Policy Review* 19 (2001): 381–443.

Fenton S. Martin and Robert U. Goehlert, *The U.S. Supreme Court: A Bibliography* (Washington, D.C.: Congressional Quarterly Books, 1990).

William H. Rehnquist, *The Supreme Court: A New Edition of the Chief Justice's Classic History* (New York: Knopf Publishing Group, 2001).

J. Samaha, *Criminal Procedure* (Belmont, Calif.: Thomson Wadsworth, 2008).

J. Scheb and J. Scheb II, *Criminal Law and Procedure* (Belmont, Calif.: Thomson Wadsworth, 2008).

Herman Schwartz, *The Rehnquist Court: Judicial Activism on the Right* (New Hork: Hill and Wang, 2003).

Mark Tushnet, *A Court Divided: The Rehnquist Court and the Future of Constitutional Law* (New York: W.W. Norton Co., 2005).

K. Urbonya, "Rhetorically Reasonable Police Practices: Viewing the Supreme Court's Multiple Discourse Paths," *American Criminal Law Review* 40 (2003): 1387–1443.

Melvin I. Urofsky, *The Supreme Court Justices: A Biographical Dictionary* (New York: Garland Publishing, 1994).

H. Walther, "Defining the Scope of the Search Incident to an Arrest Doctrine," *Maryland Law Review* 59 (2000): 1024–53.

Wikipedia.org, "William Rehnquist," http://en.wikipedia.org/wiki/William_Rehnquist.

Robert Woodward and Scott Armstrong, *The Brethren: Inside the Supreme Court* (New York: Avon Books, 1979).

V

SEARCHES OF PLACES AND THINGS

8

Wilson v. Arkansas

CRAIG HEMMENS*

INTRODUCTION

This chapter examines the history of the knock-and-announce rule and the Supreme Court decision in *Wilson v. Arkansas* and subsequent cases, that have dealt with the application of the knock-and-announce rule to police investigatory practices. In *Wilson*, the United States Supreme Court, in a nine-to-zero decision written by Justice Thomas, for the first time squarely held that the common-law knock-and-announce rule is a part of the Fourth Amendment's prohibition on unreasonable searches and seizures. At the same time, the opinion of the Court made it clear that the knock-and-announce requirement was not inflexible and that exigent circumstances might well justify police discountenance of the general rule. The Court left to another day the determination of what constitutes a valid "exigent circumstance."

THE KNOCK-AND-ANNOUNCE RULE

The knock-and-announce rule requires police officers to identify themselves, give notice of their purpose, and request entry before entering a dwelling. The rule has existed since the early common law and is considered part of the reason-

'Portions of this chapter appeared, in modified form, in Craig Hemmens, "The Police, the Fourth Amendment, and Unannounced Entry: *Wilson v. Arkansas,*" *The Criminal Law Bulletin* 33, no. 1 (1997): 29–58; Craig Hemmens, "I Hear You Knocking: The Supreme Court Revisits the Knock-and-Announce Rule," *University of Missouri-Kansas City Law Review* 66, no. 3 (1998): 559–602; and Craig Hemmens and Chris Mathias, "*United States v. Banks*: The Knock-and-Announce Rule Returns to the Supreme Court," *Idaho Law Review* 41, no. 1 (2005): 1–36.

ableness requirement of the Fourth Amendment. The rule is intended to protect people in their home from unexpected and forcible entries and is based in part on the common-law maxim that "a man's home is his castle."

Precisely what constitutes identification and notice of purpose has been the subject of some debate. Generally, what is required is that a police officer (1) identify himself as a police officer, (2) request entry of the premises, (3) inform the occupants that he has the authority to enter (based either on possession of a search or arrest warrant, or the existence of probable cause and an exigent circumstance), and (4) give the occupants an opportunity to admit him before he resorts to forcible entry.[1]

It is sufficient for police to identify themselves by merely stating "Police." The demand to enter can be as simple as "Open the door"; it may also be inferred from statements such as "I have a search warrant." Such statements also carry the implicit notice that the officer has the lawful authority to enter the premises.

Once the notice and announcement are made, the police must give the occupants a reasonable opportunity to admit them before resorting to forcible entry. While refusal to admit the police is required before forcible entry is permitted, such refusal may be inferred from the circumstances, such as no response from the dwelling or the sound of people retreating from the door. The knock-and-announce rule is not intended to prevent police entry but merely to make such entries as peaceful and nondestructive as possible under the circumstances of the case.

Entry without notice is allowed in certain circumstances. These instances, often grouped together under the heading of "exigent circumstances," include danger to the officer seeking to enter the premises, the possibility of the destruction of evidence contained on the premises, and the possibility that the occupants will escape. Announcement is also unnecessary when it would be a "useless gesture," meaning when the presence and purpose of the police is already known to the occupants. For an unannounced entry to withstand judicial scrutiny, the police officer must establish a reasonable belief that an exigent circumstance exists.[2]

Entry by force is permissible after notice and announcement are given and refused or if there is no response from within the dwelling.

KNOCK AND ANNOUNCE AND THE COMMON LAW
The knock-and-announce rule was first discussed in *Semayne's Case* in 1603. While the case dealt with the execution of a civil writ, the court broadly stated,

"In all cases when the king is a party, the sheriff (if the doors be not open) may break the party's house, either to arrest him or to do other execution of the king's process, if otherwise he cannot enter. But before he breaks it, he ought to signify the cause of his coming and to make request to open the doors."

While this is the first reported case involving notice and announcement, the language of the decision indicates that the rule of announcement is actually much older and is based on the Statute of Westminster, adopted in 1275.

While *Semayne's Case* involved a civil writ, later cases dealt with execution of criminal process. In *Curtis's Case*, decided in 1757, the court declared that "peace officers, having a legal warrant to arrest for a breach of the peace, may break open doors, after having demanded admittance and given due notice of their warrant." The court in *Curtis's Case* refused to require a "precise form of words" but held that the homeowner was entitled to notice that the officer was acting under proper authority and not as a trespasser.

Early American colonial case law followed the English tradition. Writs of assistance were commonly used (and abused) by the crown's officials searching for prohibited goods. Yet even these writs, with their broad language and scope, could be executed only after notice was given to the suspect.[3] After the American Revolution, at least ten of the original thirteen states codified the common-law rule by enacting statutes requiring notice and announcement prior to the execution of warrants. Such was the state of the common law when the Bill of Rights, including the Fourth Amendment, was drafted by Congress and adopted by the states in 1791.

While studies of the debates surrounding passage of the Bill of Rights indicate the manner of warrant execution was not discussed, and the Fourth Amendment does not mention manner of execution, it certainly seems reasonable to conclude that the standard for execution of a warrant under the federal constitution would not be any less than that which was required under the despised writs of assistance.

KNOCK AND ANNOUNCE, 1791–1958

State common law developed at a rapid rate after the passage of the Bill of Rights. Exceptions to the notice-and-announcement requirement were developed by a number of state courts during the late nineteenth and the twentieth centuries. These exceptions included danger to the police or persons within the home, potential destruction of evidence, and possible escape by the suspect, as well as occasions where notice and announcement would be a "useless gesture" because the occupant of the house is either not present or is clearly aware of the presence and purpose of the officers. These exceptions already existed in English common law; American courts merely endorsed extant exceptions to the knock-and-announce rule.[4]

During the twentieth century a number of states enacted statutes dealing with the manner of warrant service. A majority of the states passed knock-and-announce statutes that generally required notice and announcement but also codified common-law exceptions to the general rule. Prior to the decision in *Wilson*, at least forty states had either case law or a statute requiring police to knock and announce.[5]

Several states also enacted legislation authorizing the issuance of *no-knock warrants*. No-knock warrants are warrants issued by a magistrate, based on probable cause, that permit police to ignore the knock-and-announce requirement. Generally, such warrants issue only when the police can demonstrate to the magistrate that there is some exigent circumstance that justifies ignoring the knock-and-announce rule. The idea behind such warrants is that they will eliminate the problem of police officers deciding on the spot whether it is appropriate to ignore the knock-and-announce rule—here they have sought and obtained the prior approval of a neutral and detached magistrate. Critics of no-knock warrants point to the difficulty in establishing, prior to execution of a search, the need to ignore the knock-and-announce rule. Officers may not discover the circumstances, such as a fleeing suspect, which justify ignoring the knock-and-announce rule until they are in the process of executing a warrant.

KNOCK AND ANNOUNCE IN THE UNITED STATES SUPREME COURT, 1958–1995

There have been only a handful of United States Supreme Court cases dealing with the knock-and-announce rule. All of these cases have been decided within the past fifty years—three between 1958 and 1968, and five between 1995 and 2010.

Miller v. United States (1958)

In *Miller v. United States*, 357 U.S. 301 (1958), the Court held that 18 U.S.C. 3109, the federal knock-and-announce statute, codified the common-law requirement of notice and announcement. The Supreme Court, in an opinion by Justice Brennan, held that the entry and arrest in this case were illegal because the police had failed to first announce the purpose of their visit to Mr. Miller's apartment. In his opinion Justice Brennan discussed the common-law authorities and concluded that common law required an announcement of both lawful authority and purpose before the police could break into and enter a home. He also noted that a number of states had enacted knock-and-announce statutes, which adopted the common-law rule. In addition, Brennan noted that there were some exceptions to the knock-and-announce rule, both at common law and in modern court decisions. These exceptions were not at issue before the Court in this case, however, as the police did not claim that any "exigent circumstances" existed that would have justified their failure to "knock and announce." Ultimately, the decision in *Miller* was based not on Fourth Amendment principles or 18 U.S.C. 3109 but on District of Columbia law. The Court declined to expressly incorporate the knock-and-announce rule into the Fourth Amendment, preferring to decide the case on a nonconstitutional ground.

Wong Sun v. United States (1963)

In *Wong Sun v. United States*, 371 U.S. 471 (1963), the Supreme Court ruled that evidence seized by federal law-enforcement officers who broke into a home without first identifying themselves and announcing their purpose should be suppressed because there were no facts to make the officers "virtually certain" that the suspect was aware of their purpose, thereby making notice and announcement a "useless gesture." The opinion, again authored by Justice Brennan, did suggest that there might be some common-law exceptions to the knock-and-announce rule. Among these exceptions were the "imminent destruction of vital evidence or the need to rescue a victim in peril." Lower courts, both state and federal, had already recognized such exceptions to the rule, and Brennan's opinion seemed designed to invite appeals based on these grounds.

Ker v. California (1963)

The Supreme Court did not have to wait long to decide the issue left open in *Wong Sun*. The following year, in *Ker v. California*, 374 U.S. 23 (1963), the Supreme Court did not expressly hold that the common knock-and-announce rule was included in the Fourth Amendment but did hold that a failure to knock and announce was acceptable only in certain circumstances and that these circumstances should be judged based on the Reasonableness Clause of the Fourth Amendment. Unfortunately for lower courts looking for guidance, however, the Court's decision was badly splintered. While eight justices agreed that under certain circumstances failure to knock and announce was justified, the justices split four-to-four on whether the particular circumstances of this case justified ignoring the knock-and-announce rule. Justice Harlan concurred only in the result of Justice Clark's plurality opinion, basing his decision on the Fourteenth Amendment and "fundamental fairness" rather than the Fourth Amendment and the Reasonableness Clause. With Harlan's vote and the four votes in the *Clark* opinion, Ker's conviction was upheld, but lower courts searching for guidance were left to choose from Clark's opinion or Brennan's opinion, both of which commanded four votes.

Los Angeles police officers went to Ker's apartment to arrest him. They entered the apartment without announcement, seized Ker, and searched his apartment, finding narcotics, which were used in evidence at Ker's trial. The police defended their failure to knock and announce prior to entry on the grounds that they believed Ker would attempt to destroy evidence if he were made aware that the police were trying to enter the apartment.

Justice Brennan's opinion held that the police in this case were not justified in ignoring the knock-and-announce rule. He argued that unannounced entry into a home violated the Fourth Amendment, except in three limited situations: "(1) the persons within already know of the officers' authority and purpose, or (2) where the officers are justified in the belief that persons within are in imminent peril of bodily harm, or (3) where those within, made aware of the presence of someone outside (because, for example, there has been a knock on the door), are then engaged in activity which justifies the officers in the belief that an escape or the destruction of evidence is being attempted."

According to Brennan, absent one of these three situations, unannounced entry, with warrant or without, violated the Fourth Amendment. All three of the exceptions he mentioned were commonly used in lower-court decisions prior to *Ker*. Justice Brennan based his argument that the knock-and-announce rule is part of the Reasonableness Clause of the Fourth Amendment on his analysis of the common law at the time of the framing of the Bill of Rights. He concluded that the knock-and-announce rule was firmly established by 1791. The exceptions to the rule, he concluded, were created after passage of the Bill of Rights. Any such exceptions should consequently be narrowly tailored.

Justice Clark's plurality opinion held that the police in this case were justified in ignoring the rule that police must knock and announce before lawfully entering a home. Police could evade this rule whenever "exigent circumstances" mandated it. Clark did not specify what sort of activity would constitute exigent circumstances per se, focusing instead on the specific facts in *Ker*. Confusion was created, however, by his apparent endorsement of the police officer's knowledge of narcotics possession as a justification for ignoring the knock-and-announce rule. Prior to this, the exceptions to the knock-and-announce rule, at common law and modern cases, were generally limited to situations where there was danger to the officers or someone inside the home, the possibility of the suspect escaping, or the possibility that evidence would be destroyed.

Did Clark's opinion mean that any time a suspect was in possession of easily destructible evidence (such as narcotics) that the knock-and-announce rule did not apply? Prior cases suggested there must be some indication that suspects would destroy evidence, regardless of its form, if police gave notice prior to entry. Clark's language suggested that the very nature of some contraband (such as narcotics) might create an exigency, absent any indication that the suspects were prepared to destroy it. Considerable confusion in state and federal courts following this decision suggests lower courts were unsure how far the destruction-of-evidence exception should be extended. According to one commentator, the only conclusion that can be drawn from the decision in *Ker* is that there are exceptions to the knock-and-announce rule, but what these exceptions were, and in what circumstances they applied, was undetermined.[6]

Sabbath v. United States (1968)

In *Sabbath v. United States*, 391 U.S. 585 (1968), the Supreme Court held that federal law-enforcement officers who fail to knock and announce must have a "substantial basis" for their belief that following the knock-and-announce rule will in some way imperil them. In this case federal customs officers apprehended a Mr. Jones attempting to smuggle cocaine into the country. The customs officers persuaded Jones to deliver the cocaine to its intended recipient, petitioner Sabbath. While the officers watched, Jones went to Sabbath's apartment with the drugs and was admitted. Shortly thereafter, the officers knocked on the door and, getting no response, opened the unlocked door and entered without announcement. They arrested Sabbath and searched his apartment, seizing evidence that was used to convict him at trial.

On appeal, Sabbath asserted that the customs officers had violated 18 U.S.C. 3109 by "breaking and entering" into his apartment without notice. The court of appeals disagreed, saying that the officers did not violate the requirements of Section 3109 because they merely opened an unlocked door—they did not "break and enter." The Supreme Court disagreed and held that opening the unlocked door constituted "breaking and entering" in violation of Section 3109.

The decision in this case turned on an interpretation of 18 U.S.C. 3109 rather than the Fourth Amendment, however, so it was not clear that state law-enforcement officers were required to meet the "substantial basis" standard. The Court did make it clear, however, that, as Section 3109 codified the common-law knock-and-announce rule, it was subject to those exceptions to the principle that were recognized at common law.

THE CASE OF *WILSON V. ARKANSAS* (1995)

The Facts

According to *Wilson v. Arkansas* (514 U.S. 927 [1995]), on December 31, 1992, four police officers went to Sharlene Wilson's home to serve a search warrant for narcotics. When the officers arrived, they found the front door of Wilson's house open. They looked inside and saw a man sitting on the living room sofa. Without first knocking on the door or announcing their presence and purpose, they opened an unlocked screen door and entered the house, announcing themselves only after they had crossed the threshold. As they entered, they identified themselves as police officers and stated that they had a search warrant. The officers then conducted a search, finding marijuana and other illegal drugs in Wilson's home. Based in part on the evidence seized during this search, Wilson was arrested and charged with several drug crimes. At a pretrial suppression hearing, Wilson sought to have the evidence that had been seized by the police during the search of her house excluded from trial, on the grounds that the police had failed to "knock and announce." The trial court refused to exclude the evidence, and Wilson was eventually convicted of drug possession and sentenced to thirty-two years in prison.

On appeal, the Arkansas Supreme Court affirmed Wilson's conviction, holding that the rule that police knock and announce is not part of the Fourth Amendment. This decision was unsupported by citation to precedent. The Arkansas Supreme Court did not discuss whether the unannounced entry by the police was reasonable or justified by any exceptions to the knock-and-announce rule. Rather, the court baldly asserted that the Fourth Amendment was entirely inapplicable to the facts of this case.

The United States Supreme Court, in a unanimous opinion written by Justice Thomas (514 U.S. 927 [1995]), held (1) that the Fourth Amendment requirement that searches be reasonable includes as a factor whether the police gave notice and announcement prior to entry and (2) that there are exceptions to the general rule that police should "knock and announce."

To determine whether the knock-and-announce rule is part of the Fourth Amendment, Justice Thomas looked to "the traditional protections against unreasonable searches and seizures afforded by the common law at the time of the framing." After examining the common law at the time of the framing of the Bill of Rights, Thomas concluded there is "no doubt that the reasonableness of a search and seizure may depend in part on whether the law-enforcement officers announced their presence and authority prior to entering." For the first time the Court clearly held that the knock-and-announce rule was an element of the reasonableness inquiry under the Fourth Amendment.

Justice Thomas did not stop there, however. He went on to say that just as the knock-and-announce rule was subsumed in the Reasonableness Clause of the Fourth Amendment, so too were possible exceptions to the general rule of notice and announcement. Said the justice, "the Fourth Amendment's flexible requirement of reasonableness should not be read to mandate a rigid rule of announcement that ignores countervailing law-enforcement interests."

Rather than choosing to delineate exactly what circumstances might make an unannounced entry reasonable, Justice Thomas decided to "leave to the lower courts the task of determining the circumstances under which an unannounced entry is reasonable under the Fourth Amendment." Thomas did indicate, however, that some of the more common exceptions to the knock-and-announce rule already existing in case law might well withstand constitutional scrutiny. Among these were the traditional exceptions of danger to the police and the hot pursuit. The decision in *Wilson* made explicit what many courts already assumed—that the knock-and-announce rule is a constitutional requirement, not just a common statutory provision or common-law principle, and that there are some exceptions to the general rule.

POST-*WILSON* CASES
Since *Wilson*, the Supreme Court has revisited the knock-and-announce rule five times in little more than a decade—a rather shocking trend, given the paucity of attention paid to the rule prior to 1995. This sudden interest is perhaps a result of increased police use of entry without notice and attempts to avoid the knock-and-announce rule. Between 1995 and 2005 the Supreme Court attempted to provide some guidance to police and lower courts on the applicability of the knock-and-announce rule.

Richards v. Wisconsin (1997)

Writing for a unanimous court, Justice Stevens held in *Richards v. Wisconsin* (520 U.S. 385 [1997]) that the Fourth Amendment does not permit a blanket exception to the knock-and-announce requirement for felony drug investigations. The Wisconsin State Supreme Court had held, per Justice Clark's opinion in *Ker v. California*, that there was a blanket exception to the knock-and-announce rule for drug cases. The Wisconsin court justified doing away with judicial scrutiny of police executing felony-drug-possession search warrants based on the special circumstances of today's drug culture.

Stevens took issue with the creation of an exception to the general rule of knock and announcement based on the culture surrounding a general category of criminal behavior. First, the blanket exception contains considerable overgeneralization. Stevens acknowledged that "while drug investigation does pose special risks to officer safety and the preservation of evidence, not every drug investigation will pose these risks to a substantial degree." Second, creation of an exception for one category of criminal behaviors leads all too easily to the creation of exceptions for other categories. Basing a per se exception to the knock-and-announce rule on the hypothetical risk of danger to officers or evidence would render the Fourth Amendment's reasonableness requirement meaningless, as it would remove law-enforcement conduct from judicial scrutiny.

While the Court's opinion found disfavor with the Wisconsin court's blanket rule, it stopped short of requiring knock and announcement in all instances. Instead, the Court held that a no-knock entry was justified when the police "have a reasonable suspicion that knocking and announcing their presence, under the particular circumstances, would be dangerous or futile or that it would inhibit the effective investigation of crime." Requiring the police to demonstrate a reasonable suspicion, the Court felt, struck "the appropriate balance between the legitimate law-enforcement concerns at issue in the execution of search warrants and the individual privacy interests affected by no-knock entries." While this stopped far short of Wisconsin's blanket approach, the reasonable suspicion showing is, by the Court's own admission, not a difficult standard for the police to meet.

United States v. Ramirez (1998)

In *United States v. Ramirez* (523 U.S. 65 [1998]) the Ninth Circuit Court of Appeals held that when a law-enforcement officer executes a no-knock warrant by entering a dwelling without knocking and announcing, "more specific inferences of exigency are necessary" to justify the entry if property will be destroyed than if property will not be destroyed. The Supreme Court, in an opinion by Justice Rehnquist, unanimously rejected the Ninth Circuit's attempt to hold law-enforcement officers to a higher standard of reasonableness when property damage occurs during the execution of a search warrant. The Court, in rejecting the Ninth Circuit's approach, explained that the reasonableness standard is the same regardless how the entry is made. The key is whether a forcible entry is justified, not how a forcible entry happens. Once officers have determined that a forcible entry is justified, that ends the reasonableness inquiry. The Supreme Court acknowledged that while the manner of execution is a factor in determining the validity of a search warrant, here there was only minor damage. The Court noted, however, that unnecessary, excessive property damage could make an otherwise lawful entry unlawful.

United States v. Banks (2003)

After the decision in *Wilson,* lower courts continued to struggle with determining what amount of time constitutes a reasonable waiting period when officers knock and announce and do not receive a response. A number of state courts and lower federal courts upheld forcible entries when officers waited approximately twenty to thirty seconds.

As indicated in *United States v. Banks* (540 U.S. 31 [2003]), in July 1998, a joint federal and state drug task force received information from a confidential informant that a person identified as "Shakes" was selling cocaine from an apartment in Las Vegas. Officers of the Las Vegas Police Department corroborated the accuracy of this tip and were then able to obtain a search warrant for drugs and drug paraphernalia from a Nevada justice of the peace. Las Vegas police and FBI officers executed the search warrant one week later at the apartment, which was rented by LaShawn Banks.

The Ninth Circuit panel next asserted that because the officers in *Banks* had not been explicitly denied entrance, they were required to delay their forceful entrance for a "sufficient period of time." The court failed to provide explicit directions as to what would constitute a "sufficient" period of time, however, preferring to resolve that issue on a case-by-case basis. The Ninth Circuit decision was in conflict with the decision in several other circuits, all of whom had held that a waiting period of approximately twenty seconds was sufficient.

Writing for a unanimous court, Justice Souter held that the law-enforcement officers' twenty-second wait prior to their forcible entry was reasonable under the totality of the circumstances. The majority opinion held that the totality of the circumstances can, and must, be assessed to determine whether "the significance of exigency revealed by circumstances" warrants, at that time from the perspective of the officers on scene, "not with the 20/20 vision of hindsight," a requirement or dispensing of the knock and announcement. The Court determined that the police were justified in not waiting any longer or not waiting for an explicit refusal before breaking down the door to Banks's apartment. This is because the police had a search warrant for drugs, which are easily and quickly disposed of. The exigent circumstance of the possible destruction of evidence justified not waiting any longer. The case might well be different if the items in the search warrant were different: "Police seeking a stolen piano may be able to spend more time to make sure they really need the battering ram."

Hudson v. Michigan (2006)

After *Banks*, it was clear that the Supreme Court saw the knock-and-announce rule as of only tangential importance in determining whether police acted reasonably when entering a dwelling, either to make an arrest or conduct a search. In 2006, in *Hudson v. Michigan* (547 U.S. 586 [2006]), the Court went even further and held that evidence seized in violation of the knock-and-announce rule could still be admitted at a criminal trial. Until this time, it was assumed that if a knock-and-announce violation occurred the appropriate remedy was the exclusion of the evidence seized as a direct result of that violation. The debate had been not over the remedy but over *when* the knock-and-announce rule applied. In *Hudson* Justice Scalia, writing for a narrow five-to-four majority, declared that the exclusionary rule was not the appropriate remedy.

In this case Detroit police officers with a search warrant for drugs and weapons had entered Booker T. Hudson's home after shouting "Police, search warrant," but waiting at most only five seconds—hardly time enough for Hudson to open his door. The police stormed in and found Hudson sitting on a chair. A subsequent search turned up a significant amount of cocaine and a weapon. Hudson argued that the police had violated the Fourth Amendment by failing to wait an appropriate amount of time before entering. While the Supreme Court in *Banks* had held that twenty seconds was sufficient, the Court had noted that it was a close case. The trial court, assuming five seconds was not long enough to satisfy the requirements of *Banks*, held that the fast entry violated the Fourth Amendment and suppressed the evidence seized. On appeal, the state court of appeals reversed, holding that suppression was not appropriate. Hudson was convicted, and he appealed to the United States Supreme Court.

The case was originally argued before the Supreme Court with Justice O'Connor sitting, but when she retired and was replace by Justice Alito the Court heard re-argument. With Justice Alito sitting, the Court voted five to four that the exclusionary rule should not apply to violations of the knock-and-announce rule. Justice Scalia's majority opinion argued that the interests protected by the knock-and-announce rule (protecting privacy and people from harm during surprise entries) were adequately protected by police professionalism and training and that civil remedies for damages would serve as at least as effective a deterrent as exclusion of the evidence, without the costs to society associated with exclusion.

The dissenting opinion, by Justice Breyer, argued that the deterrent effect of the exclusionary rule made it the most appropriate remedy for violations of the knock-and-announce rule.

CONCLUSIONS

From its early adoption at common law, the knock-and-announce rule has played a not insignificant role in balancing citizens' rights to be left alone and the government's right to engage in and effect law enforcement. The war on drugs has brought the police into many homes. This has led to a reappraisal and reexamination of the knock-and-announce rule, once a long-ignored bit of criminal-procedure esoterica.

After years of being ignored by the United States Supreme Court, the knock-and-announce rule has been the subject of intense scrutiny over the past decade. The high court has rendered five decisions regarding the knock-and-announce rule since *Wilson v. Arkansas* was decided in 1995. In these decisions the Court has moved haltingly, taking its familiar case-by-case approach to criminal-procedure issues.

The Court first declared the knock-and-announce rule and its common-law exceptions part and parcel of the Fourth Amendment. The Court then refused to create a blanket exception to the rule but has made it clear that the rule is relatively easy on law enforcement. Most recently, the Supreme Court has essentially gutted the rule by separating it from the most common remedy for violations of the Fourth Amendment, the exclusionary rule. With the recent decision in *Hudson v. Michigan*, the Supreme Court signaled that while it still pays lip service to the principle that a person's home is their castle, and that violations of the sanctity of the home are to be treated as serious infringements of individual liberty, the reality is that police who ignore the knock-and-announce rule will still be able to use the evidence they seize in a subsequent criminal trial. What survives of the knock-and-announce rule remains to be seen.

FURTHER READING

G. Robert Blakey, "The Rule of Announcement and Unlawful Entry: *Miller v. United States* and *Ker v. California*," *University of Pennsylvania Law Review* 112 (1962): 499–555.

Craig Hemmens, "The Police, the Fourth Amendment, and Unannounced Entry: *Wilson v. Arkansas*," *The Criminal Law Bulletin* 33 (1997): 29–58.

Craig Hemmens, "I Hear You Knocking: The Supreme Court Revisits the Knock-and-Announce Rule," *University of Missouri-Kansas City Law Review* 66 (1998): 559–602.

Craig Hemmens and Chris Mathias, "*United States v. Banks*: The Knock-and-Announce Rule Returns to the Supreme Court," *Idaho Law Review* 41 (2005): 1–36.

Wayne LaFave, Jerold Israel, Nancy J. King, and Orin S. Kerr, *Hornbook on Criminal Procedure* (Minneapolis: West Publishing, 2009).

Nelson B. Lasson, *The History and Development of the Fourth Amendment to the Constitution of the United States* (New York: Da Capo Press, 1937/1970 reprint).

Payton v. New York

Claire Nolasco

INTRODUCTION

In an earlier case, *United States v. Watson* (423 U.S. 411 [1976]), the Court held that a police officer may make a warrantless arrest of a suspect in a public place if he or she has probable cause to do so. The Court left open the issue whether a warrantless arrest in the suspect's house was valid under the Fourth Amendment. There was no consensus among both common-law scholars and states as to the validity of warrantless home arrests when there is probable cause but "exigent circumstances" are not present. Some scholars opined that these types of arrests were illegal, while others declared them valid. State law also varied, some authorizing such warrantless arrests, others prohibiting them.

The issue was directly addressed four years later in *Payton v. New York* (445 U.S. 573 [1980]), in which the Court held that a warrantless arrest of the suspect in the latter's home absent "exigent circumstances" violated the Fourth Amendment of the Constitution, even if the police officer had probable cause to make the arrest. In establishing this rule, the Court examined common law, state practice, federal rules, and the history and intent of the Fourth Amendment.

THE CASE OF *PAYTON V. NEW YORK* (1980)

The Facts

Payton and its companion case, *New York v. Riddick* (445 U.S. 573 [1980]), challenged the constitutionality of New York statutes authorizing police officers to enter a private dwelling without warrant in order to make a routine felony arrest.

In *Payton v. New York* (445 U.S. 573 [1980]), police officers arrived at Payton's house to make a warrantless arrest for his involvement in the murder of the manager of a gas station. They knocked on the door after noticing that light and music were coming from the apartment. When Payton did not respond, they called for emergency assistance and opened the door with crowbars. They entered the apartment, but Payton was not there. They seized a .30-caliber shell casing that was in plain view and used this as evidence at Payton's murder trial. The trial court admitted the evidence and convicted him for murder.

In *Riddick*, the companion case to *Payton*, police officers arrested Riddick without warrant for two armed robberies that had occurred three years earlier. The officers arrived at Riddick's house where Riddick's young son opened the door. Riddick was in bed, covered by a sheet. Before allowing Riddick to change, the officers searched a chest of drawers two feet from the bed and found narcotics and drug paraphernalia. The evidence was admitted in Riddick's trial for narcotics charges. The trial court held that the warrantless arrest was authorized by the New York statute and that the incidental search was admissible under *Chimel v. California*, 395 U.S. 752 (1969).

The New York Court of Appeals affirmed both convictions. The majority opinion stated that the issue had not been previously settled by either that court or the Supreme Court and that both in common law and state practice there was "apparent historical acceptance of warrantless entries to make felony arrests."

The Issue before the Court

Can police officers make a warrantless entry into a suspect's dwelling to conduct a routine felony arrest despite the absence of exigent circumstances?

The Court's Holding

Voting six to three, the Court held that the Fourth Amendment "prohibits police officers from making warrantless and nonconsensual entries" in a suspect's house to make a "routine felony arrest" in the absence of exigent circumstances. The New York statutes authorizing these types of arrests were declared unconstitutional.

The Majority Opinion

Justice Stevens, writing the majority opinion for the Court, distinguished the case from the circumstances in *United States v. Watson* (423 U.S. 411 [1976]), where the validity of a warrantless arrest in a public place was upheld based on

(1) "the well-settled common-law rule" that allowed police officers to make such arrests when they had "probable cause to believe the suspect is a felon," (2) the clear consensus among states "adhering to that well-settled common-law rule," and, (3) congressional determination of the reasonableness of such arrests.

The Court considered each of the three reasons enumerated in *Watson*.

First, they noted that there was "lack of judicial decisions and a deep divergence among scholars" on the issue of whether a "constable had the authority to make warrantless arrests in the home on mere suspicion of a felony." The most cited evidence of this common-law rule is mere dicta in the *Semayne's Case* (5 Co. Rep. 91a, 81b, 77 Eng. Rep. 194 [1603]), where the Court stated that in all cases where "the king is party, the sheriff (if the doors be not open) may break the party's house, either to arrest him or to do other execution of the king's process, if otherwise he cannot enter." Although other scholars have interpreted this as a grant of authority to enter without warrant, the Court said that the passage was "describing the extent of authority in executing the king's writ."

Thus, entry in the house was allowed only either to "arrest him or to do *other* execution of the king's process." They also noted that common-law scholars disagreed on the subject. One group of scholars, including Lord Cook, viewed a warrantless entry into the house to make an arrest as illegal. Another group believed that a warrantless entry into the house to arrest the suspect is illegal, but the officer may be immune from liability if the suspect was actually guilty. The Court believed, though, that "the weight of authority as it appeared to the framers was to the effect that a warrant was required."

Second, although a majority of the states allow warrantless entries into the home to arrest even in the absence of "exigent circumstances," there is a "significant decline" in such numbers. State practice, however, will not bind the Court, since a "longstanding, widespread practice is not immune from constitutional scrutiny." The Court also noted that this state practice is not "virtually unanimous," since "only twenty-four of the fifty states currently sanction warrantless entries into the home to arrest" and that such practice is an "obvious[ly] declining trend."

Third, there has been no congressional determination and no federal statute that considers such warrantless home entries as "reasonable."

The Dissenting Opinion

Justice White, with whom the chief justice and Justice Rehnquist concurred, dissented from the majority opinion. They stated that the majority ruling is not supported by common law or by the text or history of the Fourth Amendment. White proposed an alternative rule: after "knocking and announcing" their purpose, police officers may enter the suspect's house to make a daytime warrantless arrest if they have "probable cause to believe" that the person arrested has committed a felony and is physically present inside. White argues that this rule is supported by common law, state practice, and the history and policies of the Fourth Amendment.

The dissent explained that under common law the constable had the inherent and original power to make warrantless arrests of felons and those who were "probably suspected of felonies." The constable was also a subordinate public official who "performed ministerial tasks" under a superior's authority and direction. As a subordinate official, the constable was required to execute warrants on behalf of justices of the peace. The warrant protected the constable from liability for any damages arising in the performance of his duty under the terms of the warrant. The dissent argued that a majority of the common-law scholars would "probably" allow warrantless arrests on probable suspicion "even if the person arrested were not in fact guilty."

The dissent clarified that the warrant requirement under the Fourth Amendment was "not intended to derogate from the constable's inherent common-law authority." Instead, the Fourth Amendment assumes an "existing right" of the peace officer to make warrantless arrests and searches. The "background, text, and legislative history of the Fourth Amendment demonstrate that the purpose was to restrict the abuses that had developed with respect to warrants" but preserves the "common-law rules of arrest."

The dissent also pointed out the consensus of a majority of the states allowing the practice of "warrantless entry into the home to arrest even in the absence of exigent circumstances." They argued that such consensus is "entitled more deference than the Court today provides." They further argued that federal statutes recognize the authority of federal agents to break doors to make warrantless arrests in any place, including the suspect's dwelling.

Finally, the dissent enumerated the following safeguards under common law of the rule allowing police officers to make warrantless arrests in the absence of exigent circumstances: (1) the arrestee must be suspected of committing a felony, (2) the officer must knock on the door of the suspect's house and announce his or her presence, (3) the warrant must be executed in daytime, and (4) there must be probable cause to arrest. The dissent argues that all of these safeguards were present in *Payton* and *Riddick*.

Case Significance

Payton ruled that police officers may not, without warrant, arrest a suspect in his or her dwelling in the absence of exigent circumstances. The rule is clearly limited to warrantless arrests made in the private dwelling of the suspect and does not cover warrantless arrests in a public place. The Court, however, did not enumerate or provide guidelines as to what constituted "exigent circumstances" but left this open to interpretation by lower federal and state courts. The Court also did not require the additional safeguards provided under common law—namely, that the officers should knock and announce their purpose, the suspect must be suspected of a felony, the warrant must be executed at daytime, and there must be probable cause for the arrest.

Due to the lack of clarification on what constitutes "exigent circumstances," this phrase is susceptible to various interpretations by lower courts. It is also unclear to law-enforcement officers what "exigent circumstances" would allow them to make warrantless arrests in the suspect's home. The dissent argues that the majority rule would "impose burdens on the judicial system" due to the "endless litigation with respect to the existence of exigent circumstances, whether it was practicable to get a warrant, whether the suspect was about to flee, and the like."

To some extent, the Court clarified what constitutes "exigent circumstances" in subsequent cases. These decisions hold that police officers may make warrantless house arrests when they are engaged in hot pursuit of the suspect, to prevent destruction of evidence, and to prevent serious threat of bodily injury.[1] These cases suggest that police officers must be confronted with a dire emergency or a sense of urgency when making the warrantless arrest, therefore preventing adequate time to apply for a warrant.

Further Analysis

The Court emphasized that the Fourth Amendment "applies equally to seizures of persons and to seizures of property," rejecting the trial court's assertion that a house entry for the purpose of making an arrest is less intrusive than an entry to search. The Court further stated that a house arrest violates the suspect's expectations of privacy, observing that "the zone of privacy [is never] more clearly defined than when bounded by the unambiguous physical dimensions of an individual's home." The Fourth Amendment seeks to protect the right of a person to "retreat into his own home and there be free from unreasonable government intrusion, and this is true as against seizures of property and seizures of person."

The dissent argued that the rule established by the majority would "severely hamper effective law enforcement." Since the phrase "exigent circumstances" was not clearly defined in the majority opinion, police officers can make mistakes when trying to decide whether to arrest a suspect in his house without a valid warrant. The dissent's fears are partly allayed, however, by subsequent decisions interpreting the term. Although the Court failed to provide guidelines in *Payton* as to what constitutes "exigent circumstances," subsequent decisions as noted above have allowed warrantless house arrests in situations involving the hot pursuit of a fleeing felon or the threat of evidence destruction or to prevent serious threat or bodily injury to occupants in the private dwelling. While law-enforcement officers must show that exigent circumstances existed to justify the warrantless house arrest, they are usually given wide latitude when responding to "swiftly developing situations" (*United States v. Sharpe*, 470 U.S. 675 [1985]).

SIGNIFICANT CASES SINCE *PAYTON*

Subsequent cases have further addressed the issue of these types of arrests. The most significant rulings are detailed in the following.

Rulings That Affirm *Payton* (Chronologically)

Warrantless arrest of a suspect in a public place is valid as long as probable cause exists: A police officer may arrest a suspect in a public place without a warrant when the officer has reasonable grounds to believe that the suspect is guilty of a felony (*United States v. Watson*, 423 U.S. 411 [1976]). In *Watson*, a postal inspector received information from a credible informant that Watson had stolen several credit cards. The postal officers made a warrantless arrest of Watson after arranging a meeting in a restaurant. The officers then conducted a consensual search of Watson's nearby car and found two additional stolen credit cards. The evidence was used as evidence in Watson's trial, which resulted in his conviction for possession of stolen mail. The court of appeals reversed.

On appeal, the Supreme Court declared the warrantless arrest of the suspect valid. According to the Court, the Fourth Amendment reflected the "ancient common-law rule" allowing police officers to arrest without a warrant for "a misdemeanor or felony committed in his presence as well as for a felony not committed in his presence if there was reasonable ground for making the arrest."

A warrantless arrest that starts in a public place but ends in the house of the individual who tried to flee is valid: Police officers could validly arrest without warrant a suspected armed felon who they pursued into his house only minutes before they arrived (*Warden, Md. Penitentiary v. Hayden*, 387 U.S. 294 [1967]). In *Warden*, the police were informed that an armed robbery had occurred and that the suspect had thereafter entered a certain house. Minutes after they arrived, they searched the house with the consent of the suspect's wife. The officers arrested the suspect in an upstairs bedroom. They then searched the house and found weapons, ammunition, and clothing linking the suspect to the crime. The evidence was admitted in the respondent's trial resulting in his conviction. The district court denied habeas corpus. The court of appeals found the search lawful but reversed.

The Court held that the warrantless arrest was valid due to the "exigencies of the situation." Since they were "in pursuit" of a "suspected armed felon" in the house where the felon entered, they could validly make a warrantless entry and search of the premises.

A warrantless arrest in a house while the police officer is engaged in hot pursuit is valid: A warrantless arrest of a suspect who retreated to her house after police officers pursued her from the doorway was valid (*United States v. Santana*, 427 U.S. 38 [1976]). In *Santana*, police officers planned a buy-bust operation wherein a drug dealer purchased heroin from Santana with marked money from the police. The officers then went to Santana's house to arrest her for involvement in narcotics. Santana was standing in the doorway, but when the officers approached she retreated into her house, where they caught her. Police officers found in a paper bag envelopes containing heroin as well as the marked money used in the undercover operation. The district court suppressed the evidence and ruled that the arrest was illegal. The court of appeals affirmed.

The Supreme Court declared the warrantless arrest valid. According to the Court, the doorway of a house is "public place" for purposes of the Fourth Amendment. The defendant did not have any expectation of privacy while standing in the doorway since she was "not merely visible to the public but was exposed to public view, speech, hearing, and touch as if she had been standing completely outside her house." The warrantless arrest of the defendant based on probable cause in a public place did not violate the Fourth Amendment. The Court also stated that defendant could "not defeat an otherwise proper arrest that had been set in motion in a public place" by retreating into her house. Since police officers needed to "act quickly to prevent destruction of evidence," there was a "true hot pursuit," which does not need to be "an extended hue and cry in and about [the] public streets."

A confession obtained from a suspect outside the house where he was arrested without warrant is admissible as evidence against him: Although police officers make an invalid warrantless arrest of a suspect in his house, a confession obtained outside the house is not barred by the exclusionary rule (*New York v. Harris,* 495 U.S. 14 [1990]). In *Harris,* police officers, "having probable cause to believe that Harris committed murder," entered his house without a warrant and obtained a confession. Harris was then brought to the police station where he signed a written inculpatory statement. The state trial court suppressed the first statement under *Payton v. New York,* which held that "the Fourth Amendment prohibits the police from effecting a warrantless and nonconsensual entry into a suspect's home in order to make a routine felony arrest." The trial court, however, admitted the second statement and convicted Harris of second-degree murder. The Appellate Division affirmed, but the State Court of Appeals reversed.

The Supreme Court held that "the rule in *Payton* was designed to protect the physical integrity of the home, not to grant criminal suspects protection for statements made outside their premises where the police have probable cause to make an arrest." The police officers were justified in questioning Harris prior to his arrest. His subsequent statement at the precinct was "not an exploitation of the illegal entry into his home." The Court also stated that "suppressing that statement would not serve the purpose of the *Payton* rule," since the first confession obtained from Harris's in-home arrest was already excluded.

Rulings That Modify *Payton* (Chronologically)

The offense must be sufficiently serious in nature to justify a warrantless arrest in a house even if probable cause exists: A civil, nonjailable traffic offense is not sufficiently serious enough to constitute "exigent circumstances." Even if police officers have probable cause to arrest the suspect, they cannot validly enter his house without a warrant (*Welsh v. Wisconsin,* 466 U.S. 740 [1984]). In *Welsh,* a witness saw a car swerve off the road and stop in a field without causing damage to anyone. The driver did not wait for assistance in moving his car and instead walked away from the scene. The police proceeded to the petitioner's house, entered, and found the petitioner lying in bed. The officers then arrested him for driving a motor vehicle while under the influence of alcohol, a noncriminal offense under state law. The trial court held that the warrantless arrest was lawful. The state court of appeals vacated the order, holding that the warrantless arrest violated the Fourth Amendment because although there was probable cause to arrest, there was no "exigent circumstance" to justify it. The state supreme court reversed.

The Supreme Court held that the warrantless, nighttime arrest of Welsh for a civil, nonjailable traffic offense was prohibited by the Fourth Amendment. Before government agents may make warrantless house arrests, they must show the presence of exigent circumstances. One factor to be considered in determining the presence of "exigent circumstances" is the "gravity of the underlying offense for which the arrest is being made." The Court cautioned, however, that "exigency" is not created "simply because there is probable cause to believe that a serious crime has been committed." Also, the application of the exigent-circumstances exception to warrantless house arrests should "rarely be sanctioned" when the "underlying offense of arrest" is a "minor offense."

The Court explained that the warrantless arrest for a noncriminal traffic offense cannot be justified on the basis of the hot-pursuit doctrine, since there was "no immediate or continuous pursuit" of the petitioner from the site of the accident. Neither could it be justified on the ground of a "threat to public safety," because the petitioner was already at his house and had left his car at the accident site. Finally, the arrest could not be justified as "necessary to preserve evidence of petitioner's blood-alcohol level," since under state law a first offense for driving while intoxicated is as a noncriminal, civil forfeiture offense, not punishable by imprisonment.

An overnight guest has a reasonable expectation of privacy on the premises where he is staying; therefore, a warrantless house arrest in the absence of exigent circumstances is invalid: In *Olson*, police officers suspected Olson of involvement in a robbery-murder (*Minnesota v. Olson*, 495 U.S. 91 [1990]). They went to the house of two women with whom Olson was staying. They then entered the house without a warrant, where they arrested Olson, who was hiding in a closet. His later confession was admitted in evidence at trial where he was convicted of murder, armed robbery, and assault. The state supreme court reversed, holding that Olson had "sufficient interest" in the women's house to challenge the legality of his warrantless arrest. The state supreme court also held that the warrantless arrest was illegal because of the absence of exigent circumstances.

The Supreme Court held that the arrest was unlawful. It stated that "Olson's status as an overnight guest was alone sufficient to show he had an expectation of privacy in the home that society is prepared to recognize as reasonable." Also, society expects that "hosts will more likely than not respect their guests' privacy interests," although the guests do not have any "legal interest in the premises" or "legal authority to determine who may enter the household." In *Olson*, the warrantless entry was not justified by exigent circumstances such as "hot pursuit of a fleeing felon, the imminent destruction of evidence, the need to prevent a suspect's escape, or the risk of danger to the police or others." In the absence of hot pursuit, the Court held that the police officers must have "probable cause to believe that one or more of the other factors were present." When "assessing the risk of danger, the gravity of the crime and likelihood that the suspect is armed should be considered."

A warrantless arrest inside a house is valid to preserve life and protect occupants from serious bodily injury: Police may enter a home without a warrant when they have an "objectively reasonable basis for believing that an occupant is seriously injured or imminently threatened with such injury" (*Brigham City, Utah v. Stuart*, 547 U.S. 398 [2006]). In *Brigham*, police officers arrived at a house after responding to a 3 A.M. call about a loud party. They heard shouting inside and saw "through a screen door and windows" a fight occurring in the kitchen where a juvenile punched an adult causing the adult "to spit blood in a sink." One officer opened the screen door and announced police presence. The officers arrested respondents and charged them with "contributing to the delinquency of a minor and related offenses." The trial court suppressed the evidence, holding that the warrantless house entry violated the Fourth Amendment. The state court of appeals and state supreme court affirmed.

The Supreme Court held that "because the Fourth Amendment's ultimate touchstone is 'reasonableness,' the warrant requirement is subject to certain exceptions." When exigent circumstances exist, a warrant is not necessary to make an arrest. One exception is when police officers need to render "emergency assistance" to occupants inside a private property who are "seriously injured or threatened with such injury." Here, the officers were faced with "*ongoing* violence occurring *within* the home," making their warrantless entry "plainly reasonable." The officers had an "objectively reasonable basis" to believe that the injured adult needed assistance to avert the violence. The Court further held that the Fourth Amendment does not require them to "wait until another blow rendered someone unconscious, semiconscious, or worse before entering." The manner of the entry was also reasonable, since it was made only after an officer repeatedly announced their presence.

Cases since *Payton* adhere to the Court's decision prohibiting warrantless house arrest without probable cause. Subsequent cases have also affirmed the lawfulness of house arrests if "exigent circumstances exist." Exigent circumstances include hot pursuit, preservation of evidence, prevention of serious threat of bodily injury to occupants, and other situations where police officers are confronted with a sense of urgency that justifies a warrantless arrest.

CONCLUSIONS

Payton established the rule that a warrantless arrest in the suspect's house without exigent circumstances is unlawful. Subsequent cases defined "exigent circumstances" to include hot pursuit of a fleeing suspect, prevention of destruction of evidence and escape of suspect, and the presence of risk of danger to police or the house occupants. These cases also clarified that the existence of probable cause alone is not sufficient to arrest the suspect in his or her house when exigent circumstances are absent.

Exigent circumstances seem to be characterized by a sense of urgency, and police officers are given latitude in determining exigent circumstances and when responding to "swiftly developing situations." The broad and ambiguous nature of the phrase "exigent circumstances" leaves open the validity of warrantless arrests conducted by police officers in the suspect's house or other private dwelling. *Payton*, however, limited its rule to a house or private dwelling and does not address the issue whether the same safeguard applies to other places where the suspect has any "reasonable expectation of privacy."

The Court in *Payton* ruled that police officers have "limited authority to enter a dwelling in which the suspect lives when there is reason to believe the suspect is within." The limited authority to enter a dwelling granted to police officers making a probable-cause arrest arises only when the officers have "reason to believe the suspect is within." What circumstances would justify such reasonable belief that the suspect is actually present in the house? Various cases have held that the presence of light, sounds, or noises from inside the house, the suspect's parked car on the driveway, and the parked cars of the suspect's friends or acquaintances outside may justify such reasonable belief. It remains to be seen what factors will guide law enforcement in their reasonable belief that the suspect is inside prior to making a house arrest.

FURTHER READING

Henry J. Abraham, *Justices and Presidents: A Political History of Appointments to the Supreme Court*, third ed. (New York: Oxford University Press, 1992).

Clare Cushman, *The Supreme Court Justices: Illustrated Biographies, 1789–1995*, second ed., Supreme Court Historical Society (Washington, D.C.: Congressional Quarterly Book, 2001).

Rolando V. del Carmen, *Criminal Procedure: Law and Practice* (Belmont, Calif.: Wadsworth/ Cengage Learning, 2010).

E. Forbes, "Warrantless Arrests in Police Standoffs: A Common Sense Approach to the Exigency Exception," *Criminal Law Bulletin* 45 (2009): 6–23.

John P. Frank, Leon Friedman, and Fred L. Israel, eds., *The Justices of the United States Supreme Court: Their Lives and Major Opinions* (New York: Chelsea House Publishers, 1995).

Kermit L. Hall, ed., *The Oxford Companion to the Supreme Court of the United States* (New York: Oxford University Press, 1992).

J. Marino, "Punishment and Crime: Does *Payton* Apply: Absent Consent or Exigent Circumstance, Are Warrantless, In-Home Police Seizures and Arrests of Persons Seen through an Open Door of the Home Legal," *University of Chicago Legal Forum* (2005): 569–96.

Fenton S. Martin and Robert U. Goehlert, *The U.S. Supreme Court: A Bibliography* (Washington, D.C.: Congressional Quarterly Books, 1990).

B. Murray, "After *United States v. Vaneaton*, Does *Payton v. New York* Prevent Police from Making Warrantless Routine Arrests inside the Home?" *Golden Gate University Law Review* 26 (1996): 135–63.

C. Papapetrou, "*Payton*, Practical Wisdom, and the Pragmatist Judge: Is *Payton*'s Goal to Prevent Unreasonable Entries or to Effectuate Home Arrests?" *Fordham Urban Law Journal* 34 (2007): 1517–55.

C. Radis, "Open Doorway Arrests: Has *McClish v. Nugent* Truly Changed the Analysis?" *Valparaiso University Law Review* 43 (2009): 815–70.

J. Samaha, *Criminal Procedure* (Belmont, Calif.: Thomson Wadsworth, 2008).

J. Scheb and J. Scheb II, *Criminal Law and Procedure* (Belmont, Calif.: Thomson Wadsworth, 2008).

Melvin I. Urofsky, *The Supreme Court Justices: A Biographical Dictionary* (New York: Garland Publishing, 1994), 590.

A. Yarcusko, "*Brown* to *Payton* to *Harris*: A Fourth Amendment Double Play by the Supreme Court," *Case Western Reserve Law Review* 43 (1992): 253–90.

Oliver v. United States

CRAIG HEMMENS*

THE OPEN-FIELDS DOCTRINE

The Fourth Amendment protects "houses, papers, and effects" against unreasonable searches and seizures. Items that do not fall into one of these three categories are not covered by the Fourth Amendment. The open-fields doctrine states that items located in "open fields" are not covered by the Fourth Amendment's prohibition of unreasonable searches and seizures. Consequently, items in open fields can be lawfully seized by a law-enforcement officer without a warrant or probable cause.

It is one thing to say that items in "open fields" are not covered by the Fourth Amendment's protections. It is another altogether to define precisely what constitutes an open field. The open-fields doctrine was developed at common law and was first examined by the United States Supreme Court in *Hester v. United States* (265 U.S. 57 [1924]). In *Hester* the Court made it clear that open fields were not included in "houses, papers, and effects," and so were not protected by the Fourth Amendment. In *Oliver v. United States* (466 U.S. 170 [1984]), the United States Supreme Court attempted to clarify what constituted an open field and to determine whether the physical location of an area was the key factor in determining whether the Fourth Amendment applied to that area.

---

*Portions of this chapter are derived from Rolando V. del Carmen, *Criminal Procedure: Law and Practice*, eighth ed. (Belmont, Calif.: Wadsworth/Cengage, 2010).

OPEN FIELDS AND CURTILAGE: SOME DEFINITIONS

So what exactly are open fields? They are defined more by what they are not than by what they are. Certain areas come under the protection of the Fourth Amendment and therefore cannot be classified as open fields. Other areas are not protected. In this section some examples of areas that are (and are not) protected by the Fourth Amendment are provided.

Houses

Houses are specifically mentioned in the Fourth Amendment, so they are obviously protected. There has been some debate about what constitutes a house, however. Courts have interpreted the term *houses* under the Fourth Amendment broadly, applying it to homes (owned, rented, or leased), apartments, hotel or motel rooms, hospital rooms, and even sections not generally open to the public in places of business.

Houses (however they are defined) are protected by the Fourth Amendment, while open fields are not protected. These two distinctions are simple enough. But what about areas that are neither clearly house nor open field? This is where the fun begins, legally speaking. According to the Supreme Court, the protections of the Fourth Amendment are not limited precisely to houses as stated in the text of the amendment but include some of the area around a house, known as the *curtilage*.

Curtilage is typically defined by courts as "the area to which extends the intimate activity associated with the sanctity of a man's home and the privacies of life" (*Boyd v. United States*, 116 U.S. 616 [1886]). Curtilage is considered a part of the home and is therefore protected against unreasonable searches and seizures. Officers need a warrant and probable cause to seize items in the curtilage. Curtilage may encompass a variety of places, including outbuildings, garages, residential yards, and fenced areas.

Outbuildings

Courts typically consider all buildings in close proximity to a dwelling to be part of the curtilage, so long as these buildings are used for domestic activities. Outbuildings are usually considered part of the curtilage if they are used extensively by the family, are enclosed by a fence, or are close to the house. The farther such buildings are from the house, the less likely it is that they will be considered part of the curtilage. Precisely what constitutes a "domestic activity" has been the subject of some debate. Courts have generally held that domestic activities are those that are routinely engaged in inside a home, such as eating and sleeping.

Garages

Garages are usually considered part of the curtilage unless they are far from the house and seldom used.

Residential Yards

Courts disagree on whether yards are part of the curtilage. If members of the public have access to the yard at any time, it is probably not curtilage. But if only members of the family have access to it, it may be part of the curtilage. If there is a fence around the yard that clearly defines it, the yard is more likely to be considered curtilage.

Fenced Areas

A fence around a house makes the immediate environs within that fence a part of the curtilage, because the owner clearly intended that area to be private and not open to the general public.

Apartment Common Areas

Areas of an apartment building that are used in common by all tenants are not considered part of any tenant's curtilage. However, if the apartment building is of limited size (such as a four-unit building), and each apartment has its own backyard or front yard that is not accessible to the general public, such areas would be part of the curtilage.

THE CASE OF *OLIVER V. UNITED STATES* (1984)

For many years, *Hester* remained the law regarding searches of open fields. In 1967, however, in *Katz v. United States* (389 U.S. 347 [1976]), the Supreme Court moved away from its traditional reliance on what something was or where it was located in determining if the Fourth Amendment applied. In the words of the Court, "the Fourth Amendment protects people, not places." The Court in *Katz* determined that the Fourth Amendment applied regardless of the location, so long as a person had a "reasonable expectation of privacy" in that location. So did a person have a reasonable expectation of privacy in their yard? In an outbuilding?

In *Oliver v. United States* (466 U.S. 170 [1984]) the Supreme Court addressed the open-fields doctrine for the first time since *Hester*. In doing so it gave the doctrine a clearer and broader meaning and made it clear that the *Katz* "reasonable expectation of privacy" analysis did not preclude the affording of protection to some places. In *Oliver* the Court said that it is legal for the police to enter and search unoccupied or underdeveloped areas outside the curtilage without either a warrant or probable cause, as long as the place comes under the category of "open fields," even if the police had to pass a locked gate and a no-trespassing sign.

The Facts

Acting on reports that marijuana was grown on Oliver's farm, but without a search warrant, probable cause, or exigent circumstances, police officers went to Oliver's farm to investigate. They drove past Oliver's house to a locked gate with a no-trespassing sign but with a footpath around one side. Officers followed the footpath around the gate and found a field of marijuana more than a mile from Oliver's house. He was charged with and convicted of manufacturing a controlled substance. The field was secluded and not visible from any point of public access.

The Issue before the Court

Is a place that is posted with a no-trespassing sign, has a locked gate (with a footpath around it), and is located more than a mile from the owner's house considered an open field?

The Court's Holding

A place where the property owner posts a no-trespassing sign and has a locked gate but with a footpath around it, located more than a mile from the house, has no reasonable expectation of privacy and is considered an open field. Therefore, it is legal for the police to enter that area without a warrant or probable cause, because it is unprotected by the Fourth Amendment.

The Majority Opinion

The opinion, authored by Justice Powell, made it clear that the Fourth Amendment did not apply to open fields but only to the curtilage. In this case, while Oliver had taken steps to conceal his field from public view and to keep trespassers out, this was not enough to convert the area into curtilage. The Court acknowledged that there was no single factor that determined whether an area was curtilage, instead saying it was a combination of factors and that the primary factor was the use being made of the area. The Court also noted that curtilage is typically limited to the area immediately surrounding the home.

The Court defined the term *open fields* to include "any unoccupied or under-developed area outside the curtilage"—a definition sufficiently broad to include the heavily wooded area where Oliver's marijuana crop was discovered by the police. The Court noted that "open fields do not provide the setting for those intimate activities that the amendment is intended to shelter from government interference or surveillance. There is no societal interest in protecting the privacy of those activities, such as the cultivation of crops, that occur in open fields."

As the area in question in *Oliver* was not in close proximity to the house, and it was not used for domestic activities, it fell into the category of open fields and thus was not covered by the Fourth Amendment. While this determination may seem obvious, it is important to note that in making this determination the Supreme Court explicitly endorsed the continuing vitality of the curtilage/open-fields distinction rather than discarding them in favor of complete reliance on the *Katz* "reasonable expectation of privacy" formulation for determining the applicability of the Fourth Amendment.

Case Significance

This case makes clear that the reasonable expectation of privacy doctrine does not apply when the property involved is an open field. The Court defined what areas enjoy the protection extended by the reasonable-expectation-of-privacy doctrine. The Court stressed that steps taken to protect privacy, such as planting marijuana on secluded land and erecting a locked gate (but with a footpath along one side) and posting no-trespassing signs around the property, do not establish any reasonable expectation of privacy, so the property comes under open fields. Therefore, the police could enter the property without a warrant or probable cause. The test to determine whether the property comes under a reasonable expectation of privacy or is considered an open field is not whether the individual chooses to conceal assertedly "private activity but whether the government's intrusion infringes upon the personal and societal values protected by the Fourth Amendment."

The significance of *Oliver* is that it reaffirms the doctrine that the "reasonable expectation of privacy" standard in Fourth Amendment cases does not control when the property involved is an open field. The Court stressed that steps taken to protect privacy—such as planting the marijuana on secluded land, erecting a locked gate (but with a footpath along one side), and posting no-trespassing signs around the property—do not necessarily establish any reasonable expectation of privacy. The test, according to the Court, is not whether the individual chooses to conceal assertedly "private activity but whether the government's intrusion infringes upon the personal and societal values protected by the Fourth Amendment." The fact that the government's intrusion upon an open field (as in this case) is a trespass according to common law does not make it a "search" in the constitutional sense, so the Fourth Amendment does not apply.

SUBSEQUENT OPEN-FIELDS CASES

In *Oliver* the Supreme Court defined open fields more clearly and broadly than had been done traditionally. *Oliver* left several unanswered questions, which the Supreme Court returned to in cases decided in the years afterward. These cases are discussed below.

United States v. Dunn (1987)

In *Oliver* the Supreme Court provided a definition of open fields but left unaddressed how curtilage is determined. The Court in *United States v. Dunn* (480 U.S. 294 [1987]) created a four-factor test for determining whether an area is considered a part of the curtilage and therefore covered by the Fourth Amendment. In *Dunn*, after learning that a codefendant had purchased large quantities of chemicals and equipment used in the manufacture of controlled substances, drug agents obtained a warrant to place an electronic tracking beeper in some of the equipment. The beeper ultimately led agents to Dunn's farm. The farm was encircled by a perimeter fence, with several interior fences of the type used to hold livestock. Without a warrant, officers entered the premises and climbed over two barbwire fences and one wooden fence before reaching a barn, approximately fifty yards from Dunn's home. Without entering the barn, the officers stood at a locked gate and shone a flashlight into the barn where they observed what appeared to be a drug laboratory. Officers returned twice the following day to confirm the presence of the laboratory, each time without entering the barn. Based on information gained from these observations, officers obtained a search warrant and seized incriminating evidence from the barn.

Dunn was arrested and eventually convicted of conspiracy to manufacture controlled substances. On appeal, he sought exclusion of the evidence, arguing that (1) a barn located sixty yards from a house and fifty yards from a second fence surrounding the house is part of the curtilage and therefore could not be searched without a warrant, and (2) the officers committed trespass en route to the barn.

The Supreme Court disagreed, in an opinion by Justice Powell, holding that this particular barn could not be considered a part of the curtilage, despite the presence of three fences. The Court noted that the concept of physical trespass was no longer the test that determines whether the Fourth Amendment applies. Instead, the test is whether there exists a reasonable expectation of privacy that deserves protection. In this case, despite the presence of fences, there was none. But the Court added that, although the barn itself was part of the open field, the inside of the barn was protected by the Fourth Amendment, and so a warrant was needed for a lawful entry. The Court created a four-factor test for determining whether an area is considered a part of the curtilage and therefore covered by Fourth Amendment protections:

1. the proximity of the area to the home,
2. whether the area is in an enclosure surrounding the home,
3. the nature and uses of the area,
4. the steps taken to conceal the area from public view.

The Court quickly added this caution, however:

> We do not suggest that combining these factors produces a finely tuned formula that, when mechanically applied, yields a "correct" answer to all extent-of-curtilage questions. Rather, these factors are useful analytical tools only to the degree that, in any given case, they bear upon the centrally relevant consideration—whether the area in question is so intimately tied to the home itself that it should be placed under the "umbrella" of Fourth Amendment protection.

Applying these factors in *Dunn*, the Court concluded that the barn in this case could not be considered part of the curtilage. The good news about *Dunn* is that for the first time the Court laid out the tests that lower courts should use to determine whether a barn, building, garage, or the like is part of the curtilage. The bad news is that these factors are difficult for trial courts to apply with precision. Given the existing tests, what is curtilage to one court may not be curtilage to another. Nonetheless, they are an improvement over the complete absence of a standard under which the lower courts decided cases prior to *Dunn*.

The *Oliver* case involved a warrantless observation of a marijuana patch located more than a mile from Oliver's house. The *Dunn* case involved the warrantless observation of a barn located just sixty yards from a house and fifty yards from a wooden fence that, in turn, was within a bigger perimeter fence. In both cases, the Court concluded that neither property could be considered a part of the curtilage and therefore became open field.

California v. Ciraolo (1986)

The original open-fields cases dealt with physical entry onto private property. But as technology advanced, the courts were forced to deal with how new technology impacted the application of the open-fields doctrine. In *California v. Ciraolo* (476 U.S. 207 [1986]), the Court decided that the constitutional protection against unreasonable search and seizure is not violated by the naked-eye aerial observation by the police of a suspect's backyard, which admittedly is a part of the curtilage.

In *Ciraolo*, police in Santa Clara, California, received an anonymous phone tip that marijuana was being grown in Ciraolo's backyard. The backyard was shielded from public view by a six-foot outer fence and a ten-foot inner fence completely enclosing the yard. On the basis of the tip, officers trained in marijuana identification obtained a private airplane and flew over Ciraolo's house at an altitude of one thousand feet. They readily identified the plants growing in the yard as marijuana. A search warrant was obtained on the basis of the naked-eye observation by one of the officers, supported by a photograph of the surrounding area taken from the airplane. Officers executed the warrant and seized the marijuana plants. In a motion to suppress the evidence, Ciraolo alleged that the warrantless aerial observation of the yard violated the Fourth Amendment.

The Supreme Court, in a narrow five-to-four decision written by Chief Justice Burger, rejected Ciraolo's contention, saying that no Fourth Amendment right was violated because the observations took place within navigable airspace, where the officers had a right to be. The Court admitted that Ciraolo took precautions to maintain his privacy by erecting the fence, and that fenced areas in close proximity to the home were historically treated as curtilage, but added that just because an area is within the curtilage does not bar police from observing it. Under the *Katz* formulation, the physical location of an area was no longer determinative—the key instead was whether there existed a reasonable expectation of privacy in that area. In the words of the Court, "The Fourth Amendment protection of the home has never been extended to require law-enforcement officers to shield their eyes when passing by a home on public thoroughfares." Since the yard was plainly visible from the sky, the majority reasoned, Ciraolo did not have a reasonable expectation of privacy in it.

The dissent in *Ciraolo* was written, interestingly enough, by Justice Powell, the author of the *Oliver* opinion. Justice Powell wrote only two dissents in Fourth Amendment cases in twenty-five years on the Supreme Court. Justice Powell argued that the majority was giving undue weight to the reasonable expectation of privacy formulation and insisted that in *Oliver* the Court had made clear that the physical location of an area was still a crucial factor in determining whether the Fourth Amendment applied.

Florida v. Riley (1989)

In *Ciraolo*, the private airplane flew over the suspect's house at an altitude of one thousand feet to make the observations. Suppose the flight had been made by the police in a helicopter at a height of four hundred feet. Would the evidence still have been admissible? In *Florida v. Riley* (488 U.S. 445 [1989]), the Supreme Court answered yes, saying that, as long as the police are flying at an altitude at which the Federal Aviation Administration (FAA) regulations allow members of the public to fly (the FAA sets no minimum for helicopters), such aerial observation is valid, because, in the absence of FAA prohibitions, the homeowner would have no reasonable expectation of privacy from such flights. Note, however, that these cases involved mere "looking" or "peering" but not entering, so the degree of intrusion was minimal.

Kyllo v. United States (2001)

The most recent Supreme Court decision involving the open-fields doctrine dealt with the impact of another form of technology on open fields and curtilage. In *Kyllo v. United States* (533 U.S. 27 [2001]), the Court held that using a technological device to explore the details of a home that would previously have been unknowable without physical intrusion is a search and is presumptively unreasonable without a warrant.

In *Kyllo*, officers suspected Kyllo of growing marijuana in his home. They used a thermal-imaging device from across the street (therefore an open field) to examine the heat radiating from his house. The scan showed that the roof over the garage and a side wall of the house were relatively hot compared to the rest of his house and substantially hotter than neighboring homes. Based on this information, on utility bills, and on tips from informants, the officers obtained a search warrant for Kyllo's home. The search revealed more than one hundred marijuana plants. Appealing his conviction, Kyllo argued that what the police did without a warrant constituted an illegal search of his home. The federal prosecutor argued that thermal imaging does not constitute a search because (1) it detects "only heat radiating from the external surface of the house," and therefore there was no entry, and (2) it did not detect private activities occurring in private areas, because "everything that was detected was on the outside."

The Court disagreed, saying that the Fourth Amendment draws "a firm line at the entrance of the house." The Court said further:

> At the very core of the Fourth Amendment stands the right of a man to retreat into his own home and there be free from unreasonable governmental intrusions. With few exceptions, the question whether a warrantless search of a home is reasonable and hence constitutional must be answered no. . . . We think that obtaining by sense-enhancement technology any information regarding the interior of the home that could not otherwise have been obtained without physical intrusion into a constitutionally protected area constitutes a search, at least where (as here) the technology in question is not in general public use. . . . On the basis of this criterion, the information obtained by the thermal images in this case was the product of a search.

The significance of *Kyllo* for the open-fields doctrine is that the use of electronic devices from an open field may constitute a violation of the Fourth Amendment if such use obtains information that would not otherwise be obtainable from the open field alone. The use of thermal imaging in *Kyllo* was deemed by the Court as equivalent to physical intrusion into a home, although through the use of sense-enhancing technology. Nonetheless, this constitutes physical entry and is prohibited by the Fourth Amendment.

CONCLUSIONS

In the past the definition of open fields was simpler—everything outside the wall or fence that surrounded a dwelling was open fields, and everything inside the wall or fence was curtilage. And everyone had a wall or fence. We do not live in such simple times. Suburban homes often have no fences, apartments no yards, and what is protected by the Fourth Amendment depends in part on when one is said to enjoy a reasonable expectation of privacy, regardless of the presence of fences and no-trespassing signs.

The *Dunn*, *Ciraolo*, and *Oliver* cases all tell us that the concept of curtilage has become restricted while that of open fields has been significantly expanded by the Court, thus giving law-enforcement officials greater leeway in search-and-seizure cases. The relationship among houses and buildings, curtilage, and open fields may generally be stated as follows: Houses and buildings are the most protected, followed by curtilage, and then open fields. Houses, buildings, and curtilage are protected by the Fourth Amendment; open fields are not.

FURTHER READING

Catherine Hancock, "Justice Powell's Garden: The *Ciraolo* Dissent and Fourth Amendment Protection for Curtilage-Home Privacy," *San Diego Law Review* 44 (2007): 551–71.

Carrie Leonetti, "Open Fields in the Inner City: Application of the Curtilage Doctrine to Urban and Suburban Areas," *George Mason University Civil Rights Law Journal* 15 (2005): 297–320.

Jake Linford, "The Right Ones for the Job: Divining the Correct Standard of Review for Curtilage Determinations in the Aftermath of *Ornelas v. United States*," *University of Chicago Law Review* 75 (2008): 885–910.

Brendan Peters, "Fourth Amendment Yard Work: Curtilage's Mow-Line Rule," *Stanford Law Review* 56 (2004): 943–80.

Vanessa Rownaghi, "Driving into Unreasonableness: The Driveway, the Curtilage, and Reasonable Expectations of Privacy," *American University Journal of Gender, Social Policy and the Law* 11 (2003): 1165–98.

Rowan Themer, "A Man's Barn Is Not His Castle: Warrantless Searches of Structures under the Open Fields Doctrine," *Southern Illinois University Law Journal* 32 (2008): 139–55.

Schneckloth v. Bustamonte

Sue Carter Collins

INTRODUCTION

Throughout America people are approached by police officers on a daily basis and asked the proverbial questions: "Do you mind if I search you?" "Do you mind if I search your car?" "Do you mind if I search your property?" Although, currently, the law does not require compliance, the target of the search almost always allows it. By far, consent searches are the most popular and the most frequent form of search undertaken by the police. Police officers love consent searches for three reasons: First, in many jurisdictions, an officer may request consent to search without having a suspicion or any reasonable belief that a person is engaged in criminal activity. Second, consent searches lack the administrative inconveniences and risks associated with obtaining and executing search warrants. When an individual voluntarily consents to a search, the officer executes it immediately with no judicial oversight and few, if any, limitations on the scope of the search. Lastly, while it is often incomprehensible, many people voluntarily consent to be searched by the police while knowingly possessing evidence of a crime. Therefore, from the point of view of police officers, consent searches are an important and irreplaceable crime-fighting tool that should be protected at all costs.[1]

This chapter begins with a comprehensive analysis of *Schneckloth v. Bustamonte*, 412 U.S. 218 (1973), the Supreme Court's seminal decision on consent searches. It next discusses the theoretical origins of the consent-search doctrine and identifies legal principles that have evolved over time. The chapter concludes with observations on the continuing viability of the consent-search doctrine and its impact on police searches and individual rights.

THE CASE OF *SCHNECKLOTH V. BUSTAMONTE* (1973): THE CONSENT-SEARCH DOCTRINE

The Facts

According to *Schneckloth v. Bustamonte* (412 U.S. 218 [1973]), early one morning while on routine patrol Police Officer James Rand spotted a car with a burned-out headlight and license-plate light. Six men occupied the vehicle. Alcala and Bustamonte were passengers in the front seat together with Gonzales, the driver. Three older men occupied the back seat. In response to the officer's questions, only Alcala—who said that the car belonged to his brother—could produce a driver's license. After backup officers arrived, the six men exited the car at the officers' request. Officer Rand then asked Alcala for permission to search the car, and Acala replied, "Sure, go ahead." Prior to the search, no one was threatened with arrest, and "it was all very congenial." Alcala participated in the search by voluntarily opening the trunk and the glove compartment. Pursuant to the search the officers found three checks under the left rear seat that had been stolen from a car wash.

Bustamonte was arrested and charged with possessing checks with intent to defraud in violation of section 475a of the California Penal Code. At his trial he moved to suppress the checks, arguing that they were obtained through an unlawful search. The trial court denied the motion, and Bustamonte was convicted. He appealed to the California Court of Appeal for the First District, which affirmed the lower court's decision. Applying a totality-of-the-circumstances test that had been adopted earlier by the Supreme Court of California, the appellate court held that "there were clearly circumstances from which the trial court could ascertain that consent had been freely given without coercion or submission to authority." The California Supreme Court denied review, and Bustamonte appealed to the Ninth Circuit Court of Appeals, which set aside the district court's order. The Ninth Circuit Court held that "consent was a waiver of a person's Fourth and Fourteenth Amendment rights, and the state was [required] to demonstrate not only that the consent had been uncoerced, but that it had been given with the understanding that it could be freely and effectively withheld. Consent could not be found . . . solely from the absence of coercion and a verbal expression of consent." The United States

Supreme Court granted certiorari to determine if the Constitution required the showing specified by the circuit court.

The Issue before the Court

Is the state required to demonstrate that a suspect has knowledge of the right to refuse consent in order for a search based on consent to be valid?

The Majority Opinion

Bustamonte was argued before the Court on October 10, 1972, and decided on May 29, 1973. Justice Stewart wrote the majority opinion expressing the views of six members of the Court. He began by acknowledging that the lower courts had rendered conflicting opinions on the facts of the case. To aid in resolving the conflict, Stewart sought guidance from the Court's numerous opinions on the voluntariness of confessions. After reviewing more than thirty decisions, Stewart concluded that "in determining whether a defendant's will was overborne . . . the Court has assessed the totality of all the surrounding circumstances—both the characteristics of the accused and the details of the interrogation." Among the many factors that the Court has considered are age of the accused, lack of education, lack of advice regarding constitutional rights, length of detention, prolonged questioning, and physical punishment including deprivation of food and sleep. Stewart found it particularly significant that "none [of the Court's decisions] turned on the presence or absence of a single controlling criterion; [instead,] each reflected a careful scrutiny of all the surrounding circumstances." Stewart observed that the Court has never held that due process required the prosecution to prove that a suspect knew of the right to refuse to answer questions as part of the state's initial burden. Rather, although a suspect's state of mind and the failure of the police to inform him of the right to refuse were factors that the Court considered when assessing voluntariness, they were not determinative. Consistent with the state court's ruling, Stewart concluded that voluntariness of consent "is a question of fact to be determined from the totality of all the circumstances. While knowledge of the right to refuse consent is one factor to be taken into account, the government need not establish such knowledge as the sine qua non of an effective consent."[2]

The Dissenting Opinion

Justices Douglas, Brennan, and Marshall each wrote dissenting opinions. Since Marshall's dissent is the most comprehensive and the most critical of the majority opinion, it is the focus of this discussion. First, Marshall took issue with the majority's holding declaring that the Court had "reache[d] the curious result that one can choose to relinquish a constitutional right—the right to be free from unreasonable searches—without knowing that he has the alternative of refusing to accede to a police request to search." Next, Marshall reframed the issue that the Court should have been addressing, stating that it "is not, as the Court suggests, whether the police overbore Alcala's will in eliciting his consent but rather whether a simple statement of assent to search, without more, should be sufficient to permit the police to search and thus act as a relinquishment of Alcala's constitutional right to exclude the police."

Finally, Marshall rejected as inappropriate the Court's use of the voluntariness standard, which had been developed in confession cases, to resolve the consent-search issue in *Bustamonte*. Noting that the policies underlying the two standards are entirely different, Marshall stated that

> freedom from coercion is a substantive right, guaranteed by the Fifth and Fourteenth Amendments. Consent, however, is a mechanism by which substantive requirements . . . are avoided. In the context of the Fourth Amendment, the relative substantive requirements are that searches be conducted only after evidence justifying them has been submitted to an impartial magistrate for a determination of probable cause.

While acknowledging that exceptions to the probable-cause and warrant requirement do exist, Marshall argued that "none of the exceptions relating to the overriding needs of law enforcement are applicable when a search is justified solely by consent. . . . Rather, consent searches are permitted, not because such an exception . . . is essential to proper law enforcement, but because we permit our citizens to choose whether or not they wish to exercise their constitutional rights."

Further Analysis

Writing for the majority, Stewart identified two competing needs that must be addressed when determining whether consent is voluntary—"the legitimate need for such searches and . . . assuring the absence of coercion." Balancing the pendulum in favor of the police, Stewart argued that sometimes the only way officers have to obtain evidence against a criminal suspect is through a consent search. Furthermore, a consent search "may result in considerably less inconvenience to the subject of the search and, properly conducted, is a constitutionally permissible and wholly legitimate aspect of effective police activity." Seeing no reason to depart from the traditional definition of *voluntariness*, Stewart concluded that "just as was true with confessions, the requirement of a 'voluntary' consent reflects a fair accommodation of the constitutional requirements involved" in consent searches.

Stewart adamantly rejected the opinion of the Ninth Circuit Court of Appeals, which held that for a search based on consent to be valid the state must demonstrate that consent is not coerced and that the subject of the search is aware of the right to refuse. In addition to stating that the circuit court's ruling is not supported by judicial precedent, Stewart opined that a decision of this nature would have a negative impact on whether consent searches could still be conducted and would place a heavy burden on the prosecution that is nearly impossible to meet.

Although Stewart acknowledged that one way to prove a subject was aware of the right to refuse consent would be to tell him before the search, he spurned this idea as being "thoroughly impractical," due to the need of police to act quickly and often under unstructured circumstances. Stewart also rejected the contention that a different decision is mandated by the Court's ruling in *Johnson v. Zerbst*, 304 U.S. 458 (1938), which requires the state to demonstrate that the consenter intentionally waived a known right or privilege. Stewart observed that "almost without exception" the demand for a knowing and intelligent waiver has only been invoked in criminal cases involving the defendant's constitutional right to a fair trial. Noting that "there is a vast difference between [the Sixth Amendment right to a fair trial] . . . and the rights guaranteed under the Fourth Amendment," Stewart said he found no evidence to suggest that the "knowing" and "intelligent" waiver requirement ought to be extended to the guarantee against unreasonable searches and seizures. Related to this, Stewart also rejected outright the contention that the Court's holding in *Miranda v. Arizona* dictates that a subject be informed of his right to refuse to consent to a search. Stating that "there is no evidence of any inherently coercive tactics" in the *Bustamonte* case, Stewart determined that the factors informing the Court's holding in *Miranda* simply do not apply to this case. In setting forth the Court's ruling Stewart noted that the decision in *Bustamonte*

> is a narrow one. We hold only that when the subject of a search is not in custody and the state attempts to justify a search on the basis of his consent, the Fourth and Fourteenth Amendments require that it demonstrate that consent was in fact

voluntarily given, and not the result of duress or coercion, express or implied. Voluntariness is a question of fact to be determined from all the circumstances, and while the subject's knowledge of the right to refuse is taken into account, the prosecution is not required to demonstrate such knowledge as a prerequisite to establishing a voluntary consent.

Disagreeing totally with Stewart's assessment, Marshall declared that he was at a loss to understand why "consent cannot be taken literally to mean a 'knowing choice.'" He argued,

> If consent to search means that a person has chosen to forgo his right to exclude the police from the place they seek to search, it follows that his consent cannot be considered a meaningful choice unless he knew that he could in fact exclude the police. . . . I can think of no other situation in which we would say that a person agreed to some course of action if he convinced us that he did not know that there was some other course he might have pursued. I would therefore hold, at a minimum, that the prosecution may not rely on a purported consent to search if the subject of the search did not know that he could refuse to give consent.

Marshall asserted that if one accepts this view the only fair allocation of the burden of proof would be to place it on the prosecution. Yet, he noted, "The Court responds to this suggestion by overinflating the [state's] burden . . . [and] refusing to require the *police* to make a 'detailed' inquiry." According to Marshall, "If the burden [of proof] is placed on the defendant, all the subject can do is testify that he did not know of his rights" and, it is not likely "that many trial judges will find for the defendant" based on that.

Responding to Stewart's contention that adoption of the waiver requirement would place too heavy a burden on the state, Marshall stated that there are many ways by which the prosecutor could show that the subject had knowledge of his rights such as where the subject has affirmatively demonstrated knowledge of his rights or had prior experience or training in this area. He noted, however, that the prosecutor's burden would disappear "if the police, at the time they requested consent to search, also told the subject that he had a right to refuse consent and that his decision to refuse would be respected." Regarding the Court's assertion that "if an officer paused to inform the subject of his rights, the informality of the exchange would be destroyed," Marshall expressed doubt that this would happen and added, "it is not without significance that for many years the agents of the Federal Bureau of Investigation have routinely informed subjects of their right to refuse consent when they request consent to search." In a final assault on the majority opinion, Marshall announced that,

> when the Court speaks of practicality, what it really is talking of is the continued ability of the police to capitalize on the ignorance of citizens so as to accomplish by subterfuge what they could not achieve by relying on the knowing relinquishment of constitutional rights. . . . But such a practical advantage is achieved only at the cost of permitting the police to disregard the limitations that the Constitution places on their behavior, a cost that a constitutional democracy cannot long absorb.

Case Significance

Bustamonte is significant for holding that the Fourth and Fourteenth Amendments do not require police to inform individuals of the right to refuse consent as a prerequisite to conducting a valid search in which consent is voluntarily given. The standard for determining voluntariness is the totality of the circumstances of which knowledge of the right to refuse consent is simply one factor that courts will consider when determining if consent is valid. Although the Court looked to the confession cases for guidance on the appropriate standard to apply to consent searches, the majority concluded that, unlike *Miranda v. Arizona*, which involves a waiver of a constitutional right and requires that individuals be warned of the right to remain silent, the Fourth and Fourteenth Amendment policy concerns underlying consent searches simply do not require such a warning. Therefore, there is no legal mandate that requires the police to tell persons "you have a right to refuse consent" as a prerequisite to conducting a valid search.

THEORETICAL ORIGINS OF THE CONSENT-SEARCH DOCTRINE

The precise origin of the consent-search doctrine has never been explicitly defined.[3] At least three different theoretical bases have been offered as justifications for this exception. Historically, consent searches have been justified as an exception to the warrant and probable-cause requirement. This theoretical basis was articulated by the majority justices in *Schneckloth v. Bustamonte.*

A second explanation suggests that consent searches are permissible because, technically, they are not searches at all but are a relinquishment of an individual's privacy interests that are protected under the Fourth Amendment. Justice Marshall expressed this justification in his dissenting opinion in *Bustamonte* when he stated, "Consent searches are permitted, not because such an exception to the probable cause and warrant is essential to proper law enforcement, but because we permit our citizens to choose whether or not they wish to exercise their constitutional right."

Consent searches also have been justified based on whether they are "reasonable" under the Fourth Amendment. This position was enunciated by the Court recently in both *Illinois v. Rodriguez*, 497 U.S. 177 (1990), and *United States v. Drayton*, 536 U.S. 194 (2002). Undergirding this explanation is the principle that the Fourth Amendment does not prohibit all searches, only those that are per se unreasonable. An individual who voluntarily agrees to be searched forgoes the right to complain that it is unreasonable.

THE SCOPE OF POLICE AUTHORITY IN CONSENT SEARCHES

Currently, there is no rule of law that prohibits police officers from approaching individuals and requesting consent to search their persons, houses, papers, and effects. Whether the initial contact is made pursuant to a police-citizen encounter or as the result of a lawful detention, the police may request consent from anyone to search anything, at any time or place, and for any or no reason. In most states there is no requirement that police officers possess reasonable suspicion or probable cause as a prerequisite to seeking consent. Additionally, police officers are not required to inform individuals that they have a right to refuse assent. Consistent with the Court's holding in *Bustamonte*, evidence obtained by police officers during a warrantless search that is without probable cause and based on consent is admissible in court as long as consent is voluntarily given.

GENERAL RULES PERTAINING TO CONSENT SEARCHES

Since 1973, courts have continued to build upon the judicial framework governing consent searches that was first announced in *Bustamonte*. This section identifies and summarizes relevant legal principles and cases in the consent-search area.

Express or Implied Consent

The general rule regarding the giving of consent is that it may be express or implied but need not be knowing or intelligent (*United States v. Garcia*, 56 F.3d 418 [2d Cir. 1995]). The fact that a person is under the influence of drugs or alcohol, or suffering from various forms of mental stress or anxiety, will not invalidate consent that is voluntarily obtained. Neither will the fact that a defendant was suicidal, delusional, and admitted to a mental facility (*United States v. Barbour*, 70 F.3d 580 [11th Cir. 1995]). In such cases, the court will still find that consent is voluntary as long as there is no evidence of police coercion or intimidation and the person understands the nature of the police questioning or interrogation.

Scope of Consent

The scope of a consent search is generally defined by the nature of the object that is the focus of the search; however, where a general consent to search is given, the scope of the search is defined by what a reasonable person would expect under the circumstances. It is this general principle that underlies the Court's holding in *Florida v. Jimeno*, 500 U.S. 248 (1991). The issue in *Jimeno* involved the scope of the search authorized when a person consents to the search of his motor vehicle. When Jimeno was stopped for a traffic violation, the officer informed him that he thought drugs were in the car and asked for consent to search. After receiving Jimeno's permission the officer saw a brown paper bag on the floor, opened it, and discovered cocaine. The trial court suppressed the drugs, ruling that mere consent to search the car did not carry with it specific consent to search the bag. The Supreme Court reversed, holding that the appropriate standard for assessing the scope of a person's consent under the Fourth Amendment is objective reasonableness—that is, "what would the typical reasonable person have understood by the exchange between the officer and the suspect?" In *Jimeno* the Court held that it was permissible for the officer to search the bag since a reasonable person would have believed that it could contain drugs, which were the object of the search.

The scope of the search may not exceed the scope of the consent given. For example, an officer's request to "see" or to "enter" a person's residence is not a request to search it. To conduct a lawful search under these circumstances the police must make a specific request to search the premises; however, any contraband that an officer observes after lawfully gaining entry may be seized and provides probable cause for arrest and for obtaining a warrant to search. Similarly, if a person voluntarily consents to the search of a vehicle or container within his possession any other containers found within the vehicle or container may also be searched; however, the police may not break open a closed or locked container without specific permission to conduct the search.

Revocation of Consent

Consent to search may be revoked by the giver at any time before or during the search without giving a reason. If consent is withdrawn before the search is completed the officers must stop searching immediately (*United States v. Ho*, 94 F.3d 932 [5th Cir. 1996]). Any evidence found by the police prior to consent being withdrawn may still be used against the suspect. Typical behaviors indicating that consent is withdrawn include snatching the item from the officer, saying "no, wait!" before the officer initiates the search, and slamming the trunk or car door before the search gets underway; however, refusing to sign a written waiver form after oral consent is given does not withdraw consent.

Written Consent

The law does not require individuals to provide written consent in order for consent to be valid. The existence of written consent is simply one factor that courts will consider in the totality of the circumstances. A person who responds to a request for consent by writing "reluctantly" on the consent form will not invalidate consent that is lawfully acquired (*United States v. Rivas*, 99 F.3d 170 [5th Cir. 1996]). Even in cases where the consenter experiences a language barrier, some courts will still find that consent was voluntarily obtained (*United States v. Cedano-Medina*, 366 F.3d 682 [8th Cir. 2004]).

Third-Party Consent

Not everyone to whom a request for consent is made is legally authorized to give it. In general, the following principles apply in third-party-consent cases.

Spouses

In cases involving spouses, courts have held that husbands and wives have coequal rights of ownership and that either may authorize a search of marital property based on consent (*United States v. Matlock*, 415 U.S. 164 [1974]); however, where both spouses are physically present and one refuses consent, the police may not reasonably act on the authorization of the other (*Georgia v. Randolph*, 547 U.S. 103 [2006]).

Parents and Children

Either parent may authorize the search of property belonging to minor children (*Colbert v. Kentucky*, 2001 WL 174809 [Ky. 2001]); however, children may not authorize the search of property belonging to their parents. Some courts also have ruled that parents may not consent to the search of an adult child's property if the child pays for room and board and exhibits a reasonable expectation of privacy.

Roommates, Co-owners, and Co-users of a Property

Either roommate may consent to a search by police of the entire apartment or house except in the areas where the nonconsenting person has exhibited a reasonable expectation of privacy, such as in a separate bedroom. The absent roommate assumes the risk that the consenting roommate will permit the search. The assumption-of-the-risk principle also applies to consent given by co-owners or co-users of joint property (*Frazier v. Cupp*, 394 U.S. 731 [1969]).

Landlord and Tenant

A landlord may consent to the search of common areas used by tenants but may not authorize a search of the tenant's private residence even though he has the right to access the property in order to inspect for damage and make repairs (*Chapman v. United States*, 365 U.S. 610 [1961]).

Hotel Employee and Guest

A hotel room takes on the same characteristics as a guest's home during the rental period. Therefore, hotel employees may not authorize police to search a guest's room (*Stoner v. California*, 376 U.S. 483 [1964]).

Employer and Employees

Employers may search an employee's office for a work-related reason; however, they may not authorize a police search where the employee has exhibited a reasonable expectation of privacy in his office or at his desk (*United States v. Block*, 188 F.2d 1019 [D.C. Cir. 1951]). Whether an employee may authorize a search of the employer's property depends on the employee's status at work and the scope of his authority. The general rule is that employees may not authorize such searches; however, if the employee is left in charge of the employer's business for an extended period some courts have held that the employee may waive his employer's rights under these limited circumstances.

In summary, the law governing third-party consent is still developing. The apparent theme that binds the courts' decisions in this area is objective reasonableness. This standard ignores the subjective intent of the officer and the individual and instead asks whether a reasonable person would have believed that the person granting consent to search was authorized to do so (see *Illinois v. Rodriguez*, 497 U.S. 177 [1990], for the apparent-authority doctrine) and whether the scope of the search conducted by the police was consistent with the consent given. Where these questions are answered in the affirmative, searches conducted pursuant to consent will most likely be upheld.

COURT-IMPOSED LIMITATIONS: WHEN IS A CONSENT SEARCH INVALID?

Despite Justice Marshall's assertion that the effect of the Court's decision in *Bustamonte* is to "sanction[] a game of blindman's bluff, in which the police always have the upper hand, for the sake of nothing more than the convenience of the police," there are numerous cases in which the courts have invalidated consent searches. This section provides several examples and discusses reasons for the invalidation.

Mere Silence and Ambiguous Responses

Lower courts are split on the issue of whether consent can be inferred from mere silence with some courts holding that it can and others holding that it cannot. When the person from whom consent is sought responds with ambiguous behavior, lower courts consider the totality of the circumstances to decide if consent was voluntary. For example, in *United States v. Worley*, 193 F.3d 380 (6th Cir. 1999), the court held that consent was not voluntary when, in response to the officer's request to search a bag, the subject responded, "You've got the badge; I guess you can." Similarly, in *United States v. Albrektsen*, 151 F.3d 951 (9th Cir. 1998), the court held that consent was not voluntary when the defendant opened the hotel door but moved out of the officer's way to avoid being knocked down.

Acquiescence to Authority

The general rule of law is that consent to search may not be inferred from acquiescence to authority (*United States v. Hidalgo*, 7 F.3d 1566 [11th Cir. 1993]). Where the only reason that a suspect consents to a search is because the officer tells him it is required or threatens to get a warrant, courts have held that such consent is invalid (*Bumper v. North Carolina*, 391 U.S. 543 [1968]). Consent also has been invalidated where the warrant on which the officer relied was subsequently declared invalid (*United States v. Hotal*, 143 F.3d 1223 [9th Cir. 1998]); however, where additional circumstances are present some courts have upheld searches involving acquiescence to authority as valid. For instance, in *United States v. Lee*, 317 F.3d 26 (1st Cir. 2003), the court ruled that a consent search was voluntary where police informed the defendant that if he did not consent they would obtain a warrant since they had sufficient probable cause to do so.

Coercion and Intimidation

The courts have invalidated numerous searches based on the presence of coercion or intimidation. For example, in *United States v. Morales*, 171 F.3d 978 (5th Cir. 1999), the court held that consent was not voluntary when four officers with guns drawn banged on the door, yelled "open up," and ordered the residents to the floor. Similarly, in *United States v. Ivy*, 165 F.3d 397 (6th Cir. 1998), where officers threatened to take the defendant's child into custody and to arrest his girlfriend and family members, the court held that the defendant's consent was involuntarily obtained; however, the mere fact that a person is in custody may not be sufficiently coercive to invalidate consent (*United States v. Watson*, 504 F.2d 849 [9th Cir. 1974]).

WHAT DOES THE FUTURE HOLD FOR THE CONSENT-SEARCH DOCTRINE?

The consent-search doctrine is alive and well and strongly favored by law-enforcement officers. Indicative of this, more than 90 percent of warrantless police searches are accomplished using consent searches.[4] The fact that most people that are subjected to consent searches are entirely innocent of criminal conduct has not slowed the rate at which such searches are conducted. To be sure, one can only speculate the true extent to which the Court's refusal to adopt a standard requiring police officers to inform individuals of their right to refuse consent has contributed to the increased use of consent searches. If news reports and anecdotal stories are any indication, the use of consent searches in citizen encounters, *Terry* stops, and motor-vehicle searches involving police profiling borders on rampant.

To date there is no evidence that the Supreme Court is considering adopting standards governing consent searches that are more supportive of individual rights. On the contrary, although the *Bustamonte* Court stated that an individual's subjective characteristics would be considered when determining the voluntariness of consent, recent judicial decisions such as *Rodriguez* and *Randolph* have adopted a different rule that focuses on "objective reasonableness." This new standard, when viewed in conjunction with the fact that the police are not required to inform individuals of their right to refuse consent, sends a strong signal that today's courts will consider the totality of the circumstances primarily from the perspective of police officers. The likely result is that more consent searches will take place and few will be invalidated because consent was involuntarily obtained.

CONCLUSIONS

This chapter examines *Schneckloth v. Bustamonte*, the Court's seminal decision on consent searches. *Bustamonte*'s significance derives from the Court's holding that police are not required to inform individuals of the right to refuse consent as a prerequisite to conducting a valid search. The test for determining the validity of consent searches is voluntariness, which is determined based on the totality of the circumstances. The precise origin of the consent-search doctrine has not been defined; however, three theoretical bases have been identified, including as an exception to the probable-cause and warrant requirement, a relinquishment of an individual's privacy rights, and the degree of "reasonableness" as seen through the lens of the Fourth Amendment. Since 1973 lower courts have rendered a myriad of decisions to fill out the legal framework drawn by the Court in the *Bustamonte* case. While there are still grey areas in the law, a set of general rules pertaining to the conduct of consent searches is emerging.

From the point of view of the police, consent searches are an important weapon used to fight the war against crime. More than 90 percent of police searches are based on consent. The scope of the police authority in consent searches is extremely broad. Officers may request consent to search anyone at any time and any place for any reason or no reason at all. As long as consent is voluntarily given, the state may prosecute offenders using the fruits of the search.

From the point of view of citizens, consent searches are problematic for several reasons. First, most people are unaware that they have a legal right to refuse consent. Second, even the most educated people who are knowledgeable of their rights often feel intimidated in the presence of the state's police power. Third, when the police seek consent from persons during an encounter or stop the situation is fraught with legal coercion. As Justice Marshall stated in his *Bustamonte* dissent, it is highly unlikely that individuals in these circumstances will refuse consent even if they know that they have the legal right to do so. A major concern of many who find themselves in this situation is that the exercise of their constitutional right to privacy may result in additional legal problems including physical abuse or arrest. These factors make it inherently likely that when confronted with a request by police for permission to conduct a search most people will continue to "voluntarily" acquiesce to authority.

FURTHER READING

Yale Kamisar, Wayne R. LaFave, and Jerold H. Israel, *Basic Criminal Procedure Cases, Comments and Questions*, sixth ed. (St. Paul, Minn.: West Publishing Co., 1986).

Tracey Maclin, "The Good and Bad News about Consent Searches in the Supreme Court," *McGeorge Law Review* 39 (2008): 27–90.

Cliff Roberson, *Constitutional Law and Criminal Justice* (Boca Raton, Fla.: CRC Press, 2009).

M. Strauss, "Reconstructing Consent," *Journal of Criminal Law and Criminology* 92 (2001): 211–59.

Georgia v. Randolph

DAVID BRODY

INTRODUCTION

The Fourth Amendment states, "The right of the people to be secure in their persons, houses, papers, and effects against unreasonable searches and seizure shall not be violated, and no warrants shall issue but upon probable cause, supported by oath or affirmation, and particularly describing the place to be searched, and the person or things to be seized." Paramount to the founding fathers was protecting the sanctity of a person's home from unreasonable intrusion from the government. In interpreting the Fourth Amendment the Supreme Court has repeatedly stated that a search conducted without a warrant is presumed to be unreasonable unless the basis for the search falls into one of a few specific, "carefully drawn" exceptions.

One of these exceptions permits law-enforcement officials to conduct a search of a person's home or property pursuant to valid consent. While permitting a search pursuant to consent seems logical and straightforward, over the past century the Supreme Court has been called upon to address a number of nuances of consent-based searches. Items addressed by the Court have included the voluntariness of the consent received, the scope of the consent, and who is permitted to consent to a search.

The Supreme Court has held that under certain circumstances—a third party that is a person other than the owner or occupant of the property to be searched—may provide consent to a search of the premises by the police. Over the past half century the Supreme Court has addressed the validity of third-party consent involving roommates, landlords and tenants, hotel staff and guests, live-in boyfriends and girlfriends, and husbands and wives. Over this time frame the Court has changed the manner in which it evaluates the validity of a search pursuant to third-party consent. The evolution of the Court's analysis reached a crescendo when the case of *Georgia v. Randolph* (547 U.S. 103 [2006]) addressed whether a search of a house pursuant to the consent of one spouse is constitutional despite the contemporaneous refusal of the other spouse.

In this chapter we consider the majority, concurring, and dissenting opinions issued by the Supreme Court in *Georgia v. Randolph*. We also address the precedent and case law leading up to *Randolph*, the way in which lower courts have implemented the *Randolph* holding, and practical implications and potential future problems stemming from the Court's decision.

THE HISTORY OF THIRD-PARTY-CONSENT SEARCHES

The Supreme Court heard very few cases involving a third party's consent to a warrantless search prior to the 1960s. The first time the Court directly addressed the issue was the 1961 case of *Chapman v. United States* (365 U.S. 610 [1961]). In *Chapman* police responded to a call from a landlord who smelled an odor associated with distilling alcohol coming from a house he was renting to the defendant. After knocking on Chapman's door and receiving no answer, the police obtained permission from the landlord to enter the home. Inside they discovered evidence of an illegal distillery in the house. Arguing that the warrantless search did not violate the Fourth Amendment, the government contended that property law granted the landlord the right to bring police officers and enter the house. In rejecting this argument, the Supreme Court held that a landlord cannot consent to the search of a tenant's premises. To hold otherwise, the Court noted, "would reduce the [Fourth] Amendment to a nullity and leave [tenants'] homes secure only in the discretion of [landlords]."

Several years later the Supreme Court held that consent from a hotel manager was not sufficient to allow a search of a hotel guest's room. *Stoner v. California* (376 U.S. 483 [1964]) involved a situation in which the police were searching for a robbery suspect. Following a lead they approached the night clerk of a hotel and asked if a Joey Stoner was registered there. The clerk stated that Stoner was but that he was not in at the time. The police explained why they were looking for Stoner and asked for permission to search his room. The clerk agreed and unlocked Stoner's door for the police to search. While searching the room, they found evidence of the robbery that was used against Stoner at trial. Following his conviction, Stoner appealed. The Supreme Court held that this search was unreasonable, because the clerk had no authority to consent to a search of the defendant's room since the clerk was not an agent that could waive the defendant's constitutional right against warrantless searches for him.

Following the decision in *Stoner*, it was widely assumed that the Court would consider whether or not a third person granting consent had authority to do so as an agent. This assumption changed, however, following the Court's decision in *Katz v. United States* (389 U.S. 347 [1967]). While *Stoner* and *Chapman* were based largely on property law and associated rights, in *Katz* the Court held that the Fourth Amendment protects people and not places. As such, Fourth Amendment analysis shifted from examining property rights to examining whether a search violated a person's expectation of privacy.

The Court's third-party-consent decisions following *Katz* went beyond mere property and agency considerations. In *Frazier v. Cupp* (394 U.S. 731 [1969]), the defendant, Martin Frazier, shared a room with his cousin. Frazier's cousin gave police permission to search a duffel bag that he shared with Frazier and that contained evidence linking Frazier to a murder for which he was later convicted. The Supreme Court held that "in allowing [his cousin] to use the bag and in leaving it in his house, [Frazier] must be taken to have assumed the risk that [his cousin] would allow someone else to look inside." Therefore, based on this assumed risk, the warrantless search pursuant to the cousin's consent was constitutional.

Several years later, in the 1974 case of *United States v. Matlock* (415 U.S. 164 [1974]), the Court expanded on this assumption-of-risk framework. In *Matlock* the defendant was arrested in the front yard of a residence he shared with his girlfriend, Gayle Graff. After the police put Matlock in a patrol car, they asked Graff, who was standing at the front door of the house holding a young child, for permission to search the house. Graff readily gave consent. The police entered the house and discovered evidence of Matlock's involvement in a bank robbery.

Prior to trial, Matlock moved to suppress the evidence found inside the house. The trial court denied the motion, and Matlock was convicted at trial. On appeal the Supreme Court held that "when the prosecution seeks to justify a warrantless search by proof of voluntary consent, it is not limited to proof that consent was given by the defendant but may show that permission to search was obtained from a third party who possessed common authority over or other sufficient relationship to the premises or effects sought to be inspected." In a footnote the Court elaborated on the concept of common authority and how it related to third-party consent:

> Common authority is, of course, not to be implied from the mere property inter-est a third party has in the property. The authority which justifies the third-party consent does not rest upon the law of property . . . but rests rather on mutual use of the property by persons generally having joint access or control for most purposes, so that it is reasonable to recognize that any of the co-inhabitants has the right to permit the inspection in his own right and that the others have assumed the risk that one of their number might permit the common area to be searched.

By sharing control of the premises with Graff, Matlock ran the risk that she might allow a search of the common area. Matlock therefore did not have a rea-sonable expectation of privacy that would make a search by the police pursuant to Graff's consent unconstitutional.

In 1990 not only did the Supreme Court reiterate its *Matlock* analysis, but it also expanded the scope of third-party consent to include individuals who had apparent authority to consent. In *Illinois v. Rodriguez* (497 U.S. 177 [1990]), the police responded to a call from Gail Fischer, who claimed that the defendant had assaulted her earlier that day in their apartment. The police officer accompanied her to the apartment. When they arrived she unlocked the door and gave the officers consent to enter. Upon entry the officers found Rodriguez sleeping in the bedroom, as well as drug paraphernalia. Rodriguez was arrested and charged with possession of a controlled substance with intent to deliver.

Following the arrest it was learned that Fischer did not live in the apartment, had taken the key without Rodriguez's permission, and was only an "infrequent visitor." As she did not have common authority to consent to the search, Rodri-guez moved to have the seized evidence precluded from trial, arguing that it was discovered pursuant to an unconstitutional warrantless search. The government countered that the search was not unconstitutional because the police officers reasonably believed that Fischer had common authority over the apartment.

The Supreme Court held that the search was constitutional and that police need only have a reasonable belief that a consenting third party has the au-thority to consent to a search over the premises. The Court based its holding on the concept that the Fourth Amendment does not prohibit searches con-ducted against an occupant's desires but instead prohibits only "unreasonable" searches. Thus, if police incorrectly believe a third party has common authority to consent, they may still search the premises without a warrant so long as their belief is a reasonable one.

In the aftermath of *Matlock* and *Rodriguez*, it was accepted by lower courts that a search based on the consent of a third party with common authority or apparent authority over the premises was permissible. That being said, the Supreme Court had yet to address a situation where a third party consents to a warrantless search but a co-occupant, having equal authority over the property and being present at the time of the search, objects to the search. Such incidents were considered by a number of lower courts with mixed results. While a majority of courts found that the consent was effective and permitted the warrantless search, other courts found the rights of the person objecting to the search were paramount, thereby overriding the co-occupant's consent. In *Georgia v. Randolph* the Supreme Court squarely took up and ruled on the issue.

THE CASE OF *GEORGIA V. RANDOLPH* (2006)

The Facts

According to *Georgia v. Randolph* (547 U.S. 103 [2006]), Scott Randolph and his wife, Janet, had a history of marital problems. In May 2001, the couple separated, with Janet taking their son and some belongings from their Americus, Georgia, home and moving in with her parents in Canada. Several months later Janet and their child returned to the Georgia house (for unknown reasons).

On the morning of July 6, Janet complained to the local police that her husband had absconded with their son following a domestic dispute. When law-enforcement officers reached the Randolph residence, Janet told them that the couple was having marital problems, that they were separated, and that her husband, Scott, was a cocaine user. Soon thereafter, Scott returned to the house. He explained that he had taken their son to a neighbor's house out of concern that his wife might take their son out of the country again. He also denied using cocaine and claimed that it was his wife who abused drugs and alcohol.

While this conversation was occurring, one of the officers, Sergeant Murray, went with Janet Randolph to reclaim the child. Upon returning to the house she repeated her complaints about her husband Scott's drug use and told the police that there was evidence of his drug use in the house. Sergeant Murray asked Scott Randolph, who was standing at the door to the house, for permission to search the residence. Scott "unequivocally refused" to grant consent. Sergeant Murray turned to Janet Randolph for consent to search, which she readily granted. Janet led the sergeant to an upstairs bedroom. Inside the bedroom Sergeant Murray found a drinking straw with a powdery residue that appeared to be cocaine. After this discovery, Sergeant Murray left the house to get an evidence bag from his car. When he returned to the house, Janet Randolph withdrew her consent. The police proceeded to place the straw into evidence, and obtain a search warrant to search the residence. The ensuing warrant-based search revealed additional evidence of drug use. Based on this evidence, Scott Randolph was indicted for possession of cocaine.

Randolph moved to suppress the evidence of drug use as the product of a warrantless search following refusal to consent. The trial court denied the motion, ruling that Janet Randolph had common authority to consent to the search of their joint residence. The trial court's ruling was reversed by the Georgia Court of Appeals on the grounds that Scott's express refusal to grant consent rendered the search unreasonable and in violation of the Fourth Amendment. The Georgia Supreme Court affirmed the court of appeals, and the United States Supreme Court granted certiorari.

The Issue before the Court

Is a search based on the consent of one occupant of a jointly occupied dwelling constitutional when another co-occupant, who is physically present at the time consent is requested, expressly refuses to grant consent to a search?

The Court's Holding

In a five-to-three decision (Justice Alito did not participate in the case) the Supreme Court held that when both co-occupants of a home are both present, a refusal by one of the occupants renders a search based on the consent of the other occupant unreasonable and in violation of the Fourth Amendment.

The Majority Opinion

Justice David Souter wrote the majority opinion. He began his analysis by briefly discussing the history of third-party-consent cases. The majority acknowledged that voluntary consent to a search of a resident's home can make a warrantless search reasonable under the Fourth Amendment and that this consent may come from either the suspect himself or, when the suspect is not present, a fellow resident who shares common authority over property. In discussing the holding in *Matlock*, that a co-occupant with common authority over the property may permit a warrantless search to the detriment of other absent co-occupants, the Court observed that the Supreme Court had yet to consider a case where one co-occupant consented to a search while another physically present occupant objected. Thus, the Court found that "the significance of such a refusal turns on the underpinnings of the co-occupant consent rule, as recognized since *Matlock.*"

Justice Souter then considered the meaning and significance of the "common authority" necessary under Matlock to justify a warrantless search. The majority explained that the "common authority" that allows a co-occupant to consent to a search does not stem solely from property rights but rather from "mutual use," "joint access," and "control for most purposes." The majority explained that a co-occupant's "common authority" to consent to a search comes from a social understanding about the rights an occupant has over a shared residence. The court reasoned that a joint occupant's consent makes a warrantless search reasonable provided that "widely shared social expectations" indicate that the joint occupant has the authority to give consent. As such, the Court found that the objective reasonableness of a search under *Matlock* "is in significant part a function of commonly held understanding[s] about the authority that co-inhabitants may exercise in ways that affect each other's interests."

The majority used the facts from *Matlock* to illustrate how an analysis under the "widely shared social expectations" standard would operate. The Court reasoned that when a person like Gayle Graff comes to the door of a residence holding a child, it is reasonable to expect her to be able to invite visitors into the house. The "widely shared social expectation" is that if she lives there, she has the common authority to allow visitors like most typical tenant arrangements usually allow. The Court went on to reason that if one resident is absent, it is commonly understood that the other tenant has the authority to admit guests whom the absent resident may not like.

Justice Souter distinguished the facts at hand in *Randolph* to those in *Matlock*. The Court emphasized that in *Matlock* the defendant was not present at the house when consent was requested. In *Randolph*, both occupants of the home were present and simultaneously addressed the request for consent. In such a event, where both tenants are present and one objects to a visitor entering the home, a visitor would not feel comfortable entering because there is no common understanding that one co-occupant's invitation prevails over another occupant's refusal to permit entry. Therefore, the majority concluded that no "widely shared social expectation" indicates that one co-occupant has the authority to permit visitors to enter over another occupant's objections.

After articulating the standard to be applied and finding that a Fourth Amendment violation took place, the majority opinion addressed several items raised in the dissents. To begin with, it discussed the potential impact that its decision may have on future investigations. Recognizing the competing interests of exposing criminal activities while at the same time, respecting the Fourth Amendment, the Court noted several ways that both interests may be protected in the future. The Court explained that nothing in its decision prevents future co-occupants from bringing evidence of crime directly to the police without the need for a warrantless search, and law enforcement may still act upon information provided by a co-occupant to obtain a search warrant, regardless of whether another co-occupant objects. Next in response to a concern raised in Chief Justice Roberts's dissent, Justice Souter asserted that the decision would have "no bearing on the capacity of the police to protect domestic victims" since police are always permitted to enter a home without a warrant whenever there is reason to believe that a threat of domestic violence exists.

At the end of the majority opinion, Justice Souter addressed what he viewed as "two loose ends" created by the Court's opinion. First, he addressed the language of *Matlock*, which stated that a co-occupant of shared property possesses the right to consent to a search, therefore making reliance on the co-occupant's consent by law enforcement reasonable. Justice Souter stated that even though the co-occupant may possess "his own right" to authorize warrantless police entry, the right is not superior to the competing and equal right of the other co-occupants to refuse to consent.

The second loose end addressed by the majority concerned the significance of *Matlock* and *Rodriguez* after its decision. The majority acknowledged that in *Matlock* and *Rodriguez* the defendants did not have the opportunity to object because, although they were nearby, they were not physically present at the time the search commenced. The loose end was whether police must seek out other nearby potentially objecting co-occupants in order to perform a warrantless search when they already have the consent of one co-occupant. To resolve this concern, the majority stated that there is no requirement that law enforcement proactively seek the approval of any absent, or even nearby, co-occupant prior to conducting a warrantless search based upon the consent of a present co-occupant. Rather, in order to overcome a co-occupant's consent to a warrantless search, a defendant must be physically present and objecting to the search. Moreover, the Court stated that if the defendant was in another room or asleep on the couch then he would be considered absent and would not be able to object to the search. The Court summed up its conclusion as follows: "So long as there is no evidence that the police have removed the potentially objecting tenant from the entrance for the sake of avoiding a possible objection, there is practical value in the simple clarity of complementary rules, one recognizing the cotenant's permission when there is no fellow occupant on hand, the other according dispositive weight to the fellow occupant's contrary indication when he expresses it."

The majority opinion closed with the Court acknowledging it established a formalistic rule. Such a rule however is necessary to strike the balance between the need of law enforcement to conduct warrantless searches based on consent and the rights of an objecting cotenant to be secure in his home.

The Concurring Opinions

Justice Stevens and Justice Breyer wrote concurring opinions. Justice Stevens argued that the Court's opinion validates his view that the Court should not focus solely on the original understanding of constitutional amendments and ignore the "relevance of changes in our society." Justice Stevens observed that when the Fourth Amendment was adopted, a husband would have had superior authority over premises than his wife; therefore, his consent would be all that mattered. Accordingly, if the Court followed an original understanding of the Fourth Amendment, an arbitrary, blatantly discriminatory result may prevail.

In his concurring opinion Justice Breyer noted his agreement with the majority's conclusion but articulated his own view on how that conclusion should have been reached. Rather than imposing a bright-line rule that focused on the reasonableness of the officer's actions in conducting a warrantless search, Justice Breyer endorsed a more fact-specific approach, based on consideration of the totality of circumstances. The facts and circumstances present in *Randolph* rendered the search unreasonable. The circumstances leading to this conclusion were that the search was solely for obtaining evidence rather than preventing an ongoing crime, that the objecting party was present, that there were no exigent circumstances, and that the house could have been secured while a warrant was obtained. Under these circumstances, Justice Breyer found the search to be unreasonable.

The Dissenting Opinions

In his first written dissent since joining the Supreme Court, Chief Justice Roberts, joined by Justice Scalia, emphatically disagreed with the majority. Chief Justice Roberts argued lack of justification for evaluating *Randolph* differently from earlier third-party consent cases. He contended that the facts in *Randolph* were not dissimilar to those of *Matlock* and *Rodriguez* and that therefore the outcomes should have been the same. The dissent stressed that Fourth Amendment jurisprudence could not support such an arbitrary standard that would protect the owner who happens to be present to refuse consent, while denying the right to refuse consent to the owner sleeping in the next room or sitting in a squad car in front of the house. The dissent argued that the rule laid out by the majority leaves a person's rights under the Fourth Amendment subject to mere luck and chance that they will be present when consent is asked of a co-occupant.

Instead of the standard adopted by the majority, Chief Justice Roberts argued the Court should adopt the standards used in *Matlock* and *Rodriguez*, which upheld the constitutionality of warrantless searches conducted pursuant to third-party consent because an individual "assumes the risk that those who have access and control over his shared property might consent to a search." A person who shares a residence with another has a limited expectation of privacy due to the co-occupant's ability and authority to grant the police entry in his or her own right. Based on a limited expectation of privacy, a warrantless search was constitutional if it was conducted pursuant to the voluntary consent of one occupant despite the objection of a present co-occupant.

Justices Scalia and Thomas each wrote separate dissents. Justice Scalia's dissent dealt less with the issue presented to the Court than with the refutation of Justice Stevens's attack on interpreting the Constitution based on its original intent. On the other hand, Justice Thomas dissented to opine that the Court considered the wrong issues and standards in reaching its decision.

In his dissenting opinion, Justice Thomas asserted that *Coolidge v. New Hampshire* (403 U.S. 443 [1971]) "squarely controls this case." In *Coolidge*, police officers questioned the wife of a defendant as part of a homicide investigation. The wife invited the officers into the home and permitted them to conduct a search, during which they discovered guns and clothing belonging to Mr. Coolidge. In affirming Coolidge's conviction, the Supreme Court held that "when a citizen leads police officers into a home shared with her spouse to show them evidence, that citizen is not acting as an agent of the police, and thus no Fourth Amendment search has occurred." Justice Thomas argued that the facts in *Randolph* are indistinguishable from *Coolidge*. Since Janet Randolph was not acting as an agent of the officers, no Fourth Amendment search ever occurred, and the trial court's initial denial of the motion to suppress was correct.

Further Analysis and Significance of the Case

Nearly all Fourth Amendment decisions involve the critical balance between the privacy rights of citizens and the ability of law enforcement to effectively promote public safety. Justice Souter and the other members of the *Randolph* majority based the majority opinion on three underlying premises: First, a search based on the consent of a person with common authority over shared premises is reasonable. Second, law-enforcement officers are well equipped and not unduly burdened in obtaining a search warrant when necessary. Third, a person assumes the risk that a co-occupant will allow police to search a joint residence in his absence, but there can be no such assumption when he is present and objecting.

While these three premises were accepted by the majority, and in all likelihood to the dissenting justices to some degree, widespread consensus amongst the justices regarding how best to examine the situation presented in *Randolph* stopped there. In fact, as evidenced by the narrowness of the Court's holding, and the fact that six of the eight justices wrote separate opinions, the case bitterly divided the Court. As a result of this division, the majority opinion by Justice Souter was very fact-specific and limited in its breadth.

That being said, for the first time in over half a century, the Supreme Court decided a case involving third-party consent to expand privacy rights. As a result of the fractured Court and opinions, any expansion is likely limited in scope. The Court did announce a straightforward holding that attempted to limit the scope of consent-based searches in favor of protecting the refusing defendant's privacy. However, due to the case-specific nature of the opinion, its reach will be limited to cases in which the defendant is (1) physically present when consent is requested and (2) clearly denies permission for a search to take place.

The opinion's impact on law enforcement is likely to be limited. By holding that *United States v. Matlock* or *Illinois v. Rodriguez* were not being overruled, the Court indicated that police may obtain third-party consent from a co-occupant in cases where the defendant has been arrested by the police or is not physically present at the front door when consent is requested. Moreover, as noted by the Court, even after the denial of consent, the police had the ability to secure the premises and obtain a search warrant. Had there been an actual emergency or a basis to believe that evidence was being destroyed, entry into the home without a warrant or consent would have been reasonable and constitutionally allowed.

APPLICATION OF *GEORGIA V. RANDOLPH*

Despite the apparent clarity of its holding, *Randolph* left several issues unanswered. Since the opinion was announced in 2006, state and lower federal courts have addressed a number of these issues. As shown below, the vast majority of these courts have refused to expand the rule announced by *Randolph*.

Nature of Defendant's Refusal

Courts have held that a defendant must explicitly deny permission to search the premises to fall under the rubric of *Randolph*. Standing by silently without objecting while a search takes place is insufficient to prove the refusal of consent (*Commonwealth v. Ocasio*, 882 N.E.2d 341 [Mass. App. 2008]; *Commonwealth. v. Ware*, 913 N.E.2d 869 [Mass. App. 2009]).

Location of Refusing Defendant

A defendant must be physically present at the entryway. For example, in *United States v. Weston* (67 M.J. 390 [U.S. Armed Forces 2009]), the defendant and his wife were questioned in separate rooms at the provost marshal's office about improper eavesdropping being committed by the defendant in the home. When asked for consent to search the home, the defendant refused. Officials then asked the defendant's wife for permission to search their home. She readily granted consent. Inside the home the police found evidence incriminating the defendant. The defendant moved to suppress the evidence based on his refusal to give consent. On appeal from the defendant's conviction, the United States Court of Appeals for the Armed Forces affirmed his conviction. Applying a strict reading of *Randolph*, the court held that since he was not present at the home when he refused to give consent to the search, the subsequent search was reasonable based on his wife's consent.

Ignoring Potential Objectors

Police may ignore potential objectors who are not at the entryway when consent is obtained from a co-occupant. Once they receive consent from one joint occupant, so long as the other joint occupant is not present at the entryway, the police may search based on the former's consent (*State v. Ransom*, 212 P.3d 203 [Kan. 2009]; *State v. Starks*, 846 N.E.2d 673 [Ind. Ct. App. 2006]).

Burden of Proof

Courts that have considered the issues raised in *Randolph* have uniformly held that the defendant has the burden of providing actual evidence that a search in violation of the standards set forth in *Randolph* took place (*United States v. Parker*, 469 F.3d 1074 [7th Cir. 2006]; *United States v. McKerrell*, 491 F.3d 1221 [10th Cir. 2007]; *McClelland v. State*, 155 P.3d 1013 [Wyo. 2007]).

CONCLUSIONS

Georgia v. Randolph furnishes a classic example of a court struggling to find a balance between providing practical standards for police to follow in order to effectively perform their duties while protecting the privacy interests individuals have in their homes. In striking this balance the Court established a precedent based largely on case-specific facts. In so doing, the Court clarified under what situations third-party consent is sufficient for police to conduct a warrantless search. At the same time, it also provided a road map for police to follow in instances where co-occupants may disagree on whether to provide consent. If law-enforcement officers attempt to abuse the limiting language in *Randolph*, it is likely that the Court will be called on once again to provide further guidance in this complex area of criminal procedure.

FURTHER READING

Jack Ryan, "*Georgia v. Randolph*: Entries/Searches Based on Co-occupant Consent," *Legal & Liability Risk Management Institute, Legal Updates* (2007), www.llrmi.com/articles/legal_update/georgia-randolph.shtml.

Aaron Stanley, "The Continuing Evolution of Consent and Authority in Digital Search and Seizure," *Fordham Intellectual Property, Media & Entertainment Law Journal* 19 (2008): 179–211.

Matthew W. J. Webb, "Third-Party Consent Searches after Randolph: The Circuit Split over Police Removal of an Objecting Tenant," *Fordham Law Review* 77 (2009): 371–98.

Renee Williams, "Third Party Consent Searches after *Georgia v. Randolph*: Dueling Approaches to the Dueling Roommates," *Boston University Law Review* 87 (2007): 937–94.

VI

MOTOR VEHICLES

Carroll v. United States

ROLANDO V. DEL CARMEN

INTRODUCTION

For a long time, despite decades of motor-vehicle use and thousands of vehicle searches, the United States Supreme Court did not decide any major case involving motor vehicles and the Fourth Amendment. That changed in 1925 when the Court decided *Carroll v. United States* (267 U.S. 132 [1925]). In *Carroll* the Court held that the warrantless search of an automobile is valid if probable cause is present. This ushered in what is more popularly known in legal circles as the Carroll Doctrine. The decision was not a surprise because even at that time various exceptions to the warrant requirement under the Fourth Amendment had been carved out by the Court. *Carroll* is significant, however, because it established a rule in police work that remains intact even today. The rule is that warrantless searches of motor vehicles is constitutional as long as probable cause is present. The Carroll Doctrine is the legal bedrock for police manuals and court decisions that, on a daily basis, authorize warrantless searches of motor vehicles at any time as long as probable cause exists. Its application is a part of day-to-day policing, and officers apply it routinely. It has been an effective and convenient tool for law enforcement for a long time; it will likely stay that way for years and years to come.

THE CASE OF *CARROLL V. UNITED STATES* (1925)

The Facts

According to *Carroll v. United States* (267 U.S. 132 [1925]), in 1925, on a highway in Michigan between Grand Rapids and Detroit, George Carroll and

John Kiro were arrested for transporting intoxicating liquor (sixty-eight quarts of bonded whiskey and gin) in violation of the National Prohibition Act, more popularly known as the Volstead Act. They were driving from Grand Rapids to Detroit, Michigan. This area has an international boundary where illegal liquor at that time was routinely transported. Carroll had previous encounters with the police, twice in the four months prior to this incident. On a previous occasion, the officers tried to buy illegal liquor from Carroll, but he was alerted to their identity and did not produce the contraband. Shortly thereafter, the officers saw Carroll's car returning from Grand Rapids and bound for Detroit. The officers chased the vehicle, and both men in the car were later apprehended. Carroll and Kiro were ordered out of the car. No liquor was visible in the front seat of the car. Officers opened the rumble seat and looked under the cushions, again finding no liquor. One of the officers then struck the "lazyback" of the seat, tore open the seat cushion, and discovered sixty-eight bottles of gin and whiskey. Arrested, tried, and convicted, Carroll appealed his conviction saying his arrest and the subsequent seizure of the evidence (specifically one bottle of whiskey and one bottle of gin) were unlawful and therefore the confiscated liquor should not have been admitted as evidence at trial.

The Issue before the Court

Was the warrantless search of Carroll's car that led to the seizure of the evidence a violation of the Fourth Amendment?

The Court's Holding

Voting seven to two, the Court held that the warrantless search of Carroll's vehicle was constitutional because the officers had probable cause to believe that the vehicle contained contraband; therefore, the evidence obtained was admissible against Carroll during trial. The decision gave birth to the Carroll Doctrine, otherwise known as the "automobile exception" to the Fourth Amendment warrant requirement.

The Majority Opinion

The majority opinion of seven justices was written by Chief Justice Taft. First he reviewed previous decisions of the Court in search-and-seizure cases. Acknowledging the novelty of the issue that faced the Court, Chief Justice Taft affirmed that "in none of these cases cited is there any ruling as to the validity under the Fourth Amendment of a seizure without a warrant of contraband goods in the course of transportation." He went on to say that "on reason and authority the true rule is that if the search and seizure without a warrant are made upon probable cause—that is, upon a belief, reasonably arising out of circumstances known to the seizing officer, that an automobile or other vehicle contains that which by law is subject to seizure and destruction—the search and seizure are valid."

Chief Justice Taft reviewed the various laws that he said "made a difference as to the necessity for a search warrant between goods subject to forfeiture, when concealed in a dwelling house or similar place, and like goods in course of transportation and concealed in a movable vessel where they readily can be put out of reach of a search warrant." He concluded that since the "beginning of government" the United States has always recognized "a necessary difference between a search of a store, dwelling, house, or other structure in respect of which a proper official warrant readily may be obtained and a search of a ship, motor boat, wagon, or automobile for contraband goods, where it is not practical to secure a warrant, because the vehicle can be quickly moved out of the locality or jurisdiction in which the warrant must be sought." He added, "The measure of legality of such a seizure is, therefore, that the seizing officer shall have reasonable or probable cause for believing that the automobile which he stops and seizes has contraband liquor therein, which is being illegally transported." After analyzing previous cases, the Court concluded the following:

> In the light of these authorities, and what is shown by this record, it is clear the officer here had justification for the search and seizure. This is to say that the facts and circumstances within their knowledge and of which they had reasonably trustworthy information were sufficient in themselves to warrant a man of reasonable caution in the belief that intoxicating liquor was being transported in the automobile which they stopped and searched.

This concluding statement by Chief Justice Taft embodies the definition of probable cause, then and now. In sum, since there was probable cause and the vehicle could be quickly moved out of the locality, the warrantless search was constitutional and the evidence seized admissible at trial.

The Dissenting Opinion

The majority opinion drew a strong dissent from two justices—Justice McReynolds, with the concurrence of Justice Sutherland. Justice McReynolds started by saying that "the damnable character of the bootlegger's business should not close our eyes to the mischief which will surely follow any attempt to destroy it by unwarranted methods." He observed that the Volstead Act did not authorize the arrest or seizure of things based solely on mere suspicion. Thus the evidence seized, he said, must be suppressed.

The dissent did not specifically address the issue whether a warrantless seizure of things or items in a vehicle was unconstitutional. Instead, Justice McReynolds maintained that the Volstead Act "did not authorize arrest or seizure upon mere suspicion." On the other hand, he said, the "the whole history of the legislation indicates a fixed purpose not so to do." He added,

> The history and terms of the Volstead Act are not consistent with the suggestion that it was the purpose of Congress to grant the power here claimed for enforcement officers. The facts known when the arrest occurred were wholly insufficient to engender reasonable belief that plaintiffs in error were committing a misdemeanor, and the legality of the arrest cannot be supported by facts ascertained thorough the search which followed.

Justice McReynolds then asked, "If an officer, upon mere suspicion of a misdemeanor, may stop one on the public highway, take articles away from him, and thereafter use them as evidence to convict him of crime, what becomes of the Fourth and Fifth Amendments?" He concluded that in the absence of probable cause, the arrests and subsequent search and seizure was unconstitutional.

The majority and dissenting opinions differed sharply on two issues: (1) what the Volstead Act authorized and (2) whether probable cause existed at the time of the search. The majority said that the act authorized warrantless seizure; the dissent said it did not. The majority said probable cause was present; the dissent said the search was based on mere suspicion, not the higher requirement of probable cause. It is difficult to say how the dissent would have decided were the provisions of the Volstead Act so clear that even the dissent would have had to conclude that warrantless searches were authorized by the Volstead Act. Subsequent cases, however, adhered closely to the principle that warrantless searches of motor vehicles constitute an exception to the warrant requirement. Warrantless vehicle searches, with virtually no limitations, were the rule until recently when the Court drew an important boundary.

Case Significance

Although associated in police and legal circles with motor-vehicle stops and searches, the legal issue in *Carroll* focused solely on the legality of a vehicle search. It had nothing to do with motor-vehicle stops, which is also a function of day-to-day policing but governed by different rules. In legitimizing warrantless vehicle searches, *Carroll* enhanced the power of the police under the Fourth Amendment. Given the constant use of motor vehicles, then and now, something akin to the Carroll Doctrine was inevitable. It is hard to envision any police department that does not have definitive legal guidance on vehicle searches. It is just as difficult to imagine a modern society where search warrants are required every time a motor vehicle is searched. The Carroll Doctrine is a rule that evolved out of necessity and has held its own over time.

Carroll sets an important exception to the search-warrant requirement as long as probable cause is present. Thousands of police encounters with the public every day are defined by this rule. It is hard to imagine a Court decision in law enforcement that has had more impact on police work. The Court has barely looked back since; neither has the core of the Carroll Doctrine (warrantless arrests) been seriously eroded. The automobile exception is now well established; subsequent cases have accepted its basic principle while at the same time addressing other related issues. *Carroll* makes one principle absolute: warrantless searches of motor vehicles are constitutional and constitute an exception to the warrant requirement only if the searches and seizures are based on probable cause. Without probable cause, the case would have been decided differently. It is, of course, assumed that the vehicle is mobile.

In a later case, the Court said that the automobile exception to the warrant requirement is justified by five considerations (*Robbins v. California*, 453 U.S. 420 [1981]):

- the mobility of motor vehicles,
- a diminished expectation of privacy in a motor vehicle,
- the vehicle is used for transportation and not as a residence or repository of personal effects,
- the occupants of the motor vehicle travel in plain view,
- motor vehicles are necessarily highly regulated by the government.

Of these exceptions, only the mobility of motor vehicles was noted in *Carroll*. The others evolved out of subsequent cases that upheld the Carroll Doctrine.

Further Analysis

The Fourth Amendment to the Constitution provides that "the right of the people to be secure in their persons, houses, papers, and effects against unreasonable searches and seizures shall not be violated and no warrants shall issue but upon probable cause, supported by oath or affirmation and particularly describing the place to be searched and the persons or things to be seized."

The Fourth Amendment expressly prohibits "unreasonable searches and seizures." Determining what searches and seizures are reasonable or unreasonable is left to the courts, and ultimately to the United States Supreme Court on appeal. The issue in *Carroll*, as framed by the majority, was whether the warrantless seizures, authorized by a congressional act, were reasonable. The Taft Court first analyzed five cases decided by the Court prior to *Carroll*, concluding that "in none of the cases cited is there any ruling as to the validity under the Fourth Amendment of a seizure without a warrant of contraband goods in the course of transportation and subject to the forfeiture or destruction." It was a case of first impression for the Court on warrantless motor-vehicle searches.

The defendants in *Carroll* were charged with violating the provisions of the Volstead Act (section 25, title 2), which was enacted pursuant to the Eighteenth Amendment, which "makes it unlawful to have or possess any liquor intended for use in violating the act, or which has been so used." The act itself did not explicitly authorize the warrantless searches of motor vehicles, but after a review of its various provisions and amendments the majority concluded that "the intent of Congress to make a distinction between the necessity for a search warrant in the searching of private dwellings and in that of automobiles and other road vehicles in the enforcement of the Prohibition Act is thus clearly established by the legislative history."

The Court examined past and contemporary laws passed by Congress and concluded the following:

> Thus contemporaneously with the adoption of the Fourth Amendment we find in the First Congress, and in the following Second and Fourth Congresses, a difference made as to the necessity for a search warrant between goods subject to forfeiture, when concealed in a dwelling house or similar place, and like goods in course of transportation and concealed in a movable vessel where they readily could be out of reach of a search warrant.

These statutes, said the Court,

> show that the guaranty of freedom from unreasonable searches and seizures by the Fourth Amendment has been construed, practically since the beginning of the government, as recognizing a necessary difference between a search of a store, dwelling house, or other structure in respect of which a proper official warrant

readily may be obtained and a search of a ship, motor boat, wagon, or automobile for contraband goods, where it is not practical to secure a warrant, because the vehicle can be quickly moved out of the locality or jurisdiction in which the warrant must be sought.

As noted above, the ruling in *Carroll* required both (1) the presence of probable cause and (2) vehicle mobility. Probable cause was a major issue in the case and an issue over which the majority and the dissent differed. Vehicle mobility, however, was assumed by the majority and left unaddressed by the dissent. Subsequent Court decisions, however, make clear that mobility must be present for the Carroll Doctrine to apply.

THE CURRENT SCOPE OF POLICE AUTHORITY TO CONDUCT WARRANTLESS SEARCHES OF MOTOR VEHICLES

Over the many decades since 1925, the Court has upheld and expanded the power of the police to conduct warrantless searches of motor vehicles. Following are the most significant Court decisions since 1925:

Search of passenger compartments is valid: After the police have made a lawful custodial arrest of the occupant of a car, they may also search the car's entire passenger compartment (referring to the front and back seats) and open any container found therein (*New York v. Belton*, 453 U.S. 454 [1981]). This includes "closed or open glove compartment, consoles, or other receptacles located anywhere within the passenger compartment, as well as luggage, boxes, bags, clothing, and the like." *Belton* is important because it defines the extent of allowable searches inside a motor vehicle after a lawful arrest. It expanded the area of allowable search inside the car, including the back seat and not just the area near the driver. It also authorized the opening of containers found in the passenger compartment that may contain the object sought. Thus, under *Belton*, searches of the passenger compartment of the car are virtually unlimited. Note, however, that Belton was recently seriously eroded, although not explicitly overruled, in *Arizona v. Gant* (2009), a case discussed later in this chapter.

The extent of the warrantless search of the whole vehicle is broad: When making a valid vehicle search, the police may search the entire car and open the trunk and any packages or luggage found in the trunk that could reasonably contain the items for which they have probable cause to search (*United States v. Ross*, 456 U.S. 454 [1982]). In *Ross*, the Court said that in warrantless searches of a motor vehicle the officers may "search every part of the vehicle and its contents that may conceal the object of the search," adding that the extent of what can be searched is "defined by the object of the search and the places in which there is probable cause to believe that it may be found." *Ross* gives officers extensive authority when making a vehicle search; that authority is limited only by what is reasonable in light of the object of the search.

Passenger-compartment searches are valid even if the person was arrested outside the vehicle: Officers may search the passenger compartment of a vehicle after a lawful arrest even if the suspect was not in the vehicle when arrested (*Thornton v. United States*, 541 U.S. 615 [2004]). *Thornton* resolves the issue whether officers can search the vehicle if the area searched is not within their "immediate control" where the suspect can possibly destroy evidence or endanger officer safety. The Court used this standard: "So long as an arrestee is the sort of 'recent occupant' of a vehicle . . . officers may search that vehicle incident to the arrest." *Thornton* stretches out the traditional concept of the "area of immediate control," which justifies vehicle or nonvehicle searches. It moves this area much farther away from where the suspect might be able to destroy evidence or grab a weapon. *Thornton*, however, was also modified recently in *Arizona v. Gant* (2009), discussed later in this chapter.

Search of a vehicle based solely on probable cause to search a container in the vehicle is valid: The police may search a container located in a car without a search warrant even though they lack probable cause to search the car as a whole and have probable cause to believe only that the container itself contains contraband or evidence (*California v. Acevedo*, 500 U.S. 565 [1991]). In some cases, officers have probable cause to search a container in a car but lack probable cause to search the car itself. The Court resolved this issue in *Acevedo*, saying, "We . . . interpret *Carroll* as providing one rule to govern all automobile searches. The police may search an automobile and the container therein within it where they have probable cause to believe contraband or evidence is contained." *Acevedo* (probable cause for the container but not for the car) is the opposite of *Ross* (probable cause for the car but not for the container). In both cases, however, the search is valid.

A warrantless search is valid even if officers have time to obtain a warrant: The police may conduct a warrantless search of a vehicle even if there is time to obtain a warrant (*Chambers v. Maroney*, 399 U.S. 42 [1970]). This resolves the issue as to whether the automobile exception is based on the presence of exigent (meaning *emergency*) circumstances or is a separate exception in itself. The "exigent circumstances exception" to the warrant requirement provides that warrantless searches and seizures are valid if exigent circumstances exists that make obtaining a warrant impractical, useless, dangerous, or unnecessary. The Court stresses that the automobile exception is not based on exigent circumstances but instead is an exception on its own.

Searches of motor homes without a warrant is valid: Motor homes are vehicles for purposes of the Fourth Amendment and may be searched without a warrant (*California v. Carney*, 471 U.S. 386 [1985]). The Court in *Carney* noted, however, that the holding did not resolve the issue whether the automobile exception applies to a motor home that is "situated in a way or place that objectively indicates that it is being used as a residence." In such cases, the vehicle must be treated as a residence and not subject to the automobile exception.

A warrantless search is valid even if vehicle is immobilized: A vehicle may be searched without a warrant under the Carroll Doctrine even if it has been immobilized and released to the custody of the police (*Florida v. Myers*, 466 U.S. 380 [1984]). *Myers* reaffirms the principle that the Carroll Doctrine is not based on the presence of exigent circumstances; instead it is a separate exception and has a life of its own completely separate from exigent circumstances.

Warrantless seizure of a vehicle from a public place is valid: No warrant is needed for the seizure of a vehicle from a public place if officers have probable cause to believe it is forfeitable contraband (as when the vehicle itself is subject to forfeiture under state law because of its being used in drug traffic [*Florida v. White*, 526 U.S. 23 (1999)]). In *White*, the Court added that "because the police seized respondent's vehicle from a public area—respondent's employer's parking lot—the warrantless seizure also did not involve any invasion of respondent's privacy."

Dog sniffs after a traffic stop are valid: Dog sniffs conducted during a valid traffic stop are constitutional (*Illinois v. Caballes*, 543 U.S. 405 [2000]). In *Caballes*, the Court said that the use of dogs in the absence of "specific and articulable facts to suggest drug activity" did not change the character of a traffic stop that was otherwise lawful. The Court added that no privacy right was violated because "the dog sniff was performed on the exterior of respondent's car while he was lawfully seized for a traffic violation." In essence, if the stop of a motor vehicle is valid, the use of dogs to sniff the car for drugs is also valid even if the reason for the stop is not drug-related. This is because dog sniffs of the outside of motor vehicles are not protected by the Fourth Amendment and are therefore in the category of searches done in open fields.

Officers have unlimited authority to conduct warrantless border searches of vehicles: Government authority to conduct suspicionless and warrantless border searches is virtually without limits. It includes the authority to remove, disassemble, and reassemble a vehicle's fuel tank (*United States v. Flores-Montano*, 541 U.S. 149 [2004]). Officers have even wider authority in immigration and border searches of vehicles, whether the owner or driver is a citizen or not. This case holds that there is no need for suspicion or probable cause to search a vehicle in immigration borders. The extent of allowable search is limited only by reasonableness, meaning that the container searched might reasonably hold the object of the search. In drug or contraband cases, this includes just about every part or container of a motor vehicle. It is no exaggeration to state that the sky is the limit in this type of search.

Searches of vehicles after an arrest need not be contemporaneous: It is not required that a vehicle search occur immediately or soon after there is probable cause to believe a violation has occurred (*United States v. Johns*, 469 U.S. 478 [1985]). In *Johns*, the search was conducted three days after the officers placed the vehicles in a government warehouse after sealed packages, believed to contain marijuana, had been removed. The Court held that a three-day delay before making the search is permissible. The search, however, must be done within a reasonable time. The Court did not specify how much time is deemed reasonable; instead it said that the burden of proving unreasonableness is on the defendant, not the police.

To summarize, in all of the above cases, the power of law-enforcement officers to conduct warrantless searches was broadened. Prior to 2009, the Court refused to limit the power of the police in vehicle searches. Court decisions were consistently in the direction of expanding law-enforcement power and facilitating vehicle searches. That trajectory came to an end in April of 2009 when the Court decided *Arizona v. Gant*, No. 07-542 (2009). We now turn to this case, which represents the first time the Court has significantly limited the power of the police in warrantless vehicle searches.

ARIZONA V. GANT (2009): THE COURT SETS LIMITS ON WARRANTLESS VEHICLE SEARCHES

In a recent case, decided on April 21, 2009, the Court, for the first time since 1925, imposed a significant limitation on what the police can do in vehicle searches. As noted above, *New York v. Belton*, decided in 1981, held that after the police make a lawful arrest of the occupant of a car they may search the car's entire passenger compartment and open any container found during that search.

The Court set no limits on the search of the entire passenger compartment. That is no longer the rule.

In *Arizona v. Gant* (No. 07-542 [2009]), the Court held that the arresting officer can validly conduct warrantless search of the passenger compartment of a motor vehicle only if either of these circumstances is present: (1) if weapons are potentially within reach of the suspect or (2) if there is reason to believe that the car contains evidence that may be related to the arrest. Absent either of these, the police must obtain a warrant. Although the Court did not explicitly say it, *Gant*, in effect, overrules *New York v. Belton* and is a significant case.

The facts in *Gant* are clear and undisputed: Gant was arrested by the police because he drove on a suspended license. Immediately upon arrest, he was handcuffed and locked in the police patrol car. The police then searched Gant's car and found cocaine in a jacket pocket. He was tried and convicted of drug offenses. On appeal, Gant maintained that the search that led to the discovery of the cocaine was illegal because the police had no warrant. The Arizona trial court denied his motion to suppress the evidence, but the Arizona Supreme Court reversed, saying that the search was illegal because officers could not conduct a warrantless search of the vehicle once the scene had been secured, as it was in this case.

On appeal, the Court ruled that "police may search the passenger compartment of a vehicle incident to a recent occupant's arrest only if it is reasonable to believe that the arrestee might access the vehicle at the time of the search or that the vehicle contains evidence of the offense of arrest." The Court said that *Gant* differed from *Belton* in that Belton involved a single officer who had four unsecured arrestees, whereas in *Gant*, five police officers had handcuffed Gant and two other suspects before the search began. Under the circumstances of this case, there was no way Gant could have accessed his car to get a weapon or destroy evidence. A second crucial difference is that in *Belton* the suspect was arrested for a drug offense, whereas the arrest in *Gant* was for a traffic violation. There was no reasonable probability that the officers in *Gant* could have obtained any evidence related to driving without a license, whereas in *Belton* it was reasonable to assume that the search could have yielded drugs.

Gant curtails the authority of officers to conduct warrantless searches of the passenger compartment of a vehicle. Once the arrestee is handcuffed or secured, the authority to conduct warrantless searches no longer exists. Since most arrests for other than traffic offenses usually result in the offender being handcuffed, the authority to conduct a further search either for officer safety or destruction of evidence is no longer warranted. The second condition set by the Court is just as restrictive: the search must be related to the offense for which the suspect was arrested. For example, if the arrest is made for robbery or murder, a contemporaneous warrantless vehicle search is justified because it is reasonable to assume that evidence of the robbery or murder might be found during the search. But if the arrest is for failure to heed a stop sign, there is no justification for further vehicle search unless there is reason to suspect that failure to stop is somehow related to an alcohol or drug offense. Note, however, that this rule applies only to searches without a warrant; searches with a warrant are governed by the reasonableness rule. It is still valid for the officer to look around the car and confiscate items that are in plain view because that falls under a different rule. What officers cannot now do because of *Gant* is conduct an automatic warrantless search of the passenger compartment of a car immediately after an arrest. They were authorized to do this for a long time under *New York v. Belton* (1981).

The effect of *Gant* on searches of car trunks and containers in the trunk (authorized in *Ross v. United States* [1982]) has yet to be determined. It may be that the same twin standards of "officer protection" and "relatedness to the offense" will also be required in car-trunk and trunk-container cases. The *Gant* decision will doubtless be subjected to further scrutiny and refinement by the Court in the days ahead, particularly because of its close five-to-four vote and far-reaching effect. A change in the Court's composition might have an immediate effect on how a similar issue in the near future will be decided. In the meantime, unless *Gant* is overturned, the days of unlimited police searches of the insides of and containers of a vehicle are probably over.

DESPITE *GANT*, THE CARROLL DOCTRINE REMAINS INTACT

Gant sets boundaries but does not repudiate the automobile exception. Given the reality of an ever-growing increase in vehicular traffic in the United States and other countries, the automobile exception is perhaps an inevitable and necessary rule. Without it law enforcement becomes even more challenging. The Carroll Doctrine was promulgated in 1925, but its requirements of probable cause and mobility have remained constant. The absence of probable cause renders the search invalid unless voluntary consent is obtained. On the other hand, probable cause alone does not automatically validate the warrantless vehicle search; the vehicle must also be mobile, meaning that the vehicle can be driven away at any time, as determined by the standard of reasonableness. If a motor vehicle has been converted into an immobile residence, however, the Carroll Doctrine does not apply and a warrant is needed for a valid search. Despite *Gant*, border searches of vehicles remain unrestrained and will likely stay that way in the interest of national security.

There are only a few major Court decisions in criminal procedure and criminal justice that have lasted for so long without any major revision. *Carroll v. United States* is among the few cases that have withstood the assault of time and change. Given the ruling's longevity and because of subsequent expansion of police authority, a valid question arises: Has the Carroll Doctrine gone too far? Has the Court veered too far in the direction of expedient law enforcement at the expense of individual rights?

Over the years, there has not been any cascade of scholarly articles against the rule, nor is there any evidence of pervasive public outcry about intrusiveness into individual privacy.

An interesting article by Carol A. Chase, however—"Privacy Takes a Back Seat: Putting the Automobile Exception Back on Track after Several Wrong Turns"—features interesting observations of the motor-vehicle exception.[1] The article's main thrust is that the Carroll Doctrine may have taken several "wrong turns" along the way and gone too far. The author, a law professor and former assistant U.S. attorney, criticizes the current Carroll Doctrine as follows:[2]

1. "The original justification for the automobile exception has lost much of its force in light of changing technologies." The author maintains that because of technological developments, "telephonic search warrants can be obtained both federally and in a growing number of states." This speeds up the process of warrant issuance ("search warrants may be obtained in less than an hour"), thus the inconvenience and delay rationale used by the Court when *Carroll* was decided in 1925 is no longer valid.
2. "The 'reduced expectation of privacy' rationale does not justify warrantless searches of the entire automobile and all containers therein." The author opines that factors that allegedly diminish privacy expectations (public places, government inspections, regulating who can obtain a driver's license, and car registration) are inconsequential and do not justify privacy diminution.
3. "The automobile exception has fostered abusive police practices." The author says that the warrantless search of a vehicle has facilitated the abuse of power by the police in that "it permits the police to search an automobile merely because the persons targeted by the police—including those targeted because of

their race or for other improper reasons—are in an automobile. The absence of review as to the presence of probable cause "opens the door to abuse."

The article proposes that the "automobile exception to the warrant requirement be recast in order to preserve both the warrant requirement and the attending judicial review of probable cause whenever it would be practicable to do so." Despite these critical observations, however, no evidence supports widespread judicial or public dissatisfaction with the Carroll Doctrine. Thus, while the Carroll Doctrine may need further refinement, it may be a long time before the recommendations suggested by the author gain judicial or public support. There appears to be resigned acceptance of the automobile exception, supported perhaps by the awareness that it is difficult to fashion a viable rule that balances individual rights in a public place with the need for efficient and effective law enforcement in a society teeming daily with millions of motor vehicles.

CONCLUSIONS

The Carroll Doctrine did not raise much controversy when first promulgated more than eight decades ago. Subsequent Courts have consistently affirmed the rule. The automobile exception has gained even more importance and utility over the years because of the exponential increase in the number and use of motor vehicles. Add to that the ever-present problems of drugs and other forms of transportable contraband, and the result becomes a high-stakes clash of constitutional rights and governmental authority under the Fourth Amendment. The automobile exception is not about to change in the immediate future despite claims of abusive intrusion into people's right to privacy and its susceptibility to police abuse. In the minds of the judiciary and the public, the reality that an individual in a mobile vehicle can drive away at any time provides compelling justification to exempt motor vehicles from the full protection of the Fourth Amendment. On a pragmatic level, it is hard to imagine how much more difficult this aspect of law enforcement would have been had the Court decided *Carroll* differently. Then, as now, the automobile exception is grounded on the need for more expedient law enforcement. Nonetheless, the Court has recently manifested second thoughts and has ruled that the Carroll Doctrine, after all, has limits. It will be interesting to see what other constraints, if any, the Court will impose in the future on a practice that has long been a convenient and enduring tool for law enforcement.

FURTHER READING

Carol A. Chase, "Privacy Takes a Back Seat: Putting the Automobile Exception Back on Track after Several Wrong Turns," *Boston College Law Journal* 41 (1999), www.bc.ed/bc_org/avp/law/lwsch/journals/bclawr/41_1/02_TXT.htm.

Kendra Hillman Chilcoat, "The Automobile Exception Swallows the Rule: *Florida v. White,*" *Journal of Criminal Law and Criminology* (Spring 2000), at http://findarticles.com/p/articles/mi_hb6700/is_3_90/ai_n28810814/.

Clare Cushman, *The Supreme Court Justices: Illustrated Biographies, 1789–1993* (Washington, D.C.: Congressional Quarterly, 1993).

Rolando V. del Carmen, "Motor Vehicle Stops, Searches, and Inventories," in *Criminal Procedure: Law and Practice* (Belmont, Calif.: Wadsworth/Cengage Learning, 2010).

Wayne R. LaFave, "'The Routine Traffic Stop' from Start to Finish: Too Much 'Routine,' Not Enough Fourth Amendment," 2 *Michigan Law Review* 2 (2004): 1843–1905.

Susan E. McPherson, "Constitutional Law: Fourth Amendment; Warrantless Arrest for Misdemeanor Traffic Violation Does Not Violate Fourth Amendment Protection against Unreasonable Seizure," *Cumberland Law Review* 32 (2002): 265–94.

M. I. Urofsky, *Biographical Encyclopedia of the Supreme Court: The Lives and Legal Philosophies of the Justices* (Washington, D.C.: CQ Press, a division of Congressional Quarterly, Inc., 2006).

United States v. Ross

DAVID BRODY

INTRODUCTION

The Fourth Amendment to the Constitution prohibits unreasonable searches and seizures. In considering what constitutes a reasonable search one must balance the competing interests of the privacy rights of individuals against the government's need to investigate crimes and enforce the criminal law. While the Supreme Court has repeatedly stated the preference that a warrant be obtained prior to a search or seizure, it has established several specific exceptions to this preference.

As discussed in the previous chapter, it has been nearly a century since the Supreme Court established the automobile exception to the warrant requirement (*Carroll v. United States*, 267 U.S. 132 [1925]). Since *Carroll*, the Court has been asked to consider a number of nuances related to searches of automobiles. One such area involves the ability of police to search containers located within an automobile. Over the last several decades the Court has wrestled with how to treat such containers. In *United States v. Ross* (456 U.S. 798 [1982]), the Supreme Court broke from precedent and established a bright-line rule for when a container may be opened and searched without a warrant. In establishing this bright-line rule the Supreme Court shifted the balance significantly in favor of law enforcement and opened the door to decreasing the protections provided citizens under the Fourth Amendment.

THE AUTOMOBILE EXCEPTION

As noted above, the automobile exception to the warrant requirement was established by the Supreme Court in *Carroll v. United States*. In *Carroll*, federal agents had probable cause to believe that an automobile being driven by known bootleggers was carrying contraband liquor. After stopping the car the agents conducted a warrantless search of the vehicle's interior. The agents found that the filling had been removed from the seats and been replaced by dozens of bottles of illegal alcoholic beverages. After being convicted of violating the National Prohibition Act, the defendants appealed on the grounds that the warrantless search and seizure of the automobile violated the Fourth Amendment.

The Supreme Court held that if law-enforcement agents have probable cause to believe an automobile contains contraband, they may stop, search, and seize the vehicle without a warrant. This exception to the warrant requirement was considered necessary due to the inherent mobility of automobiles and the fact that they are unlikely to remain in one place while police seek a warrant.

The automobile exception was expanded by the case of *Chambers v. Maroney* (399 U.S. 42 [1970]). The police stopped a vehicle and arrested the occupants, who matched a description of the suspects in a gas-station robbery. The car was seized without a warrant and taken to the police station where the police conducted a warrantless search, during which they found guns and other evidence linked to the robbery. At trial, Chambers was found guilty. Following his conviction, Chambers filed a petition for a writ of habeas corpus on the grounds that the search of the vehicle violated the Fourth Amendment. On appeal from the denial of the petition, the Supreme Court held that so long as there is probable cause that contraband or evidence related to a crime is present, police may conduct a warrantless search of an automobile that is securely in police custody. The Court based its holding on the fact that so long as probable cause exists, there is no difference between the police seizing and holding a car while a warrant is obtained and searching a previously seized car without a warrant. The Court found the only difference between *Carroll* and *Chambers* was the location of the search. As the same rights are implicated, the cases should be decided similarly; therefore, the search at the police station is permissible under the automobile exception.

SEARCHES OF CONTAINERS WITHIN AUTOMOBILES

While *Carroll* and *Chambers* established that automobiles may be stopped and searched without a warrant if probable cause exists, the cases did not address the constitutionality of the search and seizure of items and containers located inside the vehicle. The Court addressed this issue for the first time in the 1977 case of *United States v. Chadwick* (433 U.S. 1 [1977]). In *Chadwick*, federal agents had probable cause to believe that that two people were carrying marijuana in a footlocker on a train bound for Boston. Chadwick met the train at the station and helped two men place the footlocker in the trunk of Chadwick's car. Before the car was started and while the trunk was still open, federal agents arrested the three men. The agents took the footlocker from the car and moved it to a secure location. Over an hour later the agents unlocked the footlocker and opened it without obtaining a search warrant. Inside the footlocker they discovered a large amount of marijuana. The district court granted the defendants' motion to suppress the evidence taken from the warrantless search of the footlocker.

The Supreme Court agreed, finding the search of the footlocker to be unconstitutional. The government did not contend that the footlocker's brief contact with the car's truck placed it within the automobile exception to the warrant requirement. Rather, the government argued that luggage, which can be moved with ease, should be treated the same as automobiles and similarly not require a warrant be obtained before it is searched. The Court disagreed, holding that items such as luggage, while easily movable, are not inherently mobile in the same fashion an automobile is. Additionally, since cars are used for transportation and not for the holding of personal effects, must be registered with the state, and are subject to licensing and safety requirements, there is a lower expectation of privacy in automobiles. Luggage and footlockers on the other hand, are designed to hold personal items. As such, the Court reaffirmed the general principle that closed containers may not be searched without a warrant.

In *Arkansas v. Sanders* (442 U.S. 753 [1979]) the police received reliable information that Sanders would arrive at a local airport carrying a green suitcase full of marijuana. Sanders was met at the airport by a companion who placed the suitcase in the trunk of a taxi. Police officers stopped the cab after several blocks and instructed the driver to open the trunk. Without obtaining a search warrant, the officers searched the defendant's suitcase, which contained several pounds of marijuana. The trial court denied Sanders's motion to suppress the evidence based on the warrantless search, and he was convicted of possession of marijuana with intent to deliver. The Arkansas Supreme Court reversed the trial court on the basis of *Chadwick*.

The United States Supreme Court affirmed. The Court held that absent exigent circumstances, the police must obtain a warrant before searching any luggage taken from an automobile even when the vehicle itself is legitimately searched pursuant to the *Carroll* criteria. The Court held that the fact that luggage is placed inside a car does not change the nature of the privacy interests maintained by the owner. Accordingly, the Court refused to broaden the scope of the automobile exception to include luggage found within a vehicle.

In *Robbins v. California* (453 U.S. 420 [1981]) police lawfully stopped Robbins's station wagon. When Robbins opened the car door, the officers smelled marijuana smoke. In a search of the interior of the car, marijuana was discovered. The police officers then opened the tailgate of the station wagon. In a recessed luggage compartment they found two packages wrapped in green opaque plastic. The police unwrapped the packages and discovered a large amount of marijuana in each. Robbins was convicted at trial. On appeal the Supreme Court reversed, finding that the evidence obtained during the search of the packages should have been suppressed.

Justice Stewart, writing the plurality opinion, held that all closed, opaque containers should be treated the same for Fourth Amendment purposes. The fact that the green plastic packages were not luggage is irrelevant. The plurality held that once a closed container was discovered in the trunk of a lawfully searched automobile, the container could not be opened without a valid search warrant unless its contents were clearly revealed by its appearance. Justice Powell concurred in the judgment only. Rejecting the rule that all containers should be viewed equally, Justice Powell found that Robbins had a reasonable expectation of privacy in the packages, and for that reason alone the warrantless search was unconstitutional.

THE CASE OF *UNITED STATES V. ROSS* (1982)

It is under the backdrop of confusing, fact-specific opinions and rules that the Court took up the case of *United States v. Ross* (456 U.S. 798 [1982]).

The Facts

On the evening of November 27, 1978, a reliable informant called the District of Columbia Police Department and told them that an individual known as "Bandit" was selling narcotics kept in the trunk of a car parked at 439 Ridge Street. The informant stated that he had just observed "Bandit" complete a sale and that "Bandit" had told him that additional narcotics were in the trunk. The informant provided a detailed description of "Bandit" and stated that the car was a "purplish maroon" Chevrolet Malibu with District of Columbia license plates.

Shortly thereafter several District of Columbia police detectives drove to the area and found a maroon Malibu parked in front of 439 Ridge Street. Computer checks showed that the car was registered to Albert Ross, that Ross fit the informant's description, and that he used the alias "Bandit." After circling the block for several minutes the officers observed the Malibu driving in the neighborhood. They pulled up next to the Malibu, saw that the driver matched the informant's description, and stopped the car. One officer discovered a bullet on the car's front seat and a pistol in the glove compartment. The driver, Albert Ross, was placed under arrest and handcuffed. Detective Cassidy took Ross's keys and opened the trunk, where he found a brown paper bag. He opened the bag and discovered a number of glassine bags containing a white powder, later identified as heroin. Cassidy replaced the bag, closed the trunk, and drove the car to the police station. At the station a more thorough search of the car revealed a zippered red leather pouch in the trunk. He unzipped the pouch and discovered $3,200 in cash. No warrant to search the car or its contents was ever obtained.

Ross was charged with possession of heroin with intent to distribute. Prior to trial, he moved to suppress the heroin found in the paper bag and the currency found in the leather pouch. After an evidentiary hearing, the trial court denied the motion to suppress, and Ross was eventually convicted by a jury. The District of Columbia Circuit Court of Appeals reversed the conviction, holding that neither container should have been searched without a warrant and therefore the heroin and currency seized by the police were inadmissible.

The Issue before the Court

May police, who have legitimately stopped an automobile and who have probable cause to believe that contraband is concealed somewhere in the vehicle, conduct a search of containers found inside the vehicle without obtaining a search warrant?

The Court's Holding

If police have probable cause to search an automobile for an object, they may search containers found in the automobile that might contain the object without first obtaining a search warrant.

The Majority Opinion

Justice John Paul Stevens wrote the opinion for a six-member majority. The Court's analysis began with a brief examination of *Carroll* and its justifications of the automobile exception to the warrant requirement. Emphasizing that probable cause is a prerequisite of warrantless searches, the majority opinion noted that the automobile exception provides that a search is "not unreasonable if based on facts that would justify the issuance of a warrant, even though a warrant has not actually been obtained." Justice Stevens noted that the search in *Carroll* was reasonable since it was based on probable cause and did not exceed the area a magistrate could have authorized to be searched pursuant to a search warrant.

After examining the rationale behind the automobile exception to the warrant requirement, the majority opinion discussed the standards applicable to searches of containers located within an automobile. After discussing the precedent established in *Chadwick* and *Sanders*, the Court carefully distinguished them from the facts presented in *Ross*. In *Chadwick* and *Sanders* the police had probable cause to believe contraband was contained within particular containers that happened to be located within an automobile. As the probable cause in those cases was associated with the container and not the car, a warrant was required as it would be for the search of a container in a public place. In *Ross*, however, the probable cause did not involve the bags but the entire vehicle itself. As such, the automobile exception was applicable and included the containers.

The Court proceeded to explain why containers contained within a vehicle are treated as if they were part of the car when the automobile exception is the basis for a search. The Court explained that the scope of a search authorized by a warrant is controlled by the object of the search and the locations where there is probable cause to believe that the object may be found. Moreover, if a magistrate issued a warrant to search a vehicle based on probable cause that there was contraband or evidence somewhere in the vehicle, the scope of the search would extend to all parts of the vehicle as well as any containers in the vehicle that could contain the object described in the warrant.

The majority opinion held that the standards that apply to searches with warrants should also apply to warrantless automobile searches. Based on this premise, the Court held that when a warrantless search of an automobile is conducted based on probable cause, the scope of the search extends to all parts of the vehicle and allows the opening of any container found in the vehicle that could contain the object of the search. The scope of such a search is based on the object of the search, not the area to be searched.

By using this reasoning, the Court did not abandon the precedent established in *Chadwick* and *Sanders* but merely distinguished them from *Ross*. On the other hand, the Court explicitly found that *Robbins* was "decided wrongly" and stripped it of any precedential value it carried.

The Dissenting Opinion

Justice Marshall wrote a dissenting opinion in which Justice Brennan joined and with which Justice White agreed. Justice Marshall wrote that the majority opinion unnecessarily disregarded the value of having a neutral, detached magistrate make probable-cause determinations. He opined that the majority decided as it did to foster the expediency of police investigations rather than based on constitutional principle. While automobiles are readily mobile, containers, once seized by law enforcement, are likely to remain under the control of the police until a warrant is obtained. As such, the exigent nature of cars, which is a key component of the automobile exception, is not applicable to searches of containers seized from within a car.

Further Analysis

The majority opinion set out to address a practical problem routinely encountered by police officers. Prior to *Ross*, it was unclear under what circumstances police were required to obtain a search warrant before they could open a container seized from within a car. This uncertainty led to overcautious police officers taking the time to obtain a search warrant for containers they had already seized. This inefficiency was a key component of the Court's decision. It was not disputed that if police had probable cause to search a car and discovered a container that might hold the object being sought, a warrant would almost certainly be issued. Given this fact, the Court reasoned that it was a waste of time and effort to require police go through the effort of obtaining a warrant rather than simply opening the container as part of an initial investigation.

Case Significance

With its decision in *Ross*, the Supreme Court signaled a shift in the manner in which it would consider cases involving Fourth Amendment issues. In the years following *Ross*, the Court established new, pro-law-enforcement standards relating to the establishment of probable cause (*Illinois v. Gates*, 462 U.S. 213 [1983]), the good-faith exceptions to the exclusionary rule (*United States v. Leon*, 468 U.S. 897 [1984]), warrantless searches of open fields (*Oliver v. United States*, 466 U.S. 170 [1984]), warrantless searches of students' belongings while at school (*New Jersey v. T.L.O.*, 469 U.S. 325 [1984]), warrantless search of a prison cell (*Hudson v. Palmer*, 468 U.S. 517 [1984]), and warrantless searches from the air (*Dow Chemical Co. v. United States*, 476 U.S. 227 [1986] and *California v. Ciraolo*, 476 U.S. 207 [1986]). In each of these cases, the need to allow law-enforcement officers and prosecutors to advance crime-control efforts with minimal constitutional limitations took precedence over Fourth Amendment protections. The tilt toward a police-focused, practical application, as opposed to a citizen-based, due-process-focused application of the Fourth Amendment, has yet to level.

POST-*ROSS* TREATMENT OF SEARCHES INVOLVING CONTAINERS IN VEHICLES

In the years since *Ross* the Supreme Court has expanded the authority of law enforcement to conduct warrantless searches of containers seized from automobiles. This expansion has focused on when the warrantless search can take place, the object of the probable cause giving rise to the warrantless search, and the nature of the container involved in the search.

In 1985 the Supreme Court decided the case of *United States v. Johns* (469 U.S. 478 [1985]). In *Johns*, customs officers seized two pickup trucks they encountered that smelled of marijuana and contained multiple packages that appeared to contain marijuana. The officers transported the trucks to DEA headquarters, where the unopened packages were unloaded into a warehouse. Three days later, officials opened the packages without a warrant and found marijuana. The trial court and Ninth Circuit Court of Appeals ruled that the search of the packages was unconstitutional due to the delay in the search.

The Supreme Court reversed. In its opinion the Court used the rationale from *Ross* to justify the warrantless search of the packages and the *Chambers* rationale for considering a delayed search of a seized object. As the customs agents had probable cause to search the entire truck, the fact that they did not do so immediately did not render the search unreasonable. Additionally, *Johns* established that once probable cause to search a vehicle is present, the scope of the search is not limited because that probable cause can later be focused on particular containers.

The Supreme Court took the holding in *Ross* a step further in *California v. Acevedo* (500 U.S. 565 [1991]). In *Acevedo*, detectives observed Charles Acevedo entering an apartment to which a package of marijuana had delivered several hours earlier. Ten minutes after entering the apartment Acevedo departed carrying a bag approximately the size of one of the packages of marijuana. Acevedo placed the package in the trunk of his car and drove away. The police stopped the car and opened both the trunk and the bag, which was found to contain marijuana. The California Court of Appeals ruled that the marijuana should have been suppressed by the trial court under the rule established in *Sanders*.

The United States Supreme Court reversed the California court. In an opinion written by Justice Blackmun, the Court eliminated the distinction between whether there was probable cause to believe contraband was within the car in general and a specific container. Instead, the Court held that police may search any closed container located within a car without a warrant so long as it may contain the items for which probable cause has been established. Under this bright-line rule, if a suspect places a closed container in a vehicle, the police no longer need to obtain a search warrant. The outgrowth of this is that a police officer who could not search the container before it was placed in the vehicle may now open it and seize its contents without a warrant.

In *Wyoming v. Houghton* (526 U.S. 295 [1999]), the Supreme Court considered the issue of whether a distinction should be drawn regarding the ownership of containers found in a vehicle for which there is probable cause to justify a search under the automobile exception. In *Houghton* a Wyoming highway patrol officer stopped a car for speeding and a faulty brake light. The driver was found to possess a hypodermic syringe in his pocket. He admitted to using it to take drugs and was placed under arrest. The officers then ordered Sandra Houghton, a passenger in the car, out of the vehicle. Houghton complied, leaving her purse in the car. A police officer proceeded to search the car for drugs. He found a purse in the back seat, which Houghton claimed belonged to her. The officer searched the purse and found a brown pouch and a black wallet-type container, which contained drug paraphernalia and a syringe filled with methamphetamine. Houghton was arrested and later convicted at trial for possession of a controlled substance.

On appeal, the Wyoming Supreme Court reversed Houghton's conviction. The court held that a container is outside the scope of a lawful search where the officer knows or should know that the container belongs to a passenger who is not suspected of criminal activity. The Supreme Court, in an opinion written by Justice Scalia, reversed. The Court held that police officers with probable cause to search a car may inspect all containers, including a passenger's belongings found in the car, that are capable of concealing the object of the search.

CONCLUSIONS

United States v. Ross is a prime example of the importance single opinions can have on shaping the manner in which an area of law is analyzed for years to come. By distinguishing the facts presented from the facts of prior cases, the

Court was able to accept legal precedent while laying the groundwork for a doctrinal shift. In doing so, the Court was able to adopt a bright-line rule for police and courts to follow, and for future opinions to build upon.

FURTHER READING

Bruce Newman, *Against That Powerful Engine of Despotism: The Fourth Amendment and General Warrants at the Founding and Today* (Lanham, Md.: University Press of America, 2006).

Martin L. O'Connor, "Vehicle Searches: The Automobile Exception; The Constitutional Ride from *Carroll v. United States* to *Wyoming v. Houghton,*" *Touro Law Review* 16 (2000): 393–435.

Catherine A. Shepard, "Search and Seizure: From *Carroll* to *Ross*, the Odyssey of the Automobile Exception," *Catholic University Law Review* 32 (1982): 221–67.

New York v. Belton

JEFFERY T. WALKER

INTRODUCTION

This case brings together a number of cases involving warrantless searches incident to an arrest, and to a lesser degree warrantless searches of automobiles. The foundation of the case comes from *Chimel v. California*, 395 U.S. 752 (1969). That case held that the search of the entire house after a person was arrested in the front room was an unreasonable search, but a search of the "area within the immediate control" of the person arrested was reasonable under the Fourth Amendment.

Even though the Court in *Belton* relied more on the doctrine of search incident to an arrest (*Chimel*) rather than an automobile exception (*Carroll v. United States*, 267 U.S. 132 [1925]) to the Fourth Amendment, the history of searches incident to an arrest goes back to the seminal case in automobile searches. In *Carroll*, the Court intimated in dicta that officers could search a person and items within his or her control incident to a lawful arrest, stating "When a man is legally arrested for an offense, whatever is found upon his person or in his control which it is unlawful for him to have and which may be used to prove the offense may be seized and held as evidence in the prosecution." The Court confirmed this rationale in *Agnello v. United States*, 269 U.S. 20 (1925), in the statement that "the right without a search warrant . . . to search the place where an arrest is made . . . is not to be doubted."[1]

Over time, lower courts interpreted the decision in *Chimel* and often expanded the authority of police to conduct warrantless searches incident to an arrest. At the same time, the authority to search automobiles (whether incident to an arrest or not) was also the subject of many court cases. Although there was discussion of warrantless searches in general prior *Carroll,* the greater use of automobiles in the 1920s created circumstances where they were used in a larger number of criminal actions. As such, officers often needed to conduct searches of the automobiles. While the Fourth Amendment provided as much detail as possible given the time it was written, it obviously did not cover automobile searches. The terms "persons, houses, papers, and effects" also did not address the mobility of automobiles and the potential for them to be driven away and the evidence destroyed while officers sought a search warrant. The need to search, particularly automobiles, was a central part of the debate in Congress over passage of the National Prohibition Act. Conference proceedings from passage of that act indicated that Congress was aware of warrantless searches in other circumstances and stated in the discussion that "it will be impossible to get a warrant to stop an automobile. Before a warrant could be secured the automobile would be beyond the reach of the officer with its load of illegal liquor disposed of."[2] As a result of the conference committee report, Congress provided punishment for officers who searched a home without a warrant but left open the possibility of searching an automobile without a warrant as long as the search was not malicious and there was probable cause for the search.

In addition to warrantless searches related to automobiles, the courts were also wrestling with the appropriate scope and authority to search when police had made a lawful arrest. The decisions of even the Supreme Court, however, were often conflicting. For example, in *Harris v. United States,* 331 U.S. 145 (1947), the Court expanded its ruling in *Agnello* and allowed officers to search an entire four-room apartment following a lawful arrest. Only a year later, the Court somewhat reversed this thinking in *Trupiano v. United States,* 334 U.S. 699 (1948), holding officers should obtain a warrant whenever reasonably practical. The Court then expressly overruled *Trupiano* in *United States v. Rabinowitz,* 339 U.S. 56 (1950).

Because lower courts were struggling to interpret the disparate decisions of the Supreme Court, the Court took the case of *Chimel v. California* in 1969 to establish a bright-line rule related to searches incident to an arrest. In this case, Chimel was suspected of robbing a coin shop. After obtaining an arrest warrant (but not a search warrant), police officers went to Chimel's house and were admitted by his wife. Chimel was not at home but was arrested upon arrival. The police asked Chimel if they could "look around." Chimel denied the request, but the officers searched the entire house anyway and discovered stolen coins. At the trial, the coins were admitted as evidence over Chimel's objection. Chimel was convicted of robbery. The Supreme Court ruled that

> when an arrest is made, it is reasonable for the arresting officer to search the person arrested in order to remove any weapons that the latter might seek to use in order to resist arrest or effect his escape. Otherwise, the officer's safety might well be endangered and the arrest itself frustrated. In addition, it is entirely reasonable for the arresting officer to search for and seize any evidence on the arrestee's person in order to prevent its concealment or destruction. And the area into which an arrestee might reach in order to grab a weapon or evidentiary items must, of course, be governed by a like rule.

This case, therefore, established that officers may search the area within the immediate control of the suspect for weapons, and also seize any evidence they find during this search. *Chimel* established a seemingly bright-line rule of the area that could be searched incident to a lawful custodial arrest. Many lower courts, however, had difficulty determining the true extent of the area authorized to be searched, especially as it pertained to automobile searches (even within the same courts).

In 1973, the Fifth Circuit in *United States v. Frick* (490 F.2d 666 [1973]) upheld the search of an attaché case lying on the back seat of an automobile when the offender was arrested outside his vehicle. The Ninth Circuit reached a similar conclusion in *United States v. Dixon* (562 F.2d 1138 [9th Cir. 1977]). In this case, officers arrested Dixon while he was still in his automobile. They then ordered him out of his vehicle. Officers then observed a revolver and bag on the floorboard of the vehicle and seized the items. Seemingly overturning its decision in *Frick*, the Fifth Circuit in *United States v. Rigales* (630 F.2d 364 [5th Cir. 1980]) ruled a search inadmissible when officers found several unspent bullets on Rigales and believed a leather case lying in the floorboard would contain a weapon. In this case, the court ruled the seizure of the leather case was beyond the scope of the search incident to the arrest because Rigales was only stopped for a traffic violation.

The Eighth Circuit Court of Appeals had conflicting rulings within two years of each other on similar cases. In *United States v. Stevie* (578 F.2d 204 [8th Cir. 1978]), the court ruled that officers could not open a suitcase on the floor of an automobile after a suspect was ordered out of his rented vehicle and arrested for suspicion of possession of marijuana. The court also ruled a search illegal where one officer arrested a suspect and removed him from his automobile while another officer opened the back door of the vehicle and seized the person's tote bag (*United States v. Benson*, 640 F.2d 1336 [8th Cir. 1980]). That same year, the court seemingly contradicted itself when it upheld the search in *United States v. Sanders* (631 F.2d 1309 [8th Cir. 1980]). In this case, officers removed Sanders from his automobile after observing suspicious behavior while he was parked on the street. During a subsequent frisk of Sanders, officers observed a brown packet on the passenger-side floorboard and seized it. The packet contained heroin.

THE CASE OF *NEW YORK V. BELTON* (1981)

As stated in the chapter in this text on *Carroll v. United States*, this case formed the basis of hundreds of cases decided by the Supreme Court. *Chimel* also resulted in a great number of cases attempting to interpret the Court's findings. Each case addressed a slightly different aspect of searches related to automobiles, search incident to an arrest, or both. The case that is the focus of this chapter, *New York v. Belton* (453 U.S. 454 [1981]), expanded the ability of police officers to not only search an automobile suspected of containing contraband but also to search containers in the passenger compartment of the automobile.

The Facts

This case arose when police stopped an automobile, of which Belton was an occupant, for speeding. A check of driver's licenses and automobile registration revealed that none of the occupants owned the vehicle or were related to the owner. While attempting to determine the owner of the vehicle, the officer smelled burnt marijuana and saw an envelope marked "Supergold" on the floor of the automobile, which the officer associated with marijuana.

After administering *Miranda* warnings, the officer placed the occupants under arrest, picked up the envelope, and found marijuana. He then searched the passenger compartment of the automobile and, on the back seat, found a jacket belonging to Belton. He unzipped one of the pockets of the jacket and discovered cocaine. Belton was arrested for possession of a controlled substance.

After his motion to suppress the evidence was denied, he plead guilty to a lesser included offense but retained the right to appeal the seizure as violating his Fourth and Fourteenth Amendment rights. The Appellate Division of the New York Supreme Court upheld the constitutionality of the search, ruling that "once the defendant was validly arrested for possession of marijuana, the officer was justified in searching the immediate area for other contraband."[3] The New York Court of Appeals reversed the decision, holding that "a warrantless search of the zippered pockets of an inaccessible jacket may not be upheld as a search incident to a lawful arrest where there is no longer any danger that the arrestee or confederate might gain access to the article."[4] The Supreme Court accepted the case to address the potential conflict between these rulings.

The Issue before the Court

The Court took this case to determine if, following a lawful arrest, an officer could search the passenger compartment of an automobile, and the containers within it, for contraband or weapons.

The Court's Holding

Justice Stewart wrote the opinion of the Court, joined by Chief Justice Burger and Justices Blackmun, Powell, and Rehnquist. The holding of the Court essentially combined the decisions in *Carroll* and *Chimel* and created a rule that officers may search, incident to a lawful arrest, the immediate area of an automobile (the passenger compartment) from which those arrested were taken. In addition, officers may search containers and clothing found in the passenger compartment as longs as they were within reach of those arrested.

The Majority Opinion

The Court based its ruling on two issues: preventing the destruction of evidence and protecting the officer. Drawing from *Chimel*, the Court offered the following logic in relation to preventing the destruction of evidence in an automobile following a lawful arrest.

> Our reading of the cases suggests the generalization that articles inside the relatively narrow compass of the passenger compartment of an automobile are in fact generally, even if not inevitably, within "the area into which an arrestee might reach in order to grab a weapon or evidentiary ite[m]." *Chimel*, 395 U.S., at 763. In order to establish a workable rule this category of cases requires, we read *Chimel's* definition of the limits of the areas that may be searched in light of that generalization. Accordingly, we hold that when a policeman has made a lawful custodial arrest of the occupant of an automobile, he may, as a contemporaneous incident of that arrest, search the passenger compartment of that automobile. It follows from this conclusion that the

police may also examine the contents of any containers found within the passenger compartment, for if the passenger compartment is within the reach of the arrestee, so also will containers in it be within his reach. *United States v. Robinson*, supra; *Draper v. United States*, 358 U.S. 307. Such a container may, of course, be searched whether or not it is open or closed, since the justification for the search is not that the arrestee has no privacy interest in the container but that the lawful custodial arrest justifies the infringement of any privacy interest the arrestee may have.

In addressing the potential for a person to gain control of a weapon, the Court seemed to foreshadow the decision it would make only two years later in *Michigan v. Long* (463 U.S. 1032 [1983]). In that case, the Court ruled that an officer could make a limited search of the passenger compartment of an automobile following a valid stop (even before an arrest) to check for weapons that could potentially be used against the officer. In *Belton*, officers seemed to draw an additional comparison with *Terry v. Ohio* (932 U.S. 1 [1968]), where they found that the risks associated with the extended time an officer would be involved with a person who is arrested increased the likelihood the offender might be able to obtain a weapon. Such precaution warranted the search of the passenger compartment of a vehicle.

The Court also addressed potential arguments that a container searched by officers was not of sufficient size to hold a weapon. Drawing again from *United States v. Robinson* (414 U.S. 218 [1973]), the Court held the following:

> It is true, of course, that these containers will sometimes be such that they could hold neither a weapon nor evidence of the criminal conduct for which the suspect was arrested. . . . "The authority to search the person incident to a lawful arrest, while based upon the need to disarm and to discover evidence, does not depend on what a court may later decide was the probability in a particular arrest situation that weapons or evidence would in fact be found upon the person of the suspect." *Robinson* 1974, 235.[5]

The Court, therefore, held that the officer's actions in *Belton* constituted a reasonable intrusion based on search incident to an arrest and required no additional justification.

The Concurring and Dissenting Opinions

A case decided the same day as *Belton* and containing similar circumstances found a different outcome in the Court. In *Robbins v. California* (453 U.S. 420

[1981]), police stopped an automobile for driving erratically. When Robbins opened the car door to retrieve the vehicle registration, officers smelled burnt marijuana. One officer patted down Robbins while the other officer searched the passenger compartment of the automobile and found marijuana. Robbins was placed in custody in the patrol car. Officers then opened the tailgate of the station wagon and located the handle that led to a recessed luggage compartment. In the compartment were a tote bag and two packages wrapped in green opaque plastic. The officers unwrapped the plastic and found marijuana.

The Court declared the search of the packages a violation of the Fourth Amendment because they were considered in a closed container. The government sought to have them fall under the automobile exception, but the Court made the bright-line distinction between luggage and other items found in an automobile.

Justice Rehnquist and Justice Stevens concurred in the opinion in *Belton* based on their dissents in *Robbins*. Justice Rehnquist dissented in *Robbins* because he argued that all searches of vehicles should fall under the automobile exception, stating "If 'contraband goods concealed and illegally transported in an automobile or other vehicle may be search for without a warrant' *Carroll v. United States*, 267 U.S. 132, 153 (1925), then, in my view, luggage and similar containers found in an automobile may be searched for contraband without a warrant." Based on this dissent, Justice Rehnquist joined the opinion of the Court in *Belton* but believed the Court did not go far enough in allowing officers to search automobiles. Similarly, Justice Stevens concurred in *Belton* and dissented in *Robbins* because he felt the cases had similar circumstances and should have been decided "by a consistent application of the automobile exception." Justice Stevens argued,

> the scope of any search that is within the [automobile] exception should be just as broad as a magistrate could authorize by warrant if he were on the scene; the automobile exception to the warrant requirements therefore justifies neither more nor less than could a magistrate's warrant. If a magistrate issued a search warrant for an automobile, and officers in conducting the search authorized by the warrant discovered a suitcase in the car, they surely would not need to return to the magistrate for another warrant before searching the suitcase.

Both Justices Rehnquist and Stevens agreed with the decision in *Belton*, but because they did not agree with the decision in *Robbins*, they concurred here rather than joining the majority opinion.

Justice Brennan wrote a dissenting opinion joined by Justice Marshall. Their primary argument was that this case should have been decided based strictly on *Chimel*, following the ruling by the New York Court of Appeals. Justices Brennan and Marshall argued that *Chimel* offered strong guidance for police that should not change simply because the person was taken from an automobile. They argued that the relevant portion of *Chimel* would limit its applicability in automobile stops, saying that "it thus places a temporal and a spatial limitation on searches incident to arrest, excusing compliance with the warrant requirement only when the search 'is substantially contemporaneous with the arrest and is confined to the *immediate* vicinity of the arrest.'"

Applying this principle to the present facts, they argued that "the Court today disregards these principles and instead adopts a fiction—that the interior of a car is always within the immediate control of an arrestee who has recently been in the car."

They argued that the majority decision substantially expanded the scope of searches authorized by *Chimel*, allowing officers to search areas that were not within the reach of the suspect at the time of arrest.

Justice White also wrote a short dissent that Justice Marshall joined. The basis of their one-paragraph argument follows:

> In *Robbins v. California, ante*, p. 420, it was held that a wrapped container in the trunk of a car could not be searched without a warrant even though the trunk itself could be searched without a warrant because there was probable cause to search the car and even though there was probable cause to search the container as well. This was because of the separate interest in the privacy with respect to the container. The Court now holds that as incident to the arrest of the driver or any other person in an automobile the interior of the car and any container found therein, whether locked or not, may be not only seized but also searched even absent probable cause to believe that contraband or evidence of a crime will be found.

Justices White and Marshall argued that it seemed an extreme extension of *Chimel* as it related to containers and that no container ought to be allowed to be searched (whether in the interior or the trunk) without probable cause.

Case Significance

The Court in this case blended two rules to give police more authority in conducting searches of the contents of automobiles following a lawful arrest. The warrantless exception for automobile searches states that officers can search vehicles without a warrant because the vehicle could be moved and the evidence destroyed before a warrant could be obtained (*Carroll v. United States*). The search-incident-to-arrest rule states that a lawful arrest creates a situation that justifies a contemporaneous search without a warrant of the person and the immediately surrounding area (*Chimel v. California*).

Following *Chimel*, the Court created a bright-line rule in *United States v. Robinson* (1973), that officers could always search a person after a lawful custodial arrest. The Court had not addressed the issue, however, of "the proper scope of a search of the interior of an automobile incident to a lawful custodial arrest of its occupants." As a result of *Belton*, officers were allowed to search the passenger compartment of a vehicle and items in the compartment that might contain contraband. Further, the officer does not need a warrant to do so even if there would potentially be time to obtain the warrant since the occupants are already in custody. The primary rationale for these rules is to protect the officer from a weapon that might easily be retrieved by the suspect. For example, a few years after *Belton*, the Court ruled in *Michigan v. Long* (1983) that even before an arrest officers who made a valid stop of a vehicle may search areas where a weapon might be obtained if the officer has reasonable belief that the suspect is dangerous. As with *Belton*, if an officer finds other contraband while conducting this search, it is permissible to seize the contraband and use it in court.

In a reaction to the *Belton* and *Robbins* decisions, Michele D. Schultz, writing for the *Ohio Northern University Law Review* (1982), argued (following the dissents by Brennan and White) that the Court's attempt to establish a workable rule for police had failed.[6] Schultz argued that, without the decision in *Robbins*, police would have had clear-cut guidelines for searches of passenger compartments incident to arrest (even though Schultz thought it was an unnecessary infringement on Fourth Amendment rights). Given the similarity between *Robbins* and *Belton*, however, and the fact that the Court handed down seemingly conflicting rules, Schultz argued that police were no better off than before in the proper scope of their searches.

Writing for the *Pepperdine Law Review*, Glen D. Forcucci (1982) extensively reviewed the history of warrantless searches (especially those related to searches incident to arrest).[7] He concluded from his review of case law that *Belton* was not consistent with *Chimel* because occupants of a vehicle are not within the area of the arrest as outline in *Chimel*, even under the most liberal definitions of "area within the immediate control." Since the occupants are no longer in the passenger compartment of the automobile, nor able to gain access to the interior of the vehicle, Forcucci argued that this was an unnecessary extension of *Chimel*.

Forcucci returned to *Chimel* to support his assertion. In *Chimel*, the Court stated there was no justification "for routinely searching any room other than that in which an arrest occurs."[8] Forcucci argued that a person standing outside of an automobile while officers searched the interior is tantamount to officers searching a room away from where the offender was arrested.

Forcucci argued that, once the persons and automobile were under the control of police, the exigency of the offender potentially obtaining a weapon or destroying evidence was lessened. Even using the automobile exception, Forcucci argued that officers had control of the vehicle and could retain control while a search warrant was obtained.

Forcucci concluded that lower courts would rely on *Belton* rather than *Chimel* when making decisions related to the warrantless search of an automobile. He argued that the *Belton* decision unnecessarily expands the scope of searches incident to an arrest and creates a situation where officers will be able to search in areas that would not be allowed by *Chimel*. This logic was born out in subsequent cases, resulting in the Supreme Court having to revisit *Belton*.

SIGNIFICANT SUBSEQUENT CASES

The bright-line rule of *Belton* was far from being a bright line. Lower courts struggled with application of the rule, trying to balance the words of the Court citing *Chimel* and the holding of the Court that seemingly went beyond *Chimel*. There were also significant cases at the Supreme Court level following *Belton*. None was perhaps more significant than *Arizona v. Gant* (556 U.S. ___ [2009]). This case either overturned *Belton* (according to the dissent by Alito, joined by Roberts, Kennedy, and Breyer) or substantially distinguished it (as stated in the majority opinion). Because of the significance of *Gant*, we will address it here first, followed by other significant cases related to *Belton*.

Arizona v. Gant (2009)

In *Arizona v. Gant*, 556 U.S. ___ (2009), police went to a house, acting on an anonymous tip that the residence was being used to sell drugs, knocked on the door, and asked to speak to the owner. Gant answered the door and, after identifying himself, stated that the owner was gone and would be back later. The officers left but, while waiting on the owner to return, checked Gant's records and found that he had an outstanding warrant for driving on a suspended license. The officers returned to the house later and made arrests for drugs and other offenses. The arrestees were handcuffed in patrol cars when officers spotted Gant returning. Gant stopped his vehicle and got out. Officers approached Gant at about ten feet from his car, arrested him, and handcuffed him. After another patrol unit arrived, Gant was placed in the back of that patrol car. Officers then searched Gant's car. They found a gun and also found cocaine in the pocket of a jacket on the back seat. Gant was charged with drug offenses.

At trial, Gant moved to suppress the drugs, stating *Belton* did not authorize the search of the vehicle because he posed no threat to the officers and because he was arrested for a traffic offense, and no evidence of that offense could have been found in the vehicle. Officers admitted that the reason they conducted the search was because the law allowed it. The trial court ruled that *Belton* permitted the search incident to the arrest and denied the motion. The Arizona Supreme Court held the search unreasonable, ruling that the search went beyond the holding in *Chimel* because Gant could not possibly pose a threat to the officers or could not gain access to the vehicle to destroy evidence because he was handcuffed in the back of the patrol car.

The Supreme Court began its analysis with the assumption from *Katz v. United States* (1967), that warrantless searches are per se unreasonable outside "a few and specifically established and well-delineated guidelines."[9] The Court then noted that the rationale in the warrantless exception in *Chimel* was to protect the arresting officers and prevent destruction of evidence. The Court then foreshadowed its holding by stating that if there is no possibility the arrestee could reach into the passenger compartment of the vehicle, then the justifications of *Chimel* are absent.

In the discussion that followed, the Court distinguished both the proper interpretation of *Belton* and how *Belton* was distinguished from the present case. In *Belton*, there were four occupants. The officer's initial probable cause was smelling burnt marijuana and seeing an envelope marked "Supergold" on the floor. The officer removed the occupants, frisked them, and separated them but could not handcuff them because he only had one pair of handcuffs. The officer then conducted the search of the vehicle. In its brief in *Belton*, the state argued that it was possible for the occupants to have gained access to the passenger compartment of the vehicle, making the search permissible under *Chimel*. The Court compared these facts to *Gant* and found two distinctions: First, it would not have been possible for Gant to gain access to the passenger compartment of his vehicle since he was handcuffed in the backseat of a patrol car. Second, Gant was arrested for a traffic offense, and no evidence to support the arrest could be found in the process of the search of his vehicle.

Based on this analysis, the Court held that "police may search a vehicle incident to a recent occupant's arrest only if the arrestee is within reaching distance of the passenger compartment at the time of the search or it is reasonable to believe the vehicle contains evidence of the offense of arrest." Specifically for this case, the Court held that "because police could not reasonably have believed either that Gant could have accessed his car at the time of the search or that evidence of the offence for which he was arrested might have been found therein, the search in this case was unreasonable."

Other Significant Cases and Holdings

The search of a passenger compartment incident to the arrest of a recent occupant of the vehicle is valid even if the person was not in the vehicle when the officer first made contact: In *Thornton v. United States* (541 U.S. 615 [2004]), an officer attempted to stop Thornton's vehicle after Thornton exhibited suspicious behavior and the officer determined the vehicle license plates did not match the vehicle. Before the officer had an opportunity to stop Thornton, Thornton drove into a parking lot, parked, and got out of the vehicle. The officer stopped Thornton as he walked away from his vehicle. As the officer questioned Thornton about his license plate, Thornton appeared nervous. Concerned for his safety, the officer asked Thornton if he had any narcotics or weapons on him or in his vehicle. When Thornton said no, the officer asked if he could frisk him, to which Thornton agreed. After the frisk revealed narcotics, the officer handcuffed Thornton and placed him in the back seat of the patrol car. He then searched Thornton's vehicle and found a handgun. The Court held that the holding in *Belton* governs even when an officer does not make contact until the person arrested has left the vehicle. They based this decision on the finding that the span of the area within the arrestee's immediate control (as defined in *Chimel*) is not determined by whether the arrestee exited the vehicle or whether the officer initiated contact while the arrestee was in the car. The Court argued that "in all relevant aspects, the arrest of a suspect who is next to a vehicle presents identical concerns regarding officer safety and evidence destruction as one who is inside."

Given the decision in *Gant*, it is likely that *Thornton* would now be decided differently. In this case, Thornton was handcuffed in the back of the patrol car when the search took place. While this was deemed acceptable, even by the

Supreme Court at one time, it is likely this would not be tolerated following the *Gant* ruling.

A search of an automobile, after a valid stop but no arrest, is permissible to search for weapons for which a suspect might gain control: Not long after the decision in *Belton*, the Court accepted *Michigan v. Long* (463 U.S. 1032 [1983]) to determine whether an officer could conduct a limited search of the passenger compartment of a vehicle even if no arrest had yet been made. In this case, officers stopped Long's vehicle after observing it driving erratically, eventually swerving into a ditch. Officers approached Long, who was by that time at the rear of his vehicle. He appeared under the influence of something and did not respond to initial requests for his license. Upon a second request for his license, Long began to return to his vehicle. The officers followed him and noticed a large hunting knife on the floorboard. Officers then stopped and frisked Long. Another officer observed marijuana in the vehicle, and Long was arrested. A further search of his vehicle produced more marijuana in the trunk. The Court ruled that officers may conduct a search of a vehicle after a stop, limited to areas where weapons may be hidden, if the officer has reasonable belief that the suspect is dangerous and might gain control of a weapon. The Court based this ruling on the premise that "articles inside the relatively narrow compass of the passenger compartment of an automobile are in fact generally, even if not inevitably, within the area into which an arrestee might reach in order to grab a weapon." The Court further held that any evidence of a crime found during this search could also be seized.

CONCLUSIONS

One comment made by the Court in *Belton* was that there was no straightforward rule on "the proper scope of a search of the interior of an automobile incident to a lawful custodial arrest of its occupants." The Court noted the large number of lower court cases where the intricacies of the search had been litigated. The Court then established a desire to establish a workable rule for police to follow in these kinds of cases. Even though many inisisted that this effort resulted in overbroad police powers,[10] the case did establish a rule police could follow in conducting searches of vehicles incident to an arrest. This served police well for many years, and still does in some circumstances. The practice of many lower courts, however, allowing all searches incident to an arrest, following their interpretation of *Belton*, led to the decision in *Gant* that limited or refined the permissible scope of searches of the passenger compartment of vehicles incident to an arrest.

FURTHER READING

Glen D. Forcucci, "*New York v. Belton*: The Scope of Warrantless Searches Extended," *Pepperdine Law Review* 9 (1982): 919–38.

Michele D. Schultz, "*New York v. Belton*: A Man's Car Is Not His Castle: Fourth Amendment Search and Seizure," *Ohio Northern University Law Review* 9 (1982): 153–61.

Whren v. United States

JEFFERY T. WALKER

INTRODUCTION

The term *war on drugs* is used far too loosely in the media and among those who have a point to prove. That said, there truly is a war of sorts going on in relation to drugs. Drug dealers and users do everything possible to avoid being discovered by the police, including using loopholes in the law. To counter this, the police have marshaled their forces in efforts to control drug sales, use, and possession. Even for uniformed patrol officers, much of their focus is typically on activities related to drugs. Most police agencies also have special units that have the sole focus of drug interdiction. These plainclothes officers, often bearded and undercover, work exclusively in drug efforts. They do very little, if any, other types of police work. That is the foundation of the arguments in this case, *Whren v. United States*. As discussed below, Whren and others were stopped by plainclothes officers who pulled them over for traffic violations. Once stopped, the officers discovered drugs (which was the real reason for the stop). At trial, Whren argued that the plainclothes officers would not normally make traffic stops and should not be allowed to use that excuse to initiate an investigation for drugs.

THE CASE OF *WHREN V. UNITED STATES* (1996)

The Facts

According to *Whren v. United States* (517 U.S. 806 [1996]), plainclothes officers in an unmarked vehicle were patrolling an area known for drug activity when they noticed a truck with temporary license plates remaining an unusually long time at a stop sign while an occupant stared into the lap of the driver. When officers made a U-turn and headed toward the vehicle, the vehicle made a sudden right turn without signaling and sped off at a high speed. The officers stopped the vehicle, and when the officers approached the vehicle, one officer saw what appeared to be crack cocaine in Whren's hands.

At trial, Whren sought to suppress the evidence, saying that plainclothes officers would not normally make a traffic stop and that there was no probable cause to make a stop for drugs. Whren argued the traffic stop was simply a pretext to determine if there were any drugs. The motion to suppress was denied, and Whren was convicted. The court of appeals upheld the verdict.

The Issue before the Court

"In this case we decide whether the temporary detention of a motorist who the police have probable cause to believe has committed a civil traffic violation is inconsistent with the Fourth Amendment's prohibition against unreasonable seizures unless a reasonable officer would have been motivated to stop the car by a desire to enforce the traffic laws."

The Court's Holding

The temporary detention of a motorist upon probable cause to believe that he has violated the traffic laws does not violate the Fourth Amendment's prohibition against unreasonable searches and seizures, even if an officer would not normally have stopped the motorist absent some additional law-enforcement objective.

The Majority Opinion

Justice Scalia delivered the opinion of the unanimous court. The Court began by examining previous decisions related to this type of action by the police. Drawing from *Delaware v. Prouse* (440 U.S. 648 [1979]), among other cases, the Court acknowledged that the "temporary detention of individuals during the stop of an automobile by the police, even if only for a brief period and for a limited purpose, constitutes a 'seizure' of 'persons' within the meaning of this provision." As such, any actions by police must be reasonable within the Fourth Amendment. The Court then restated that an automobile stop is reasonable if the officer had probable cause to believe criminal activity was taking place—even if that criminal activity was a traffic violation.

The basis of Whren's argument was that even though the officer had probable cause to make the stop because of traffic violations, probable cause is not enough. His attorneys argued that "the use of automobiles is so heavily and minutely regulated that total compliance with traffic and safety rules is nearly impossible, [and] a police officer will almost invariably be able to catch any given motorist in a technical violation." They argued this allows officers to use traffic stops as a means of investigating other law violations, even when the officer has no probable cause that other criminal activity has occurred. Whren argued that the standard for a stop should be that the officers would have made the stop for the reason given—and in this case that plainclothes officers would not have made a traffic stop. Whren also implied that the ability of officers to use these kinds of stops was a part of racial profiling. The Court largely refused to address this last issue.

After a brief recitation of previous cases related to inventory searches of automobiles, the Court stated, "not only have we never held, outside the context of inventory search or administrative inspection, that an officer's motive invalidates objectively justifiable behavior under the Fourth Amendment, but we have repeatedly held and asserted the contrary." This statement foreshadowed the decision of the Court. The Court drew its strongest support for this argument from *United States v. Robinson* (414 U.S. 218 [1973]) and its ruling there that "a traffic-violation arrest (of the sort here) would not be rendered invalid by the fact that it was 'a mere pretext for a narcotics search.'" The Court further drew from *Robinson*, whose decision argued that "the fact that the officer does not have the state of mind which is hypothecated by the reasons which provide the legal justification for the officer's action does not invalidate the action taken as long as the circumstances, viewed objectively, justify that action."

The Court returned to *Prouse* to support a balancing test between the need for effective law enforcement and protection of Fourth Amendment rights. The Court compared the actions in *Prouse* against those in the present case to show support for their holding. In *Prouse*, the officer made a random traffic stop (for the purpose of checking a motorist's license and vehicle registration) as a pretext for a further intrusion without probable cause—in effect using the stop as a pretext when no initial traffic violation had occurred. The Court then distinguished *Prouse* from *Whren* by stating, "Our opinion in *Prouse* expressly distinguished the case from a stop based on precisely what is at issue here: 'probable cause to believe that a driver is violating any one of the multitude of applicable traffic and equipment regulations.'" The Court noted that it is the requirement that officers have the probable cause for the stops (even if for traffic violations) "which afford the 'quantum of individualized suspicion' necessary to ensure that police discretion is sufficiently constrained."[1] The Court concluded from this analysis that "the making of a traffic stop out of uniform does not remotely qualify as such an extreme practice and so is governed by the usual rule that probable cause to believe the law has been broken 'outbalances' private interest in avoiding police contact."

Based on this line of logic, the Court concluded, "Here the district court found that the officers had probable cause to believe that petitioners had violated the traffic code. That rendered the stop reasonable under the Fourth Amendment, the evidence thereby discovered admissible, and the upholding of the convictions by the Court of Appeals for the District of Columbia Circuit correct."

Case Significance

The primary effect of *Whren* was to judicially permit police to make valid traffic stops, even if their primary intention may be investigation of other crimes rather than issuing a citation. This is important for police officers because a traffic stop can often lead to additional investigation. For example, the officer may be able to speak to the driver and discern whether or not the driver is intoxicated; or the officer may be able to smell the presence of marijuana. Perhaps more important, the officer will be able to use the plain-view doctrine of warrantless searches to look for evidence of criminal activity that might be visible during the stop. This could result in further investigation and searches by the officer. The officer could also take the opportunity of the stop to receive consent to search the person's vehicle. While the driver can refuse this consent, it is common police practice to make such requests—and these requests often bear fruit in terms of the evidence of a crime.

Not everyone was happy with the decision in *Whren*. Civil-rights groups and others saw the decision as just another degradation of rights by a law-enforcement-oriented Supreme Court. For example, writing for the *Florida Law Review*, Kenneth Gavsie quoted *Terry v. Ohio* (392 U.S. 1 [1968]), that "intrusions upon constitutionally guaranteed rights based on nothing more substantial than inarticulate hunches [are] a result this Court has consistently refused to sanction."[2] Gavsie argued that while *Terry* reduced a person's right to privacy in favor of police effectiveness, at least that decision required reasonable suspicion for police actions. He went on to argue that *Whren* went beyond the ruling in *Terry*, giving officers the right to stop based on nothing more than a hunch [and traffic violations]. He argued, "in holding that such stops could be made regardless of an officer's true intentions, however, the Court enabled the police to do what they clearly could not do prior to *Whren*—stop and investigate criminal activity unrelated to the traffic violation with less than reasonable suspicion."

Gavsie saw the underlying problem (consistent with Whren's arguments) to be that vehicle operation is so extensively regulated that officers can always find a reason to stop a person. He cited a case out of Florida (*Florida* v. *Corvin*, 677 So.2d 947 [Fla. App. 1996]) as an example of how far *Whren* could be stretched to justify a traffic stop, ultimately leading to the discovery of drugs. In this case, an officer stated that Corvin's license tag was bent in the corner to the extent that the yearly validation sticker was unreadable. The trial court found the officer's rationale unconvincing: the stop had been made at 4 A.M., and thus it would have been virtually impossible to read anyone's validation sticker. The trial court's decision was handed down before *Whren*, and the court ruled that the officer's actions were an unconstitutional pretext. The case was overturned on appeal, however, based on the *Whren* decision.

Writing for the *Pacific Law Journal*, Matthew J. Saly found similar issues with *Whren*, stating that "with the pretext issue gone, this Casenote argues that the Fourth Amendment no longer affords meaningful protection from intrusive police searches while a person is in a motor vehicle."[3] Saly went on to argue that *Whren* allowed officers to conduct a variety of intrusions based simply on the pretext stop. In addition to those cases discussed above, Saly drew back to *Belton*, arguing that a traffic stop for improperly changing lanes would result in the detention of the driver and/or passenger(s), which would then provide officers an opportunity to search the entire automobile, including containers found therein. Saly continued, pointing out that "prior to *Whren*, the defendants would at the minimum have an argument that the stop was unreasonable and, therefore, the subsequent fruits of the search should be inadmissible." Saly concluded by arguing that given the line of cases related to automobile searches, motorists did not have strong Fourth Amendment protection even prior to *Whren*, but *Whren* went on to destroy what little protection remained. An argument could be made that since *Whren* some of these protections have been reestablished,[4] but the protection of persons while in an automobile are still substantially less than in almost any other location.

An even larger issue with *Whren* (or occurring about the same time as *Whren* and fueled by the decision) was racial profiling. Gavsie, in arguing that *Whren* would lead to additional infractions by police, cited a 1992 study made in

Volusia County, Florida, in which over 140 hours of videotape were compiled consisting of almost 1,110 traffic stops. The results showed that more than 70 percent of all the traffic stops involved African American drivers, even though African Americans made up less than 10 percent of the drivers on that particular highway. The study further found that African American drivers were detained twice as long, on average, as were white drivers and also were twice as likely to have their cars searched subsequent to the stop.

Saly suggested that legislation be passed mandating that officers issue a citation every time they stop a vehicle as a way of balancing the effects of *Whren*. Writing for the *University of Miami Law Review*, Angela J. Davis correctly argued that the public would not stand for such a mandate, and, even if they did, it would be an administrative nightmare.[5] Plus, there is nothing to guarantee that officers would not simply write a citation for the traffic offense as a part of a *Whren* stop anyway. Davis pointed out that not writing each motorist a citation necessarily involves discretion on the part of officers. She noted, however, that "the obvious drawback of police discretion is that it inherently involves treating similarly situated motorists differently. A police officer may stop and ticket one driver even when he observes several motorists exceed the speed limit."

As evident from the discussion here, *Whren* has become a central element in the debate of racially motivated policing. Davis pointed out that beyond any issue of overt police discrimination, "the legal standard governing a police officer's decision to stop a suspect has become so flexible and loosely defined that it is difficult to know whether, and to what extent, race influences the decision." Even though the research of Brian L. Withrow, published in 2007 in *Police Quarterly*, found little effect of *Whren* circumstances on police pretextual stops,[6] most considered *Whren* a considerable blow dealt by the Supreme Court on the rights of motorists. Similar concerns were voiced following *Brown v. Mississippi* (297 U.S. 278 [1936]), *Miranda v. Arizona* (384 U.S. 436 [1966]), *Terry v. Ohio* (392 U.S. 1 [1968]), and other cases, however; so the true effect of *Whren* will be demonstrated in police behavior over time.

SIGNIFICANT SUBSEQUENT CASES

At the time of this writing, the Supreme Court has not decided any significant cases exactly like *Whren*. Four significant Court decisions, however, are closely related to *Whren* in that they deal with the actions of officers when making stops for traffic offenses: *Maryland v. Wilson* (519 U.S. 408 [1997]), *Ohio v. Robinette*

(519 U.S. 33 [1996]), *Knowles v. Iowa* (525 U.S. 113 [1998]), and *Brendlin v. California* (551 U.S. 249 [2007]). These cases are briefed in the following.

Police officers do not have to inform motorists who are stopped for traffic violations that the stop has concluded before any subsequent interrogation or search is considered consensual: In *Ohio v. Robinette* (1996), a deputy stopped Robinette for speeding, and he then asked Robinette to step out of the car, where Robinette was issued a verbal warning. After the deputy returned Robinette's license, he asked, "One question before you get gone: are you carrying any illegal contraband in your car?" When Robinette replied "No," the deputy asked if he could search the car. Robinette consented, and the deputy searched the car, where he found a small amount of marijuana and a pill that turned out to be methamphetamine. The evidence was admitted over Robinette's objection, and he was convicted of possession of a controlled substance. Robinette later claimed that he should have been informed that he was "free to go" in order for the consent to search the vehicle to be valid. The Court ruled that the Fourth Amendment does not require "police officers to inform motorists lawfully stopped for traffic violations that the legal detention has concluded before any subsequent interrogation or search will be found to be consensual." The Court based this ruling on the totality-of-circumstances test for searches and seizures. Here, the Court ruled that (1) "voluntariness is a question of fact to be determined from all the circumstances," that (2) while "knowledge of the right to refuse consent is one factor to be taken into account, the government need not establish such knowledge as the sine qua non of an effective consent," and that (3) it would "be unrealistic to require police officers to always inform detainees that they are free to go before a consent to search may be deemed voluntary." The result of the case was that the Court ruled that officers may obtain consent to search a vehicle from stopped motorists without the requirement to first inform them that they are free to go.

An officer making a traffic stop may order passengers out of the car pending completion of the stop: In *Maryland v. Wilson* (1997), a state trooper attempted to stop an automobile, in which Wilson was a passenger, for speeding and an irregular license plate. The trooper followed the vehicle with his lights on for over a mile before the vehicle stopped. During this time, two of the three passengers in the automobile kept looking at the trooper, ducking below the line of site, and then reappearing. As the trooper approached the vehicle after it stopped, the driver got out of the car and met him halfway. The driver was trembling and appeared very nervous but did produce a valid driver's license.

When the driver returned to the car to retrieve the rental papers, the trooper noticed that Wilson was sweating and appeared very nervous. The trooper ordered Wilson out of the vehicle, at which time a quantity of crack cocaine fell to the ground. Wilson was arrested and charged with possession of cocaine with intent to distribute. The Supreme Court accepted the case to determine whether officers may order the passenger of a lawfully stopped vehicle out the car. The Court relied in this case on its ruling in *Pennsylvania v. Mimms* (434 U.S. 106 [1977]). In *Mimms*, the Court had ruled "that once a motor vehicle has been lawfully detained for a traffic violation, the police officers may order the driver to get out of the vehicle without violating the Fourth Amendment's proscription of unreasonable searches and seizures." Here, the Court ruled that "on the public-interest side of the balance, the same weighty interest in officer safety is present regardless of whether the occupant of the stopped car is a driver or passenger." The Court did concede that passengers may have more privacy interests than the driver, stating,

> On the personal-liberty side of the balance, the case for the passengers is in one sense stronger than that for the driver. There is probable cause to believe that the driver has committed a minor vehicular offense, but there is no such reason to stop or detain the passengers. But as a practical matter, the passengers are already stopped by virtue of the stop of the vehicle. The only change in their circumstances which will result from ordering them out of the car is that they will be outside of, rather than inside of, the stopped car.

As a result, the Court extended the rule in *Mimms*, that officers can order the driver out of a car pursuant to a lawful stop of the vehicle to include passengers of the vehicle. The Court stopped short, however, of ruling that officers could detain the passenger for the duration of the stop absent exigent circumstances (a finding of illegalities, for example).

Officers may not conduct a search incident to the issuance of a traffic citation absent consent or probable cause: In *Knowles v. Iowa* (1998), officers stopped Knowles for speeding and issued him a citation (although the officer had the authority to arrest him). The officer then conducted a full search of Knowles's car, where he found marijuana and drug paraphernalia. At trial, the officer conceded that he had neither consent nor probable cause for the search and that he relied on state law that permitted "searches incident to citation." The evidence was admitted over Knowles's objection, and he was convicted of possession of drug paraphernalia. The Supreme Court accepted this case to determine if the ruling in *New York v. Belton* (453 U.S. 454 [1981]) should be extended to allow officers to conduct a search incident to issuing a traffic citation. The Court ruled that while officers may search a vehicle incident to an arrest, a search incident to issuance of a traffic citation, absent consent or probable cause, violates the Fourth Amendment, even if authorized by state law. In making this ruling, the Court compared its holdings and the conditions of the officer in *Belton* (1981) and *United States v. Robinson* (1973) to those of an officer issuing a traffic citation. The Court argued, "In *Robinson*, we stated that a custodial arrest involves 'danger to an officer' because of 'the extended exposure which follows the taking of a suspect into custody and transporting him to the police station.'" This line of reasoning was extended in *Belton*, allowing officers to search the passenger compartment of a vehicle and containers found therein for weapons and evidence. The Court reasoned that "the threat to officer safety from issuing a traffic citation, however, is a good deal less than in the case of a custodial arrest." Citing *Berkemer v. McCarty* (468 U.S. 420 [1984]), the Court stated that "a routine traffic stop, on the other hand, is a relatively brief encounter and 'is more analogous to a so-called 'Terry stop' . . . than to a formal arrest," and "while the concern for officer safety in this context may justify the 'minimal' additional intrusion of ordering a driver and passengers out of the car, it does not by itself justify the often considerably greater intrusion attending a full field-type search."

The passenger of a vehicle is seized within the meaning of the Fourth Amendment during a traffic stop: In *Brendlin v. California* (2007), officers stopped a vehicle of which Brendlin was a passenger, in order to verify a temporary license tag, even though the officers admitted that there was nothing unusual about the permit. The officer recognized Brendlin as probably on parole and asked him to identify himself. After verifying that Brendlin was a parole violator and obtaining a warrant for his arrest, the officer arrested him. A search incident to the arrest revealed a syringe cap. A pat-down search of the driver revealed syringes and marijuana. Drug-production equipment was also found in a search of the vehicle. After Brendlin's motion to suppress the evidence as fruits of a stop without probable cause was denied, he pleaded guilty to drug charges.

Even though this case seems to favor the police, it does not. The Court ruled that Brendlin, along with the driver, was seized at the moment the stop was effected. As such, Brendlin had a proper interest in whether or not the subsequent searches were reasonable. The Court, therefore, overturned the lower court ruling, stating that "it was error to deny [Brendlin's] suppression motion on the ground that seizure occurred only at the formal arrest." The Court based this ruling on the rationale that "a person is seized by the police and thus entitled to challenge the government's action under the Fourth Amendment when the officer, 'by means of physical force or show of authority,' terminates or restrains his freedom of movement '*through means intentionally applied.*'"[7] The Court also stated that

> the law is settled that in Fourth Amendment terms a traffic stop entails a seizure of the driver "even though the purpose of the stop is limited and the resulting detention quite brief." *Delaware v. Prouse*, 440 U.S. 648, 653 (1979). And although we have not, until today, squarely answered the question whether a passenger is also seized, we have said over and over in dicta that during a traffic stop an officer seizes everyone in the vehicle, not just the driver. . . . We resolve this question by asking whether a reasonable person in Brendlin's position when the car stopped would have believed himself free to "terminate the encounter" between the police and himself. We think that in these circumstances any reasonable passenger would have understood the police officers to be exercising control to the point that no one in the car was free to depart without police permission.

In view of the reasonableness of this belief, the Court ruled that Brendlin was seized under the Fourth Amendment and therefore could assert his Fourth Amendment right against unreasonable search and seizure.

CONCLUSIONS

Like many other Supreme Court cases, *Whren* was viewed as a great step forward for some and a severe degradation of constitutional rights by others. Naturally, police officers saw the decision as correct, giving them really no more power than they already had—the ability to make a stop for violations of traffic laws and to conduct further inquiry based on probable cause. Detractors saw this as the Supreme Court giving law enforcement much more power because no one can follow all traffic laws and therefore a police officer could find a reason to stop almost anyone for a traffic violation. *Whren* also fueled the discussion of race-based policing activity, arguing that the decision would further allow officers the ability to stop minorities based on little more than hunches and to conduct searches leading to arrest. Whether or not *Whren* created these conditions, police activity appears to have changed little based on this ruling.

FURTHER READING

Angela J. Davis, "Race, Cops and Traffic Stops," *University of Miami Law Review* 51 (1996–1997): 425–43.

Kenneth Gavsie, "Making the Best of *Whren*: The Problems with Pretextual Traffic Stops and the Need for Restraint," *Florida Law Review* 50 (1998): 385–403.

Matthew J. Saly, "*Whren v. United States*: Buckle Up and Hold On Tight Because the Constitution Won't Protect You," *Pacific Law Journal* 28 (1996–1997): 595–628.

Brian L. Withrow, "When *Whren* Won't Work: The Effects of a Diminished Capacity to Initiate a Pretextual Stop on Police Officer Behavior," *Police Quarterly* 10, no. 4 (2007): 351–70.

VII

INTERROGATION AND LINEUPS

Miranda v. Arizona

MARVIN ZALMAN

INTRODUCTION

Miranda v. Arizona (384 U.S. 436 [1966]) is probably the most famous Supreme Court case known to the general public today, largely because its famous warnings are repeated in countless police procedurals on TV: "You have the right to remain silent. Anything you say can and will be used against you in a court of law. You have a right to have an attorney present during questioning. If you cannot afford an attorney, one will be appointed for you." The *Miranda* decision held that a confession made during custodial interrogation without police getting a waiver of rights, after reading these warnings to a suspect, is inadmissible in court. The warnings were required by the Fifth Amendment prohibition of compelled self-incrimination.

Miranda was a highly controversial case in its time. Its decision in 1966 brought a roar of disapproval from police chiefs and politicians throughout the land. They thought that *Miranda* would put an end to police interrogation and let criminals go free. Indeed, within two years Congress passed a law to nullify the decision, saying that an otherwise voluntary confession is admissible even if the warnings are not read. This law conflicted with the Supreme Court's power to determine the Constitution's meaning. The issue lay dormant for three decades. Then, in 2000 the Supreme Court ruled that Congress could not could nullify a constitutional ruling by ordinary legislation and upheld *Miranda*'s constitutionality (*Dickerson v. United States*, 530 U.S. 428 [2000]), saying, "*Miranda* has become embedded in routine police practice to the point where the warnings have become part of our national culture." *Dickerson* was based in part on the principle of *stare decisis*, a Latin phrase meaning "to stand by that which is decided." Stare decisis embodies the principle of precedent by which prior decisions are to be followed by the courts. Later in this chapter we'll return to this principle when discussing the arguments for and against *Miranda*.

Miranda focused on a critical police function: the interrogation of suspects to (1) determine whether they are guilty of the crimes for which they were arrested and (2) obtain confessions that can be used as evidence to convict them. Interrogation has been used throughout history to get information and confessions from suspects. It has also been subject to the worst abuses, including torture. In fact, the use of torture to obtain confessions was legal in ancient and medieval societies. Strange as it may seem, a brief discussion of torture and interrogation in those societies helps us understand *Miranda*'s underpinnings.

TORTURE AND INTERROGATION: A HISTORICAL BACKGROUND

Ancient Practice

In ancient Greek city-states and in ancient Rome, using torture to get the truth from a slave about a serious crime was not only allowed but also required. This seems bizarre today, but in those hierarchical societies it was commonly believed that a slave, typically a farm worker, would be so afraid of testifying against an owner that torture was deemed necessary to ensure the truth. Generally, free persons and nobles were not subject to torture. As Rome shifted from a republic to a principate ruled by the emperor and became a polity with a state-police apparatus, torture also came to be used against free persons in the investigation of crime.

Medieval Practice

This usage was carried into medieval continental Europe, where serious crimes were tried in inquisitorial trials. Continental judges required "full proof" before a suspect could be executed for a serious crime like murder. One reason was to protect suspects. Another was to protect judges, who, as devout Christians, feared eternal damnation if they spilled the blood of innocent people. Full proof was obtained by two eyewitnesses to a crime, a rule derived from the Hebrew Bible. Without full proof, even substantial circumstantial evidence could not lead to guilt and execution. Only a confession also constituted full proof. As few spontaneous confessions occurred, interrogation and torture, if necessary, were needed to get suspects to admit guilt. To ensure accuracy, torture could be used only if a great amount of circumstantial evidence also pointed to guilt. Questioning under threats had to precede the application of torture. The judge had to personally question the suspect being tortured. If a confession was obtained under torture, the suspect had to appear in court within twenty-four hours and freely confess under oath. A person who withstood the torture was supposed to be freed.

The Common-Law Trial-by-Jury Adversary System

In contrast to criminal trials in continental Europe, English criminal trials from the thirteenth century for crimes punishable by death were conducted by twelve-person juries presided over by royal circuit judges. The jury's verdict was the judgment of "the country" and treated as sacred, relieving the judge of any bloodguilt for an incorrect verdict. The important point is that guilty verdicts could be based on circumstantial evidence. Because of this, there was no need to apply torture to obtain full proof in common-law trials.

This does not mean that English law was unconcerned with the accuracy of verdicts. A common-law rule developed by the eighteenth century said that guilt could not be based on a confession alone; corroboration (additional evidence) of guilt was required, or else the "extrajudicial" confession (i.e., a confession that was not made in court) was inadmissible.[1] The rule was provoked by a 1660 case in which John Perry, a servant, was interrogated in the disappearance of his employer, William Harrison. Harrison's body was not found, and no facts pointed to Perry's having killed Harrison, like threats, arguments, known grudges, or found weapons. Under incessant questioning by a magistrate, Perry confessed to killing Harrison and implicated his mother and brother. All three hanged for the crime. A few years later, William Harrison reappeared, claiming to have been kidnapped.

Values that Underlie *Miranda*

The modern law of confessions that led to the *Miranda* decision is based on two distinct but related legal rules and principles that originated in England: the exclusionary rule against involuntary confessions and the privilege against self-incrimination. Before discussing the origin and content of these rules in detail, it is important to understand the values that underlie them. The first value that supports rules that limit the use of confessions, and that absolutely prohibits the use of torture to obtain them, is a concern for accuracy. It does not take much fancy reasoning to recognize that a person who is tortured or interrogated under conditions of great stress might confess simply to stop the physical or psychological pressure. A second value that has been expressed by judges is that extreme pressure on a suspect tends to turn him or her into a tool being manipulated by the interrogator, which in turn tends to destroy the suspect's human dignity, autonomy, and privacy.

Support for the adversary system of justice is the third value. This system, with its origin in the English trial by jury, is firmly embedded in the U.S. Constitution and every state constitution. It provides many rights that assure defendants the ability to meaningfully confront the power of the state. A defendant has the right to an attorney, to subpoena witnesses, to confront and cross-examine accusers, to have charges decided by a jury of citizens drawn from the locality rather than by state officers, and more. A criminal-justice process in which police can have the unfettered ability to interrogate suspects at will to solve crimes, rather than by gathering objective evidence of guilt by collecting facts, tends to corrupt the investigation process and undermine the adversary system.

This leads to the final value supported by the legal and constitutional limits on police interrogation practices: restraining the state's power. An abiding lesson of history is that government officers are in positions to abuse their power rather than apply it for the public good. The most obvious danger is personal corruption and making partisan decisions to support the narrow interests of family, friends, and loyal supporters. But history also teaches that the misuse of state power can occur when officials believe that they are working for the public good but are in fact advancing harmful policies. This is more likely to happen when government power is not checked by countervailing forces and by the ability of people to have a say in policies that affect them.

These lessons have led to the development of the rule of law—the idea that the government must rule through law and be controlled by law; constitutionalism—stable procedures and political rules that allow various government and social interests to participate in law making and check one another; and ultimately democratic government—which gives all citizens a voice in making policies that will affect them. Criminal justice is the state's most powerful instrument of coercion, and keeping it in check and focused on providing public safety is a vital part of maintaining a balanced and democratic government.

The Privilege against Self-Incrimination

All of these values came into play and were forcefully expressed in Chief Justice Earl Warren's majority opinion in *Miranda v. Arizona* (1966). The decision was preceded by two streams of common-law legal developments and by rules that reached back several centuries; both rules were distrustful of confessions. As stated above, the *Miranda* decision was based on the privilege against self-incrimination. The privilege has its origins in a sort of medieval common law (*ius commune*) practiced in ecclesiastical (church) and lay courts in Europe and England, which contained a rule against forced self-incrimination. People brought into court had to swear an oath to tell the truth before knowing the nature of the charges against them. This allowed the authorities to engage in fishing expeditions to gather all kinds of evidence about immorality, disputed paternity, or heresy. To counter this, the *ius commune* allowed people to refuse to answer such questions unless there was substantial evidence of guilt of a specific crime.

In sixteenth- and seventeenth-century England, this rule was strengthened and led to the privilege against self-incrimination. The Latin maxim *nemo tenetur prodere seipsum* ("no one is bound to betray or accuse oneself") became a rallying cry by those accused of heresy in the sixteenth century and those charged with political crimes in the seventeenth century. Perhaps the most famous defender of the right of silence was John Lilburne (1614–1657), a political and religious activist and radical who was tried both by the Stewart royal regime prior to the English civil war and by courts under Oliver Cromwell, who became the lord protector of the English commonwealth during the Interregnum. Lilburne was tried for treason in 1649 in a major public trial that was a cause célèbre. He had no defense lawyer. In the trial he berated his prosecutors and the judges, demanding many trial rights that would eventually be enshrined in the American Bill of Rights. Chief among these was the privilege against self-incrimination, which he invoked in order to refuse answering questions that could incriminate him. Lilburne's acquittal raised the visibility of the right to remain silent in court.

In reality, the privilege as we know it today did not fully emerge until defense lawyers became standard features of criminal trials. But as a constitutional provision secured in the Fifth Amendment, the privilege against self-incrimination guaranteed a defendant the absolute right to silence during a trial. Before the United States Constitution was framed, the privilege against self-incrimination had been included in the charters of several English North American colonies. After the nation was established, the privilege became law in the states of the new republic, typically included in their own constitutions or bills of rights. The privilege supported all of the values listed above. However, while the privilege made the trial an arena where rights were upheld, there was a risk that the values of accuracy, human dignity, support of the adversary system, and limiting abusive state power could be undermined by extrajudicial interrogation and confessions.

The Voluntary-Confession Exclusionary Rule

The second limiting rule, developed in mid-eighteenth-century English courts, provided that an extrajudicial confession was admissible only if made voluntarily, without inducements, threats, tricks, or force. A confession obtained by threats or promises of leniency was inadmissible. By the early nineteenth century the rule appeared in American cases and by the early twentieth century was an established common-law rule on both sides of the Atlantic Ocean.

In 1912, at the request of the English government, the Court of King's Bench issued a set of guidelines, known as the Judges' Rules, that summarized the legal rules for interrogation. The Judges' Rules allowed police to question suspects with a view to finding out whether, or by whom, an offense had been committed. However, before questioning a suspect in custody, the suspect had to be cautioned that he or she was not obliged to say anything and that whatever was said would be taken down and could be admitted into evidence. The use of cautioning suspects became the practice in a few American law-enforcement agencies, including the FBI, by the 1930s.

By the early twentieth century every state prohibited the introduction of coerced confessions as evidence against a defendant. That said, the federal rule was not highly developed, as most crimes and most criminal-procedure doctrines were matters of state law. Furthermore, at this time the Supreme Court decided that the Bill of Rights, including the privilege against self-incrimination, were restraints only on the federal government and its law-enforcement apparatus. The Bill of Rights did not, at that time, apply to state courts, prosecutors, or police officers. In 1897 the Supreme Court did decide that involuntary confessions were inadmissible in federal criminal trials, in a case of a murder occurring on board a U.S. ship (*Bram v. United States*, 168 U.S. 532 [1897]). The *Bram* rule, oddly, was decided under the privilege against self-incrimination. The rule, that the privilege encompassed the voluntariness test, had little traction and was ultimately repudiated by the Court.

The Third Degree

The real problem with interrogations and confessions in the period from the 1890s to the 1930s was not with the content of the legal rules but with the fact of the so-called third degree in police interrogations. By 1910 it was widely known that police departments across the nation routinely got confessions from suspects by measures that ranged from rough handling to outright torture. Third-degree methods, dispensed in secret in the back rooms of police stations, included brutal beatings with nightsticks and other implements, beatings with telephone books and rubber hoses designed to not leave marks, choking, tear gas, forcing suspects to stand for hours while handcuffed, placing suspects in sweat boxes, water boarding, extensive questioning for over thirty hours without sleep, deprivations of food, and more.

Because third-degree methods violated legal and social norms, they were practiced in secret, mostly against poor people and people without influence. Nevertheless, these practices were an "open secret" and even led to a congressional hearing in 1910, but nothing came of it. In 1930 the Wickersham Commission, a national crime commission established by President Hoover, exposed the third degree in a detailed report. This time the report caused national shock, and matters began to change. Over the next few decades, police practices slowly became less harsh; by the 1960s the routine use of force to get confessions, with rare exceptions, disappeared.

The Supreme Court's Due-Process Voluntariness Cases

Soon after the Wickersham report the Supreme Court began to decide cases of involuntary confessions coming from local police departments that had been upheld by state courts. Because the Bill of Rights did not apply to the states, the Supreme Court ruled that police brutality imposed on suspects violated the Due Process Clause of the Fourteenth Amendment. The amendment was ratified after the Civil War in 1868 and prohibited *states* from violating the due-process rights of its citizens, who were also U.S. citizens. The first due-process voluntariness case, *Brown v. Mississippi* (297 U.S. 278 [1936]), held that confessions obtained from three black defendants after being whipped on the back with a metal-studded belt, tearing the flesh, and being hung by the neck and threatened with death, were involuntary. Between 1936 and the 1966 *Miranda* case, it decided over thirty state voluntariness cases, finding that involuntary confessions were produced not only by physical torture but by prolonged questioning for thirty-six hours, keeping the suspect incommunicado for days, threatening a suspect with mob violence, using "truth serum," degrading a suspect by keeping him naked, having a medical doctor ask incriminating questions under the guise of treatment, telling a mother that her children's welfare assistance would be cut off and her children taken from her if she failed to cooperate with police, and the like.

By 1966, a majority of the Supreme Court felt that continuing to decide such cases under the Due Process Clause, which required weighing all of the facts and circumstances of a case, allowed the police to continue to find new methods of creating undue pressure to force confessions from suspects' lips. All of the history and values involved in the use of interrogation and the taking of confessions came to the fore in *Miranda v. Arizona* (1966). Writing for a five-justice majority, Chief Justice Earl Warren expressed the view that the time had come for the Court to establish firm rules to end the perceived game playing by police departments seeking to avoid the ban on coerced confessions and "to give concrete constitutional guidelines for law-enforcement agencies and courts to follow."[2]

The Incorporation of the Bill of Rights

The Court had the option of bringing the constitutional law of interrogation confessions under one of three doctrines: the due-process voluntariness test, the Sixth Amendment right to counsel, or the Fifth Amendment privilege against compelled self-incrimination. The majority was clearly fed up with the voluntariness approach as the primary method of controlling police practices. Until the 1960s, however, the Court had refused to apply the Bill of Rights to actions of state and local officers. This refusal was based on an interpretation going back to the 1830s that those rights applied only as limitations against the federal government.

This interpretation changed in a massive reappraisal of the constitutional relationship between the states, the federal government, and the courts in the 1960s, in which most Bill of Rights provisions were extended as protections of individual liberties against local and state authorities. This change, known as the Due Process Revolution, meant that local and state police, prosecutors, judges, and correctional officers, had to grant criminal suspects, defendants, and prisoners rights guaranteed in the Bill of Rights. The Due Process Revolution was based on a reassessment of the meaning of the post–Civil War Fourteenth Amendment, holding that the amendment was intended to create a more unified nation in which the rights of all citizens were guaranteed by the Bill of Rights. To accomplish this, the Supreme Court would hold the states to minimum standards of rights by "incorporating" components of the Bill of Rights into the Due Process Clause.

The Choice of Constitutional Doctrine in *Miranda*

Thus, having "incorporated" the right to counsel and the privilege against self-incrimination in 1963 and 1964, the Court had the option of applying either of these rights to the interrogation process. In 1964 the Court tentatively extended a limited right to counsel to an in-custody suspect who was questioned by police in *Escobedo v. Illinois* (378 U.S. 478 [1964]). That case was limited to the particular circumstances of an attorney being present at the police station and requesting that interrogation cease until he could speak to his client. The question confronting the Court in *Miranda* was whether to expand *Escobedo* and make attorney-mediated interrogations mandatory. If the Court had taken this direction, it likely would have severely limited the ability of police to interrogate suspects and obtain confessions in secret. Instead, the Court took a more moderate position and ruled that "custodial interrogations"—the questioning of suspects who had been detained or arrested—came under the strictures of the Fifth Amendment privilege against compelled self-incrimination.

THE CASE OF *MIRANDA V. ARIZONA* (1966)

The Facts

Miranda v. Arizona (384 U.S. 436 [1966]) consisted of four consolidated cases. The facts in the cases were essentially simple: criminal suspects were in police custody, effectively under arrest. Without the advice of counsel, and before seeing a magistrate, they were questioned in private. There was no indication of beatings or excessive pressure. Ernesto Miranda was questioned for about two hours concerning the rape of a mentally retarded teenage girl, and he confessed. The important fact in each case was that the suspects were not warned that they in fact had the right to remain silent in the face of police interrogation.

Compulsion in the Majority Decision

The first problem confronting the majority was the need to establish the compulsion required by the privilege. Involuntary-confessions cases, decided under the Due Process Clause, typically involved high-pressure tactics, like the in-custody intermittent questioning over four days of Arthur Culombe, an illiterate mental defective with low intellectual functioning who became upset upon seeing his wife and sick daughter and being urged by his wife to tell the truth, thereafter confessing to participation in a holdup in which two men had been murdered (*Culombe v. Connecticut*, 367 U.S. 568 [1961]). But in *Miranda* there were no such tactics. The confessions were probably admissible under the due-process voluntariness test.

Chief Justice Warren, a former experienced prosecutor, drew on police manuals that instructed police in the methods of psychological interrogation, in order to establish that the atmosphere of police custody is inherently compelling. Investigators are instructed to keep the suspect secluded in a small room, create an atmosphere of dominance, project confidence in his guilt, provide explanations that the suspect can use to justify his crime and downplay its moral seriousness, and interrogate relentlessly for hours at a time over a period of days if needed. If the suspect claims the right to remain silent, the officers are to agree but continue to ask questions. If the suspect asks for an attorney, they are to suggest that he tell the truth and spare his family unnecessary expenses. Tricks and lies are recommended, including false identification in a so-called reverse lineup.

Historical Underpinnings and Precedent for the Majority Decision

Having established the precondition for applying the privilege—compulsion—the decision then recalled the history of the privilege and how the travails of John Lilburne brought it to popular consciousness and that it is so central to constitutional liberty to have been included in the Bill of Rights as a "hallmark of our democracy."[3] Chief Justice Warren, drawing on Supreme Court precedent, pointedly asserted that a variation on the common-law maxim *nemo tenetur seipsum accusare* had been transformed from "a mere rule of evidence" to become "clothed in this country with the impregnability of a constitutional enactment."[4] Further, the Court relied on *Bram* (1897) as the precedent for applying the privilege to police interrogation and, noting that the privilege had recently been incorporated, for extending that rule to state courts. The Court then laid out its method for balancing the absolute right to silence against the need of the police to investigate. As the majority opinion noted, "we are not unmindful of the burdens which law-enforcement officials must bear, often under trying circumstances. . . . Our decision does not in any way preclude police from carrying out their traditional investigatory functions."[5]

The Court's central innovation was to seek "a protective device to dispel the compelling atmosphere of the interrogation," and it found it by adopting the practice of warnings, innovated by the Judges' Rules in England, as a way to preserve the privilege but to open the door to lawful questioning.[6] In doing so the Court simply extended the waiver rule that existed regarding the right to counsel: that a constitutional right can be waived by a person who is fully informed that he or she has the right and understands the consequences of a waiver. In the Court's reasoning, without proper safeguards the process of in-custody interrogation of persons suspected or accused of crime contains inherently compelling pressures which work to undermine the individual's will to resist and to compel him to speak where he would not otherwise do so freely. In order to combat these pressures and to permit a full opportunity to exercise the privilege against self-incrimination, the accused must be adequately and effectively apprised of his rights and the exercise of those rights must be fully honored.[7]

Hence, the familiar four warnings or cautions listed at beginning of this article.

The Warnings in the Miranda Rule

The first warning tells a suspect that he or she is clothed with an absolute, constitutionally grounded right to silence, as absolute as that which may be claimed by a defendant in a criminal trial. The second warning "is needed in order to make [the suspect] aware not only of the privilege but also of the consequences of forgoing it. It is only through an awareness of these consequences that there can be any assurance of real understanding and intelligent exercise of the privilege."[8]

The next warning, regarding the right to counsel, should not be confused with the Sixth Amendment right to an attorney, which is granted only during a criminal prosecution; police interrogation precedes "prosecution." The Court had held that under the Sixth Amendment counsel is not required unless a pretrial process constitutes a "critical stage."[9] The *Miranda* Court created a special Fifth Amendment rule for the right to "consult with a lawyer and to have the lawyer with him during interrogation"[10]:

The circumstances surrounding in-custody interrogation can operate very quickly to overbear the will of one merely made aware of his privilege by his interrogators. Therefore, the right to have counsel present at the interrogation is indispensable to the protection of the Fifth Amendment privilege under the system we delineate today. Our aim is to assure that the individual's right to choose between silence and speech remains unfettered throughout the interrogation process. A once-stated warning, delivered by those who will conduct the interrogation, cannot itself suffice to that end among those who most require knowledge of their rights. A mere warning given by the interrogators is not alone sufficient to accomplish that end.[11]

Finally, as for providing counsel for indigents, "financial ability of the individual has no relationship to the scope of the rights involved here. The privilege against self-incrimination secured by the Constitution applies to all individuals. The need for counsel in order to protect the privilege exists for the indigent as well as the affluent. In fact, were we to limit these constitutional rights to those who can retain an attorney, our decisions today would be of little significance."[12]

If a suspect at any time before or after the warnings says that he wishes to remain silent, the interrogation must cease, even if he had begun to answer questions. The suspect may waive the rights and agree to answer the interrogator's questions, but the waiver has to be explicit and preferably on the record.

The Values Underlying the Miranda Rule

Chief Justice Warren spoke eloquently about the values that underlie the privilege against self-incrimination and the extension of the privilege to the interrogation of suspects. The case begins by reminding readers that our government is founded on the rule of law, individual liberties, and constitutional restraints on government: "The cases before us raise questions which go to the roots of our concepts of American criminal jurisprudence: the restraints society must observe consistent with the federal Constitution in prosecuting individuals for crime."[13] He noted

> that the privilege against self-incrimination—the essential mainstay of our adversary system—is founded on a complex of values. . . . All these policies point to one overriding thought: the constitutional foundation underlying the privilege is the respect a government—state or federal—must accord to the dignity and integrity of its citizens. To maintain a fair state-individual balance, to require the government to shoulder the entire load, to respect the inviolability of the human personality, our accusatory system of criminal justice demands that the government seeking to punish an individual produce the evidence against him by its own independent labors rather than by the cruel, simple expedient of compelling it from his own mouth. In sum, the privilege is fulfilled only when the person is guaranteed the right "to remain silent unless he chooses to speak in the unfettered exercise of his own will."[14]

The majority opinion expresses an awareness of history, an impassioned defense of hard-won constitutional liberties, alertness to the dangers of convicting the innocent, and the need to make rights effective while balancing the need of the public for safety through police investigation of crimes.

The Dissenting Opinions

The Supreme Court split bitterly in this landmark case. Four dissenting justices eloquently challenged the majority decision. Great cases are often decided by narrow majorities, as they do not resolve easy technical questions but speak to controversial issues and conflicting ideals. An acute challenge to the Court was that its decision was unprecedented and thus violated the principle of stare decisis. Justice Tom Clark noted that the Supreme Court had on several previous occasions rejected the need to impose a warnings requirement on the police. He and Justice Byron White made the case that the *Miranda* decision did not rest on the historical lineage of the privilege against self-incrimination, which applied only to in-court testimony. Justice White trenchantly observed that the decision "is at odds with American and English legal history."[15] As noted above, the history of the privilege has medieval and early modern roots and focused mainly on the right to silence in judicial proceedings. Justice White, capitalizing on this historical knowledge, pointed out that the involuntary-confessions rule came into play about a century after the privilege against self-incrimination was established, thus seeking to undermine the majority's historical analysis.

Justice White made a sophisticated observation about stare decisis. It is easy to show that the *Miranda* decision was a legal innovation. But to argue that the law should never change through the Court's opinions, or that changes ought to be left to the slow and politically charged purview of Congress, misunderstands the common-law method and would create real problems.

That the Court's holding today is neither compelled nor even strongly suggested by the language of the Fifth Amendment, is at odds with American and English legal history, and involves a departure from a long line of precedent does not prove either that the Court has exceeded its powers or that the Court is wrong or unwise in its present reinterpretation of the Fifth Amendment. It does, however, underscore the obvious—that the Court has not discovered or found the law in making today's decision, nor has it derived it from some irrefutable sources; what it has done is to make new law and new public policy in much the same way that it has in the course of interpreting other great clauses of the Constitution. This is what the Court historically has done. Indeed, it is what it must do and will continue to do until and unless there is some fundamental change in the constitutional distribution of governmental powers.[16]

However, according to Justice White the Court did not adequately explain the reason for the new rule, beyond resting on "syllogism, metaphysics, or some ill-defined notions of natural justice."[17]

Justice White poked a few more holes in the majority opinion. He challenged the finding of compulsion based on police manuals, without the Court examining any transcripts of police interrogations. Also, if the atmosphere of police custody were inherently coercive, the Court should not allow the introduction of purely spontaneous confessions, but it did so in its opinion. Additionally, the majority's decision is irrational in another way. The Miranda rule asserts that the coercive nature of custodial interrogation is so great that it cannot constitutionally proceed without the warnings. If that is so, there is no logic to believing that a suspect is free from compulsion to make a voluntary waiver of rights. Finally, Justice White passionately expressed the view that the Miranda regime of warnings would hamper police investigations to the extent that it would lead to some failed prosecutions resulting in more serious crimes.

MIRANDA'S AFTERMATH

Chief Justice Warren's hope that the Miranda decision would put an end to disputes over police-induced confessions was not borne out by subsequent events. The Miranda decision proved to be so toxic at the time that, in addition to the Congressional Act purporting to overturn it (as discussed above), the ruling became a major issue in the 1968 presidential campaign. Richard Nixon, the Republican nominee, made overturning the case a campaign pledge. When as president he nominated four conservative justices to the Supreme Court by 1972, it appeared that Miranda might be overruled. However, the Court for the most part prevented any expansion of suspects' rights during interrogation, interpreted the case in ways favorable to the police, and thus upheld a truncated version of the interrogation regime hoped for by Earl Warren. Ironically, instead of reducing the number of confession-based appeals to the Supreme Court, the thirty years following Miranda generated twice the number of confessions cases that came to the Court in the thirty years prior to Miranda.

In numerous cases the Supreme Court under Chief Justices Burger and Rehnquist ruled to uphold confessions and made interrogation easier for police. Warnings were thus upheld even where they seemed to imply that a lawyer would not be provided until a suspect went to court (Duckworth v. Eagan, 492 U.S. 195 [1989]). A confession was admissible after a suspect said he did not want to talk, under circumstances where questioning ceased but was later resumed by police, who again administered warnings, for a different crime (*Michigan v. Mosley*, 423 U.S. 96 [1975]). A confession was admissible where a juvenile asked for and did not get the assistance of his probation officer; the request for help under the Miranda rule would not be extended beyond a request for a lawyer (*Fare v. Michael C.*, 442 U.S. 707 [1979]). Questioning in private at the police station is not deemed to be custodial interrogation if the police invite a person to come to the station on his own, a ploy that often tangles a person into a confession (*Oregon v. Mathiason*, 429 U.S. 492 [1977]). A confession was upheld where a suspect did not know that his family hired an attorney who got the police to promise not to interrogate him; although the interrogation could have been interpreted as interference with the attorney-client relationship, the Court held that events occurring outside the police station had no bearing on whether a suspect can waive his rights, including his ignorance that he is represented; the Court also held that the right to counsel for Miranda-warning purposes is not the same as the more general right to counsel under the Sixth Amendment (*Moran v. Burbine*, 475 U.S. 412 [1986]).

Not all post-*Miranda* cases were decided in favor of the police. In several cases the Supreme Court supported the suspect's claims, especially where the suspect invoked a request for counsel. In *Edwards v. Arizona* (451 U.S. 477 [1981]) a suspect told police that he wanted to make a deal and then said he wanted an attorney before making the deal. The police terminated the interrogation but came back the next day, reinitiated the questioning, and obtained a confession. The Supreme Court held that the interrogation violated the Miranda rule and that the resulting confession must be excluded. When a suspect invokes counsel, the police may not reinterrogate the suspect unless he reinitiates further communications. This is so even if the invocation for a lawyer is made in court at an initial appearance (*Michigan v. Jackson*, 475 U.S. 625 [1986]) or after a suspect has had an opportunity to consult with a lawyer (*Minnick v. Mississippi*, 498 U.S. 146 [1990]). Nevertheless, the Court ruled that an interrogated suspect who says "Maybe I should talk to a lawyer" has not invoked counsel; a suspect must clearly request a lawyer (*Davis v. United States*, 512 U.S. 452 [1986]).

A fascinating set of cases nearly led to *Miranda* being overruled before it was "saved" in *Dickerson v. United States* (530 U.S. 428 [2000]). In these cases the Supreme Court said that the Miranda warnings are not in themselves constitutional rights but only prophylactic devices designed to protect the underlying privilege against self-incrimination. As such, confessions taken where the Miranda warnings were violated could still be admitted for collateral purposes but not for proving the crime. This reasoning was applied to introducing a confession to impeach a

defendant who testified at trial (*Oregon v. Hass*, 420 U.S. 714 [1975]) and to intro-
duce evidence derived from confessions that violated the Miranda rules (*Michigan v. Tucker*, 417 U.S. 433 [1974]; *United States v. Patane*, 542 U.S. 630 [2004]).

The Supreme Court also ruled that a confession made when no warnings were given did not invalidate a later confession that was preceded by Miranda warnings, even though in the first, unconstitutional confession, the suspect "let the cat out of the bag" and may have thought that he had to talk thereafter (*Oregon v. Elstad*, 470 U.S. 298 [1985]). The Supreme Court, however, has found such a procedure to be a violation of the suspect's rights where the second interrogation, preceded by warnings, was part of a police plan to "soften up" the suspect by getting an admission of guilt in a previous interview that was essentially part of the same interrogation process (*Missouri v. Seibert*, 542 U.S. 600 [2004]). Lastly, the Supreme Court carved out an exception, allowing the introduction of an unwarned confession to prove guilt where the police asked a question to preserve public safety from immediate harm (*New York v. Quarles*, 467 U.S. 649 [1984]).

As these cases were proceeding, police continued to perfect the psychological interrogation and discovered that about four-fifths of all suspects waived their rights. Generally speaking, police have come to accept the Miranda warning system, finding that it provides them with professionalism and legitimacy. More recently, however, research has uncovered a disturbing number of false confessions. While police techniques of psychological pressure may be necessary to obtain lawful confessions that do not violate the due-process (which still applies to confessions) or self-incrimination clauses, it is a very powerful technique that can pressure innocent people into confessions, especially teenagers or those who are mentally or emotionally challenged. This realization has led to a widespread call for videotaping entire interrogation sessions.

FURTHER READING

Liva Baker, *Miranda: Crime Law and Politics* (New York: Atheneum, 1985).

Peter Brooks, *Troubling Confessions: Speaking Guilt in Law & Literature* (Chicago: University of Chicago Press, 2000).

R. H. Helmholtz, Charles M. Gray, John H. Langbein, Eben Moglen, Henry E. Smith, and Albert W. Alschuler, *The Privilege against Self-Incrimination: Its Origins and Development* (Chicago: University of Chicago Press, 1997).

Richard A. Leo, *Police Interrogation and American Justice* (Cambridge, Mass.: Harvard University Press, 2008).

Leonard Levy, *The Origins of the Fifth Amendment: The Right against Self-Incrimination* (London: Oxford University Press, 1968).

Schmerber v. California

Marvin Zalman

INTRODUCTION

Can officers of the state invade a person's body to extract evidence of a crime? If they can, are there any limits to when they can do so and how far they can go? English law faced a parallel question in earlier times when dealing with when and under what conditions the king's officers could invade a person's home to seize evidence. The general answer worked out in English and American law was that officers could not willy-nilly force their way into a person's home or place of business on a whim, on the basis of rumors, or even on probable cause. True, a criminal might store criminal evidence in a private place, but government officers could make mistakes in seeking it or could act on corrupt motives. Honest persons had to be protected against the casual invasion of state officers. At the same time, officers had to have some power to enforce the law lest criminals turn their homes into crime sanctuaries. The answer was to authorize home invasions for evidence only if a judge was convinced that probable cause existed and issued a search warrant to the police. Modern conditions have led to a greater scope for warrantless searches where law-enforcement officers arrest or search under emergency conditions, expanding exigency exceptions to the search-warrant requirement.

A somewhat similar problem concerned knowledge of a crime held by alleged suspects who nevertheless refused to talk when questioned by officers. Could a suspect be forced to explain whether he had a connection to a crime? As legal history showed, the English legal system decided that it was uncivilized to use compulsion to force evidence out of a suspect's mouth, so to speak.[1]

The resolution of these potential conflicts between citizens and the state, established in English common law, became bedrock constitutional principles in the United States. Searches and seizures were limited by the Fourth Amendment, and interrogations were controlled by rules of due process (in the Fifth and Fourteenth Amendments) and the Fifth Amendment privilege against self-incrimination.

But time does not stand still, and as society progresses new ideas and technologies raise new legal problems. In the era when the common law of England was formed all could understand that evidence of crime could be secreted in a cottage or knowledge of a crime secured in the mind of a tight-lipped man. But blood was not evidence. Yet with developments of modern science and medicine, blood could and indeed did become evidence. Specifically, it became possible to measure the alcohol content of blood in percentage terms, and a series of experiments correlated that amount with such factors as body weight, food consumption, and time elapsed between the time of alcohol consumption and testing, to assess the extent to which a person's functions, such as the ability to safely direct the movement of an automated vehicle weighing a ton or more, could be carried out with safety to the bodily integrity and lives of people who happened to come into the path of such a vehicle.

And so police came to desire the extraction of blood to prove suspects guilty of driving under the influence of liquor. But suspects resisted and raised legal objections. The specific issue was new, but the courts responded to the new question by using the time-honored method, fundamental to the growth of law, of reasoning by analogy. Is a medical procedure to extract blood more like entering a home to obtain evidence or more like torturing a suspect to force him to talk? If more like a search, could blood be taken if probable cause existed? But if alcohol-laden blood is more like spoken testimony, is taking it a more serious invasion of privacy that is absolutely protected by the privilege against self-incrimination? Or is blood simply physical evidence, like a person's appearance, that can be viewed no matter how incriminating?

THE CASE OF *SCHMERBER V. CALIFORNIA* (1966)

In the case of *Schmerber v. California* (384 U.S. 757, 758 [1966]), a Los Angeles police officer came on the scene soon after an automobile accident in which a passenger was injured. He smelled liquor on the breath of Armando Schmerber, the apparent driver, and saw that his eyes appeared bloodshot and glassy. Schmerber was transported to a hospital. Two hours later, in the hospital, the officer noticed similar symptoms of drunkenness and arrested Schmerber for driving under the influence of intoxicating liquor. Schmerber was told that he had a right to counsel, that he could remain silent, and that anything he said would be used against him. A lawyer apparently advised Schmerber to refuse to consent to a blood test. Despite his objection, "a blood sample was . . . withdrawn from [Schmerber's] body by a physician at the hospital [at] the direction of a police officer." A report of the blood's chemical analysis, indicating intoxication at the time he drove the car, was admitted into evidence to convict Schmerber of driving under the influence of liquor.

On appeal to the Supreme Court Schmerber raised four constitutional objections to the introduction of the evidence, arguing that it deprived him of liberty without due process of law, violated his privilege against self-incrimination, deprived him of the right to counsel, and violated his right to be free from unreasonable searches and seizures. As noted above, a court may have to resolve an issue because technological changes create new situations, like scientific blood-alcohol testing, that were unknown to an earlier period. But a court may also have to address a question because the legal landscape has changed. The Supreme Court decided, only nine years before the *Schmerber* case, that the medical withdrawal of blood in a reasonable manner from an unconscious person believed to have been a drunk driver, at the order of a state police officer who had probable cause of intoxication, for chemical testing that established a blood alcohol level of .17 percent, and the use of that evidence in court to convict the driver of involuntary manslaughter, did not violate the petitioner's right to due process under the Fourteenth Amendment (*Breithaupt v. Abram*, 352 U.S. 432 [1957]).

What changed since *Breithaupt* was that the Court had incorporated the Fourth Amendment exclusionary rule in *Mapp v. Ohio* (367 U.S. 643 [1961]) and the privilege against self-incrimination in *Malloy v. Hogan* (378 U.S. 1 [1964]).[2] Challenges in *Breithaupt* on the claims that his privilege against self-incrimination was violated or that the taking of his blood was an illegal search and seizure were brushed aside because those provisions simply did not apply to the actions of state or local officers. The extension of these rights to limit state and local officials raised the question whether police could continue to gather blood evidence of intoxication. As a general matter the Bill of Rights had been interpreted in a more "liberal," or defendant-friendly, way, especially by the five liberal justices of the Warren Court. Justice Brennan, in many ways the intellectual driver of the Due Process Revolution, wrote the opinion in *Schmerber*.[3] But in this case he upheld the power of the police to gather blood evidence, joined by

Justices Clark, Harlan, Stewart, and White. The other purportedly liberal justices (Chief Justice Warren and Justices Black, Douglas, and Fortas) dissented.

The Privilege-against-Self-Incrimination Claim

In the case of *Schmerber*, the petitioner clearly objected to the withdrawal of blood, so for Fifth Amendment purposes there was no question as to whether he was compelled to give evidence by a state officer. The issue in this case was, rather, "whether petitioner was thus compelled 'to be a witness against himself.'"[4] In answering the question, Justice Brennan set a test that might have subjected blood testing to the self-incrimination limitation: "If the scope of the privilege coincided with the complex of values it helps to protect, we might be obliged to conclude that the privilege was violated."[5] He then turned to the four values underlying the privilege: accuracy, human dignity, support of the adversary system, and limiting abusive state power.[6] The forced puncturing of the skin to extract blood can be seen as failing "to respect the 'inviolability of the human personality'" and undermines the adversary system by allowing "the state to [not] procure the evidence against an accused 'by its own independent labors.'"[7]

Against these factors that weigh in favor of the petitioner, Justice Brennan noted the following:

> The privilege has never been given the full scope which the values it helps to protect suggest. History and a long line of authorities in lower courts have consistently limited its protection to situations in which the state seeks to submerge those values by obtaining the evidence against an accused through the cruel, simple expedient of compelling it from his own mouth. . . . In sum, the privilege is fulfilled only when the person is guaranteed the right to remain silent unless he chooses to speak in the unfettered exercise of his own will.[8]

In short, the privilege was limited to speech and speech-like acts. It would not be extended to physical evidence.

In his dissent in *Schmerber*, Justice Hugo Black, the other architect of the Due Process Revolution, wrote that

> to reach the conclusion that compelling a person to give his blood to help the state convict him is not equivalent to compelling him to be a witness against himself strikes me as quite an extraordinary feat. . . . The compulsory extraction of petitioner's blood for analysis so that the person who analyzed it could give evidence

to convict him had both a "testimonial" and a "communicative nature." The sole purpose of this project that proved to be successful was to obtain "testimony" from some person to prove that petitioner had alcohol in his blood at the time he was arrested. And the purpose of the project was certainly "communicative" in that the analysis of the blood was to supply information to enable a witness to communicate to the court and jury that petitioner was more or less drunk.[9]

Justice Brennan answered by asserting that

of course, all evidence received in court is "testimonial" or "communicative" if these words are thus used. But the Fifth Amendment relates only to acts on the part of the person to whom the privilege applies, and we use these words subject to the same limitations. A nod or head-shake is as much a "testimonial" or "communicative" act in this sense as are spoken words. But the terms as we use them do not apply to evidence of acts noncommunicative in nature as to the person asserting the privilege, even though, as here, such acts are compelled to obtain the testimony of others.[10]

Prior Supreme Court precedent made it clear that not only was there no violation of the privilege by witnesses being able to look at and identify a suspect, but that the suspect could be made to participate in the prosecution by having to wear an article of clothing like one worn at the scene of the crime, stand in a particular way in a lineup, be photographed and fingerprinted, made to speak words so that the timbre of his voice can be noted, and the like. All of this is "communicative" but comes under the heading of "real" or physical evidence and is allowed into evidence at the trial. To put a fine point on the distinction, Justice Brennan noted that although the so-called lie-detector test (polygraph) measures "changes in body function during interrogation," its real purpose is to elicit "responses which are essentially testimonial" and therefore could not be compelled. The basic principle that helps to decide which kinds of communications are protected is that "the privilege 'is as broad as the mischief against which it seeks to guard.'"[11] In this case not "even a shadow of testimonial compulsion . . . was involved either in the extraction or in the chemical analysis" of the blood.[12] Schmerber was simply a donor of physical evidence that was subjected to chemical analysis to determine a blood-alcohol level indicative of guilt of driving while under the influence.

Justice Black made a prescient observation in his dissent. Justice Brennan said he did not agree to a formulation of the privilege that was championed by

Professor John Henry Wigmore (1863–1943), the greatest scholar of evidence law. Wigmore was famous for trying to reduce the scope of the privilege as a protection for defendants. Justice Black noted that despite Brennan's disclaimer, the Court's interpretation of the privilege in *Schmerber* would undermine the liberal interpretation that had been established by *Boyd v. United States* (116 U.S. 616 [1886]). "The refined, subtle reasoning and balancing process used here to narrow the scope of the Bill of Rights safeguard against self-incrimination provides a handy instrument for further narrowing of that constitutional protection, as well as others, in the future."[13] This would prove to be true.

The Court dispensed with Schmerber's right to counsel claim by noting that as he had no right under the privilege to refuse the blood test, "he has no greater right because counsel erroneously advised him that he could assert it."[14]

The Majority Opinion Addresses the Search-and-Seizure Claim

Because the Fourth Amendment was applied to seizures by local officers, the Court had to reconsider "whether the chemical analysis introduced in evidence . . . should have been excluded as the product of an unconstitutional search and seizure."[15] Justice Brennan begins with a value analysis of the search-and-seizure amendment: "The overriding function of the Fourth Amendment is to protect personal privacy and dignity against unwarranted intrusion by the state. . . . The values protected by the Fourth Amendment thus substantially overlap those the Fifth Amendment helps to protect."[16] The privilege, nevertheless, did not prevent the seizure of blood. "But if compulsory administration of a blood test does not implicate the Fifth Amendment, it plainly involves the broadly conceived reach of a search and seizure under the Fourth Amendment," which, after all specifically protects *persons* (as well as houses, papers and effects) against unreasonable searches and seizures.[17]

At this point Justice Brennan found that analogies are not entirely helpful. This new situation involved seizing a kind of evidence not found in prior cases. There was little doubt, however, that "compelled intrusions into the body for blood to be analyzed for alcohol content" are searches. The Fourth Amendment does not prohibit all police intrusions into premises "but . . . intrusions which are not justified in the circumstances, or which are made in an improper manner. In other words, the questions we must decide in this case are whether the police were justified in requiring petitioner to submit to the blood test and whether the means and procedures employed in taking his blood respected relevant Fourth Amendment standards of reasonableness."[18]

What, then, justifies a blood seizure as a "reasonable" search and seizure under the Fourth Amendment? The first factor is the existence of probable cause, the basic evidentiary standard triggering lawful police impositions like arrests and seizures. In this case the smell of alcohol and other "symptoms of drunkenness" supplied the constitutionally required evidence necessary for a lawful arrest. However, "the mere fact of a lawful arrest does not end our inquiry."[19] A classic kind of warrantless search recognized at common law is a "search incident to arrest." The reasons for not requiring a warrant to search an arrested person are to seize weapons that pose dangers to the officer, the arrestee, and bystanders and to prevent destruction of evidence under the person's control. Once an officer can reach into pockets or bags held by an arrestee to seize a weapon, it is "both impractical and unnecessary" to say that the officer cannot also seek incriminating evidence. This reasoning, however, cannot apply to a procedure that punctures the person's skin and extracts bodily fluids. The majority continued,

> The interests in human dignity and privacy which the Fourth Amendment protects forbid any such intrusions on the mere chance that desired evidence might be obtained. In the absence of a clear indication that in fact such evidence will be found, these fundamental human interests require law officers to suffer the risk that such evidence may disappear unless there is an immediate search.[20]

Probable cause supplied the "clear indication" for the search.

The next question was whether the police officer alone could authorize the medical extraction or if the officer had to apply for a judge's search warrant to obtain blood: "The importance of informed, detached, and deliberate determinations of the issue whether or not to invade another's body in search of evidence of guilt [by a neutral and detached magistrate] is indisputable and great."[21] The seizure of blood for evidence of alcohol, however, becomes an exigency search that allows dispensing with a warrant because blood alcohol is evanescent and fleeting: "We are told that the percentage of alcohol in the blood begins to diminish shortly after drinking stops, as the body functions to eliminate it from the system."[22] At least two hours elapsed between the time of the accident and the arrest in the hospital, and seeking a magistrate may have taken hours longer. Under "these special facts," the Supreme Court held that "the attempt to secure evidence of blood-alcohol content in this case was an appropriate incident to petitioner's arrest."[23]

That did not end the question of whether the search and seizure was reasonable in its effectiveness and in the manner in which it was conducted: "Extraction of blood samples for testing is a highly effective means of determining the degree to which a person is under the influence of alcohol."[24] Chemical analysis of the blood is a precise, scientific, and an effective way of resolving the issue of impairment with greater accuracy than observing the suspect's affect. A medical procedure that involves physically entering a person's body might be viewed more critically by the courts if the evidence extracted were equivocal. The manner of extraction was reasonable. As a general matter, blood tests "are a commonplace," and "experience with them teaches that the quantity of blood extracted is minimal and that for most people the procedure involves virtually no risk, trauma, or pain."[25] As for the blood extraction from Schmerber himself, "the record shows that the test was performed in a reasonable manner. Petitioner's blood was taken by a physician in a hospital environment according to accepted medical practices."[26]

It is worth noting that the Court was asked to consider a number of issues that it did not answer in the present case. How, for example, would the Court rule if a suspect had an enormous fear of syringes? Had health problems that could be exacerbated by blood extraction? Or held religious scruples against the taking of blood? Could a "breathalyzer" test be required as an alternative? Or does the result of this case apply if an extraction involves a more complicated and invasive medical procedure? Or if blood is taken by someone other than medical personnel or not in a hospital? While suggesting that to "tolerate searches under these conditions might be to invite an unjustified element of personal risk of infection and pain," the Court left such questions for a later day.

There are two reasons why appellate courts do not answer such hypotheticals: First, the issues may not have been fully briefed and argued, and to answer hypotheticals without considering all the questions and angles that could arise would be inadvisable. A preliminary response to a legal question, by failing to consider all problems, might need revision in the future. Such revisions tend to make the law less certain and weaken the respect for a particular court. For this reason, the Supreme Court sometimes refuses to grant certiorari so that an issue can "ripen," by coming before federal circuit courts, so as to better see all of the issues that arise in arguments over an issue. A more fundamental reason why appellate courts do not resolve hypothetical issues goes to the nature of the court as a law-making institution. In our system it is the role of Congress and state legislatures to enact broad laws intended to cover a variety of acts. In a sense, legislation can be considered as something like a word formula meant to cover a variety of behaviors that come within its meaning. Appellate courts in the common-law system also make law. But to be legitimate they are not supposed to overstep the role of the popularly elected legislature, and answering hypothetical issues that arise when a case is decided offers courts the opportunity to do something like legislating. That is why courts are supposed to answer only the issue that arises in a case, bounded by the specific facts of the case. This also why students should be aware that while cases are often said to stand for or establish abstract rules, the actual "holding" of a case is a rule that it intimately tied to its facts. Lastly, the nature of case law as an amalgam of rules and facts allows for a dynamic system of rules that can evolve to meet new conditions or new judicial perspectives, as an appellate court at times "distinguishes" prior precedent by finding that facts deemed essential in earlier cases are only dictum, and vice versa.

The Court concluded that Schmerber's right to be free from an unreasonable search and seizure was not violated and emphasized that its decision was based "only on the facts of the present record." Its decision was, therefore, that "the Constitution does not forbid the states minor intrusions into an individual's body under stringently limited conditions" but that it "in no way indicates that . . . more substantial intrusions, or intrusions under other conditions," are permitted."[27] By emphasizing the limits of the holding and the value that the "integrity of an individual's person is a cherished value of our society," Justice Brennan's opinion sought to forestall some unjustifiable extensions.

The Fourth Amendment decision also resolved the due-process claim that had been decided in favor of the state in *Breithaupt v. Abram* (1957), where the blood extraction was conducted "by a physician in a simple, medically acceptable manner in a hospital environment."[28] The *Breithaupt* decision was based on the rule of *Rochin v. California* (342 U.S. 165 [1952]), which held that evidence was excluded under the Due Process Clause where the way in which it was obtained "shocked the conscience."

The Dissenting Opinion: Regarding the Search-and-Seizure Claim

The four dissenters who objected on self-incrimination grounds also dissented on Fourth Amendment grounds, referring to Chief Justice Warren's Due Process Clause–based dissent in *Breithaupt v. Abram* (1957) (with Justice Douglas adding that the due-process reasoning also applied to the Fourth Amendment issue). Chief Justice Warren's *Breithaupt* dissent suggested that the shocks-the-conscience test had two elements: "the character of the invasion of the body and the expression of the victim's will."[29] In *Rochin* the petitioner objected to the search by physical resistance. The *Breithaupt* dissent argued that the lack of consent, whether by physical resistance (the situation in *Rochin*), inability to refuse (the situation in *Breithaupt*), or voicing an objection (the factual situation in *Schmerber*), constitutes part of the shocks-the-conscience test, and so the result in *Rochin*, excluding the seized evidence, should also apply in the other cases. Furthermore, both blood extraction and stomach pumping are common medical procedures that took place in hospitals in these cases, and neither procedure normally causes lasting ill effects. In each of the three cases the goal was to secure incriminating evidence from the suspect's body. The dissenters make the point that there is no essential difference between the three cases except the "personal reaction" of the justices to stomach pumping (which under *Rochin* shocks the conscience) and blood extraction (which does not in *Breithaupt* and *Schmerber*). This is not law. In the *Breithaupt* dissent Chief Justice Warren wrote,

> To base the restriction which the Due Process Clause imposes on state criminal procedures upon such reactions is to build on shifting sands. We should, in my opinion, hold that due process means at least that law-enforcement officers in their efforts to obtain evidence from persons suspected of crime must stop short of bruising the body, breaking skin, puncturing tissue, or extracting body fluids, whether they contemplate doing it by force or by stealth.[30]

CONCLUSIONS

Thus, by a close majority, the Supreme Court made it easier for police to gather identification and biological evidence, although the reasoning in *Schmerber* created some guidelines that could limit the level of intrusiveness.

Schmerber's Precedent: Limits to Surgery for Evidence

Schmerber's caution that only "minor intrusions into an individual's body under stringently limited conditions" are allowed and that its decision "in no way indicates that it permits more substantial intrusions, or intrusions under other conditions," came to the fore in *Winston v. Lee* (470 U.S. 753 [1985]). Justice Brennan, writing for a unanimous Court, put that limit into effect in a case where the state tried to compel Rudolph Lee, an armed robbery suspect, "to undergo a surgical procedure under a general anesthetic for removal of a bullet lodged in his chest." The Supreme Court upheld the decision of the lower courts barring the surgery on Fourth Amendment grounds.

Police believed that Lee shot the victim of an attempted robbery, who in turn shot the robber. The victim claimed to have hit the robber in his left side. Police, responding to a different call eight blocks away, found Lee twenty minutes after the attempted robbery, claiming that he was shot by men trying to rob him. Lee was spontaneously identified by the robbery victim when both were brought to the hospital to attend to their respective gunshot wounds. After investigation the police believed the robbery victim and charged Lee with crimes arising out of the attempted robbery.

The state sought a court order to subject Lee to surgery to remove the bullet lodged in him to be used as evidence. Several evidentiary hearings were held. Initially a state expert testified that surgery to retrieve the bullet would be intrusive (e.g., under general anesthesia, last forty-five minutes, create a 3 to 4 percent chance of temporary nerve damage) but after reexamination asserted that the bullet was close to the skin requiring a small incision under local anesthesia to retrieve it. After additional hearings and appeals, surgery to get the bullet was ordered over Lee's objection. Presurgery x-rays showed the bullet lodged about one-inch deep into muscular tissue in Lee's chest, requiring general anesthetic. Further legal proceedings led federal courts to block the surgery, and the state brought the case to the Supreme Court.

The Court noted that the "reasonableness of surgical intrusions beneath the skin depends on a case-by-case approach, in which the individual's interests in privacy and security are weighed against society's interests in conducting the procedure."[31] The Fourth Amendment requires a balancing of these interests. Typically, where the state can establish probable cause, its interest in obtaining evidence outweighs the individual's privacy interests. "A compelled surgical intrusion into an individual's body for evidence, however, implicates expectations of privacy and security of such magnitude that the intrusion may be 'unreasonable' even if likely to produce evidence of a crime."[32] Therefore, the seriousness of the bodily intrusion and its reasonableness must be closely examined.

The federal district and circuit courts and the Supreme Court examined a number of factors in detail in deciding that the Fourth Amendment barred the surgery in this case. The four factors were probable cause, the threat to the suspect's safety and health, the "extent of intrusion upon the individual's dignitary interests in personal privacy and bodily integrity," and "the community's interest in fairly and accurately determining guilt or innocence."[33]

The state had probable cause in this case that Lee was the robber who shot the victim. There was conflicting evidence about the health risks to Lee created by the surgery, with estimates of the time it would take ranging from fifteen minutes to two-and-a-half hours. A surgeon testified that it could be difficult to find the bullet's exact location, requiring "extensive probing and retracting of the muscle tissue." This raised "risks of injury to the muscle as well as injury to the nerves, blood vessels, and other tissue in the chest and pleural cavity."[34] The courts found that Lee "would suffer some risks associated with the surgical procedure."[35]

The conclusion regarding the intrusion to Lee's dignitary interests was more forceful. Surgery with a patient's consent is not demeaning because the surgeon is carrying out the patient's wishes. Forced surgery for evidence is another matter.

> In this case, however, the court of appeals noted that the commonwealth proposes to take control of respondent's body, to "drug this citizen—not yet convicted of a criminal offense—with narcotics and barbiturates into a state of unconsciousness," and then to search beneath his skin for evidence of a crime. This kind of surgery involves a virtually total divestment of respondent's ordinary control over surgical probing beneath his skin.[36]

On close examination, it turned out that the state's need for the bullet as evidence was not so strong. By the time of the surgery the bullet's marking might have corroded. Additionally, the state did not test-fire the victim's gun to determine whether it could give consistent markings. The state also had sufficient evidence to go to trial based on the victim's spontaneous identification of Lee. While the bullet might have been of use to the state, the state's "assertions of a compelling need for the bullet are hardly persuasive."[37] Putting all these factors together led the Court to conclude that surgery for the bullet was not reasonable under the circumstances.

The Impact of *Schmerber*: Lineups

The self-incrimination portion of *Schmerber* was brought into action in the lineup case of *United States v. Wade* (388 U.S. 218 [1967]), in which the majority opinion was also authored by Justice Brennan.[38] The prime issue in that case was whether a lawyer was constitutionally required to participate in a lineup by the Sixth Amendment. Wade claimed that making him (along with other lineup participants) wear strips of tape on his face (as did the robber) and speak words so as to identify his voice violated his right against self-incrimination. Justice Brennan dismissed the Fifth Amendment argument on the basis of *Schmerber*'s holding that the privilege protects an accused only from being compelled to give testimony or evidence of a testimonial or communicative nature. He drew on the opinion of Justice Oliver Wendell Holmes in *Holt v. United States* (218 U.S. 245 [1910]) for the proposition that the "prohibition of compelling a man in a criminal court to be witness against himself is a prohibition of the use of physical or moral compulsion to extort communications from him, not an exclusion of his body as evidence when it may be material." The majority concluded that the tape and spoken words in *Wade* were designed exclusively to identify him as the robber and in no way involved having him communicate information about his whereabouts on the day of the crime or whether he knew anything about the robbery.

Chief Justice Warren and Justices Black, Douglas, and Fortas dissented from this portion of *Wade*, expressing the view that the dissents in *Schmerber* were correct. Justice Black reasoned that supplying the blood in *Schmerber* or actively participating in the lineup in *Wade* violated the privilege against self-incrimination because it allowed the government to force a "person to supply proof of his own crime" before trial in ways that would not have been possible at the trial.[39] Justice Fortas agreed with the last point, adding that what Wade was compelled to do in the lineup "is more than passive, mute assistance to the eyes of the victim or of witnesses. It is the kind of volitional act—the kind of forced cooperation by the accused—which is within the historical perimeter of the privilege against compelled self-incrimination."[40] In his view the only thing that the state can demand from a suspect or a defendant is to "stand mute."

FURTHER READING

Hadley Arkes, *Beyond the Constitution* (Princeton, N.J.: Princeton University Press, 1990).

Kim Isaac Eisler, *Justice for All: William J. Brennan, Jr., and the Decisions That Transformed America* (New York: Simon and Schuster, 1993).

United States v. Wade, Kirby v. Illinois, United States v. Ash: The Identification Trilogy

Marvin Zalman

INTRODUCTION

A trilogy of Supreme Court cases decided between 1967 and 1972 considered whether there is a constitutional right to the presence of a defense lawyer at a live and a photographic lineup. These cases display the Court's attempt to deal with mistaken eyewitness identification, a major cause of wrongful convictions. But the cases also show the Court to be a political and even an ideological institution and show that its decisions operate on multiple levels, dealing not simply with the immediate problem at hand (e.g., the fairness of lineups) but with concerns about the Court's capacity to effect change in a fragmented federal system.

The three decisions, *United States v. Wade* (388 U.S. 218 [1967]), *Kirby v. Illinois* (406 U.S. 682 [1972]), and *United States v. Ash* (413 U.S. 300 [1973]) held that (1) counsel is required at a *post-indictment* live lineup, (2) counsel is *not* required at a *pre-indictment* live lineup or showup, and (3) counsel is not required at a pre- or post-indictment *photographic* lineup. These legal rules appear arbitrary and do not make sense in relation to one another. They can only be understood by examining the reasoning in each case and appreciating the external political and ideological milieu that shaped the justices' reasoning.[1]

The context of the cases can be summarized in two sentences: The 1960s was a period of explosive liberal reform in Supreme Court decisions that expanded the rights of suspects and defendants as never before and that generated a furious negative reaction from conservative politicians, jurists, and a substantial portion of the American public. Between 1969 and 1972 (and later), as the Supreme Court's ideological center shifted from center-left to center-right because President Nixon reshaped the Court with four appointments, and fueled by an anti–Warren Court agenda centering on turning back the expansion of criminal-procedure rights, the Court acted to limit the expansion of defendant's rights but did not reverse the precedents of the 1960s outright.

The claims made by the defendants in these cases, that their convictions had to be reversed and new trials held because defense lawyers were not present at identification lineups, were truly novel and in a way expressed the innovations of the 1960s. That decade was rife with social and political upheaval—the culmination of the civil-rights movement, the eruption of the baby-boomers' youth culture that was expressed in actions as diverse as the Summer of Love and the bringing down of a sitting president, the explosive rise in use of recreational drugs, the increase in crime, the massive, vocal, and even violent reactions against the war in Vietnam, political assassinations, and hundreds of inner-city race riots every summer by disaffected African Americans. It was also the decade of the Supreme Court's Due Process Revolution, by which the liberal Warren Court extended constitutional rights to criminal suspects and defendants. Most of these rights, like the right to appointed counsel in criminal cases for indigents, were long overdue. Some were widely accepted, but most, like the incorporation of the Fourth Amendment exclusionary rule, had been the subject of debate for decades if not longer and were opposed by the police. These rights had roots in constitutional doctrines going back hundreds of years.

But the right to counsel *at a lineup* came out of thin air, or, more accurately, out of the imagination of defense lawyers infused with the innovative spirit that characterized the 1960s. To the Warren Court majority the claim was an attempt to "do something" about the terrible problem of mistaken identification, that even then was known to have sent innocent men to prison. To conservative justices on the Court, in the minority in the late 1960s, the newfangled idea of lawyers at the lineup was a bizarre and even outrageous experiment that tinkered with the traditional ways of the adversary system and that extended the heavy hand of the federal courts into the preserve of the states in running their local justice systems as they saw fit. When the ideological orientation of the Court flipped in a more conservative direction by 1972, the conservatives of the Burger Court lost little time in slamming the door on any further judicial experimentation in lineups.

WADE V. UNITED STATES (1967)

Five justices joined in Justice William Brennan's majority opinion holding that a defendant in a post-indictment lineup has a right to have a lawyer present, including four other "liberal" justices—Chief Justice Earl Warren and Justices Hugo Black (who did not fully agree with its consequences, as discussed below), William O. Douglas, and Abe Fortas—and center-right Justice Tom Clark. The more "conservative" justices, John M. Harlan (II), Potter Stewart, and Byron White, dissented from this portion of the case.

Wade was indicted for a bank robbery before he was arrested. A lineup was conducted in which all lineup members had to wear strips of tape, as did the robber, and say something like "Put the money in the bag." The essential contention is that the lineup was conducted without notice to Wade's lawyer and without a defense lawyer being present. Bank employees identified Wade at the lineup and at his trial. *Wade* was decided together with a companion case, *Gilbert v. California* (388 U.S. 263 [1967]), with similar essential facts—a post-indictment lineup without the presence of Gilbert's lawyer, and identifications made at the lineup and during Gilbert's trial.

As Wade's right-to-counsel argument was novel, Justice Brennan emphasized that the right to counsel is not simply a stand-alone benefit but was "indispensable" because it was needed "to protect Wade's most basic right as a criminal defendant—his right to a fair trial at which the witnesses against him might be meaningfully cross-examined."[2] Anticipating the counterargument that there was no old rule that guaranteed a lawyer at the lineup, Justice Brennan wrote that "the framers of the Bill of Rights envisaged a broader role for counsel than under the practice then prevailing in England of merely advising his client in 'matters of law' and eschewing any responsibility for 'matters of fact.'"[3] This clever and sound point connected the lawyer's role at lineup to her vital role at trial—to probe the prosecution's presentation of facts in an attempt to ensure that the prosecution is based on *accurate* facts.

The Critical-Stage Analysis

This analysis set the stage for the majority opinion's doctrinal foundation: Wade had a Sixth Amendment right to counsel at the lineup because the lineup is a *critical stage* of the prosecution. The critical-stage doctrine was adopted by the Supreme Court in a series of earlier cases. What is a critical stage? It is a proceeding where presentation of facts or the making of arguments can determine the guilt or innocence of a defendant. The trial is without doubt a critical stage, and the provision of competent counsel to indigent defendants has become an absolute requirement (*Powell v. Alabama*, 287 U.S. 45 [1932]; *Gideon v. Wainwright*, 372 U.S. 335 [1963]). But the Court also held that pretrial stages of the prosecution could be critical stages. The critical-stage doctrine "has since been applied to require the assistance of counsel at the type of arraignment—for example, that provided by Alabama—where certain rights might be sacrificed or lost: 'What happens there may affect the whole trial. Available defenses may be irretrievably lost, if not then and there asserted'" (*Hamilton v. Alabama*, 368 U.S. 52, 54 [1961]). The majority decided that a pretrial, post-indictment lineup is such a critical stage. There were no lineups before the creation of organized police forces in the late nineteenth century. When the Bill of Rights was ratified in 1791 witnesses identified suspects at the trial itself. "In contrast, today's law-enforcement machinery involves critical confrontations of the accused by the prosecution at pretrial proceedings where the results might well settle the accused's fate and reduce the trial itself to a mere formality."[4]

Is the Lineup a "Mere Preparatory Step"?

In coming to this conclusion the majority had to overcome two major objections raised by dissenting justices. The first was that if a lawyer had to be present at a lineup, the effect of precedent would lead later courts to require defense counsel to accompany police when they collected fingerprints, blood samples, clothing, hair, and similar evidence that could be subjected to forensic analysis. The prosecution argued that the lineup, along with these kinds of evidence-gathering procedures, constituted "a mere preparatory step" that did not require a lawyer. The majority differed: lineups are *not* like fingerprinting and the like. Any problems in evidence gathering could be effectively confronted by the defense at trial: "Knowledge of the techniques of science and technology is sufficiently available, and the variables in techniques few enough, that the accused has the opportunity for a meaningful confrontation of the Government's case at trial through the ordinary processes of cross-examination of the Government's expert witnesses and the presentation of the evidence of his own experts."[5] In contrast, so many things could go on at a lineup that are not regulated by precise procedures, like taking evidence samples, that the majority felt a lawyer should be present to observe and report possible unfairness that could taint the eyewitnesses' identification. Gilbert's lineup, for example, took place in an auditorium where a hundred witnesses to various robberies sat, a situation rife with the possibility of cross-witness contamination. In sum, the inability of a lawyerless defendant at a lineup to know what was going on "deprived [him] of that right of cross-examination which is an essential safeguard to his right to confront the witnesses against him."[6]

State Action

The other objection was a fundamental challenge to the Court's jurisdiction. It may be that the real problem causing miscarriages of justice is that eyewitness identification is an inherently weak *human* process subject to inevitable error. The role of cross-examination at trial is designed to expose such problems to a jury. But the purpose of *constitutional* rights, such as the right to counsel, is to prevent illegal and improper *governmental* actions that could lead to tyranny. This is the *state-action doctrine* and requires that a constitutional remedy be applied only against state, or governmental, action. The majority answered this objection by asserting that the "evil" to which the *Wade* rule was directed was "improper suggestion" by the police. "A major factor contributing to the high incidence of miscarriage of justice from mistaken identification has been the degree of suggestion inherent in the manner in which the prosecution presents the suspect to witnesses for pretrial identification."[7] Justice Brennan backed up the assertion that improper suggestion supplied the necessary state action to establish a constitutional rule by citing pages of examples and citations of improper and unfair lineups that could easily lead to the conviction of innocent defendants.

The Court also brushed away the argument that defense lawyers would delay or interfere with the conduct of lineups: Wade and Gilbert had lawyers who could be summoned, in other cases substitute lawyers could stand in for defendants' counsel, and lawyers are professionals who are obligated not to interfere with proper governmental procedures.

The *Wade* Remedy

Finally, the Court had to deal with the proper remedy for violations of defendants' rights where lineups occur without lawyers present. In all such cases the witness is barred from testifying about any identification made at the lineup. The real issue was whether the lineup witness could point out the defendant at the trial as the perpetrator of the crime. The lower circuit court, ruling in Wade's favor, held that all courtroom identifications by participants in lawyer-less lineups were not allowed at trial. Justice Brennan held that such a per-se rule was not "justified without first giving the Government the opportunity to establish by clear and convincing evidence that the in-court identifications were based upon observations of the suspect other than the lineup identification."[8] Various factors could be applied for a judge to determine whether a witness's recall of the defendant came from the crime itself or from his or her memory of the lineup: "for example, the prior opportunity to observe the alleged criminal act, the existence of any discrepancy between any pre-lineup description and the defendant's actual description, any identification prior to lineup of another person, the identification by picture of the defendant prior to the lineup, failure to identify the defendant on a prior occasion, and the lapse of time between the alleged act and the lineup identification."[9]

Justice Black, who concurred in the holding that there is a right to counsel at lineups, objected to this remedy:

> I think it is practically impossible. How is a witness capable of probing the recesses of his mind to draw a sharp line between a courtroom identification due exclusively to an earlier lineup and a courtroom identification due to memory not based on the lineup? What kind of "clear and convincing evidence" can the prosecution offer to prove upon what particular events memories resulting in an in-court identification rest? How long will trials be delayed while judges turn psychologists to probe the subconscious minds of witnesses?[10]

Nevertheless, the majority ruling of *Wade* established a right to counsel at *post-indictment* lineups with the remedy agreed on by five justices.

THE CASE OF *KIRBY V. ILLINOIS* (1972)

The Facts

The treatment of the *Wade* rule in *Kirby v. Illinois* (406 U.S. 682 [1972]) was an early example of the Nixonian counterrevolution in criminal procedure carried out by the Burger Court. Between 1969 and 1972 the composition of the Court shifted, with the replacement of four justices—the ostensibly liberal Chief Justice Warren and Justices Black and Fortas, and the ostensibly conservative Justice Harlan—with four more or less conservative justices appointed by President Nixon—Chief Justice Warren Burger and Justices Harry Blackmun, Lewis Powell, and William Rehnquist. Earlier, in 1967, middle-of-the-road Justice Tom Clark had resigned, and his seat went to the liberal Thurgood Marshall. In 1972, then, the ideological configuration of the Court could be described as three liberal justices (Douglas, Brennan, and Marshall), two middle-of-the-road justices (Stewart and White), and four conservatives (Burger, Blackmun, Powell, and Rehnquist).

Justice Stewart wrote the deciding opinion in *Kirby*, joined by three justices (Chief Justice Burger and Justices Blackmun and Rehnquist). When the Court's opinion is joined by less than a majority, it is a "plurality" opinion and does not carry the same precedential weight as a majority opinion. In *Kirby*, Justice Powell simply concurred in the result in a terse but important statement: "As I would not extend the *Wade-Gilbert* per se exclusionary rule, I concur in the result reached by the Court."[11] This seems to say that the plurality justices considered overruling *Wade* and *Gilbert*. If that occurred, the law would have been consistent. Justice Powell may have thought that a sudden overruling of a precedent only five years old would have appeared to the nation as an overtly political decision that could have tarnished the Supreme Court's image in public opinion. If this speculation is correct, it suggests that justices consider institutional as well as narrowly legal issues in deciding cases.

The identification procedure in *Kirby* differed in two essential facts from that in *Wade*, and one would prove crucial to the decision. A day after a Chicago robbery of Willie Shard, police stopped Kirby, and a search turned up papers and identification cards belonging to Shard. Shard was brought to the police station and immediately upon his entry identified Kirby. This was not a lineup of a suspect and fillers but a *showup*, where a witness is shown only the suspect. A showup is rightly considered to be quite suggestive by the Supreme Court. Nevertheless, this difference in the identification procedures was not legally significant. What did matter to the Court's plurality, in Justice Stewart's opinion, was that the identification took place before Kirby was indicted or formally charged. The extent of the legal process against Kirby at that point was his arrest on probable cause of having committed a robbery.

Kirby sought to reverse his conviction, having been identified at the trial by Shard, by arguing to the Supreme Court that his Sixth Amendment right to counsel at a lineup or other identification procedure, supposedly established in *Wade*, had been violated. The Court upheld the Illinois appellate court, which had ruled "that the *Wade-Gilbert* per se exclusionary rule is not applicable to pre-indictment confrontations."[12]

A Supreme Court case, like every legal contest, can be analogized to military combat. Legal opponents can fight over the proof of facts and on the grounds of legal rules and doctrines and try to position themselves for victory by selecting the best "terrain" on which they will fight. In *Wade*, the defendant waged a battle to get the courts to accept the applicability of the right to counsel at a lineup, and won, winning a new trial. The prosecution tried to position the case facts as "mere preparatory steps," while Wade positioned his case on doctrinal grounds as a "critical stage." In *Kirby*, the state did not fight on the same critical-stage "terrain"; instead, it fastened on the difference between a post-indictment lineup versus a pre-indictment lineup (or showup) to make the case that this difference was substantial. Kirby, and the dissenters in the Supreme Court, argued that the difference was a mere formalism, without legal significance. The plurality in *Kirby*, nevertheless, based its decision on that distinction.

The Court held that a lawyer was not required in a pre-indictment lineup:

> In a line of constitutional cases in this Court, stemming back to the Court's land-mark opinion in *Powell v. Alabama*, it has been firmly established that a person's Sixth and Fourteenth Amendment right to counsel attaches only at or after the time that adversary judicial proceedings have been initiated against him.
>
> This is not to say that a defendant in a criminal case has a constitutional right to counsel only at the trial itself. . . . But the point is that, while members of the Court have differed as to existence of the right to counsel in the contexts of some of the above cases, *all* of those cases have involved points of time at or after the initiation of adversary judicial criminal proceedings—whether by way of formal charge, preliminary hearing, indictment, information, or arraignment.[13]

The plurality believed that it was wrong "to import into a routine police investigation an absolute constitutional guarantee historically and rationally applicable only after the onset of formal prosecutorial proceedings."[14] In response to the dissent, the plurality reasoned the following:

> The initiation of judicial criminal proceedings is far from a mere formalism. It is the starting point of our whole system of adversary criminal justice. For it is only then that the government has committed itself to prosecute and only then that the adverse positions of government and defendant have solidified. It is then that a defendant finds himself faced with the prosecutorial forces of organized society, and immersed in the intricacies of substantive and procedural criminal law. It is this point, therefore, that marks the commencement of the "criminal prosecutions" to which alone the explicit guarantees of the Sixth Amendment are applicable.[15]

The Dissenting Opinion

Justice Brennan, dissenting in an opinion joined by Justices Douglas and Marshall, argued that the pre-indictment/post-indictment distinction was a

mere formalism that was not significant to the holding of *Wade*. The plurality
had asserted that Kirby's arrest was simply part of a routine police investigation
and not the initiation of charges, but to the dissent this made no sense, because a
lineup is designed to gather information to convict a suspect: "In view of *Wade*,
it is plain, and the plurality today does not attempt to dispute it, that there
inhere in a confrontation for identification conducted after arrest the identical
hazards to a fair trial that inhere in such a confrontation conducted 'after the
onset of formal prosecutorial proceedings.'"[16] The dissent quoted from *Wade* at
length to reassert the primacy of its reasoning based on critical-stage reasoning.
After a lengthy exposition showing that the dangers of convicting an innocent
person are the same in all identification procedures, whether occurring before or
after formal charges, and clearly exasperated at the plurality's reasoning, Justice
Brennan wrote, "If these propositions do not amount to 'mere formalism,' it is
difficult to know how to characterize them."[17] However logical the dissent's argument, it was in a sense irrelevant because the justices who voted for the result
and joined the plurality opinion fought the battle on different terrain.

Finally, Justice White, who had dissented in regard to the Sixth Amendment
issue in *Wade*, now joined the dissent in *Kirby*. His terse opinion simply stated,
"*United States v. Wade* (1967) and *Gilbert v. California* (1967) govern this case
and compel reversal of the judgment below."[18] This signified a position that
was based on stare decisis and the values of precedent. Having lost the battle
on this issue in *Wade*, Justice White was saying that the Court (he included)
ought to abide by the Court's prior precedents and not overrule them without
a really good reason or ought not try to create inconsistent exceptions, as this
author believes the Court did in *Kirby*. Like Justice Powell's lone position,
Justice White's vote and reason were based on institutional concerns and a
stronger belief in precedent.[19]

UNITED STATES V. ASH (1973)

Justice Harry Blackmun opened his majority opinion by stating the issue in the
case, which included its two essential facts: "In this case the Court is called upon
to decide whether the Sixth Amendment grants an accused the right to have
counsel present whenever the Government conducts a post-indictment photographic display, containing a picture of the accused, for the purpose of allowing
a witness to attempt an identification of the offender."[20] The Court held that Ash
had no right to have a lawyer present at a photographic lineup. *Wade* and *Kirby*,

in contrast, involved live lineups; one involved a post-indictment lineup, the other a pre-indictment identification.

In *Ash*, four witnesses to a bank robbery viewed five black-and-white photos of similarly appearing black males before the indictment was handed up: "All four made uncertain identifications of Ash's picture."[21] Three years later, after Ash and Bailey were indicted, the prosecutor showed the witnesses five color photographs prior to trial. This photo lineup included both suspects, Ash and Bailey. Three witnesses made positive identifications of Ash and one could not. None of the witnesses selected Bailey. In a hearing, the trial judge ruled that by "clear and convincing" evidence the witnesses' in-court identifications were based on observation of the crime and not the lineups. Ash was convicted and Bailey acquitted.

The decision in *Ash* was six to three, with Justice Blackmun writing the opinion joined by Chief Justice Burger and Justices White, Powell, and Rehnquist. Justice Stewart wrote a concurring opinion. Justice Brennan's dissenting opinion was joined by Justices Douglas and Marshall. Initially, it would appear that since the identification in *Ash* was post-indictment, the precedent of *Wade* would require counsel at a lineup. Indeed, the lower court in this case, the U.S. Court of Appeals for the District of Columbia Circuit, so held. However, the circuit court's en banc decision (a decision of the entire bench instead of a three-judge panel) was split five to four, and a majority of other federal circuit courts sided with the government's position. Clearly, there had to be something about photographic lineups that was so different that *Wade* was not a precedent.

What the Court did in *Ash* was to distinguish the holding of *Wade* to limit it to live lineups, by concluding that the essential element of the right to counsel at a post-indictment lineup is that "the lineup constituted a trial-like confrontation, requiring the 'assistance of counsel' to preserve the adversary process by compensating for advantages of the prosecuting authorities."[22] What *Wade* did not depend on as absolutely essential to its holding were "the dangers of mistaken identification."[23] Therefore, while there may be dangers of mistaken identification in a photo lineup, counsel is not required as a constitutional right. The Court supported this conclusion with two strategies: First, it analyzed *Wade* to demonstrate that it was based primarily on the adversary-like process of a live lineup. Second, it listed the ways in which the photo lineup is not such an adversarial process and that the absence of the defendant makes it less likely that photo lineups will lead to miscarriages of justice.

As to the first strategy, Justice Blackmun noted several reasons why the Supreme Court first extended the assistance of counsel to indigent criminal defendants at trial: to help the "unaided layman [who] had little skill in arguing the law or in coping with an intricate procedural system"; that "the core purpose of the counsel guarantee was to assure 'assistance' at trial, when the accused was confronted with both the intricacies of the law and the advocacy of the public prosecutor"; that the "extension of the right to counsel to events before trial has resulted from changing patterns of criminal procedure and investigation that have tended to generate pretrial events that might appropriately be considered to be parts of the trial itself"; and that the assistance of counsel "envisioned the lawyer as advising the accused on available defenses in order to allow him to plead intelligently."[24] Thus, in *Coleman v. Alabama* (399 U.S. 1 [1970]) the right to counsel was extended to a preliminary hearing because lawyerly skills like "examining witnesses, probing for evidence, and making legal arguments" were required.[25] A weakness of these arguments (given that the Court did not overrule *Wade*) is that none of these lawyerly skills are needed at the post-indictment lineup where the lawyer's primary function is to observe and report. Therefore, Justice Blackmun explained the *Wade* rule by saying that a live lineup

> offer[s] opportunities for prosecuting authorities to take advantage of the accused. Counsel was seen by the Court as being more sensitive to, and aware of, suggestive influences than the accused himself, and as better able to reconstruct the events at trial. Counsel present at lineup would be able to remove disabilities of the accused in precisely the same fashion that counsel compensated for the disabilities of the layman at trial.[26]

The next part of the majority-opinion strategy was to prove that these problems are not present in a photographic-identification procedure where the defendant is not present. The opinion basically likened a photographic lineup to preparatory steps in gathering evidence like fingerprints, hair, clothing, and blood samples. A live lineup differs because of the "lack of scientific precision and inability to reconstruct" its events. After a photographic lineup, to the contrary, "accurate reconstruction is possible. [Although] the risks inherent in any confrontation still remain . . . the opportunity to cure defects at trial [by cross-examination] causes the confrontation to cease to be 'critical.'"[27] "Since the accused himself is not present at the time of the photographic display, and asserts no right to be present, no possibility arises that the accused might be misled by his lack of familiarity with the law or overpowered by his professional adversary."[28] The Court next noted that while pretrial photographic identification is relatively new, the pretrial examination of witnesses by prosecutors was part of the common law, and the defense can challenge unfairness of either kind of pretrial-evidence process through the mechanism of cross-examination at the trial.

In his concurrence, Justice Stewart added that "a photographic identification is quite different from a lineup, for there are substantially fewer possibilities of impermissible suggestion when photographs are used, and those unfair influences can be readily reconstructed at trial."[29] Even if the first part of his assertion seems unrealistic, like Justice Blackmun's opinion, Justice Stewart trusted cross-examination at trial to cure any injustices.

The Dissent in *Ash*

Justice Brennan's dissent repeated the dangers of miscarriages of justice that can result from lineups. His main point was stated by the court of appeals: "the dangers of mistaken identification . . . set forth in *Wade* are applicable in large measure to photographic as well as corporeal identifications."[30] He elaborated on this point:

> First, the photographs themselves might tend to suggest which of the pictures is that of the suspect. For example, differences in age, pose, or other physical characteristics of the persons represented, and variations in the mounting, background, lighting, or markings of the photographs all might have the effect of singling out the accused.
>
> Second, impermissible suggestion may inhere in the manner in which the photographs are displayed to the witness. The danger of misidentification is, of course, "increased if the police display to the witness . . . the pictures of several persons among which the photograph of a single such individual recurs or is in some way emphasized." And, if the photographs are arranged in an asymmetrical pattern, or if they are displayed in a time sequence that tends to emphasize a particular photograph, "any identification of the photograph which stands out from the rest is no more reliable than an identification of a single photograph, exhibited alone."
>
> Third, gestures or comments of the prosecutor at the time of the display may lead an otherwise uncertain witness to select the "correct" photograph. For example, the prosecutor might "indicate to the witness that [he has] other evidence that one of the persons pictured committed the crime," and might even point to a particular photograph and ask whether the person pictured "looks familiar." More subtly, the prosecutor's inflection, facial expressions, physical motions,

and myriad other almost imperceptible means of communication might tend, intentionally or unintentionally, to compromise the witness'[s] objectivity. Thus, as is the case with lineups, "improper photographic identification procedures . . . by exerting a suggestive influence upon the witnesses, can often lead to an erroneous identification."[31]

It is interesting that Justice Brennan, the author of the *Wade* opinion, wrote that "contrary to the suggestion of the Court, the conclusion in *Wade* that a pretrial lineup is a 'critical stage' of the prosecution did not in any sense turn on the fact that a lineup involves the physical 'presence of the accused' at a 'trial-like confrontation' with the Government."[32] This demonstrates a powerful factor about how the system of precedent operates: a later Court can look at an earlier opinion and interpret it in a manner that its author contradicts. The later Court is not in the business of accurately assessing the intent of the author of the opinion but is desirous of deciding a case (here, *Ash*) in a certain way, even if this means distorting the real intention of an earlier precedent (*Wade*). In his opinion, Justice Brennan expressed a flash of anger at what may have seemed to him a deliberately obtuse reading to exalt a seemingly ideological result over one designed to prevent injustice: "I must reluctantly conclude that today's decision marks simply another step towards the complete evisceration of the fundamental constitutional principles established by this Court."[33]

CONCLUSIONS

In addition to the three cases dealing with the right to counsel at live and photographic lineups, the Supreme Court at this time also decided cases under the Due Process Clause to determine whether lineups were fair. If a lineup is unfair, the conviction is reversed and a new trial is ordered. A lineup of a thin, six-foot-tall robbery suspect, wearing a leather jacket similar to the robber's, along with two other men who were approximately five-foot-five and were not wearing leather jackets was unfair (*Foster v. California*, 394 U.S. 440 [1969]). However, suggestive identification passes the due-process test, which depends on all of the facts and circumstances, where there are exigent circumstances, necessity, or indicia of reliability. Thus, showing photographs of a suspect (without fillers) during a crime investigation, which is suggestive to witnesses, is necessary to capture suspects (*Simmons v. United States*, 390 U.S. 377 [1968]). A suggestive showup is necessary where a witness is in critical condition and may not live to observe a fair lineup (*Stovall v. Denno*, 388 U.S. 293 [1967]). A suggestive showup may be allowed to stand as evidence where there are factors that counteract the suggestiveness to show that the identification was probably accurate: the witness had a good opportunity to view the perpetrator, paid attention, gave an accurate description after the crime, was sure of her identification, and viewed the suspect in the showup soon after the crime (*Neil v. Biggers*, 409 U.S. 188 [1972]; *Manson v. Brathwaite*, 432 U.S. 98 [1977]).

The move to bring lawyers into the lineup can be seen as a heroic but limited attempt to prevent the grave injustice of convicting the innocent. Recent research has shown that mistaken eyewitness identification is the leading cause of miscarriages of justice. There is not much reason to believe that the presence of lawyers can reduce any but the most egregious behaviors by police that virtually tell the witness which person to pick in the lineup. But this kind of corrupt behavior is rare. The real problem is that honest police can inadvertently signal their knowledge of the suspect in the most subtle ways with absolutely no intention of doing so.

In the 1960s there was virtually no psychological research on lineups. Since 1970 thousands of scientific experiments have established a foundation of solid knowledge and have provided police with a set of low-cost procedures that is shown by laboratory research and a few field studies to reduce errors in lineups. These include telling the witness that the perpetrator may not be in the lineup, placing only one suspect in a lineup at a time, matching fillers to the victim's or witness's description of the perpetrator (and not similarity to the suspect), having an officer of the same race as the suspect compose the lineup, ensuring that lineups are fair, conducting lineups in a double-blind manner (i.e., the officer running the lineup should not know the suspect's identity), and if the lineup is double-blind conducting the lineup sequentially (one at a time) rather than simultaneously (the suspect and fillers being viewed together). However noble was the intent of the liberal justices in *Wade*, their solution to the problem of convicting the innocent did little to solve it.

The *Wade-Kirby-Ash* trilogy of cases clearly shows how political and ideological changes on the Supreme Court causes its conclusions and even its mode of interpretation to change. This does not necessarily mean that justices decide cases in a distinctly partisan manner. It does mean that their honestly held views reflect the lifetime of experience they bring with them to the Supreme Court. These views, like those of everyone, reflect different philosophies and perspectives, both about the substantive issues that confront them and their ideas about constitutional categories like precedent and the original intent of the Constitution's framers.

It so happens that divisions in the larger society are reflected among the justices, and this split in views has been analyzed in Herbert Packer's "two models of the criminal process," published in his seminal 1969 book, *The Limits of the Criminal Sanction.*[34] A model is only a representation of reality that highlights salient features. He labeled the models of the directions taken by Supreme Court justices in criminal cases as the due-process model and the crime-control model. He stressed that the justices agreed more than they disagreed about the importance of the rule of law, legal controls on the police, and the need for an effective criminal-justice system. Disagreements did not in any way suggest that conservative justices believed there should be no controls on the police or liberal justices wanted criminals to go free.

While all justices would agree that suppressing crime increases personal freedom through public safety, those with stronger crime-control perspectives view this value as paramount. As a result they believe that the criminal-justice system is relatively free from error and are less willing to impose restrictions on the police so as to make police more efficient and effective. All justices believe in the rule of law, but those with due-process orientations are more suspicious of the accuracy and effectiveness of the police, believe that errors are more frequent, and desire greater judicial controls. These differing perspectives tend to produce "conservative" and "liberal" justices. But as can be seen in all of these chapters, the specific case opinions must be examined to assess the precise views of Supreme Court justices.

FURTHER READING

James M. Doyle, *True Witness: Cops, Courts, Science, and the Battle against Misidentification* (New York: Palgrave Macmillan, 2005).

Fred P. Graham, *The Self-Inflicted Wound* (New York: Macmillan, 1970).

Elizabeth Loftus, *Eyewitness Testimony* (Cambridge, Mass.: Harvard University Press, 1979).

Herbert L. Packer, *The Limits of the Criminal Sanction* (Stanford, Calif.: Stanford University Press, 1968).

VIII

POLICE LIABILITY

Tennessee v. Garner

JEFFERY T. WALKER

INTRODUCTION

The case of *Tennessee v. Garner* (471 U.S. 1 [1985]) holds many dichotomies. Some argue this case changed policing as much or more than any Supreme Court case in history since it constitutionally prohibited the two-hundred-plus-year practice of using deadly force against nonviolent felons who were fleeing police. Others point out that many police agencies had already changed their policies in line with the decision in *Garner* before the case was accepted by the Supreme Court. In addition, this case imposed nationwide change to police practice across the country and should have resulted in at least half of the states making changes to their laws. In reality, very few states revised their laws in response to the decision.[1] Finally, the Court made this radical change seemingly decisively and abruptly; but it is important to note that the case took five years to reach the Supreme Court, and it took almost exactly thirty years for all criminal and civil cases to be decided from this one shooting.

This chapter focuses on the background and ruling of *Tennessee v. Garner* and the influence it had on American policing. Although the Supreme Court appeared to create a bright-line rule in deciding under what conditions the police could use deadly force against citizens, *Garner* continues to present legal challenges for police, policy makers, and the legal system in this vital aspect of law enforcement.

BACKGROUND

The issue in this case has its roots in common law, upon which American law is based. At common law, police were authorized to use any force necessary, including deadly force, to apprehend a felon because (1) all felonies were punishable by death at the time, and thus officers were not inflicting anything on the person that was not possible in court, and (2) the lack of organized police forces at the time made later capture of the person less likely.[2] Early in the history of the United States, this "fleeing-felon rule" was the norm. By the 1930s, a few police and legal experts began to question the continued validity of this law, given that most felonies were no longer punishable by death and technology had greatly increased the chances that a person fleeing the police would be caught. For example, writing in defense of the American Law Institute's attempt to establish a model legal code, noted legal scholar Professor William Mikell posed the following question:

> May I ask what we are killing for when [a suspect] steals a car and runs off with it? Are we killing him for stealing the automobile? . . . It cannot be . . . because the statute provides only three years in the penitentiary for that. Is it then . . . for fleeing that we kill him? Fleeing from arrest . . . [has] a penalty much less than that for stealing the automobile. If we are not killing him for stealing the automobile and not killing him for fleeing, what are we killing him for?[3]

At that time, states and police departments were not willing to change their laws to limit deadly force against all felons. Further, many police officers and police executives believed that restricting police use of deadly force would create a situation in which no offender would submit to the demands of the police to stop.

The debate as to whether officers should be allowed to use deadly force against nonviolent felons continued during the 1970s in both academic and policy circles and began to come to a head in the early 1980s.[4] It is also relevant that the Memphis Police Department had four cases reach the court of appeals on similar circumstances prior to *Garner*'s review by the Supreme Court (*Cunningham v. Ellington*, 323 F.Supp. 1072 [W.D.Tenn. 1971]; *Beech v. Melancon*, 465 F.2d 425 [6th Cir. 1972]; *Wiley v. Memphis Police Department*, 548 F.2d 1247 [6th Cir. 1977]; and *Hayes v. Memphis Police Department*, 571 F.2d 357 [6th Cir. 1978]). Finally, as often happens with Supreme Court cases, the Court seemed to carefully select a case that would provide the most legal impact and direction on the issue.

POLICE PRACTICE PRIOR TO *GARNER*

Prior to the decision in *Garner*, there were at least four broad categories of police practice related to deadly force. These ranged from the common-law rule that allowed officers to use deadly force against any fleeing felon to a defense-of-life-only rule that allowed officers to use deadly force only to defend themselves or a third party from imminent threat of death or serious bodily harm.

As stated above, the historical rule of deadly force in the United States was the common-law rule (also called the fleeing-felon rule or any-felon rule). At the time of the *Garner* decision, nineteen states had statutes based on the common-law rule.[5] Unless otherwise limited by departmental policy, officers in these states were authorized to take the same actions as those taken by the officer in *Garner* who shot a fleeing nonviolent felon.

At the time of the *Garner* decision, seven states had laws that limited the use of deadly force to prevent escape only in commission of forcible or violent felonies.[6] This was known as the forcible-felony rule. Under this rule, police could only use deadly force against those suspected of committing a violent (or personal) felony. This was a step forward from the fleeing-felon rule but still allowed officers to use deadly force against suspects who did not necessarily represent a threat of life or serious bodily harm (such as assault).

At the time of the decision in *Garner*, fourteen states had already adopted a rule that was similar to the ruling in *Garner*.[7] The Model Penal Code rule stated in its relevant part that deadly force could only be used if "the [police officer] believes that (1) the crime for which the arrest is made involved conduct including the use or threatened use of deadly force or (2) there is substantial risk that the person to be arrested will cause death or serious bodily harm if his apprehension is delayed." This rule, discussed further in this chapter, established that deadly force could only be used against persons who threatened or used deadly force against another person or who could potentially use that force if not captured (known as "future dangerousness").

One would expect that the greatest and most legally relevant guidance in a critical area of policing would come from state law. This was not the case, however. Rules governing police practice often came from several sources (state law, court decisions, departmental policy), and oftentimes there was no state law or policy on police use of force to guide police officers. At the time of *Garner*, ten states did not have any kind of state law governing police use of deadly force. Six of those states at least had prevailing court decisions that defined the limits of police practice.[8] Each of these court decisions supported the common-law rule, allowing officers to use deadly force against any fleeing felon. This brought the total number of states with laws supporting the fleeing-felon rule to twenty-five. Louisiana and Vermont had no laws governing the police use of deadly force, but they did have justifiable-homicide laws that permitted use of deadly force only to prevent violent felonies. South Carolina and Wyoming had no laws or court decisions guiding police use of deadly force.

Especially for those ten states that did not have a state statute or court ruling delineating restrictions on police use of force, and even in those states that did, police-department policy was often the most important restriction on police use of deadly force. As discussed in the following, departmental policy often was, and is, the best method of controlling police behavior. This is in part because departmental policies can be revised more quickly in response to changes in practice or custom. That was the case with deadly force in the 1970s and 1980s. Even though there were no laws supporting a defense-of-life rule for police use of deadly force, there were police agencies that adopted this rule. In a 1977 study of the use of deadly force by police officers, authors Milton, Lardner, and Abrecht found that several large agencies in the United States, including the New York City Police Department and the Federal Bureau of Investigation, had adopted this rule.[9] Defense-of-life rules only allowed an officer to use deadly force if his or her life or the life of a third person was imminently in danger of death or serious bodily harm. This rule was more restrictive than even the ruling in *Garner*.

THE CASE OF *TENNESSEE V. GARNER* (1985)

The Facts

In *Tennessee v. Garner* (471 U.S. 1 [1985]), a Memphis Police Department officer shot and killed Garner while responding to a prowler-inside call. At the scene, police saw a woman standing on her porch, gesturing toward the adjacent house. She told them that she had heard glass breaking and that someone was breaking into the house next door to hers. While one officer radioed the dispatcher, the other went behind the adjacent house. He heard a door slam and saw someone run across the backyard. The fleeing suspect, Edward Garner, stopped at a six-foot-high chain-link fence at the edge of the yard. With the aid of a flashlight, the officer was able to see Garner's face and hands. He saw no sign of a weapon and, although not certain, was "reasonably sure" Garner was unarmed. The officer testified he believed Garner to be seventeen or eighteen years old and about 5'5" tall. While Garner was crouched at the base of the fence, the officer called out, "Police! Halt!" and took a few steps toward him. Garner then began to climb over the fence. Believing that if Garner made it over the fence he would elude capture, the officer shot him. Garner was taken by ambulance to a hospital, where he died. Ten dollars and a purse taken from the house were found on his body. In taking this deadly action, the officer had acted under Tennessee Code Annotated §40-7-108, which permitted the shooting in such circumstances, and was similarly guiltless under a departmental policy that was slightly more restrictive than the state law but nonetheless allowed the actions of the officer.

Garner's father brought suit in federal district court under 42 U.S.C. §1983, claiming the shooting violated Garner's Fourth, Fifth, Sixth, Eighth, and Fourteenth Amendment rights. After a three-day bench trial, the court dismissed the claims against the mayor and police chief for lack of evidence and ruled that the officer's actions were authorized by state law, which in turn was constitutional.

The court of appeals for the Sixth Circuit affirmed the decision for the officer, ruling that he had acted in good-faith reliance on the state statute. It remanded for reconsideration of possible liability against the city in light of *Monell v. New York City Department of Social Services* (436 U.S. 658 [1978]), which was decided after the trial.

On remand, the district court ruled that *Monell* did not affect its decision. Upon a second appeal, the court of appeals reversed and remanded the decision of the district court related to the city. The court of appeals "reasoned that the killing of a fleeing suspect is a 'seizure' under the Fourth Amendment and is therefore constitutional only if 'reasonable.'" Relying on language from the Model Penal Code, the court held that the Tennessee statute "did not adequately limit the use of deadly force by distinguishing between felonies of different magnitudes."[10] At that point, the state of Tennessee joined the suit and appealed the case to the United States Supreme Court to support its state statute.

The Majority Opinion

As if to craft language for state law or departmental policy, the Court established what many thought was a bright-line rule concerning police use of deadly force. The holding of the Court read, "We conclude that such force may not be used unless it is necessary to prevent the escape and the officer has probable cause to believe that the suspect poses a significant threat of death or serious physical injury to the officer or others." The Court based this ruling on both constitutional grounds and on police practice at the time.

In comparing the officer's actions and the state statute in this case to constitutional protections, the Court found police use of force against nondangerous felons to be unconstitutional. The majority wrote:

> The use of deadly force to prevent the escape of all felony suspects, whatever the circumstances, is constitutionally unreasonable. It is not better that all felony suspects die than that they escape. Where the suspect poses no immediate threat to the officer and no threat to others, the harm resulting from failing to apprehend him does not justify the use of deadly force to do so. It is no doubt unfortunate when a suspect who is in sight escapes, but the fact that the police arrive a little late or are a little slower of foot does not always justify killing the suspect. A police officer may not seize an unarmed, nondangerous suspect by shooting him dead. The Tennessee statute is unconstitutional insofar as it authorizes the use of deadly force against such fleeing suspect.

This portion of the ruling struck down the laws or practices in half of the states in the Union.

The Court also relied heavily on research and current policies concerning use of deadly force. Based on several amici curiae, the Court held that "in light of the rules adopted by those who must actually administer them, the older and fading common-law view is a dubious indicium of the constitutionality of the Tennessee statute now before us."

The Concurring and Dissenting Opinions

The decision was six to three, with Justice O'Connor (joined by Chief Justice Burger and Justice Rehnquist) writing the sole dissent. O'Connor reviewed the same facts as the majority but in a different light. Where the majority saw that many states and police agencies had already changed their laws to reflect stricter standards of use of deadly force, the dissent noted that half of the states still employed the common-law rule. Further, where the majority saw that offenders committing, in this case, burglary were not a particular threat to life or bodily harm, the dissent commented that "by disregarding the serious and dangerous nature of residential burglaries and the longstanding practice of many states, the Court effectively creates a Fourth Amendment right allowing a burglary suspect to flee unimpeded from a police officer who has probable cause to arrest, who has ordered the suspect to halt, and who has no means short of firing his weapon to prevent escape."

The final part of the dissent was a general adherence to the common-law standard and deference to precedence. The dissent also took exception with the focus of the holding by the majority. Justice O'Connor noted:

> The precise issue before the Court deserves emphasis, because both the decision below and the majority obscure what must be decided in this case. The issue is not the constitutional validity of the Tennessee statute on its face or as applied to some hypothetical set of facts. Instead, the issue is whether the use of deadly force by Officer Hymon under the circumstances of this case violated Garner's constitutional rights. Thus, the majority's assertion that a police officer who has probable cause to seize a suspect "may not always do so by killing him" is unexceptionable but also of little relevance to the question presented here.

The dissent agreed that Garner was "seized" under the Fourth Amendment when he was shot but disagreed with the Court's balance between crime prevention and "legitimate interests of the individual."

Case Significance

The significance of this case is simultaneously substantial and relatively nonexistent. At the constitutional level, and for many police departments and officers, the changes were dramatic and completely altered their authority to use deadly force. In practice in the states, and for many other police departments, few changes were made based on the ruling, or the departments were already using a policy at least as a restrictive as *Garner* demanded.

On the one hand, this ruling completely changed the constitutional guidance on police use of deadly force. Prior to *Garner*, officers were constitutionally supported with the common-law rule for using deadly force—they could shoot a person attempting to evade arrest as long as the person was suspected of committing a felony. Following *Garner*, the rule was that "such force may not be used unless necessary to prevent the escape and the officer has probable cause to believe that the suspect poses a significant threat of death or serious physical injury to the officer or others."

On the other hand, many states with unconstitutional laws did not change them in response to the *Garner* decision. Writing for the *American Journal of Criminal Justice*, James J. Fyfe and Jeffery T. Walker reported that five years after the *Garner* decision only four of the twenty-five states with unconstitutional statutes made changes to their laws.[11] Further, only two attorneys general in the remaining states even offered official guidance to police concerning the impact the *Garner* decision would have on officer use of deadly force.

The impact of the case on police practices was also not as significant in many departments as most would expect. As noted previously, many police departments had already changed their practices to something similar to the holding in *Garner*. For example, research cited in the *Garner* decision itself found that 86.6 percent of the agencies surveyed just prior to the Court's review of the case already had deadly-force policies at least as restrictive as outlined in *Garner*.[12]

It may be, however, that the influence of *Garner* preceded the actual ruling. The Memphis Police Department's four cases similar to *Garner* had already reached the court of appeals prior to *Garner*'s being accepted by the Supreme Court, after all. There were other cases reaching the court of appeals in other circuits as well.[13] In fact, the circumstances of *Garner* were so well known in police circles that in *Acoff v. Abston* the Eleventh Circuit Court of Appeals ruled that the *Garner* decision could be applied retroactively to cities because the decision only reinforced an already accepted policy.[14]

The overall significance of *Garner*, therefore, is somewhat subject to debate. It no doubt completely changed the way police carried out their duties in some departments. It also established with some clarity when police were not authorized to use deadly force. For other departments and officers, though, the influence of *Garner* was less felt because the changes had already been made.

SIGNIFICANT SUBSEQUENT CASES

Since the decision in *Garner*, the Court has been largely content to stand on that holding in deadly-force cases. The Court has not accepted for review any new cases in which police officers shot and killed a suspect resulting in a rule on the constitutionality of the shooting. There have been cases involving police shootings where the use of deadly force was not the issue in the case; and, as described later in the case of *Brower*, the Court did rule in one other case regarding deadly force. Rather, *Garner* has received the most attention and widest interpretation within the lower courts. Although *Garner* set specific guidelines as to when officers are not allowed to use deadly force, it did little to determine when they can; therefore, lower courts have been required to fill in the gaps left by the Supreme Court.

The decisions of the lower courts following *Garner* can be divided into three categories: procedural, factual, and circumstantial. Procedural decisions are those involving issues related primarily to the court, such as the retroactive application of *Garner* discussed above in the *Acoff* case. Additional such cases, however, will not be addressed here. Factual decisions represent the largest number of cases following *Garner* and involve determining whether the *Garner* decision is applicable to a particular case. Circumstantial issues are raised in determining whether an officer's actions are in compliance with *Garner.*

The category of factual decisions addresses whether *Garner* is applicable to a particular case. These cases often center on whether or not a seizure was made. For the Fourth Amendment provisions of *Garner* to apply, a seizure by police must be made. *Garner* ruled that when police shoot a person, the person has been seized for the purposes of the Fourth Amendment. But what if the person dies while fleeing police? Is the person seized because police are attempting to seize the person, or is the person still free? In *Cameron v. City of Pontiac, Michigan* (813 F.2d 782 [6th Cir. 1986]), the court held that even though he is shot at by police officers during a chase, an offender who runs into traffic while being chased by police is not seized under the Fourth Amendment. Even though the police were trying to seize Cameron in this instance, they were not successful before he was killed by his own decision to run into traffic.

Although not a deadly-force case, the Supreme Court supported this same assumption in *California v. Hodari D.* (499 U.S. 621 [1991]) when they ruled that a person is not seized when an officer uses a show of authority but applies no physical force and the person does not willingly submit. Which governmental actions represent a seizure was addressed by the Supreme Court in *Brower v. County of Inyo* (489 U.S. 593 [1989]). In this case, Brower stole a car and was driving at a high speed to elude police. An eighteen-wheel tractor-trailer had been parked in the road beyond a hill that blocked it from Brower's view as he approached. The police had also positioned a police car with its lights on to blind Brower. Brower crashed into the roadblock and was killed as a result. His family sued the police department, arguing that the roadblock was an excessive use of force. The Supreme Court ruled that the government's intentional termination of an individual's freedom of movement is a form of seizure; thus, any forcible action taken by the police results in a seizure subject to Fourth Amendment provisions, and any injury or death that results from that seizure, will be judged concerning the proper use of deadly force. These cases support the view that if the police are chasing a person who dies prior to being apprehended by the police, no seizure is made; but if official police action restricts the movement of the person (as in pulling the vehicle in front of Brower to stop him), a seizure is made and the Fourth Amendment and *Garner* apply.

Finally, we discuss cases applying *Garner* to specific circumstances. Often such cases involve the concept of "future dangerousness." In the *Garner* decision, the Court stated that the use of force is unconstitutional unless "the officer has probable cause to believe that the suspect poses a significant threat of death or serious physical injury to the officer or others." The Court, however, did not delineate what would constitute a threat of death or serious physical injury.

Lower courts have made several rulings that further defined what is to be considered an adequate threat. In a relatively straightforward case (*Ford v. Childers*, 1986, affirmed in *Ford v. Childers*, 855 F.2d 1271 [7th Cir. 1987]), an Illinois district court found that police noting that victims of a bank robbery were holding their hands in the air was sufficient to satisfy *Garner*'s dangerousness requirement. Perhaps the quintessential case for future dangerousness was *Ryder v. City of Topeka* (814 F.2d 1412 [10th Cir. 1987]). In this case, a young female was involved in the robbery of a pizza parlor. The police had prior knowledge of the robbery but did not know if the suspects were armed. At the scene, an officer saw one of the suspects with a knife but did not know if the other suspects were armed. When the suspects fled, one officer chased Ryder. As they neared a residential area, the officer shot Ryder, later stating he was afraid that if she made it into one of the houses she might take a hostage or injure residents. Ryder was not armed when she was shot. The court ruled that the officer reasonably could have believed that the life of others would be in danger if Ryder were to escape, so the use of deadly force was authorized. In another case, the court addressed what constituted imminent danger to the officer or others.

In *Hinojosa v. City of Terrell, Texas* (864 F.2d 401 [1989]), police were called to a pool-hall fight. At the scene, officers used force on one of the persons involved in the brawl. The owner of the pool hall, Hinjosa, stated that when he tried to prevent the officers from using force, they pointed a gun at him. Hinojosa filed suit against the officers. The court found that an officer does not make a *Garner* seizure or use excessive force when using a weapon to make someone back off with no intent to arrest him or her.

Finally, courts addressed whether or not use of other police weapons could be considered use of deadly force. In *Garcia v. Wyckoff* (615 F.Supp. 217, 223 [D. Colo. 1985]), a police officer threw a flashlight at Garcia as he was fleeing. Garcia stated that he sustained serious injuries as a result. The Tenth Circuit Court of Appeals ruled that individuals who were not killed in incidents with the police could not use *Garner* as the basis for a suit against them.

RESEARCH RELATED TO THE CASE

One of the more substantial influences of the *Garner* decision was to quiet so-cial-science research on police use of deadly force. Prior to the 1960s, little had been said about police use of deadly force (in a 1988 article for *Justice Quarterly*, James J. Fyfe found only two studies on the topic prior to 1967[15]). The police had always been able to use deadly force against a fleeing person suspected of com-mitting a felony, and most people assumed this was unlikely to change. What re-search did exist discussed deadly force as only a small part of a larger discussion. For example, studies that led up to or were a part of the President's Commission on Law Enforcement and the Administration of Justice (1967) found that almost two-thirds of even the largest police departments in the United States did not have written policies directing police use of deadly force.[16] It would have been of little comfort to the people living within those districts that officers could rely on state law for guidance since, as almost half of the states either had no law or judicial guidance on use of deadly force or else followed the fleeing-felon rule.

The discussion of police use of deadly force began to change in the late 1960s, however, with the increased occurrence of urban riots in several American cit-ies. In response to those riots, two presidential committees were formed: The President's Commission on Law Enforcement and the Administration of Justice (1967) reported that officers generally received little guidance on the use of deadly force. The commission called on states to change their laws and police departments to promulgate stronger policies guiding officers' actions. A year later, the National Advisory Commission on Civil Disorders (1968) proposed that police shootings were often the events that set off urban riots. This commis-sion also called for greater control of police use of deadly force.

The recommendations of these commissions produced a much greater dis-cussion of the proper limits on police use of deadly force. One response to the findings of the commissions was that too little was actually known about police use of deadly force. To address these concerns, research in the late 1970s and particularly in the early 1980s began to focus on the characteristics of police shootings. The findings were often just as startling as the initial discovery that large segments of law enforcement throughout the country were operating with-out the benefit of clear guidelines on the matter. This research showed that the likelihood of police use of deadly force varied greatly in different cities, rang-ing from .37 shooting per thousand in the population of Honolulu to 7.17 per thousand in the population of Jacksonville, Florida. This led to further studies designed specifically to determine why there were such discrepancies in police shootings between cities.

Such studies typically looked to the characteristics of the event (i.e., officer race or sex, offender race, crime rate of the area, etc.) for sources of difference. As expected, crime and violence of the public played a part in determining use of force. Several studies found that the rate of police shootings in an area was significantly correlated with the homicide rate, the violent-crime rate, gun density, and other measures of violence.[17] Even though it bore a relation to frequency of police use of deadly force, violence in public was only one relatively infrequent explanation for the differences in use of deadly force between departments.

Further, research related to demographic characteristics often did not produce the expected associations. For example, while a general correlation was found between the race of the officer and shootings (in most studies, black officers used deadly force at a higher rate), the correlation was quickly explained away by other factors. For example, many police departments were hiring a greater number of black officers in response to civil-rights legislation and community demands; but this meant black officers were more likely to be in patrol positions, often in the more violent parts of town, where use of deadly force was more likely. It was also expected that female officers would use deadly force more frequently because they were of smaller stature and, hence, less able to prevail in a physical confrontation. This was also found to not be true; and female officers were actually less likely to use deadly force.

By the early 1980s, many police agencies had responded to the calls for tighter restrictions on use of deadly force and had changed their policies (or, more appropriately, created policies). For example, by 1982 Kenneth J. Matulia found in his book, *A Balance of Forces: A Report of the International Association of Chiefs of Police*, that 86 percent of cities with populations over 250,000 had defined polices limiting police use of deadly force in essentially the same manner as proscribed in the rule handed down in *Garner*.[18] These studies would all come to play a large part in the 1985 *Garner* decision. Normally relying on legal documents and court cases, the Supreme Court in this case consulted over ten social-science studies in formulating the basis of its opinion.

The ruling in *Garner* quieted most social-science research. Of course, there were newspaper articles on police reactions to *Garner*, and there continue to be news articles on particular shooting incidents, especially when they are questionable. There were also a number of studies conducted before *Garner* that were taken up for fresh review; the most extensive overview was William A. Geller's *Deadly Force: What We Know.*[19]

The focus of much of the research prior to *Garner*, however, had been trained on understanding police use of deadly force and those calling for the changes the Court made in that decision. Research conducted following the *Garner* decision was often a part of a larger study. For example, officer use of deadly force was often included in studies examining higher education in policing.[20] These studies found no real relationship between higher education and use of deadly force. While this seemed to be a blow for proponents of further educating police officers, extenuating circumstances in the education/force issue accounted for much of the negative findings, such as the type of education, the job functions of many college-educated officers, and the like.

A small number of studies following *Garner* examined the effects the case had on police. Drawing on his previous research, James J. Fyfe published several works in which he proposed that police policy and actions of the chief of police were the most important factors in controlling police use of deadly force, trumping even state law and court actions.[21] Fyfe and coauthor Jeffery T. Walker furthered that argument by showing that few states had actually changed their laws in the five years following the *Garner* decision, while many police departments had changed their policies.[22] Research from Fyfe and Walker supported earlier findings that when police executives promoted a consistent policy controlling use of deadly force their incidence of use of deadly force differed most greatly from other departments.[23]

One category of police-involved deaths not explicitly addressed by *Garner* (though partially addressed in *Brower*) was police pursuits wherein the suspect is killed as a product of the pursuit, an observation made by author Geoffrey P. Alpert and Patrick Anderson, among others.[24] Suspect death as a direct result of police pursuit had not been considered in *Garner*, and at that time many courts failed to consider it police use of deadly force.

This attitude somewhat changed in 1987 in *Brower v. County of Inyo*—the case where the fleeing suspect fatally crashed his car into a police barricade—where the Supreme Court overruled lower court decisions and found that when police intentionally stop a person who is fleeing they create a seizure under the Fourth Amendment and may be liable in 42 U.S.C §1983 cases if the seizure is not justified. Research on police pursuits and deadly force continues to the present day, and the courts still struggle with the full implications of police pursuits, particularly as they relate to police use of deadly force. It may be that the

Supreme Court is waiting for a case that can establish a bright-line rule as *Garner* did before taking on this issue.

CONCLUSIONS

Despite initial claims by some that the ruling was unjust, it would appear that the *Garner* decision has gone on to have a significant and positive influence on police officers. Police now have a firm basis for determining when deadly force is authorized under many circumstances. In situations where split-second decisions are made concerning life and death matters, no rule can be adequate. In some situations, an offender may escape who should not have been allowed to. Likewise, some offenders may be unnecessarily subjected to deadly force. Simply knowing when the use of deadly force is not permissible under law, however, may prevent an officer from taking actions that will lead to unnecessary injury and litigation.

Probably the greatest, and least recognized, impact *Garner* has made is on police departments and supervisory personnel. Although many large police departments already had deadly-force policies in effect prior to *Garner*—many of which were at least as strict as the ruling—that decision set a standard on which smaller departments could base their policy. Additionally, for those departments with guidelines that had been more lenient than those in the *Garner* decision, guidance was provided as they sought to redraw policy concerning deadly force. The effect was that supervisors and policy makers were relieved of the guesswork as to what the courts would allow concerning police use of deadly force. *Garner* impacted department supervisors even more drastically than it did police on the streets, for the ruling provided clear guidelines as to what the courts would consider constitutional or violative, saving the departments time and money in lawsuits.

FURTHER READING

Geoffrey P. Alpert and Patrick Anderson, "The Most Deadly Force: Police Pursuits," *Justice Quarterly* 3 (1986): 1–13.

American Law Institute, *ALI Proceedings* (Philadelphia: The Executive Office, The American Law Institute, 1931).

American Law Institute, *Model Penal Code* (proposed official draft) (Philadelphia: The Executive Office, The American Law Institute, 1962).

David L. Carter, Allen D. Sapp, and Darrel W. Stephens, *The State of Police Education: Policy Directions for the 21st Century* (Washington, D.C.: Police Executive Research Forum, 1989).

James J. Fyfe, "Geographic Correlates of Police Shootings: A Microanalysis," *Journal of Research in Crime and Delinquency* 17 (1980): 101–13.

James J. Fyfe, "Observations on Police Use of Deadly Force," *Crime and Delinquency* 27 (1981): 376–89.

James J. Fyfe, "*Tennessee v. Garner*: The Issue Not Addressed," *New York University Review of Law and Social Change* 14 (1986): 721–31.

James J. Fyfe, "Police Use of Deadly Force: Research and Reform," *Justice Quarterly* 5, no. 2 (1988): 165–204.

James J. Fyfe and Jeffery T. Walker, "Garner Plus Five Years: An Examination of Supreme Court Intervention into Police Discretion and Legislative Prerogatives," *American Journal of Criminal Justice* 144 (1990): 167–84.

William A. Geller, *Deadly Force: What We Know* (Washington, D.C.: Police Executive Research Forum, 1991).

William A. Geller and Kevin J. Karale, "Shootings of and by Chicago Police: Uncommon Crisis, Part 1: Shootings by Chicago Police," *Journal of Criminal Law and Criminology* 72 (1981): 1813–66.

John C. Hall, "Police Use of Deadly Force to Arrest: A Constitutional Standard, Part 1," *FBI Law Enforcement Bulletin* 57 (1988): 23–30.

Kenneth J. Matulia, *A Balance of Forces: A Report of the International Association of Chiefs of Police* (Gaithersburg, Md.: International Association of Chiefs of Police, 1982).

C. Milton, J. Lardner, and G. Abrecht, *Police Use of Deadly Force* (Washington, D.C.: Police Foundation, 1977).

Monell v. New York City Department of Social Services, 436 U.S. 658 (1978).

National Advisory Commission on Civil Disorders, *Report of the National Advisory Commission on Civil Disorders* (New York: Dutton, 1968).

President's Commission on Law Enforcement and the Administration of Justice, *Task Force Report: The Police* (Washington, D.C.: U.S. Government Printing Office, 1967).

IX

THE NEXT TWENTY MOST SIGNIFICANT CASES

The Next Twenty (Or So) Most Significant Cases Dealing with Police Practices

Valerie Bell

Atwater v. City of Lago Vista, 532 U.S. 318 (2001)

Board of Education of Independent School District v. Earls, 536 U.S. 822 (2002)

California v. Greenwood, 486 U.S. 35 (1988)

Camara v. Municipal Court, 387 U.S. 523 (1967)

City of Indianapolis v. Edmond, 531 U.S. 32 (2000)

Delaware v. Prouse, 440 U.S. 648 (1979)

Florida v. Bostick, 501 U.S. 429 (1991)

Griffin v. Wisconsin, 483 U.S. 868 (1987)

Illinois v. McArthur, 531 U.S. 326 (2001)

Illinois v. Wardlow, 528 U.S. 119 (2000)

Knowles v. Iowa, 525 U.S. 113 (1998)

Kyllo v. United States, 533 U.S. 27 (2001)

Michigan v. Chesternut, 486 U.S. 567 (1988)

Michigan Department of State Police v. Sitz, 496 U.S. 444 (1990)

Minnesota v. Carter, 525 U.S. 83 (1998)

Minnick v. Mississippi, 498 U.S. 146 (1990)

New Jersey v. T.L.O., 469 U.S. 325 (1985)

Ohio v. Robinette, 519 U.S. 33 (1996)

Rhode Island v. Innis, 446 U.S. 291 (1980)

South Dakota v. Opperman, 428 U.S. 364 (1976)

United States v. Drayton et al., 536 U.S. 194 (2002)

Wyoming v. Houghton, 526 U.S. 295 (1999)

While the first twenty cases highlighted in this book are, in our opinion, the most significant cases dealing with police investigatory practices, we recognize there are others that are, if not as significant, nonetheless worthy of mention. We provide capsule summaries of this next "tier" of significant criminal-procedure cases here.

ATWATER V. CITY OF LAGO VISTA, 532 U.S. 318 (2001)

Atwater v. City of Lago Vista (2001) determines whether or not the Fourth Amendment allows an officer to arrest a person for a criminal offense that carries no jail time. Atwater was arrested for driving a vehicle without a seatbelt on herself or her children. Under Texas law the charge is a misdemeanor criminal offense, punishable by a maximum fine of $50.00 with no possibility of incarceration. Texas law does allow officers to arrest and cite for all offenses, even those that are nonjailable. Atwater posted bail shortly after arrest and eventually pled no contest to the seatbelt violation. She then brought a Section 1983 lawsuit against the officer and his employer, alleging that the arrest violated her Fourth Amendment right to be free from unreasonable seizures.

The Court held that it was not unreasonable under the Fourth Amendment for an officer who has probable cause to believe an offense has been committed in his presence to make an arrest even for a minor criminal offense that carries no jail term. The justices found no historical evidence to indicate that the framers of the Constitution intended to restrict warrantless misdemeanor arrests in such a manner. Additionally, the Court noted that actual practice has failed to support any such kind of restriction as well. The case is significant in that it allows officers a great deal of latitude in making arrests for minor criminal offenses but insignificant insofar as it is unlikely that officers will greatly increase arrests made for minor criminal offenses as a result.

BOARD OF EDUCATION OF INDEPENDENT SCHOOL DISTRICT V. EARLS, 536 U.S. 822 (2002)

The Student-Activities Drug-Testing Police implemented by the Board of Education of Independent School District No. 92 of Pottawatomie County, Oklahoma, requires students who participate in extracurricular activities to submit to random, suspicionless drug tests. Urine tests are intended to detect the use of illegal drugs. Two students and their parents brought a Section 1983 lawsuit against the school district, alleging that the drug-testing policy violated the Fourth Amendment as incorporated to the states through the Due Process Clause of the Fourteenth Amendment. The district court found in favor of the school district, but the Tenth Circuit reversed, holding that the policy violated the Fourth Amendment.

The Court held that random, suspicionless drug tests of students who participate in extracurricular activities do not violate the Fourth Amendment. The degree of intrusion caused by collecting a urine sample was negligible, and the policy clearly required that test results be kept in confidential files separate from a student's other records, to be released to school personnel only on a need-to-know basis, and that the test results are not to be turned over to any law-enforcement authority. Additionally, the only consequences of a failed drug test are to limit the student's privilege of participating in extracurricular activities.

The Court concluded that the policy in question here served the school district's interest in protecting the health and safety of its students, so the minimal intrusions did not violate the Fourth Amendment. This case is important because it carefully outlines the requirements of a constitutional regulatory drug-testing program.

CALIFORNIA V. GREENWOOD, 486 U.S. 35 (1988)

In *California v. Greenwood* (1988) the Court addressed the difference between an officer's looking for evidence of a crime and participating in a search. An investigator of the Laguna Beach Police Department gained information that a truck filled with illegal narcotics was going to Greenwood's residence. Based on this and other information, the investigator placed the Greenwood house under surveillance. Garbage was obtained from the trash collector, and evidence of narcotics use was uncovered. A warrant was obtained based on this evidence, drugs were found in a subsequent search, and Greenwood was arrested. A second warrant was issued after more evidence was retrieved from a second garbage search, and Greenwood was again arrested.

The Court held that items placed in the trash for collection on a public street can be searched without a warrant or probable cause based on the abandonment exception. The Court determined that garbage placed for collection on a public street is accessible to anyone and therefore, although an individual may have an expectation of privacy in that garbage, it is not one that society is prepared to recognize as reasonable.

CAMARA V. MUNICIPAL COURT, 387 U.S. 523 (1967)

Camara was charged with violating the San Francisco housing code for refusing to allow housing inspectors to engage in a warrantless inspection of the apartment where he resided. While awaiting trial, Camara claimed that the inspection ordinance was unconstitutional because it permitted searches without warrants or any suspicion, in violation of the Fourth Amendment.

Nonconsensual administrative searches of private residences violate the Fourth Amendment. Under the Fourth Amendment, people have a constitutional right to insist that code inspectors obtain a warrant to search their private residences. This case is important because it prohibits warrantless, nonconsensual "inspections" of private residences. The decision reinforces the Court's interest in preserving the privacy of people in their homes. Code inspections of the nature discussed in *Camara* are still permissible, but authorities are now required to obtain a warrant to "inspect" beforehand. The only time government officials are permitted to enter a residence without a warrant is either with valid consent or exigent circumstances. Neither was present in this case.

CITY OF INDIANAPOLIS V. EDMOND, 531 U.S. 32 (2000)

The city of Indianapolis operated a checkpoint program under which officers, without any suspicion, would stop certain vehicles at roadblocks throughout the city for the purpose of discovering unlawful narcotics. Once a vehicle was stopped, at least one officer would approach the car, advise the driver that he or she was stopped at a narcotics checkpoint, ask the driver for his or her license and registration, look for signs of impairment, conduct an open-view examination of the vehicle from the outside, and allow a trained drug dog to walk around the outside of the car. Two people stopped at the checkpoints filed suit in the

U.S. District Court for the Southern District of Indiana, asserting that the checkpoints violated the Fourth Amendment.

Because suspicionless vehicle checkpoints for detecting illegal drugs are "indistinguishable from the general interest in crime control," the checkpoints violate the Fourth Amendment. In other checkpoint cases the focus was on patrolling the borders and/or ensuring roadway safety. The Court held that because Indianapolis's checkpoint program served little more than a general crime-control function—instead of being concerned with broader issues of safety—it violated the Fourth Amendment's proscription against unreasonable searches and seizures.

DELAWARE V. PROUSE, 440 U.S. 648 (1979)

After making a stop for the sole purpose of checking the driver's license and registration of a vehicle, a Delaware patrol officer observed a quantity of marijuana within plain view on the floorboard. Prouse, a passenger in the vehicle, was arrested and subsequently indicted for possession of a controlled substance. Prior to trial, Prouse entered a motion to suppress the evidence as the result of an unlawful traffic stop. The officer was not acting pursuant to any established standards, guidelines, or procedures promulgated by his agency or the state for purposes of conducting such spot checks. The trial court granted the motion to suppress, and the state Supreme Court affirmed, noting that a random stop of a motorist in the absence of specific articulable facts as justification for the stop is constitutionally impermissible and violative of the Fourth and Fourteenth Amendments to the Constitution.

The Court held that the Fourth Amendment prohibits officers from stopping a vehicle being operated on a public roadway for purposes of checking the driver's license and vehicle registration in the absence of at least articulable and reasonable suspicion that a motorist is unlicensed or that a vehicle is unregistered or that either the vehicle or its occupants are subject to seizure for some violation of law. Both the Fourth and Fourteenth Amendments were triggered in this case due to the fact that stopping a vehicle and detaining its occupants, even if only for a brief period of time, constitutes a seizure. The Court noted that just as an individual does not lose all protections of the Fourth Amendment when stepping from his home onto the sidewalk, neither should these protections be lost when an individual steps from the sidewalk into a car.

This case is significant first because prior to this case traffic stops lacking the element of probable cause or at least reasonable, articulable suspicion were not unconstitutional under the Fourth Amendment as a general rule of law. Second, the case clearly requires that officers develop, at a minimum, reasonable, articulable suspicion that a violation of law has occurred before making a traffic stop. Third, the Court noted that the Fourth Amendment prohibited random spot checks but not necessarily full-scale roadblocks where every passing motorist is stopped.

FLORIDA V. BOSTICK, 501 U.S. 429 (1991)

In *Florida v. Bostick* (1991) the Court provided a slightly different definition of *seizure* for the purposes of the Fourth Amendment. During a routine stop of a bus, Bostick was asked if he would consent to a search of his luggage. The defendant consented, and the police searched his luggage and found cocaine. Bostick later sought suppression of the drugs, arguing that the cocaine was improperly seized. The question at issue in this case was if the Florida Supreme Court had erred in adopting a per se rule that every encounter on a bus is a seizure.

The Court determined that the Florida Supreme Court was in error. The Court held that, in a confined space such as a bus, more is required for a seizure to take place than that a person simply feel that they are not free to leave. The Court held that the appropriate test for such a situation was whether or not the person felt free to decline the search or to terminate the encounter. The case was remanded to the Florida State Court for a determination as to whether or not, consistent with the new definition, a seizure actually took place.

GRIFFIN V. WISCONSIN, 483 U.S. 868 (1987)

After Griffin was convicted on charges of resisting arrest, disorderly conduct, and obstructing an officer, he was placed on probation. One of the probation conditions was that he allow any probation officer to search his home without a warrant as long as the probation officer's supervisor approved and that there were "reasonable grounds" to believe contraband would be found.

After being informed by a detective in the Beloit Police Department that there might be guns at Griffin's apartment, his probation officer, accompanied by another probation officer and three plainclothes police officers, went to Griffin's apartment. Griffin answered the door, and Officer Lew told him that they were there to search his apartment. A handgun was found during the search. Griffin was convicted of possession of a firearm by a felon.

The issue in this case involved whether or not it was constitutional to force a probationer to submit to warrantless searches of his or her residence. The Court held that probationers can be forced to submit to warrantless searches of their residences if there are "reasonable grounds" to believe that contraband will be found. The Court based its decision on the special-needs exception of law enforcement.

This case is important because it treats probationers differently than ordinary citizens. The Court sanctioned warrantless searches of probationers' residences because, it argued, they enjoy a lesser expectation of privacy as part of being placed on probation. The Court has sanctioned similar searches of parolees' homes as well. The same logic applies. In this case the Court focused more on the special needs of law enforcement than on a balancing approach, weighing the individual's privacy interests with the state's interest in promoting public safety.

ILLINOIS V. MCARTHUR, 531 U.S. 326 (2001)

In *Illinois v. McArthur* (2001) the Court addresses the seizure of a place. In this case, police officers accompanied a woman to the home of her husband, where she had previously lived. The woman told the officers that her husband had marijuana in the trailer. After being denied permission to search the trailer by the man living there, one officer went to obtain a warrant to search while the other remained behind and secured the premises, refusing the man reentry. The officer returned with a warrant, marijuana was found, and the man was arrested and charged with misdemeanor possession. The trial court accepted a motion to suppress the evidence as the fruit of an unlawful seizure.

The Court overturned the decision of the trial court, stating that refusing McArthur reentry into his residence was not a violation of the Fourth Amendment seizure clause. The Court based its finding on the exigency exception, establishing that suspects do not have a constitutional right to destroy evidence of their involvement in criminal activity. This case is significant because it gives the police authority to refuse an individual entry into a dwelling if there is reason to believe that once inside she or he will attempt to destroy evidence of criminal activity.

ILLINOIS V. WARDLOW, 528 U.S. 119 (2000)

As Chicago police officers converged upon a high-crime and drug neighborhood, two officers observed Wardlow immediately flee the area on foot and, after catching up to him, seized a firearm unlawfully in his possession. A motion to suppress was denied, and Wardlow was convicted on charges of unlawful use of a weapon by a felon. After reversal by a state appellate court based on a lack of reasonable suspicion for the detention as required by *Terry v. Ohio* (1968) and affirmation by the state supreme court, the case came before the Court.

The case centered on whether sudden flight from a high-crime area was sufficient to create reasonable suspicion for a *Terry* stop and frisk. The Court held that unprovoked flight from a high-crime area combined with the characteristics of the neighborhood and the nervous and evasive behavior of the individual were enough to support a *Terry* stop and frisk. The Court noted that flight itself was not enough to provide reasonable suspicion, but combined with the other factors the stop was justified. This case addresses the long-standing question of whether or not officers are authorized to stop an individual who has done nothing more than flee the area upon becoming aware of their presence.

KNOWLES V. IOWA, 525 U.S. 113 (1998)

Iowa law authorized police officers to either cite or arrest traffic violators. After issuing Knowles a citation for speeding, the officer conducted a full search of the vehicle before releasing him. During the course of this search the officer found a quantity of marijuana and narcotic paraphernalia, resulting in Knowles's arrest. Prior to trial Knowles entered a motion to suppress the evidence on grounds that since he had received a citation and had not been arrested the search did not qualify under the incident-to-arrest exception created in *United States v. Robinson* (1973). The trial court rejected this claim, finding Knowles guilty, and the Iowa Supreme Court affirmed by creating a search-incident-to-citation exception to the Fourth Amendment.

The Court unanimously held that a full search of a vehicle incident to a traffic stop in which the officer issues a citation rather than arresting the motorist violates the Fourth Amendment. The Court's ruling was based on the fact that neither of the two historical rationales for allowing officers to conduct such searches (i.e., mobility and/or the need to disarm a dangerous suspect) was present to justify the search of Knowles's vehicle. In situations where an officer decides to let a violator leave the scene after issuing a summons, the only acceptable basis for conducting a search of the vehicle is by developing probable cause or obtaining informed consent.

KYLLO V. UNITED STATES, 533 U.S. 27 (2001)

In *Kyllo v. United States* (2001) the Court further addresses the issue of searches, but the setting here is the home, traditionally an area of greatest protection under the Fourth Amendment. Based on suspicion of marijuana cultivation, but without probable cause, law-enforcement agents used a thermal-imaging device to scan Kyllo's triplex in an effect to determine if it was radiating more heat than his neighbors. The scan determined that the triplex was producing more heat in certain areas than the neighboring homes. Based on this and other information, a warrant was issued, and one hundred marijuana plants were discovered. Kyllo was indicted and convicted in federal court following a plea agreement.

The issue in this case does not concern the legality of the use of thermal-imaging devices. Rather, the Court concerned itself, in this case, with whether or not the use of such devices, without a warrant, constituted an unreasonable search and seizure under the Fourth Amendment. The Court held that the use of such devices not in general public use requires probable cause to be a reasonable search and seizure. According to the Court, lack of a physical intrusion was no longer necessary to preclude the existence of a search. The case is important because it greatly restricts the use of thermal-imaging scans by law enforcement and may greatly affect the ability of law enforcement to detect indoor marijuana-growing operations.

MICHIGAN V. CHESTERNUT, 486 U.S. 567 (1988)

Michigan v. Chesternut (1988) addresses whether or not following a person constitutes a search and seizure according to the Fourth Amendment. Chesternut was followed by a police car while walking down the street. After a man stepped out of a car and approached Chesternut standing on a corner, Chesternut saw the police car and ran. As the police were following Chesternut, he pulled several packets out of his pockets and threw them away. The packets contained codeine pills. Chesternut was arrested for possession of narcotics.

The Court held that the appropriate test for determining whether a person is seized within the meaning of the Fourth Amendment is whether a reasonable person, viewing all the circumstances in their totality, would conclude that she or he is not free to leave. The Court's rationale stated that the police merely chased Chesternut and did not pursue him aggressively using lights or sirens or attempt to stop his progress. The Court concluded that this did not implicate Fourth Amendment protections. The case is significant because it addresses the question of when a person has been seized by the police and thus has the right to Fourth Amendment protections.

MICHIGAN DEPARTMENT OF STATE POLICE V. SITZ, 496 U.S. 444 (1990)

The Michigan Department of State Police instituted a sobriety-checkpoint program under guidelines set forth by an advisory committee. The guidelines described how the checkpoints were to be operated, where they were to be set up, and how public notice was to be provided. The checkpoint at issue in this case was one that was in operation for about seventy-five minutes, during which time 126 vehicles passed through. The average delay per car was twenty-five seconds. One day prior to operation of the checkpoint a group of drivers filed a complaint in the circuit court of Wayne County, Michigan, claiming that the checkpoints were unconstitutional.

The Court held that such checkpoints do not violate the Fourth Amendment, but it suggested that part of the reason for this was that the checkpoints were operated pursuant to clearly defined policies, every vehicle was stopped, and there was little discretion regarding who would be stopped accorded to each individual officer. The detentions were generally very brief, so the Court looked favorably on the checkpoints, even though they technically amounted to seizures within the meaning of the Fourth Amendment.

MINNESOTA V. CARTER, 525 U.S. 83 (1998)

Upon arriving at an apartment based on a tip regarding narcotics violations, through a ground-floor window a police officer observed people putting white powder into bags. Carter and Johns were stopped by the police in their car after they left the apartment. Officers observed a handgun in the car and arrested both men, and a search incident to arrest revealed drugs and drug paraphernalia. The officers returned to the apartment with an arrest warrant for the lessee, Thompson, and a search of the apartment revealed more drugs. Later information revealed that Carter and Johns were visiting from another city and were only there for a short time for the purpose of packaging drugs.

The decision by the Court in this case concerns the existence of an expectation of privacy in another's apartment with consent, for the purpose of doing business. The Court held that no such reasonable expectation of privacy exists in this situation.

The rationale for the decision was based on the conclusion that Carter and Johns were there strictly for business purposes and were not friends with the lessee, Thompson. This case is important because it clarifies the situations in which overnight guests enjoy an expectation of privacy in third-party dwellings. Overnight guests who are visiting friends have an expectation of privacy, but not those visiting for business purposes.

MINNICK V. MISSISSIPPI, 498 U.S. 146 (1990)

Minnick, wanted on capital murder charges out of Mississippi, was arrested in California and held for extradition. Federal agents questioned him and terminated their interrogation when he asked to speak with an attorney, which he was allowed to do two or three times. Upon arrival, the deputy sheriff from Mississippi resumed interrogation and told Minnick that he could not refuse to talk, and Minnick confessed to involvement in the murder.

Minnick motioned to suppress the confession and was denied, convicted, and sentenced to death. The Mississippi Supreme Court rejected Minnick's appeal based on violation of his Fifth Amendment right to counsel. The state's high court reasoned that the *Edwards* rule, which prohibits the police from reinitiating interrogation of a suspect until counsel is made available, was not applicable in Minnick's case because his request for representation had been granted before the deputy resumed questioning.

The issue addressed in this case involves whether protection established under the *Edwards* rule ceases to exist once a suspect has consulted with an attorney. The Court held that when, during the course of custodial interrogation, a suspect asks for counsel, all questioning must immediately cease and may not resume until such time as counsel is present in the room. The Court's majority literally interpreted *Edwards* to mean that before questioning by police may resume, an attorney must be physically present in the room.

This case is significant in that it clearly establishes the standard that once a suspect under custodial interrogation requests assistance of counsel, all questioning must immediately cease and be held in abeyance until such time as an attorney is physically present in the room. This expansion of the Fifth Amendment by the Court's majority drew sharp criticism from the dissenting justices who noted that, even if a suspect genuinely and freely desired to do so, she or he could never consent to an interview with police unless an attorney is present. In effect, the dissenting justices suggest that although increased protection for criminal suspects has indeed been gained as a result of this decision, that which has been lost—a certain measure of power on the part of police to find those who have violated the law—may be of greater cost in the end.

NEW JERSEY V. T.L.O., 469 U.S. 325 (1985)

A high-school teacher caught a fourteen-year-old freshman smoking in a school restroom, in violation of a school rule. The student was brought to the principal's office and was questioned by the assistant vice principal. The student denied smoking, and, after demanding her purse, the assistant vice principal found a pack of cigarettes and a pack of rolling papers. A more thorough search of the student's purse revealed a small amount of incriminating evidence. The evidence was admitted against the student in a New Jersey juvenile court proceeding. The New Jersey court held that school officials can search a student if the official has reasonable suspicion or reasonable cause to believe a search is necessary to enforce a school policy.

The Court held that school officials do not need a warrant or probable cause for a school disciplinary search. This case serves as a prime example of the Court's balancing approach used in judging the constitutionality of so-called regulatory searches. Note that this case dealt with grades K–12. The story is markedly different for college students. The courts have generally held that college students enjoy Fourth Amendment protection and cannot be searched and/or seized on less-than-probable cause.

OHIO V. ROBINETTE, 519 U.S. 33 (1996)

After being stopped for speeding and given a verbal warning, Robinette was asked before being released from the scene if his vehicle contained any contraband. Answering in the negative, he gave permission for the car to be searched. The officer discovered a small amount of marijuana and a pill that later tested positive for methamphetamine. Robinette was arrested and charged with possession of a controlled substance. The trial court rejected a motion to suppress, whereupon Robinette pleaded no contest and was convicted. The Ohio Court of Appeals reversed the conviction, and the Ohio Supreme Court affirmed on grounds that the continued detention constituted an illegal seizure, stating that officers must inform motorists that they are free to leave before asking for consent to search.

The Court held that the Fourth Amendment does not require an officer to inform a motorist that she or he is free to leave the scene before requesting consent to search the vehicle. An eight-justice majority reasoned that in assessing the validity of a given consent search is the element of voluntariness. The Court concluded that it would be unrealistic to require police officers always to inform motorists that they are free to go in order for a given consent search to be considered both voluntary and valid.

The decision in this case is one that clearly favors and facilitates the law-enforcement endeavor. By refusing to require that police officers specifically inform motorists that they are free to leave before requesting permission to search a vehicle, the Court emphasized that the determination of whether or not a particular consent to search is voluntary should not turn on a single statement. Rather, this determination should be based on a totality of the circumstances.

RHODE ISLAND V. INNIS, 446 U.S. 291 (1980)

Police arrested Innis after he was identified by a robbery victim. He was advised no less than three times of his Miranda rights by the patrol officer and two supervisory personnel on the scene. A prior robbery victim had been killed with a sawed-off shotgun, and one of the transporting officers expressed concern to another that children from a nearby school for the handicapped might find the weapon and accidentally harm themselves. Innis overheard the comment and told the officers to turn the car around so that he could show them where the weapon was hidden. He was informed of his Miranda rights another time at the scene and indicated that he understood these rights. He then led officers to a nearby field where the gun was recovered. Innis was subsequently convicted of kidnapping, robbery, and murder. On appeal, the Rhode Island Supreme Court set aside the conviction on grounds that the transporting officers had interrogated Innis without the benefit of counsel while transporting him to the jail.

The Court held that the conversation between the two officers did not constitute an interrogation or its functional equivalent, as the suspect was not directly involved in the exchange. Therefore, no Sixth Amendment right was either implicated or violated. The Courts reasoned that the conversation that had transpired between the officers did not constitute an interrogation insofar as there occurred no direct questioning of Innis and the officers at no time attempted to elicit a response from Innis. Finally, the majority also observed that there was no indication that the two officers were specifically aware of and intentionally sought to exploit Innis's concern for the safety of nearby handicapped children.

This case is important in that it helps clarify those police behaviors that constitute an interrogation and those that do not. This case differs from *Brewer v. Williams* (1977) because in that case an officer made a direct appeal to a suspect for information regarding the whereabouts of a murder victim's body. In the present matter the two officers did not directly engage the suspect in conversation—they were speaking only among themselves and did not ask him any questions. Although the distinction between these two cases may seem clear, the use of such tactics to obtain information remains risky given that the situation will be assessed not from the perspective of the officers but, instead, from that of the suspect.

SOUTH DAKOTA V. OPPERMAN, 428 U.S. 364 (1976)

Police impounded Opperman's car and, following standard department procedures, inventoried the contents of the car. In doing so they discovered marijuana in the glove compartment. Opperman was arrested and charged with narcotics offenses. He sought suppression of the evidence.

The Court held that a warrantless, suspicionless inventory search of an impounded vehicle does not violate the Fourth Amendment. However, the impoundment must be lawful, the search should follow "standard operating procedures," and the search should not be used as a pretext concealing a motive to obtain incriminating evidence. The expectation of privacy in one's automobile is significantly less than that relating to one's home or office. This case is important because it is the first to constitutionally sanction police inventory searches. Even though the Court stated that inventory searches should not be relied upon for obtaining incriminating evidence, it is clear that if the police do not have probable cause to engage in a conventional search, inventories can act as something of a fallback measure.

UNITED STATES V. DRAYTON ET AL., 536 U.S. 194 (2002)

Police conducting a bus sweep asked permission to search the defendants' carry-on luggage. After the search, which uncovered nothing, the police asked permission to search their persons. A pat-down revealed drugs taped to both thighs under their clothing. Both men were arrested and charged with conspiracy to distribute cocaine. At trial in federal district court, Drayton moved to suppress the evidence on grounds of coercive police conduct and was denied and convicted. The Eleventh Circuit Court of Appeals reversed and remanded with instructions to grant the motion to suppress.

The question before the Court was whether police can randomly approach individuals and ask for consent to search their belongings or person without any indication of criminal activity. The Court held that police can approach individuals and ask for consent to search without any justification, as compliance is not induced by coercive means.

If an individual refuses to speak with the police that person must be allowed to go along her or his way, and refusal to engage the police in conversation or consent to a search cannot be used as a basis for detention. Additionally, officers may not use coercive or intimidating tactics in order to gain consent for a search. When an individual is free to leave and go about her or his business, no seizure has occurred under the Fourth Amendment. The decision in this case reaffirms the Court's earlier ruling in *Florida v. Bostick* (1991): Once an officer has developed reasonable suspicion of criminal activity she or he has a legally justifiable basis for initiating a detention of the individual. In order to detain an individual who refuses to talk to the police, the officer must draw upon his or her unique experience as well as a totality of the circumstances to develop a reasonable and articulable suspicion that criminal activity is afoot.

WYOMING V. HOUGHTON, 526 U.S. 295 (1999)

A Wyoming state trooper stopped a vehicle in which Houghton and two others were traveling. The trooper inquired about the trio's use of illegal drugs after noticing a syringe in the driver's shirt pocket. The driver confirmed that he in fact used drugs, whereupon the trooper initiated a search of the vehicle's passenger compartment, including a purse that belonged to Houghton, which was lying on the back seat. The trooper found a quantity of methamphetamine and related narcotic paraphernalia in the purse, and Houghton was arrested and convicted for possession of a controlled substance. The Wyoming Supreme Court reversed the conviction on grounds that the officer had no justifiable basis for searching the purse.

The Court held that where officers have probable cause to conduct a warrantless vehicle search, they are also authorized to search a passenger's personal belongings where there exists the possibility that they may contain contraband. The practical significance of this case for law enforcement lies in the fact that it allows officers to search the personal belongings of all passengers in a vehicle so long as the vehicle has been lawfully stopped and there is probable cause to believe that the search will reveal evidence of criminal activity. Thus officers no longer have to obtain the consent of the passenger whose belongings are to be searched.

Appendix 1

Timeline of Significant Supreme Court Cases Dealing with Police Investigatory Practices

Top 20 Cases	Next 20 (Or So) Cases
Carroll v. United States (1925)	
Mapp v. Ohio (1961)	
Miranda v. Arizona (1966)	
Schmerber v. California (1966)	
Katz v. United States (1967)	*Camara v. Municipal Court* (1967)
United States v. Wade (1967)	
Terry v. Ohio (1968)	
Chimel v. California (1969)	
Kirby v. Illinois (1972)	
United States v. Ash (1973)	
United States v. Robinson (1973)	
	South Dakota v. Opperman (1976)
Schneckloth v. Bustamonte (1979)	*Delaware v. Prouse* (1979)
Payton v. New York (1980)	*Rhode Island v. Innis* (1980)
New York v. Belton (1981)	
United States v. Ross (1982)	
Illinois v. Gates (1983)	
Oliver v. United States (1984)	
Tennessee v. Garner (1985)	*New Jersey v. T.L.O.* (1985)
	Griffin v. Wisconsin (1987)
	California v. Greenwood (1988)
	Michigan v. Chesternut (1988)

Top 20 Cases

Next 20 (Or So) Cases
Michigan Dept. of State Police v. Sitz (1990)
Minnick v. Mississippi (1990)
Florida v. Bostick (1991)

Minnesota v. Dickerson (1993)
Wilson v. Arkansas (1995)
Whren v. United States (1996)

Ohio v. Robinette (1996)
Minnesota v. Carter (1988)
Knowles v. Iowa (1998)
Wyoming v. Houghton (1999)
City of Indianapolis v. Edmond (2000)
Illinois v. Wardlow (2000)
Kyllo v. United States (2001)
Illinois v. McArthur (2001)
Atwater v. City of Lago Vista (2001)
United States v. Drayton (2002)
Board of Education v. Earls (2002)

Georgia v. Randolph (2006)

Appendix 2

Biographies of Select United States Supreme Court Justices

This chapter provides brief biographies of the United States Supreme Court justices and chief justices who wrote the majority opinion in one or more of the top twenty cases we examine in this book. These biographies are arranged in chronological order.

WILLIAM HOWARD TAFT (1857–1930)

Chief Justice of the United States Supreme Court (1921–1930), nominated by Dwight D. Eisenhower

Taft is the only person in the history of the United States of America to have served as both president of the Executive Branch and chief justice of the Supreme Court. Born into the powerful Taft family in Cincinnati, Ohio, William Taft lived a life of privilege and graduated from Yale College in 1878. After going on to receive a degree from Cincinnati Law School and after several years of faithful courtship, Taft finally was able to marry his sweetheart Helen Herron in 1886. A year later, in 1887, Taft was appointed judge to the Ohio Superior Court in 1887, then solicitor general of the United States in 1890, judge on the United States Court of Appeals for the Sixth Circuit in 1891, governor general of the Philippines in 1900, and secretary of war in 1904.

Although Helen envisioned a powerful and prestigious political career for her husband, Taft himself treasured the Court as the "nearest thing to his heart" next to his family.[1] Less interested in politics, especially campaigning, Taft regardless spent four "uncomfortable years" in the White House, where he earned little credit for his administrative accomplishments. After an unsuccessful presidential reelection, Taft was invited to Yale University as Kent Professor of Constitutional Law. Later, he began serving on the Supreme Court, where at last he managed to integrate his unique background in administration, academia, and the judiciary. There Taft used his personal and political clout to initiate various judicial reforms in an effort to expand judiciary power, simplify procedures, and reduce political patronage, which greatly influenced the federal judiciary over the long term. Perhaps because of his staggering weight (an average of three hundred pounds at any given time, making him the heaviest American president in history), Taft become seriously ill and as a result was eventually forced to announce his resignation from the bench in 1930. He died at the age of seventy-two, five weeks after his resignation.

References

Clare Cushman, *The Supreme Court Justices: Illustrated Biographies, 1789–1993* (Washington, D.C.: Congressional Quarterly, 1993).

Wikipedia.org, "William Howard Taft," http://en.wikipedia.org/wiki/William_Howard_Taft.

THOMAS CAMPBELL CLARK (1899–1977)

Associate Justice of the United States Supreme Court (1949–1967), nominated by Harry Truman

Thomas Campbell Clark served the federal government in multiple capacities, in the Department of Justice (1937–1945), as attorney general (1945–1949), and as associate justice to the Supreme Court (1949–1967).

Clark was born in Dallas, Texas, to William and Virginia Clark, both from distinguished Southern families. William was a renowned lawyer in Dallas and president of the Texas Bar Association. Thomas was educated in local schools, where he excelled at debate and oration. After graduating from high school, with the Second World War raging, he decided to join the army. Since he was underweight, he only managed to serve in the National Guard. In college he met and married a fellow student, Mary Ramsey, whose father was a judge on the Court of Criminal Appeals and the Texas Supreme Court.

After graduation Clark joined his father and brother's law firm in Dallas. After practicing law there for five years, Clark served as assistant district attorney for Dallas County, where he excelled, never losing a single case for all the civil litigation he handled. Despite his impressive rise, at this time Clark made what he later considered to be "the biggest mistake" of his life in 1940, when, as coordinator of alien-enemy control for the Western Defense Command, he oversaw the evacuation of persons of Japanese ancestry.² Although during the anguish and confusion immediately following the attack on Pearl Harbor Clark believed national security dictated these measures, he later bitterly regretted his decision.

Around 1942, the career of the junior senator from Missouri began a precipitous rise. Harry S. Truman was a colleague and professional touchstone for Clark, and the two remained in close contact thereafter. In repayment for the wise counsel Truman had provided over the years, Clark supported the Democrat in his successful 1945 bid for the U.S. vice presidency. Mere months after assuming office, when President Roosevelt died, Truman assumed the presidency and immediately appointed Clark to be his attorney general. In 1949 President Truman again promoted his friend, this time nominating him to the Supreme Court to fill the seat vacated by Frank Murphy. Although the media termed Clark "a personal and political friend [of Truman's] with no judicial experience and few demonstrated qualifications," Truman believed Clark's appointment would strengthen Chief Justice Fred Vinson's position on the bench, anticipating a similarity in their judgments.

Although initially Clark deferred to Vinson, before long he began demonstrating remarkable independence. The most striking example of his autonomous decision making was the case of *Youngstown Sheet & Tube Co. v. Sawyer* (1952). In this case, Clark ruled that Truman's seizure of private steel mines during the Korean War was unconstitutional—this after having advised Truman as his attorney general that he had the legal authority to do so. Clark's unexpected judicial independence made Truman later bemoan that "Tom Clark was my biggest mistake"; "It isn't so much that he's a bad man," Truman explained. "It's just that he's such a dumb son of a bitch."

As a Democrat, Clark's liberal ideals were well in evidence in his written opinions on the high court. Perhaps the most important case Clark ever wrote was *Mapp v. Ohio* (1961), a major criminal-justice case. Clark ruled that the evidence obtained through an unconstitutional search could not be admitted in court. In addition to this decision, Clark frequently supported the Court's decisions to enhance the legal standing of blacks.

In 1967, Clark decided to leave the high court at the age of sixty-seven when his son Ramsey Clark was nominated to be attorney general. Clark senior felt that by stepping aside he could best avoid conflicts of interest, as many of the Court's cases came from the Justice Department. Even after his resignation Clark remained active in the judicial community and was invited to sit on federal circuits in all the judicial circuits in the country. He also traveled the country lecturing on suggested improvements to judicial administration.

References

Nigel Bowles, *The Government and Politics of the United States* (New York: Palgrave Macmillan, 1993).

Clare Cushman, *The Supreme Court Justices: Illustrated Biographies, 1789–1993* (Washington, D.C.: Congressional Quarterly, 1993).

Kim Isaac Eisler, *A Justice for All: William J. Brennan, Jr., and the Decisions That Transformed America* (New York: Simon & Schuster, 1993).

Wikipedia.org, "Tom C. Clark," http://en.wikipedia.org/wiki/Tom_C._Clark.

EARL WARREN (1891–1974)

Chief Justice of the United States Supreme Court (1953–1969), nominated by Dwight D. Eisenhower

Earl Warren was chief justice of the United States and the only person ever to have served three terms as governor of California. Warren was born in Los Angles to Scandinavian immigrants Methias and Chrystal Warren. Methias drew a thin salary from his work on the Southern Pacific Railroad, and Earl Warren's childhood opportunities modest. His father once joked, "My boy, when you were born I was too poor to give you a middle name."[3] Despite his humble beginnings, Warren gained admission to the University of California, Berkeley, where he earned his college diploma in 1912. After obtaining his law degree, he briefly worked in a law firm and then in army training camps. Then from 1925 to 1938 he was a district attorney, during which time he gained a reputation as a rough, incorruptible prosecutor and firm enforcer of corruption laws. Because of his contribution, Warren was named "the best district attorney in the United States."[4]

During this period, Warren married a young Swedish-born widow named Nina Palmquist. They grew into a handsome family with seven attractive children. His "unbeatable" family became a great asset in his burgeoning political career and also informed his values throughout his entire career; later, his colleague Justice Potter Stewart would observe that Warren reviewed each of his cases with the eternal values of "home, family, and country."[5] In 1938 Warren was elected attorney general of California, and it was during this period of his career that he agreed to the exclusion of residents of Japanese ancestry from the

West Coast after the attack on Pearl Harbor. He later told Justice Arthur Goldberg that "that is one of the worst things" he had ever done.[6]

Warren became the governor of California in 1942, twice winning reelection. He began a vigorous campaign for the presidency in 1952 but never gained serious traction. Though he had begun as a promising candidate for the Republican nomination, he eventually withdrew his bid in support of Eisenhower: "Warren was reported to have offered to support Eisenhower's campaign in return for an appointment to the Supreme Court at the first possible opportunity." Although twice Warren conducted failed campaigns for the presidency, his eventual professional accomplishments eclipsed those of most presidents with his "most profound and pervasive evolution" as chief justice on the Supreme Court. Despite his conservative beginnings, over time Warren became a liberal justice. Republican president Eisenhower admitted later that nominating Warren for the chief justice seat was "the biggest damned-fool mistake I ever made." In his role as head of the highest court in the land, Warren was a results-oriented judge rather than a legal scholar, and his pronounced leadership abilities, especially when presiding over the justices' meetings, made him one of the most effective chief justices in the history of the United States. During his tenure he also emphasized that Court opinions ought to be "short, readable by the lay public, nonrhetorical, unemotional, and . . . nonaccusatory." The Warren Court presided over some landmark decisions, especially *Brown v. Board of Education* (1954) and *Miranda v. Arizona* (1966).

References

Clare Cushman, *The Supreme Court Justices: Illustrated Biographies, 1789–1993* (Washington, D.C.: Congressional Quarterly, 1993).

Wikipedia.org, "Earl Warren," http://en.wikipedia.org/wiki/Earl_Warren.

WILLIAM J. BRENNAN JR. (1906–1997)

Associate Justice of the United States Supreme Court (1956–1990), nominated by Dwight D. Eisenhower

Known for his liberal views, including a staunch opposition to the death penalty and support for abortion rights, Brennan was considered to be among the Court's most influential members. Brennan was born in Newark, New Jersey, to Irish immigrants William and Agnes Brennan. His father had little formal education but managed to become a labor activist and in 1917 was eventually elected to the Newark Board of Commissioners, with three subsequent reelections. Brennan senior then ascended to commissioner of Public Safety for the city of Newark, where he took charge of the police and fire departments. Although young Brennan showed no interest in his father's political activities, he was indelibly marked by his father's campaign message—"A square deal for all, special privileges to none." All of his life Brennan showed a deep commitment to justice and human dignity.[7]

Perusing a career in business, Brennan attended the Wharton School of the University of Pennsylvania, where in 1928 he earned his undergraduate degree in economics. Before graduating from Penn, Brennan secretly married Marjorie Leonard, whom he had met at a Christmas dance in high school and quietly dated for two years. According to Brennan, it was not acceptable for a man of shaky financial foundation to marry a woman. It was only after Brennan finished his studies at Harvard Law School in 1931 that the couple disclosed their marriage to their families.

They had three children who all went on to enjoy varying degrees of success in their chosen professions: William became a famous lawyer in Princeton, Hugh was a high-ranking administrator at the Commerce Department, and Nancy was executive director of Baltimore's city life museums.

Equipped with his Harvard degree, Brennan entered private law practice in New Jersey, where he specialized in labor law. He gained a reputation as a "quick thinker and tireless worker."[8] As the Second World War encompassed American life, Brennan joined the army and applied his legal expertise to helping resolve labor conflicts that arose as companies were converted to wartime production. After the war, Brennan resumed private practice and became partner, his reputation in labor law ever on the rise.

In addition to his private practice, Brennan helped reform the New Jersey court system, with aims to increase its efficiency, effectiveness, and justice. Brennan was appointed to a New Jersey trial court in 1949 and in 1952 was promoted to the state Supreme Court by Governor Alfred E. Driscoll. Brennan's impressive reputation as a court reformer attracted the attention of the Eisenhower administration, and in 1956 Brennan was appointed to the United States Supreme Court shortly before the 1956 presidential election. At that time, the appointment of a Catholic Democrat from the Northeast was part of Eisenhower's concerted presidential campaign strategy, since such an inclusion would undoubtedly sway critical voters in favor of the ticket. Justice Brennan became one of twelve Catholic justices to ever serve on the Court, out of a total of 110 justices.

Brennan sat on the Court for thirty-four years and was eventually succeeded by Justice David Souter. During his tenure, Brennan sat with twenty-four justices and wrote more than 1,360 published opinions, second in number only to the opinions written by Justice William Douglas. After stepping down from the Supreme Court, Brennan taught at Georgetown University Law Center until 1994.

References

Clare Cushman, *The Supreme Court Justices: Illustrated Biographies, 1789–1993* (Washington, D.C.: Congressional Quarterly, 1993).

"Religious Affiliation of Supreme Court Justice," www.adherents.com/adh_sc.html.

Wikipedia.org, "William J. Brennan Jr.," http://en.wikipedia.org/wiki/William_J._Brennan,_Jr.

POTTER STEWART (1915–1985)

Associate Justice of the United States Supreme Court (1958–1981), nominated by Dwight D. Eisenhower

Stewart was born in Jackson, Michigan, during a family vacation. His father, James G. Stewart, was a famous lawyer and Republican politician who served as city mayor for nine years and then as a justice on the Ohio Supreme Court. Potter's mother, Harriet Potter Stewart, was a political activist in Cincinnati and served as the president of the League of Women Voters and was at the fore of the movement to reform Cincinnati's city government. Young Potter Stewart was strongly influenced by his parents and the intense family atmosphere they created. At the family dinner table, his father would pepper the meal with tales of the day's adventures in court. Stewart grew up assuming he would be a lawyer. The family's affluent lifestyle meant numerous international trips, luxury summer vacations, and private schooling for the children. While at prep school, Stewart developed a sharp sense of humor and picked up the art of mimicking, earning him the title of class wit.

In 1933 Stewart enrolled in Yale University, supported by a scholarship and earnings from his summer job as a reporter for a Cincinnati newspaper. At Yale he majored in English literature and in his senior year managed the *Yale Daily News*. He graduated cum laude in 1937 and was awarded a fellowship at the University of Cambridge. In 1938 Stewart returned to Yale where he enrolled in the law school. He excelled academically and became an editor of the *Yale Law Journal*. Upon graduation, Stewart briefly served in the army and then returned to his hometown to practice law in a leading law firm. He was elected to the Cincinnati City Council in 1949 and again in 1951.

In 1954 President Eisenhower appointed Stewart to fill a vacancy on the Sixth Circuit Court of Appeals. At the age of thirty-nine, Stewart was the youngest judge serving in the federal courts. As an appellate judge, Stewart's opinions emphasized clarity, parsimony, and careful reasoning. Dissenting from his court's conviction of a man who was arrested, tried, and sentenced on the same day, Judge Stewart asserted that "swift justice demands more than swiftness."

Stewart was next appointed by President Eisenhower to the Supreme Court in 1958, where at forty-three years of age he became the second-youngest serving justice since the Civil War. Stewart joined a Supreme Court sharply divided into two ideological camps, sitting resolutely at its center and carefully executing his role as the swing vote. He refused to be integrated into either faction and followed a selectively and cautiously independent course, voting with the liberals and the conservatives at different times. Because of his sincere appreciation for the division between personal beliefs and the requirements of the Constitution, Stewart managed his separate roles as citizen and justice with aplomb. He often voted to uphold the constitutionality of statutes that he did not favor personally. For example, he voted to uphold some death-penalty statutes, even though he opposed capital punishment personally. Stewart viewed constitutional law from a restrained perspective: he preferred narrow decisions reaching only as far as necessary to decide a particular case. As a diligent justice, Stewart often drafted his opinions at home during the late evening and into the night. His "concise, clear, and graceful writing style is evident in his more than six hundred Supreme Court opinions."

References
Clare Cushman, *The Supreme Court Justices: Illustrated Biographies, 1789–1993* (Washington, D.C.: Congressional Quarterly, 1993).

Wikipedia.org, "Potter Stewart," http://en.wikipedia.org/wiki/Potter_Stewart.

BYRON R. WHITE (1917–2002)
Associate Justice of the United States Supreme Court (1962–1993), nominated by John F. Kennedy

Byron White was famous both as a football player and an associate justice of the Supreme Court of the United States. He was born to a working-class family in Fort Collins, Colorado, to parents of little education. His brother, Clayton S. White, greatly influenced young Byron, graduating first in his high-school class and earning a state scholarship to the University of Colorado, where he went on to a starring role on their football team. Later, Clayton followed up his collegiate successes with a Rhodes Scholarship to the University of Oxford, where he studied medicine. Byron White later closely followed in his older brother's footsteps.

After graduating at the top of his own high-school class, Byron White also attended the University of Colorado on a football scholarship where he became an All-American running back. In addition, he played basketball and baseball and served as student-body president. After graduating from college in 1938, like his brother before him he won a Rhodes Scholarship to the University of Oxford in England. Simultaneously, he was offered a professional football contract with the old Pittsburgh Pirates franchise. After some deliberation, he chose to play for the Pirates and postpone his studies at Oxford for a semester. Nicknamed "Whizzer," he led the league that year in rushing and become the highest-paid player in the sport at that time.

White went on to Oxford as planned in January 1939 and stayed on for only two terms, since, due to the outbreak of the Second World War, all American students studying abroad were sent home. Determined to continue with his studies, White enrolled at Yale Law School and concurrently resumed his professional football career during the 1940 and 1941 seasons, this time playing for the Detroit Lions. After the attack on Pearl Harbor, White wished to join the Marines but was ineligible because he was born color-blind. Instead, he was able to enlist in the navy and became an intelligence officer in the Pacific theater.

In 1946, White clerked for Chief Justice of the United States Supreme Court Fred Vinson. That same year, he married Marion Sterns, daughter of the president of the University of Colorado. White then returned to Colorado in order to practice law in Denver, where he enjoyed a relatively quiet existence, indulging in skating, fishing, and other solitary pursuits.

Over the years White's reputation for humility and a sharp mind grew, and in 1962 President Kennedy appointed him to succeed retired justice Charles Evans Whittaker on the Supreme Court. Kennedy marveled that White "has excelled at everything. And I know that he will excel on the highest court in the land."

Over a period of thirty-one years on the bench, White wrote some 994 opinions, a prodigious judicial output by today's and yesterday's standards alike. He was noted for being a fierce interrogator of lawyers in court. Kennedy supporters had initially expected White to vote as part of the liberal bloc of the Court but grew disappointed by the justice's fierce independence. Especially upsetting to them were his opinions in *Miranda v. Arizona* (1966, suspects under custodial interrogation must be given warnings against self-incrimination) and *Roe v.*

Wade (1973, the decision allowing abortion). White generally avoided broad interpretation of constitutional doctrine, preferring instead to focus on judicial philosophy. He often took a narrow, fact-specific perspective of cases before the Court and left a legacy of a practical approach to law.

References

Joan Biskupic, "Ex–Supreme Court Justice Byron White dies," *USA Today*, April 15, 2002, www. usatoday.com/news/nation/2002/04/15/white-obit.htm (retrieved on October 20, 2008).

Clare Cushman, *The Supreme Court Justices: Illustrated Biographies, 1789–1995*, second ed. (Washington, D.C.: Supreme Court Historical Society, Congressional Quarterly Books, 1993).

Christopher L. Tomlins, *The United States Supreme Court* (Boston: Houghton Mifflin, 2005).

Wikipedia.org, "Byron R. White," http://en.wikipedia.org/wiki/Byron_White.

LEWIS F. POWELL JR. (1907–1998)

Associate Justice of the United States Supreme Court (1972–1987), nominated by Richard M. Nixon

While associate justice of the Supreme Court of the United States, Powell developed a reputation as a judicial moderate. He was known to be a master of compromise and consensus building, a man of gentle manners and courtesy. Justice Sandra Day O'Connor, who served with Powell for six years, said of him, "I have known no one in my lifetime who is kinder or more courteous than he. If at times he was unhappy or frustrated with one of us, he never expressed a harsh thought or criticism. Instead, he would smile and say, in his soft Southern accent, something like, 'Now, I would be pleased to have any of you join me. And I would be happy to hear any of your suggestions.'"[9]

Powell was born in Suffolk, Virginia, to a prosperous family and was able to attend private school before heading on to college. Although the headmaster of his high school wanted him to attend the University of Virginia, Powell chose Washington and Lee University in Lexington, Virginia, partly influenced by a baseball coach who led Powell to believe he could earn a spot on the team there. Though Powell failed to make the baseball team, he became quarterback on the football team. Powell earned his B.S. degree and two years later a law degree at the same university. Going to law school had been a natural next step for Powell, who said, "I was interested in history, and it seemed clear to me that soldiers and lawyers made most of the history. I entertained no ambition for a military career, and so for me the only choice was the law."

After receiving his law degree, Powell passed the Virginia bar exam and prepared to begin private practice. In the end he placed his law practice on hold for a year, while he pursued a master's of law at Harvard. While there, Powell studied under several well-known professors, such as Roscoe Pound and Felix Frankfurter. In 1932 Powell graduated, and though the country was in the midst of the Great Depression, he received a number of job offers. As his legal career commenced in the mid-1930s, Powell fully expected it to be a lifelong job. For over a quarter century Powell served as partner at Hunton, Williams, Gay, Powell and Gibson, a large Virginia law firm, where he chiefly practiced corporate law and railway-litigation law. His reputation grew and eventually took on national prominence. From 1964 to 1965, he served as president of the American Bar Association.

In 1969, President Nixon asked him to join the Supreme Court, pointing out that at sixty-four he would be among the oldest justices ever nominated. Powell initially resisted, worried about his personal financial status once he left the particularly lucrative private practice he so loved. An appeal from the president in 1971 and persuasion from his family and friends convinced him to finally accept the position. Study of his opinions demonstrates that Powell was not easily categorized by political or ideological camp. As he told one of his law clerks, "I do not regard myself as conservative or liberal," exhibiting "different instincts in different types of cases." That said, Powell proved consistently conservative on issues of criminal procedure. He was an exceptionally diligent justice, telling one of his clerks, "I've found my health is better when I work only a six-and-a-half-day week." He was never known to leave the office without a briefcase containing evening reading.

References

Clare Cushman, *The Supreme Court Justices: Illustrated Biographies, 1789–1993* (Washington, D.C.: Congressional Quarterly, 1993).

Wikipedia.org, "Lewis F. Powell Jr.," http://en.wikipedia.org/wiki/Lewis_F._Powell,_Jr.

JOHN PAUL STEVENS (1920–)

Associate Justice of the United States Supreme Court (1975–), nominated by Gerald Ford.

Stevens was born to a wealthy family in Chicago, with many family members practicing law or business. His father owned an insurance company and a series of hotels, including the Stevens Hotel, now the Chicago Hilton. During World War II, Stevens served as an intelligence officer for the U.S. Navy in the Pacific theater and was awarded a Bronze Star for his service in code breaking, which led to the downing of a Japanese plane in 1943. After an excellent academic performance in law school, Stevens was recommended to serve as a clerk to Justice Wiley Rutledge on the Supreme Court. And it was the clerkship, Stevens says, that inspired him to carefully interpret the facts of a case and present them with equal care and accuracy in his opinions.

After the clerkship, Stevens returned to Chicago, where he joined a law firm and specialized in antitrust law, where he made a name for himself and was eventually able to establish his own firm. Meanwhile, he taught antitrust law at the law schools in Northwestern University and University of Chicago. In years following, Stevens worked for the federal government in the House of Representatives' subcommittee and in the attorney general's committee. In 1970, Stevens was appointed to the Seventh Circuit Court of Appeals by President Richard Nixon. He was recognized as an able jurist. As Senator Charles Percy said, he was a "lawyer's lawyer" before and now had become a "judge's judge."[10]

Appointed by Republican president Gerald Ford to the Supreme Court, Stevens has become the oldest sitting justice. He is also the only justice currently seated to have served under three chief justices—Warren E. Burger, William Rehnquist, and John G. Roberts. His long-term service has been characterized as "well, with dignity, intellect, and without partisan political concerns." Although he has publicly referred to himself a judicial conservative, Stevens is widely considered to be on the liberal wing of the court with an idiosyncratic jurisprudence. He is one of the most active justices in the Court. Less reliant on his clerks than some of his colleagues, Stevens usually writes the first drafts of his opinions himself and personally reviews petitions for certiorari. Due to his seniority, Stevens almost always writes the dissenting opinion when in dissent. Additionally, Stevens writes concurring opinions more often than most other justices historically and has asked more questions during oral arguments than most of justices on the bench.

References

Clare Cushman, *The Supreme Court Justices: Illustrated Biographies, 1789–1993* (Washington, D.C.: Congressional Quarterly, 1993).

Wikipedia.org, "John Paul Stevens," http://en.wikipedia.org/wiki/John_Paul_Stevens.

WILLIAM H. REHNQUIST (1924–2005)

Chief Justice of the United States Supreme Court (1986–2005), nominated by Ronald Reagan

Rehnquist was born in Milwaukee, Wisconsin. He is one of two chief justices of Swedish linage, the other being Earl Warren. As a young boy, Rehnquist was precociously ambitious and, when asked by his elementary teacher about his professional plans, declared, "I'm going to change the government."[11] His lifelong conservative views were formed from a young age in his household, where the political heroes among his family, according to a *Washington Post* report, were "Republican standard bearers such as Alf Landon, Wendell Willkie, and Herbert Hoover."[12] He earned both a B.A. and M.A. in political science at Stanford University and then pursued another M.A., this in government, from Harvard. While enrolled in Stanford Law School, Rehnquist briefly dated Sandra Day O'Connor, who would later join him on the Supreme Court as the first female justice in the United States. Rehnquist was described as "the outstanding student of his law school generation" and graduated at the top of his class in 1952.[13]

Rehnquist became friendly with attorney Richard Kleindienst while campaigning on behalf of Republican presidential candidate Barry Goldwater in 1964. Kleindienst later arranged for Rehnquist to become assistant attorney general for the Justice Department's Office of Legal Counsel. Rehnquist's job was to screen candidates for a potential Supreme Court vacancy. Interestingly, when the search committee moved to find a qualified candidate to fill the position vacated by Justice John Marshall Harlan, Rehnquist was informed that he himself had been selected as a candidate. He and Justice Lewis Powell Jr. joined the Court on the same day, January 7, 1972.

Rehnquist initially served as an associate justice from 1972 to 1986, nominated by Richard Nixon, and then was nominated by Ronald Reagan for the position of chief justice, which he executed from 1986 to 2005. Nearly nineteen years' tenure made Rehnquist the fourth-longest-serving chief justice, after John Marshall, Roger Taney, and Melville Fuller. Rehnquist was called "a great chief justice" by Justice Thurgood Marshall. As a true conservative, Rehnquist supported federalism. Under him, the Supreme Court of the United States ruled for the first time since the 1930s against an act of Congress, because the Court determined it had exceeded federal authority under the Commerce Clause. In 1999, Rehnquist was the second chief justice to preside over a presidential impeachment trial, that of President Bill Clinton.

References

Clare Cushman, *The Supreme Court Justices: Illustrated Biographies, 1789–1993* (Washington, D.C.: Congressional Quarterly, 1993).

Jeffrey Rosen, "Rehnquist the Great?" *Atlantic Monthly,* April 2005, www.theatlantic.com/doc/200504/rosen/2.

Wikipedia.org, "William Rehnquist," http://en.wikipedia.org/wiki/William_Rehnquist.

"William Rehnquist: Supreme Court Justice," http://irreference.com/william-rehnquist-supreme-court-justice/.

ANTONIN SCALIA (1936–)

Associate Justice of the United States Supreme Court (1986–), nominated by Ronald Reagan

A dynamic personality, Antonin Scalia is known for his controversial, combative, and confrontational style on the Court. He delights in rhetorical extremes, bandying such terms as "perverse," which hurt his relations with fellow justices. This has resulted in a wide range of sentiments among his colleagues as well as his detachment from the mainstream of the Court. Once, after a long tirade, an offended Sandra Day O'Connor expressed her displeasure, gently chiding, "But, Nino [Justice Scalia], if it weren't for affirmative action, I wouldn't be here." However, his legal brilliance and intellectual prowess are undeniable. A Supreme Court observer pointed out that "if the mind were muscle and Court sessions were televised, Scalia would be the Arnold Schwarzenegger of American jurisprudence." Between his intellectual vigor and his confrontational style he has surprised many attorneys; one litigator described his actions as "those of a big cat batting around a ball of yarn."

Antonin Scalia is the first American of Italian heritage appointed to the Supreme Court and is the only child of Eugene and Catherine Scalia. Eugene was a professor of Romance languages, while Catherine taught school. Young Antonin was raised in Queens, New York, and then went on to receive an A.B. summa cum laude in history from Georgetown University. After that, it was off to Harvard Law School, where he served as editor of the *Harvard Law Review.* Scalia married Maureen McCarthy, with whom he shares a strong Catholic devotion. The two enjoy a large family of nine children and twenty-eight grandchildren. In fact, when Scalia moved to Chicago to teach law, his family "had grown so considerably by then that Scalia had to buy a former fraternity house to accommodate them."

Before he joined the Court, he was a private lawyer and professor of law at several universities. Nominated by Richard Nixon to serve as head of the Justice Department's Office of Legal Counsel before the Watergate scandal, Scalia was eventually tasked with determining legal ownership of the famous Nixon tapes. Scalia decided in favor of the president, reflecting his consistently sincere "respect for the executive branch, though the Supreme Court soon ruled unanimously against this conclusion." Appointed by Republican president Ronald Reagan to the Supreme Court, Scalia is currently the second-most senior associate justice and is considered a "core member of the conservative wing of the court." Justice Scalia is "a vigorous proponent of textualism in statutory interpretation and originalism in constitutional interpretation and a passionate critic of the idea of a living Constitution."

Reference

Clare Cushman, *The Supreme Court Justices: Illustrated Biographies, 1789–1993* (Washington, D.C.: Congressional Quarterly, 1993).

Oyez, "Justice Biographies, Antonin Scalia," www.oyez.org/justices/antonin_scalia.

Wikipedia.org, "Antonin Scalia," http://en.wikipedia.org/wiki/Antonin_Scalia.

DAVID HACKETT SOUTER (1939–)

Associate Justice of the United States Supreme Court (1990–2009), nominated by George H. W. Bush

Souter was born an only child in Melrose, Massachusetts, and spent much of his youth at his maternal grandparents' farmhouse in a small New Hampshire town, where everybody "knows everybody else's business."[14] Souter's intellectual abilities were well known at the local public school and then again at Harvard, where he graduated with a bachelor's degree in philosophy with a focus on jurisprudence. In 1963 Souter enrolled in law school at Harvard, where, despite the rigorous curriculum, he also served as proctor, which required him to be on call twenty-four hours a day to counsel thirty Harvard freshmen. Souter briefly practiced law in a private firm and demonstrated an interest in public service. Souter became attorney general of New Hampshire in 1971. Although a Republican, Souter showed little interest in party political activities but devoted all of his time to his legal practice. In 1978, Souter was appointed associate justice of the New Hampshire Superior Court, where he gained a reputation as a tough but fair judge. On July 23, 1990, Republican President George H. W. Bush nominated

Souter to fill the vacancy left upon Justice Brennan's retirement. Despite expectations, Souter often voted with the Court's more liberal wing.

Souter maintains a simple, solitary life in nature. He has never married, though he was briefly engaged. He was once named one of Washington's ten most-eligible bachelors by the *Washington Post*, ironically, as he is not a very social person. He maintains a simple home in New Hampshire. In the New Hampshire summers, Souter spends time repairing his own home, attending his Episcopal church, mountain climbing, enjoying classical music, and reading. Souter lives a remarkably analogue life in the digital age and is known to write with a fountain pen and does not use e-mail. He doesn't own a cell phone, answering machine, or television. He has studied martial arts, and once, in 2004, successfully fended off an attack of two youths while jogging home one night.

References

Clare Cushman, *The Supreme Court Justices: Illustrated Biographies, 1789–1993* (Washington, D.C.: Congressional Quarterly, 1993).

Tinsley E. Yarbrough, *David Hackett Souter: Traditional Republican on the Rehnquist Court* (Oxford and New York: Oxford University Press, 2005).

CLARENCE THOMAS (1948–)

Associate Justice of the United States Supreme Court (1991–), nominated by George H. W. Bush

After Justice Thurgood Marshall, Clarence Thomas is the second African American justice on the Supreme Court. He is also one of twelve Catholic justices, out of 110 justices, in the history of the Court. Known as an originalist, Thomas steadfastly pursues the "original meaning of the Constitution and statutes," which beliefs have left him the lone dissenter in many a Court opinion.

His judicial beliefs relate to his early life and background. As a descendent of slaves in the American South, Thomas was born in a small, impoverished African American community in Georgia. His father abandoned the family when Clarence was only two years old, leaving his mother to support the family with a meager maid's salary. A house fire triggered a series of moves for the family, and Thomas eventually settled down with his maternal grandfather, Myers Anderson. Thomas has called his grandfather "the greatest person I have ever known" and learned from him an ardent Catholic faith and a belief in hard work and self-reliance. Although Thomas did not become a priest as his grandfather wished, Anderson's beliefs have significantly influenced his grandson's worldview and career.

References

Clare Cushman, *The Supreme Court Justices: Illustrated Biographies, 1789–1993* (Washington, D.C.: Congressional Quarterly, 1993).

Wikipedia.org, "Clarence Thomas," http://en.wikipedia.org/wiki/Clarence_Thomas.

Notes

CHAPTER 1

1. Rolando V. del Carmen and Jeffery T. Walker, *Briefs of Leading Cases in Law Enforcement*, seventh ed. (Newark: Anderson Publishing, 2008).

2. A pen register records outgoing numbers dialed from a particular telephone line. A trap-and-trace device records incoming numbers made to a particular telephone line. Neither device records the caller's actual conversation. A caller ID box is an example of a trap-and-trace device.

3. Rolando V. del Carmen, *Criminal Procedure: Law and Practice*, seventh ed. (Belmont, Calif.: Thomson-Wadsworth, 2007), 264.

4. Ibid., 265.

5. See also *United States v. White*, 401 U.S. 745 (1971), holding that the Constitution does not prohibit the government from using an electronic device to record a telephone conversation between two parties if one of the parties consents to allow it. A person assumes the risk that what is said to others will be reported to the police (*On Lee v. United States*, 343 U.S. 747 [1952]).

6. Archal Oza, "Amend the ECPA: Fourth Amendment Protection Erodes as E-mail Gets Dusty," *Boston University Law Review* 88 (2008): 1043–73.

7. Deborah Buckner, "Internet Search and Seizure in *United States v. Forrester*: New Problems in the New Age of Pen Registers," *BYU Journal of Public Law* 22 (2008): 499–517.

8. Jeremy Brown, "Pan, Tilt, Zoom: Regulating the Use of Video Surveillance of Public Places," *Berkeley Technical Law Journal* 23 (2008): 755–82.

CHAPTER 3

1. Mapp was decided in 1961, three years prior to the Court's ruling in *Miranda v. Arizona*, which changed the rule of law regarding the admissibility of illegally obtained confessions.

2. Rolando V. del Carmen, *Criminal Procedure Law and Practice*, seventh ed. (Belmont, Calif.: Thomson Higher Learning, 2007), 108.

3. A habeas-corpus proceeding occurs after the defendant has been convicted and sentenced to jail or prison. In such proceedings the defendant argues for release on the basis that a constitutional right was violated.

4. The Court has made an exception in the case of civil-forfeiture actions where the underlying basis for the forfeiture is criminal activity. The Court treats them as criminal actions for purposes of determining applicability of the exclusionary rule (*One 1958 Plymouth Sedan v. Pennsylvania*, 380 U.S. 693 [1965]).

5. It is a Fourth Amendment requirement that police officers knock and announce their presence and wait a brief period prior to entering premises to execute a warrant.

CHAPTER 4

1. "Cop in the Hood," www.copinthehood.com/2009/02/stop-and-frisk.html.

2. The case of *Minnesota v. Dickerson* (508 U.S. 366 [1993]) is discussed more extensively in chapter 5 of this book.

3. "Cop in the Hood," www.copinthehood.com/2009/02/stop-and-frisk.html.

4. "NYPD Stop-and-Frisk Policy Challenged by Civil Rights Group," www.lawyersandsettlements.com/features/nypd-stop-and-frisk-policy.html.

CHAPTER 5

1. Parts of the discussion in this section are taken, with modification, from Rolando V. del Carmen and Jeffery T. Walker, *Briefs of Leading Cases in Law Enforcement*, seventh ed. (Newark: Anderson Publishing, 2008), 29–46.

2. Steven L. Emanuel and Steven Knowles, *Emanuel Law Outlines: Constitutional Procedure* (Larchmont, N.Y.: Emanuel, 1998), 129.

CHAPTER 8

1. Craig Hemmens, "The Police, the Fourth Amendment, and Unannounced Entry: *Wilson v. Arkansas*," *The Criminal Law Bulletin* 33 (1997): 29–58.

2. Wayne LaFave, Jerold Israel, Nancy J. King, and Orin S. Kerr, *Hornbook on Criminal Procedure* (Minneapolis: West Publishing, 2009).

3. Nelson B. Lasson, *The History and Development of the Fourth Amendment to the Constitution of the United States* (New York: Da Capo Press, 1937/1970 reprint).

4. Hemmens, "The Police, the Fourth Amendment, and Unannounced Entry."

5. Ibid.

6. G. Robert Blakey, "The Rule of Announcement and Unlawful Entry: *Miller v. United States* and *Ker v. California*," *University of Pennsylvania Law Review* 112 (1962): 499–555.

CHAPTER 9

1. See *Brigham City, Utah v. Stuart*, 547 U.S. 398 (2006); *United States v. Santana*, 427 U.S. 38 (1976); *Warden, Md. Penitentiary v. Hayden*, 387 U.S. 294 (1967); and *Ker v. California*, 347 U.S. 23 (1963).

CHAPTER 11

1. Tracey Maclin, "The Good and Bad News about Consent Searches in the Supreme Court," *McGeorge Law Review* 39 (2008): 27–90; Cliff Roberson, *Constitutional Law and Criminal Justice* (Boca Raton, Fla.: CRC Press, 2009).

2. *Sine qua non* is a legal term meaning "the main thing or the primary factor."

3. M. Strauss, "Reconstructing Consent," *Journal of Criminal Law and Criminology* 92 (2001): 211–59.

4. Maclin, "The Good and Bad News."

CHAPTER 13

1. 41 *Boston College Law Review* 71 (1999).

2. Carol A. Chase, "Privacy Takes a Back Seat: Putting the Automobile Exception Back on Track after Several Wrong Turns," *Boston College Law Journal* 41 (1999), www.bc.ed/bc_org/avp/law/lwsch/journals/bclawr/41_1/02_TXT.htm.

CHAPTER 15

1. *Agnello* 1925, 30.

2. *Carroll*, 267 U.S. at 146.

3. *People v. Belton*, 1979.

4. *State v. Belton*, 1980.

5. Citations omitted.

6. "*New York v. Belton*: A Man's Car Is Not His Castle: Fourth Amendment Search and Seizure," *Ohio Northern University Law Review* 9 (1982): 153–61.

7. "*New York v. Belton*: The Scope of Warrantless Searches Extended," *Pepperdine Law Review* 9 (1982): 919–38.

8. *Chimel* 1969, 763.

9. *Katz* 1967, 357.

10. Schultz, "A Man's Car Is Not His Castle," 1982. See also Silk, "When Bright Lines Break Down: Limiting *New York v. Belton*," *University of Pennsylvania Law Review* 136 (1987–1988): 281–313.

CHAPTER 16

1. Quoting from *United States v. Martinez-Fuerte*, 428 U.S., at 560.

2. "Making the Best of *Whren*: The Problems with Pretextual Traffic Stops and the Need for Restraint," *Florida Law Review* 50 (1998): 385–403.

3. "*Whren v. United Staes*: Buckle Up and Hold On Tight Because the Constitution Won't Protect You," *Pacific Law Journal* 28 (1996–1997): 595–628.

4. See discussion of *Arizona v. Gant*, 2009, in his chapter on *Belton v. United States*, in Saly, "Buckle Up and Hold On," 1996–1997.

5. "Race, Cops and Traffic Stops," *University of Miami Law Review* 51 (1996–1997): 425–43.

6. "When *Whren* Won't Work: The Effects of a Diminished Capacity to Initiate a Pretextual Stop on Police Officer Behavior," *Police Quarterly* 10, no. 4 (2007): 351–70.

7. Internal citations omitted.

CHAPTER 17

1. A *common-law rule* is one created by courts of law rather than by legislatures. Such rule making was characteristic of England, and the practice was carried to nations that were English colonies. Many English common-law rules formed the basis of American law. All American appellate courts, state and federal, have the power to create so-called common-law rules. Perhaps the most important examples are rules established in U.S. Supreme Court decisions interpreting the Constitution, which constitute a form of common law that we call *constitutional law*.

2. *Miranda v. Arizona* 1966, 441–42.

3. Ibid., 460.

4. Ibid., 442–43; citation omitted.

5. Ibid., 481.

6. Ibid., 465.

7. Ibid., 467.

8. Ibid., 469.

9. Additional information is provided about this point in the discussion on eyewitness identification in chapter 19.

10. *Miranda v. Arizona* 1966, 471.

11. Ibid., 469–70.

12. Ibid., 472.

13. Ibid., 439.

14. Ibid., 460; internal citations and quotations marks omitted.

15. Ibid., 531.

16. Ibid.

17. Ibid., 532.

CHAPTER 18

1. See the discussion of the history of interrogation in chapter 17.

2. See the discussion of incorporation in the discussion of *Miranda v. Arizona* in chapter 17.

3. See the discussion of the Due Process Revolution in chapter 17.

4. *Schmerber*, 761.

5. Ibid., 762.

6. See the discussion of *Miranda v. Arizona* in chapter 17.

7. *Schmerber*, 762.

8. Ibid., 762–63; internal quotation marks omitted.

9. Ibid., 773–74.

10. Ibid., 761, note 5.

11. Ibid., 764; citation and internal quotation marks omitted.

12. Ibid., 765.

13. Ibid., 778.

14. Ibid., 766.

15. Ibid., 766–67.

16. Ibid., 767.

17. Ibid.

18. Ibid., 768.

19. Ibid., 769.

20. Ibid., 769–70.

21. Ibid., 770.

22. Ibid.

23. Ibid., 771.

24. Ibid.

25. Ibid.

26. Ibid.

27. Ibid., 772.

28. Ibid., 759.

29. *Breithaupt*, 441.

30. Ibid., 442.

31. *Winston*, 760.

32. Ibid., 759.

33. Ibid., 760–63.

34. Ibid., 764.

35. Ibid., 763–64.

36. Ibid., 765.

37. Ibid., 765.

38. See the discussion of lineups and lawyers in chapter 19.

39. *Wade*, 245.

40. Ibid., 260.

CHAPTER 19

1. *Wade* also dealt with the issue of whether lineup participation violated a suspect's Fifth Amendment privilege against self-incrimination; this is discussed in chapter 18's exploration of *Schmerber v. California*.

2. *Wade v. United States* (1967), 223–34.

3. Ibid., 224.

4. Ibid., 224.

5. Ibid., 227–28.

6. Ibid., 235.

7. Ibid., 228.

8. Ibid., 240.

9. Ibid., 241.

10. Ibid., 248.

11. *Kirby v. Illinois* (1972), 691.

12. Ibid., 686.

13. Ibid., 688–89.

14. Ibid., 690.

15. Ibid., 689–90.

16. Ibid., 697–98; internal footnote omitted.

17. Ibid., 698–99.

18. Ibid., 705; citations omitted.

19. Justice White's views on stare decisis are discussed in chapter 17 in the examination of *Miranda v. Arizona* (1966).

20. *United States v. Ash*, 413 U.S. 300 (1973), 300–301; internal footnote omitted.

21. Ibid., 302.

22. Ibid., 314.

23. Ibid., 314.

24. Ibid., 307, 309, 310, and 312, respectively.

25. Ibid., 312.

26. Ibid.

27. Ibid., 316.

28. Ibid., 317; internal citation omitted.

29. Ibid., 324.

30. Ibid., 332.

31. Ibid., 333–34; internal citations and footnotes omitted.

32. Ibid., 343–44.

33. Ibid., 326; internal footnote omitted.

34. Herbert Packer, *The Limits of the Criminal Sanction* (Stanford, Calif.: Stanford University Press, 1968).

CHAPTER 20

1. James J. Fyfe and Jeffery T. Walker, "Garner Plus Five Years: An Examination of Supreme Court Intervention into Police Discretion and Legislative Prerogatives," *American Journal of Criminal Justice* 144 (1990): 167–84.

2. John C. Hall, "Police Use of Deadly Force to Arrest: A Constitutional Standard, Part 1," *FBI Law Enforcement Bulletin* 57 (1988): 23–30.

3. American Law Institute, *ALI Proceedings* (Philadelphia: The Executive Office, The American Law Institute, 1931).

4. See, for example, James J. Fyfe, "Observations on Police Use of Deadly Force," *Crime and Delinquency* 27 (1981): 376–89; and William A. Geller and Kevin J. Karale, "Shootings of and by Chicago Police: Uncommon Crisis, Part 1: Shootings by Chicago Police," *Journal of Criminal Law and Criminology* 72 (1981): 1813–66.

5. These states were Alabama, Arkansas, California, Connecticut, Florida, Idaho, Indiana, Kansas, Mississippi, Missouri, Nevada, New Mexico, Oklahoma, Oregon, Rhode Island, South Dakota, Tennessee, Washington, and Wisconsin.

6. These states were Georgia, Illinois, New Jersey, New York, North Dakota, Pennsylvania, and Utah.

7. These states were Alaska, Arizona, Colorado, Delaware, Hawaii, Iowa, Kentucky, Maine, Massachusetts, Minnesota, Nebraska, New Hampshire, North Carolina, and Texas. This rule was largely based on the Model Penal Code; see American Law Institute, *Model Penal Code* (proposed official draft) (Philadelphia: The Executive Office, The American Law Institute, 1962).

8. These states were Maryland, Michigan, Montana, Ohio, Virginia, and West Virginia.

9. *Police Use of Deadly Force* (Washington, D.C.: Police Foundation, 1977).

10. American Law Institute, *Model Penal Code* (proposed official draft) (Philadelphia: The Executive Office, The American Law Institute, 1962).

11. "Garner Plus Five Years," 1990.

12. Kenneth J. Matulia, *A Balance of Forces: A Report of the International Association of Chiefs of Police* (Gaithersburg, Md.: International Association of Chiefs of Police, 1982).

13. See, for example, *Mattis v. Schnarr*, 547 F.2d 1007 (8th Cir. 1976).

14. *Acoff v. Abston*, 762 F.2d 1543, 1548 (11th Cir. 1985).

15. "Police Use of Deadly Force: Research and Reform," *Justice Quarterly* 5, no. 2 (1988): 165–204.

16. *Task Force Report: The Police* (Washington, D.C.: U.S. Government Printing Office, 1967).

17. James J. Fyfe, "Geographic Correlates of Police Shootings: A Microanalysis," *Journal of Research in Crime and Delinquency* 17 (1980): 101–13.

18. Matulia, *A Balance of Forces.*

19. William A. Geller, *Deadly Force: What We Know* (Washington, D.C.: Police Executive Research Forum, 1992).

20. For example, David L. Carter, Allen D. Sapp, and Darrel W. Stephens, *The State of Police Education: Policy Directions for the 21st Century* (Washington, D.C.: Police Executive Research Forum, 1989).

21. See, for example, his "*Tennessee v. Garner:* The Issue Not Addressed," *New York University Review of Law and Social Change* 14 (1986): 721–31.

22. "Garner Plus Five Years," 1990.

23. Ibid.

24. Geoffrey P. Alpert and Patrick Anderson, "The Most Deadly Force: Police Pursuits," *Justice Quarterly* 3 (1986): 1–13.

APPENDIX 2

1. Clare Cushman, *The Supreme Court Justices: Illustrated Biographies, 1789–1993* (Washington, D.C.: Congressional Quarterly, 1993), 342.

2. Cushman, *Supreme Court Justices,* 427.

3. Ibid., 436.

4. Ibid., 437.

5. Ibid.

6. Ibid.

7. Ibid., 447.

8. Ibid.

9. Ibid.

10. Ibid., 503.

11. Ibid., 496.

12. Ibid.

13. Ibid., 497.

14. Ibid., 521.

Selected Bibliography

Abraham, Henry J. *Justices and Presidents: A Political History of Appointments to the Supreme Court*, third ed. New York: Oxford University Press, 1992.

Alpert, Goeffrey P., and Patrick Anderson. "The Most Deadly Force: Police Pursuits." *Justice Quarterly* 3 (1986): 1–13.

American Law Institute. *ALI Proceedings*. Philadelphia: The Executive Office, The American Law Institute, 1931.

———. *Model Penal Code* (proposed official draft). Philadelphia: The Executive Office, The American Law Institute, 1962.

Arkes, Hadley. *Beyond the Constitution*. Princeton, N.J.: Princeton University Press, 1990.

Avergun, Jodi Levine. "The Impact of *Illinois v. Gates*: The States Consider the Totality of the Circumstances Test." *Brooklyn Law Review* 52 (1987): 1127–69.

Baker, Liva. *Miranda: Crime Law and Politics*. New York: Atheneum, 1985.

Barnett, Helaine M., Janice Goldman, and Jeffrey B. Morris. "A Lawyer's Lawyer, a Judge's Judge: Potter Stewart and the Fourth Amendment." *University of Cincinnati Law Review* 51 (1982): 509–91.

Barnett, Helaine M., and Kenneth Levine. "Mr. Justice Potter Stewart." *New York University Law Review* 40 (1965): 526–82.

Berman, Daniel M. "Mr. Justice Stewart: A Preliminary Appraisal." *University of Cincinnati Law Review* 28 (1959): 401–55.

Blakey, G. Robert. "The Rule of Announcement and Unlawful Entry: *Miller v. United States* and *Ker v. California*." *University of Pennsylvania Law Review* 112 (1964): 499–555.

Brooks, Peter. *Troubling Confessions: Speaking Guilt in Law & Literature.* Chicago: University of Chicago Press, 2000.

Brown, Jeremy. "Pan, Tilt, Zoom: Regulating the Use of Video Surveillance of Public Places." *Berkeley Technical Law Journal* 23 (2008): 755–82.

Buckner, Deborah. "Internet Search and Seizure in *United States v. Forrester:* New Problems in the New Age of Pen Registers." *BYU Journal of Public Law* 22 (2008): 499–517.

Carter, David L., Allen D. Sapp, and Darrel W. Stephens. *The State of Police Education: Policy Direction for the 21st Century.* Washington, D.C.: Police Executive Research Forum, 1989.

Cushman, Clare. *The Supreme Court Justices: Illustrated Biographies, 1789–1995,* second ed. Washington, D.C.: Supreme Court Historical Society, Congressional Quarterly Books, 2001.

Davis, Angela, J. "Race, Cops and Traffic Stops." *University of Miami Law Review,* 51 (1996–1997): 425–43.

Del Carmen, Rolando V. *Criminal Procedure: Law and Practice.* Belmont, Calif.: Wadsworth/Cengage Learning, 2010.

Del Carmen, Rolando V., and Jeffery T. Walker. *Briefs of Leading Cases in Law Enforcement,* seventh ed. Newark: Anderson Publishing, 2008.

Deters, K. "The Evaporation Point: *State v. Sykes* and the Erosion of the Fourth Amendment through the Search Incident to Arrest Exception." *Iowa Law Review* 92 (2007): 1901–27.

DiKalk, D. "Stop-and-Frisk Limitations Exist." *The Law Enforcement Magazine* 21, no. 12 (December 1997): 44–45.

DiPietro, Louis. "The 'Plain Feel' Doctrine: Frisking Suspects." *The FBI Law Enforcement Bulletin* (February 1994).

Doyle, James M. *True Witness: Cops, Courts, Science, and the Battle against Misidentification.* New York: Palgrave Macmillan, 2005.

Dripps, D. "The Fourth Amendment and the Fallacy of Composition: Determinacy versus Legitimacy in a Regime of Bright-Line Rules." *Mississippi Law Journal* 74 (2004): 341–423.

Eisler, Kim Issac. *Justice for All: William J. Brennan, Jr., and the Decisions That Transformed America.* New York: Simon and Schuster, 1993.

Forbes, E. "Warrantless Arrests in Police Standoffs: A Common Sense Approach to the Exigency Exception." *Criminal Law Bulletin* 45 (2009): 6–23.

Forcucci, Glen D. "*New York v. Belton:* The Scope of Warrantless Searches Extended." *Pepperdine Law Review* 9 (1982): 919–38.

Fox, S. "Protective Sweep Incident to a Lawful Arrest: An Analysis of Its Validity under the Federal and New York State Constitutions." *Touro Law Review* 8 (1992): 761–95.

Frank, John P. *The Justices of the United States Supreme Court: Their Lives and Major Opinions.* Edited by Leon Friedman and Fred L. Israel. New York: Chelsea House Publishers, 1997.

Fyfe, James J. "Geographic Correlates of Police Shootings: A Microanalysis." *Journal of Research in Crime and Delinquency* 17 (1980): 101–13.

———. "Observations on Police Use of Deadly Force." *Crime and Delinquency* 27 (1981): 376–89.

———. "*Tennessee v. Garner:* The Issue Not Addressed." *New York University Review of Law and Social Change* 14 (1986): 721–31.

———. "Police Use of Deadly Force: Research and Reform." *Justice Quarterly* 5, no. 2 (1988): 165–204.

Fyfe, James J., and Jeffery T. Walker. "Garner Plus Five Years: An Examination of Supreme Court Intervention into Police Discretion and Legislative Prerogatives." *American Journal of Criminal Justice* 144 (1990): 167–84.

Gavsie, Kenneth. "Making the Best of *Whren:* The Problems with Pretextual Traffic Stops and the Need for Restraint." *Florida Law Review* 50 (1998): 385–403.

Geller, William A., and Kevin J. Karale. "Shootings of and by Chicago Police: Uncommon Crisis." Pt 1 of "Shootings by Chicago Police." *Journal of Criminal Law and Criminology* 72 (1981): 1813–66.

———. *Deadly Force: What We Know.* Washington, D.C.: Police Executive Research Forum, 1992.

Graham, Fred P. *The Self-Inflicted Wound.* New York: Macmillan, 1970.

Grano, Joseph D. "Probable Cause and Common Sense: A Reply to the Critics of *Illinois v. Gates.*" *University of Michigan Journal of Law and Legal Reform* 17 (1984): 465–521.

Hall, John C. "Police Use of Deadly Force to Arrest: A Constitutional Standard, part 1." *FBI Law Enforcement Bulletin* 57 (1988): 23–30.

Hall, Kermit L., ed. *The Oxford Companion to the Supreme Court of the United States.* New York: Oxford University Press, 1992.

Hancock, Catherine. "Justice Powell's Garden: The Ciraolo Dissent and Fourth Amendment Protection for Curtilage-Home Privacy." *San Diego Law Review* 44 (2007): 551–71.

Harris, David A., "Driving while Back and All Other Traffic Offenses." *Journal of Criminal Law and Criminology* (Winter 1997), 544–605.

Helmholtz, R. M., Charles M. Gray, John H. Langbein, Eben Moglen, Henry E. Smith, and Albert W. Alschuler. *The Privilege against Self-Incrimination: Its Origins and Development.* Chicago: University of Chicago Press, 1997.

Hemmens, Craig. "The Police, the Fourth Amendment, and Unannounced Entry: *Wilson v. Arkansas.*" *The Criminal Law Bulletin* 33 (1997): 29–58.

———. "I Hear You Knocking: The Supreme Court Revisits the Knock and Announce Rule." *University of Missouri-Kansas City Law Review* 66 (1998): 559-602.

Hemmens, Craig, and Chris Mathias. "*United States v. Banks*: The Knock and Announce Rule Returns to the Supreme Court." *Idaho Law Review* 41 (2005): 1–36.

Hudson, David L. *The Rehnquist Court: Understanding Its Impact and Legacy*. New York: Raeger Publishers, 2006.

Kamisar, Yale, Wayne R. LaFave, and Jerold H. Israel. *Basic Criminal Procedure Cases, Comments and Questions*, sixth ed. St. Paul, Minn.: West Publishing Co., 1986.

LaFave, Wayne, Jerold Israel, Nancy J. King, Orin S Kerr. *Hornbook on Criminal Procedure*. Minneapolis: West Publishing, 2009.

Lasson, Nelson B. *The History and Development of the Fourth Amendment to the Constitution of the United States*. New York: Da Capo Press, 1937 (reprint 1970).

Leo, Richard A. *Police Interrogation and American Justice*. Cambridge, Mass.: Harvard University Press, 2008.

Leonetti, Carrie. "Open Fields in the Inner City: Application of the Curtilage Doctrine to Urban and Suburban Areas." *George Mason University Civil Rights Law Journal* 15 (2005): 297–320.

Levy, Leonard. *The Origins of the Fifth Amendment: The Right against Self-Incrimination*. London: Oxford University Press, 1968.

Linford, Jake. "The Right Ones for the Job: Divining the Correct Standard of Review for Curtilage Determinations in the Aftermath of *Ornelas v. United States*." *University of Chicago Law Review* 75 (2008): 885–910.

Loftus, Elizabeth. *Eyewitness Testimony*. Cambridge, Mass.: Harvard University Press, 1979.

Logan, W. "An Exception Swallows a Rule: Police Authority to Search Incident to Arrest." *Yale Law and Policy Review* 19 (2001): 381–443.

MacIntosh, Susanne M. "Fourth Amendment: The Plain Touch Exception to the Warrant Requirement." *Journal of Criminal Law and Criminology* (Winter–Spring 1994), 743–75.

Maclin, Tracey. "The Good and Bad News about Consent Searches in the Supreme Court." *McGeorge Law Review* 39 (2008): 27–90.

Marino, J. "Punishment and Crime: Does *Payton* Apply; Absent Consent or Exigent Circumstance, Are Warrantless, In-Home Police Seizures and Arrests of Persons Seen through an Open Door of the Home Legal?" *University of Chicago Legal Forum* (2005), 569–96.

Martin, Fenton S., Robert U. Goehlert. *The U.S. Supreme Court: A Bibliography*. Washington, D.C.: Congressional Quarterly Books, 1990.

Matulia, Kenneth J. *A Balance of Forces: A Report of the International Association of Chiefs of Police*. Gaithersburg, Md.: International Association of Chiefs of Police, 1982.

Melilli, Kenneth J. "What Nearly a Quarter Century of Experience Has Taught Us about *Leon* and 'Good Faith.'" *Utah Law Review* 2 (2008): 519–62.

Milton, C., J. Lardner, and G. Abrecht. *Police Use of Deadly Force.* Washington, D.C.: Police Foundation, 1977.

Minzner, Max. "Putting Probability Back into Probable Cause." *Texas Law Review* 87, no. 5 (2009): 913–78.

Moran, R. "Motorists Are People Too: Recalculating the Vehicular Search Incident to Arrest Exception by Prohibiting Searches Incident to Arrests for Nonevidentiary Offenses." *Criminal Law Bulletin* 44 (2008): 3–20.

Moylan Jr., Charles E. "*Illinois v. Gates:* What It Did and What It Did Not Do." *Criminal Law Bulletin* 20 (1984): 93–118.

Murray, B. "After *United States v. Vaneaton,* Does *Payton v. New York* Prevent Police from Making Warrantless Routine Arrests inside the Home?" *Golden Gate University Law Review* 26 (1996): 135–63.

National Advisory Commission on Civil Disorders. *Report of the National Advisory Commission on Civil Disorders.* New York: Dutton, 1968.

Newman, Bruce. *Against That Powerful Engine of Despotism: The Fourth Amendment and General Warrants at the Founding and Today.* Lanham, Md.: University Press of America, 2006.

O'Connor, Martin L. "Vehicle Searches—The Automobile Exception: The Constitutional Ride from *Carroll V. United States* to *Wyoming V. Houghton.*" *Touro Law Review* 16 (Winter 2000): 393–435.

Oza, Archal. "Amend the ECPA: Fourth Amendment Protection Erodes as E-mails Get Dusty." *Boston University Law Review* 88 (2008): 1043–73.

Packer, Herbet L. *The Limits of the Criminal Sanction.* Stanford: Stanford University Press, 1968.

Papapetrou, C. "*Payton,* Practical Wisdom, and the Pragmatist Judge: Is *Payton*'s Goal to Prevent Unreasonable Entries or to Effectuate Home Arrests?" *Fordham Urban Law Journal* 34 (2007): 1517–55.

Peters, Brendan. "Fourth Amendment Yard Work: Curtilage's Mow-Line Rule." *Stanford Law Review* 56 (2004): 943–80.

President's Commission on Law Enforcement and the Administration of Justice. *Task Force Report: The Police.* Washington, D.C.: U.S. Government Printing Office, 1967.

Radis, C. "Open Doorway Arrests: Has *McClish v. Nugent* Truly Changed the Analysis?" *Valparaiso University Law Review* 43 (2009): 815–70.

Rehnquist, William H. *The Supreme Court: A New Edition of the Chief Justice's Classic History.* New York: Knopf Publishing Group, 2001.

Roberson, Cliff. *Constitutional Law and Criminal Justice.* Boca Raton, Fla.: CRC Press, 2009.

Rownaghi. Vanessa. "Driving into Unreasonableness: The Driveway, the Curtilage, and Reasonable Expectations of Privacy." *American University Journal of Gender, Social Policy and the Law* 11 (2003): 1165–98.

Ryan, Jack. "*Georgia v. Randolph*: Entries/Searches Based on Co-occupant Consent." *Legal & Liability Risk Management Institute, Legal Updates,* 2007, www.llrmi.com/articles/legal_update/georgia-randolph.shtml.

Saly, Matthew J. "*Whren v. United States*: Buckle Up and Hold On Tight Because the Constitution Won't Protect You." *Pacific Law Journal* 28 (1996–1997): 595–628.

Schultz, Michele D. "*New York v. Belton*: A Man's Car Is Not His Castle—Fourth Amendment Search and Seizure." *Ohio Northern University Law Review* 9 (1982): 153–61.

Schwartz, Herman. *The Rehnquist Court: Judicial Activism on the Right.* New Hork: Hill and Wang, 2003.

Shepard, Catherine A. "Search and Seizure: From *Carroll* to *Ross*, the Odyssey of the Automobile Exception." *Catholic University Law Review* 32 (1982): 221–67.

Stanley, Aaron. "The Continuing Evolution of Consent and Authority in Digital Search and Seizure." *Fordham Intellectual Property, Media & Entertainment Law Journal* 19 (2008): 179–211.

Strauss, M. "Reconstructing Consent." *Journal of Criminal Law and Criminology* 92 (2001): 211–59.

Themer, Rowan. "A Man's Barn Is Not His Castle: Warrantless Searches of Structures under the Open Fields Doctrine." *Southern Illinois University Law Journal* 32 (2008): 139–55.

Tomkovicz, J. "Divining and Designing the Future of the Search Incident to Arrest Doctrine: Avoiding Instability, Irrationality, and Infidelity." *University of Illinois Law Review* (2007): 1417–76.

Trupp, A. "*Maryland v. Buie*: Extending the Protective Search Warrant Exception into the Home." *Journal of Contemporary Law* 17 (1991): 193–210.

Tushnet, Mark. *A Court Divided: The Rehnquist Court and the Future of Constitutional Law.* New York: W.W. Norton Co., 2005.

Urbonya, K. "Rhetorically Reasonable Police Practices: Viewing the Supreme Court's Multiple Discourse Paths." *American Criminal Law Review* 40 (2003): 1387–1443.

Urofsky, Melvin I. *The Supreme Court Justices: A Biographical Dictionary.* New York: Garland Publishing, 1994.

Walther, H. "Defining the Scope of the Search Incident to an Arrest Doctrine." *Maryland Law Review* 59 (2000): 1024–53.

Webb, Matthew W. J. "Third-Party Consent Searches after Randolph: The Circuit Split over Police Removal of an Objecting Tenant." *Fordham Law Review* 77 (2009): 371–98.

Williams, Renee. "Third Party Consent Searches after *Georgia v. Randolph*: Dueling Approaches to the Dueling Roommates." *Boston University Law Review* 87 (2007): 937–94.

Withrow, Brian L. "When *Whren* Won't Work: The Effects of a Diminished Capacity to Initiate a Pretextual Stop on Police Officer Behavior." *Police Quarterly* 10, no. 4 (2007): 351–70.

Woodward, Robert, and Scott Armstrong. *The Brethren: Inside the Supreme Court.* New York: Avon Books, 1979.

Yarbrough, Tinsley E. "Justice Potter Stewart: Decisional Patterns in Search of Doctrinal Moorings." In *The Burger Court: Political and Judicial Profiles.* Edited by Charles M. Lamb and Stephen C. Halpern, 375–406. Urbana: University of Illinois Press, 1991.

Yarcusko, A. "*Brown* to *Payton* to *Harris*: A Fourth Amendment Double Play by the Supreme Court." *Case Western Reserve Law Review* 43 (1992): 253–90.

Index

About the Authors

Rolando V. del Carmen is a distinguished professor of criminal justice (law) and Regents Professor in the College of Criminal Justice at Sam Houston State University. He has written many books and numerous articles in law and criminal justice. His book *Criminal Procedure: Law and Practice* has been translated into various languages and widely used in criminal-justice programs. His other books include *The Death Penalty: Constitutional Issues, Commentaries and Case Briefs* (with colleagues); *Juvenile Justice: The System, Process, and Law* (with Chad Trulson); *Civil Liabilities in American Policing*; and *Community-Based Corrections* (with Leanne Fiftal Alarid and Paul Cromwell). He is the recipient of three awards from the Academy of Criminal Justice Sciences: The Academy Fellow Award (1990), the Bruce Smith Award (1997), and the Founder's Award (2005).

Craig Hemmens is a professor in the Department of Criminal Justice at Boise State University. He holds a J.D. from North Carolina Central University School of Law and a Ph.D. in Criminal Justice from Sam Houston State University. Professor Hemmens has published more than fifteen books and one hundred articles on a variety of criminal justice–related topics. His primary research interests are criminal law and procedure. He has served as the editor of the *Journal of Criminal Justice Education*. His publications have appeared in *Justice Quarterly*; the *Journal of Criminal Justice, Crime and Delinquency*; the *Criminal Law Bulletin*; and the *Prison Journal*.

Valerie Bell is an assistant professor at Loras College in Dubuque, Iowa. She is currently completing her dissertation for doctorate degree in criminal justice at the University of Cincinnati. She received her M.A. in criminal-justice administration from Boise State University in 2004. Valerie worked as a graduate assistant for the Center for Criminal Justice Research at the University of Cincinnati. She coauthored the curriculum for training and implementation of the Women's Risk/Needs Assessment created by the University of Cincinnati and the National Institute of Corrections. She has also been involved in the training of actors in the correctional systems in the states of Rhode Island and California. Her research interests include women in corrections, risk assessment, and Supreme Court law.

David Brody is an associate professor and academic director of the criminal-justice program at Washington State University, Spokane. He received a J.D. from the University of Arizona College of Law and a Ph.D. in criminal justice from the State University of New York at Albany. He is author of casebooks on criminal law and criminal procedure and over twenty other scholarly works that have been published in such journals as the *American Criminal Law Review, Denver University Law Review, Hastings Women's Law Journal, Justice System Journal,* and *Judicature.* His research focuses on judicial selection and performance evaluation, jury reform, the effect of social capital on the criminal-justice system, and the interaction between law and criminal-justice policy.

Sue Carter Collins is an associate professor in the Department of Criminal Justice at Georgia State University. Dr. Collins has more than two decades of professional experience in law enforcement and criminal justice. She is a former correctional officer, deputy sheriff, and felony investigator. She also served as assistant public defender, assistant state attorney, and senior police legal advisor for a large metropolitan police agency. She received her J.D. from the Florida State University College of Law, where she served on the *FSU Law Review.* She received her Ph.D. in criminology and criminal justice from Florida State University. Her research interests include legal issues in criminal justice with specific emphasis on sexual harassment, law enforcement, and criminal-justice policy. She teaches a variety of courses, including legal issues in law enforcement, legal aspects of criminal justice, policing, and criminal-justice management.

Claire Nolasco is a doctoral teaching fellow in the College of Criminal Justice at Sam Houston State University where she teaches criminal law and global organized crime. She obtained her J.D. from the University of the Philippines College of Law, where she was a member of the Order of the Purple Feather, the law school's honor society. She is authorized to practice law in California and the Philippines. She has extensive corporate and litigation experience, having worked first in private practice in the Philippines and Japan. Upon leaving private practice, she joined the Philippine government as chief legal officer for Senate majority floor leader Francis Pangilinan. At Senator Pangilinan's request, Nolasco wrote several pieces of legislation, including a judicial-reform bill, an anti–money laundering law, a dual-citizenship law, and a juvenile-justice law. Her research interests include court systems, organized crime, and white-collar crime.

Jeffery T. Walker is a professor in the Department of Criminal Justice at the University of Arkansas in Little Rock. Dr. Walker also holds a joint appointment with the University of Arkansas Medical School. Dr. Walker has written six books, over fifty journal articles and book chapters, and seventeen technical reports and has delivered over eighty professional papers and presentations. He has obtained over $9 million in grants from the Department of Justice, National Institute of Drug Abuse, and other agencies. He is a past president of the Academy of Criminal Justice Sciences. His editorial experience includes service as editor of the *Journal of Criminal Justice Education*, editor-in-chief of *Journal of Critical Criminology*, and editor of *Crime Patterns and Analysis*. Previous publications include articles in *Justice Quarterly*, *Journal of Quantitative Criminology*, and *Journal of Criminal Justice Education* and the books *Leading Cases in Law Enforcement* (seventh edition), *Statistics in Criminal Justice and Criminology: Analysis and Interpretation* (third edition), and *Myths in Crime and Justice*.

Marvin Zalman is a professor in the Department of Criminal Justice at Wayne State University in Detroit, where he teaches classes on constitutional criminal procedure, criminal-justice policy, the judicial process, and wrongful convictions. His casebook text, *Criminal Procedure: Constitution & Society* (2010), is in its sixth edition. He has written numerous criminal-procedure articles on such subjects as confessions law under *Miranda*, Justice Sandra Day O'Connor's Fourth Amendment decisions, fleeing from the police and stop and frisk, the selection of jurors during voir dire, and trial venue. He has written entries for the *CQ Encyclopedia of the Fourth Amendment*. His sole- and coauthored articles on a number of policy issues include studies of assisted suicide, sentencing, the police reaction to the *Miranda* rules, and the relationship of criminal procedure and civil liberties. His most recent work has been on wrongful convictions, including a survey of criminal justice–system officers regarding the frequency of miscarriages of justice.

Breinigsville, PA USA
20 July 2010
242126BV00003B/2/P